BARNARDO

BARNARDO

Gillian Wagner

WEIDENFELD AND NICOLSON
LONDON

ISBN 0 297 77561 8

Set, printed and bound in Great Britain by
Cox & Wyman Ltd, London, Fakenham and Reading

Contents

Illustrations

The author and publishers are grateful to the following for the loan of illustrations: 1, National Library of Ireland; 11, Mr E. N. Sheppard; 23, Lady Glendevon; and the Barnardo Archives for the others.

Preface

WHEN a caring organisation like Barnardo's has used the name of its founder for over a hundred years, the problems that face any biographer take on an extra dimension. Although Dr Barnardo, whose actions aroused controversy as well as admiration during his lifetime, is well known by name, Thomas Barnardo the man has been eclipsed by his public image. This partly reflects his personal choice, for it was his work, not his life, that he wished to be remembered by: but it also reflects something of the dilemma to which I have referred. To attempt a critical assessment of the life and achievements of the man whose name is synonymous with the work of a charitable organisation might seem a reflection on the work of the organisation itself; or in other words, there has been a tendency to put a favourable interpretation upon all his actions and to mute criticism, to avoid causing any loss of goodwill to an organisation which is dependent on public support for its survival.

All previous biographies of Barnardo have been affected to a certain degree by these considerations. They have also been influenced by the way in which Mrs Barnardo, Dr Barnardo's widow, wished to see her husband's work perpetuated. Mrs Barnardo was a lady with very decided views. Her husband's work had made great demands on his time and energy, demands which, sharing his beliefs, she had accepted as necessary. When he died he left to her all his private letters and papers, giving her complete discretion as to their future use. Almost immediately after his death she announced her intention of writing his life story and asked those who had known him to let her have their reminiscences. James Marchant, who cooperated with her over the book, had been one of Barnardo's deputation secretaries and had been, therefore, professionally involved in putting over to the public the needs and claims of the organisation. In addition he had become secretary of the national memorial fund, set up to commemorate Barnardo's work but also to relieve the organisation of the huge debt, amounting to nearly a quarter of a million pounds, which had accumulated during Barnardo's life. It was therefore inevitable that the book, *The Memoirs of the late Dr Barnardo*, should take the form of a tribute and a justification of Thomas Barnardo's life and work.

The Memoirs remain one of the most valuable sources of information about Barnardo, but as a work of reference, one that needs to be used with discretion. Barnardo himself was not unmindful of what future historians might write, and in his later years he wrote his own account of his early struggles as he wished them remembered. Mrs Barnardo has based her account of his early days on his later recollections, which, when compared with contemporary evidence, sometimes tell a slightly different story. It seems probable that many if not all of Barnardo's private letters have been destroyed, which gives an added importance to the selected few that form part of *The Memoirs*. *Night and Day*, Barnardo's own journal, which he edited from 1877 until his death, is the other major source of information about his life and work. Here again it must be remembered that Barnardo used *Night and Day* to enlist the support of the public for his work and inevitably it presents a one-sided point of view.

Later biographers have tended to follow the outlines of the story as presented in *The Memoirs*. Mrs Barnardo died in 1944, and in her lifetime she had been able to exercise a certain amount of control over what was written. Two books by former members of his staff, A. R. Newman's *Dr Barnardo as I knew him* and A. E. Williams' *Barnardo of Stepney*, both add valuable insights to the information available. J. Wesley Bready in *Doctor Barnardo, Physician, Pioneer, Prophet* and Norman Wymer in *Father of Nobody's Children* have both been able to use new material made available by members of the family. Norman Wymer is the only author so far to have written about Barnardo since the death of Mrs Barnardo.

At this point I feel I must declare my own hand; as a member of the Barnardo Council as chairman of the executive/finance committee and now as Chairman of Council, I am very conscious of the danger of being over-defensive in my writing. In a sense it is all too easy to revere Barnardo for the way in which he dedicated his life to helping children and to inquire no further. Yet one of the strangest episodes in his life centred on the arbitration case of 1877. His activities had aroused passionate opposition, opposition which nearly shattered his work; the arbitration settled the quarrel, but it also imposed restrictions on Barnardo which had far-reaching consequences. It was when I was writing an account of his life for the catalogue to the exhibition, 'The Camera and Dr Barnardo', which was held at the National Portrait Gallery in 1974, that I realised that no one had yet dealt satisfactorily with the events which led to the crisis of 1877. I was also troubled by other seeming inconsistencies in the existing accounts of his life. For this reason I felt it essential to try to understand the causes and consequences of the arbitration and to look at the role played by Barnardo during his early years as dispassionately as possible before attempting a new assessment of his life and work. I am extremely grateful to the London School of Economics for allowing me to make the arbitration case of 1877 the central episode of my Ph.D. thesis, *Dr Barnardo and the Charity Organisation Society: a re-assessment of the Reynolds–Barnardo Arbitration Case of 1877* (University of London, 1977). I am deeply indebted to Dr José Harris, who became my supervisor, for her guidance, patience and interest, but above all for her skill in directing my attention to material and sources which enabled me to see the episode in a wider perspective.

During the course of my research I was fortunate enough to discover a considerable amount of previously unknown material. I have made use of the many letters, reports and articles concerning Barnardo which appeared in *The Revival* and *The Christian* from 1867 to 1877; the two East London papers, the *East London Observer* and the *Tower Hamlets Independent*, also contain letters and reports. The most important new sources of information concerning Barnardo's early life are in the two supplements to the *East London Observer* of 8 and 15 September 1877, which gave the verbatim report of Alfred Thesiger's summing-up speech in Barnardo's defence, and which I have used exclusively when quoting from that speech. In spite of extensive searches I have been unable to find a complete copy of the award of the arbitrator, but fortunately I discovered that the *Tower Hamlets Independent* had issued the whole of the award together with a description of the arbitration in a free supplement on 20 October 1877.

The Barnardo archives house one of the great national collections of children's records. To this must be added the unique collection of photographic records which Barnardo started in 1870. To look at the thousands of photographs of destitute children is to be poignantly reminded both of the appalling conditions in which so many children lived in his day and of the magnitude of the task that faced Barnardo. Few of his own private papers have survived, although the number of letters returning to the organisation is slowly increasing. A valuable collection of Barnardo's sermon notes dating from 1870 until his death was returned anonymously to the organisation while this book was in preparation. My aim in writing Barnardo's life has been to present a portrait of the man both as a public figure and a private individual, making use of such material as is at present available.

Acknowledgements

WITHOUT generous cooperation this book could not have been written. My first thanks must be to the former chairman, Sir Ian Scott, and the Council of Dr Barnardo's, who allowed me to make use of all relevant records, letters and publications. I would also like to place on record my deep appreciation of the help that I have been given by very many members of staff both past and present. I am grateful to the three directors, Miss Joynson, Mr Lowe and Mr Manley, for their encouragement and support. Mr Nowell, Barnardo's librarian, never failed to respond promptly and efficiently to my many requests for information; Mr Ainsworth, chief photographer, traced many of the children's records and supplied me with their photographs; Mr Clough and the after-care department produced much vital information. I should also like to thank Miss Lefroy, senior social worker, Dublin; Miss Dixon, social work adviser; Mr Singleton, deputy director of child care; Dr Bywaters; and Miss Eve Soar, who not only typed and retyped the manuscript, but helped me in so many other ways.

Owing to the paucity of personal papers I am particularly grateful to members of the family who have talked to me about the Barnardos and who have lent me family papers. I am much indebted to the late Mr Harry Barnardo of Dublin, Mrs Cyril Barnardo, Mr Kenward Barnardo, Lady Glendevon and Mrs Hannaford for all their help.

I am most grateful to all those who have given me access to letters and other unpublished material. I would like to thank Mr Kenward Barnardo for allowing me to quote from a diary in his possession written by T. J. Barnardo while in Canada in 1890, and from a letter to his wife from Canada written in 1900, and to make use of the *Reminiscences* of Sophie Salbach and Abbie

Fulwood; the late Mr Harry Barnardo for the loan of family papers and letters; the Overseas Missionary Fellowship for allowing me to use letters from Hudson Taylor, W. T. Berger and T. J. Barnardo, and Dr Broomhall for bringing them to my attention; the Family Welfare Association for allowing me to make use not only of their collection of Barnardo papers but also of papers relating to Mr Fegan's homes, the Home for Little Boys, Farningham, and the National Refuge for Homeless and Destitute Children, as well as their other records now housed in the Greater London Records Office and Goldsmiths Library, University of London; the Shaftesbury Society for permission to quote from the minutes of the management committee of 1870; the Church of England's Children's Society and I wish to thank the trustees of the Broadlands Archive for permission to quote from Shaftesbury's diary.

Very many people have given me help in different ways and I would particularly like to thank Dr Joy Parr of the University of British Columbia who not only allowed me to read her thesis, *Home Children, Juvenile Immigrants to Canada, 1868–1924*, but also helped me to find the most important Barnardo papers in the Public Archives of Canada during my short stay in Ottawa, and with whom I have had many enjoyable discussions on the subject of juvenile emigration; Mr Brian Corbett, archivist, Public Archives of Canada; Mr John Bovey, archivist, Provincial Archives of Manitoba; Mr W. H. Popple, supervisor of records, Department of Renewable Resources, Manitoba; Miss Smith, archivist, Hudson Bay Company, Winnipeg; Mr Andrew Munday, barrister at law, for his valuable help in explaining the legalities involved in the custody of children cases and for checking all the points of law; Dr John Bourke, Munich University; Dr Anderhub, archivist, Giessen University; Mr J. Hutton, Durham University; Miss Dorothy Wardle, librarian, Royal College of Surgeons, Edinburgh; Mr J. P. Entract, librarian, London Hospital Medical College; Mrs Goodbody, curator, Religious Society of Friends in Ireland; Professor Gordon Dunstan and Mr Eamon Duffy, Kings College, London; Sir Edward Singleton; Mr Paul Richardson, librarian, The Law Society; Mr F. M. Watts and Mr Peter Smith, management committee, Dr Barnardo's in Australia; Col. Peter Smeaton, administrator, Dr Barnardo's in Australia;

Acknowledgements

Mr A. N. Falder and the Wellcome Foundation; Professor James Findlay, University of Rhode Island; Mr Walter Osborn and Mr Gordon Loux, Moody Bible Institute; Professor H. R. Cathcart, Queen's College, Belfast; Canon Mark Ruston; Dr Louis Hyman; Mr K. Newton, county archivist, Essex; Mr Sedley Andrus and Mr Thomas Woodcock of the College of Arms; Mr E. N. Sheppard; Mrs E. A. Hennessy; Mr Edward Malari; Mr Anthony Howard; Sir Gerald Thesiger; Mrs Georgina Battiscombe; Mrs Bonython; Mrs Pat Thomas; Mr Bowles; Mrs A. Heath; Mr Roger Wagner. I would also like to thank the staff of the Evangelical Library, the British Library Newspaper Division, Colindale, the British Library, the London Library, the Greater London Records Office, Goldsmiths Library, University of London and the library of the Royal College of Surgeons.

I owe very much to Miss Betty Askwith, who read an early draft of the manuscript, for her helpful suggestions; to Dame Eileen Younghusband and Lord Briggs who both kindly read the typescript at a later stage and gave me much valuable help and criticism. To my husband, Sir Anthony Wagner, I owe thanks not only for his help with all the genealogical research involved, but for his unfailing interest and encouragement at all stages of the work. I am indebted to Sue Philpott for help in the preparation of the manuscript and to my publishers for their patience and cooperation. Finally my grateful thanks to Mr Laurens van der Post for putting at my disposal the room in the South Lookout Tower, Aldeburgh, where this book was written in near-perfect surroundings.

1

Birth and Boyhood
1845-66

JOHN Michaelis Barnardo and Abigail Matilda O'Brien were married in the German church in London[1] on 23 June 1837 on a fine and nearly cloudless day. Thomas John Barnardo was born eight years later on 4 July 1845. Many families embellish their history with myths and stories said to be traditional but often bearing little relation to fact, and the Barnardo family history as recorded is not unusual in this respect. What does make the story unusual is the extent to which certain facts have been suppressed concerning Thomas Barnardo's background and parentage. John Michaelis, born in the town of Havelberg in 1800, was thirty-seven years of age when he married Abigail O'Brien. Nothing is known of his parents except that they were both Prussian subjects and have been assumed to have been Lutherans. If he had brothers and sisters they have left no trace. No record of his early life in Prussia has been found nor are the reasons that made him leave his native land known. He is thought to have arrived in Ireland some time in 1823 and, because his trade was to be that of a furrier, it has been supposed that he had connections with the Hudson Bay Company and indeed to have spent some time in Canada. But a careful survey of the company's records makes any such connection seem improbable.[2]

With so few facts to build upon it is not surprising that a more romantic and interesting background has been woven into the Barnardo story. Although no mention is made of the subject in any of the published biographies, Jewish historians writing of the period have assumed the family to be of Jewish extraction.[3] The late Mr Edgar Samuel, the authority on English-Jewish genealogy to whom I am indebted for this information, believed that both the name Michaelis and the trade of furrier suggest an

Ashkenazi Jewish origin. Barnard was a common nineteenth-century German-Jewish personal name in England and an equivalent for the Hebrew Baruch which means blessed. Michaelis is a Yiddish patronymic. It is possible that John Michaelis Barnardo was the first or second bearer of the name Barnardo. Ashkenazi Jews have never treated surnames very seriously and change them readily, relying more on personal names and patronymics. John Michaelis Barnardo could be the equivalent of Jacob son of Michael and the surname Barnardo or Bernardi could have been adopted in Dublin for business purposes, or else it could be the name under which his father registered the family in Germany after the Napoleonic decree of 1808 by which the Jews of Germany were ordered to register surnames, in which case his father may have been Michael son of Baruch. Although there are no hard facts to support this theory it is interesting that Barnardo believed, as did Disraeli, that their families originated in Spain and that they were expelled during the persecution of 1650.

Dr Barnardo's widow, co-author with James Marchant of his memoirs, which were published soon after his death wrote as though a branch of the family had settled in Venice. The Palazzo Bernardi on the Grand Canal is seen as the original home of the Barnardos, and a certain Count John is given ancestral status. However, in the only published account of his family background,[4] Barnardo himself did not include the claim to a noble Venetian ancestor, but said that one branch of his family went to Germany and another went to Russia. It was from the German branch that Barnardo claimed to be descended, and this would seem to accord most nearly with the limited number of known facts. Mr Samuel mistrusted the stories of Spanish or Venetian origin and believed them to be an attempt to raise the social standing of a rather humble family. There is some evidence that Mrs Barnardo was aware of a Jewish background which she wished suppressed, hence her wide generalisations on the family's Spanish and Italian origins designed to divert attention.

The family was not only concerned about its history: the marriage of John Michaelis also had its awkward aspects. John Michaelis, at the time of his marriage, was a widower with five children under ten years old. His first wife Elizabeth, Abigail's sister, had died giving birth to her sixth child, another Elizabeth, who only survived her mother by a month. The obvious practical solution was for John to find a new wife to take care of his motherless children – and who more suitable than Abigail, who had in all probability been in charge of the household since her sister's death? However, the bill which was to permit marriage with a deceased wife's sister had not yet been passed, and according to the law as it stood it would have been illegal for John Michaelis to marry his wife's sister, although in Dublin there was less stigma attached to those who disregarded the law than there was in England. By coming to London and by having the ceremony performed in a German church by a German pastor, John Michaelis was able to avoid the legal impediment to his marriage, for as a Prussian subject he was not bound by the law. The marriage certificate is signed by five witnesses, Jos Tabrum, Fanny and James Connell and Mary and Ellen Bryan, possibly Abigail's two sisters who may subsequently have gone to America.

Very little is known about the O'Briens and it is interesting that it was only after Mrs Barnardo's death that the true facts about Thomas Barnardo's mother were made known by Norman Wymer in his book *Father of Nobody's Children*. Until then Abigail Barnardo's maiden name was given as Drinkwater, a family said to be Quakers although no record of them as such exists in Ireland.[5] Little is known about the O'Brien sisters except that they themselves were the daughters of a romantic union; in a memoir written by two of Thomas Barnardo's half-sisters, their grandmother, Elizabeth Drinkwater, is said to have met and fallen in love with a certain Philip O'Brien,[6] one of the many Roman Catholic O'Briens of County Clare, descendants of Brian Boru. She not only fell in love, but committed the indiscretion of eloping and marrying him, with the result that she was cut off by her scandalised family without the proverbial penny. Although Miss Drinkwater may have married into a Catholic family, she brought up her daughters to be devout Protestants. The deliberate omission of the O'Briens in *The Memoirs*, and the substitution of the maternal grandmother's name Drinkwater, can probably be ascribed in part to the almost pathological dislike Irish Protestants felt for Roman Catholics at that time. A strong evangelical, Mrs Barnardo could evidently not bring herself to admit that her husband had been related by marriage to the Catholic O'Briens, and for many years succeeded in keeping the fact from becoming public. Even in the Dictionary of National Biography Thomas Barnardo's mother's maiden name is wrongly given as Drinkwater: further evidence of a strong desire to foster the illusion that Thomas Barnardo's forbears were all of impeccable Protestant stock.

After the marriage, which was followed by a civil ceremony on 14 July, John Michaelis brought his wife back to the house in Dame Street where he carried on his business as a furrier. Number 4, a plain Georgian four-storied house with two windows to each storey, was similar to many of the premises in Dame Street, which were mostly occupied by traders in material, perfumes and furs. It was well placed for trade, since the vice-regal residence was just up the street on the left and Trinity College could be seen from the front door looking to the right. Here Abigail settled down to care for her new family. The Barnardos must have been a self-reliant pair; as a foreigner John Barnardo had no relations in Dublin, and Abigail's mother was estranged from her family, so that in time of need the couple had only O'Brien relations to call on for help. The house in Dame Street was not a large one, and while Elizabeth was alive John Michaelis had let off a room to increase the family income. So when Abigail started a family of her own, even without a lodger, conditions must have been somewhat cramped. A son, Adolphus, was born a year after the marriage, but he only survived to the age of two. The following year a second son, George, was born, and two more sons, Frederick and Thomas John, were later added to the family.

Thomas John's birth on 4 July 1845 was by all accounts a difficult one and he was so delicate that he was not expected to live. His mother was too ill to nurse him and on the doctor's recommendation he was put in the care of a wet nurse who lived in a suburb of Dublin. By one of those strange ironies of history the man who was later on to take every opportunity to attack Roman Catholicism was himself suckled by a Roman Catholic nurse.

Abigail, although too ill after the birth of Thomas to care for him, immediately became pregnant again and was sent to the country to be cared for by relatives. The baby, a girl, born the following May, survived only a few hours. During Abigail's absence, Sophie, then aged seventeen and the eldest of Elizabeth's children, took over the responsibility of running the household; she was devoted to 'dear Tom', as the child became known to the family, and visited him constantly. Arriving unexpectedly at the nurse's home one day, Sophie found Thomas unattended, lying in his cot under an open window. Filled with indignation at this careless disregard for the baby's wellbeing she forthwith carried him back to Dame Street, where a short time later the nurse arrived greatly alarmed at the sudden disappearance of her charge. Sophie refused to allow Thomas to return and told the nurse she could only continue to care for him if she came to live at Dame Street where she could be supervised, to which she agreed and where she remained until Thomas was ten months old.[7]

The Barnardos worshipped at St Werburgh's Church which had been rebuilt in 1719. The façade to St Werburgh's Street dates from this time, and owing to the loss of the tower and spire in 1836 presents a somewhat truncated appearance. The interior is one of the most dignified and gracious in Dublin and the vice-regal pew is distinguished by fine royal arms in high relief, the church being the parish church of the castle.[8] It was just round the corner from Dame Street and many members of the Barnardo family were both baptised and buried there, the latter including John Michaelis and his first wife Elizabeth who occupy one of the vaults. Tradition has it that Thomas John was baptised at St Andrew's Church by the Rev. Mr Slater, a curate who lived near to the Barnardos, and his godparents were his father, his sister Sophie and Mr Maguire, a family friend. There is no evidence to substantiate this story as St Andrew's was subsequently burnt down and all the records were lost. A lot of work was done to St Werburgh's between 1840 and 1860, and Thomas Barnardo may have been christened at St Andrew's because St Werburgh's was out of commission at the time.

The following year another baby, Henry Lionel, joined Thomas in the nursery. Thomas's nursery days cannot have been easy; the new baby had a sunny disposition and grew into an attractive child with curly hair and a musical voice. Thomas, who was plain and whose early experience probably contributed to his reputation for being difficult, must have felt doubly chagrined when the younger Henry was called down to be shown off to admiring visitors while he remained upstairs, and not unnaturally took his revenge when Henry reappeared in the nursery.

Sophie remained his special friend, and it was she who taught him his first lessons. He was quick and bright and learned to read and write at an early age, in spite of having more than his share of illness during his childhood, and several times his health gave his family cause for anxiety. His first school was St Ann's Sunday School, which he seems to have enjoyed. When he was about ten years old he was sent to St John's parochial school in Fishamble Street, a stone's throw from Dame Street, and there was taught by one of the curates, the Rev. James Andrews. He next followed his brothers, George and Frederick, to the Rev. William Dundas's school. Dundas's school was, in fact, St Patrick's Cathedral Grammar School, the oldest school in Ireland, and records show that George was a most successful scholar.[9] The school at 112 Stephen's Green gave instruction in 'every branch of study requisite for preparation for the University, the Queen's Colleges, the Naval and Military Colleges, the Army, the Counting-House, the profession of Civil Engineering etc.'. The Rev. Dundas wrote in a prospectus to the school that the unremitting exertions of the principal were devoted to the improvement of the pupils in every department, and that he 'made it his chief aim to enforce, without resorting to severity, habits of system, attention, propriety and self control, without which education is at best but half completed'. Thomas Barnardo, however, remembered him as one of the biggest and most brutal bullies, 'the most cruel man as well as the most mendacious that I have ever in all my life seen! He seemed to take a savage delight in beating his boys and there were two or three unfortunate lads in the school who were the special subjects of his increasing persecution.'

The feelings of loathing and disgust at the scenes he witnessed remained with Thomas all his life, and he ascribed his violent reaction to and detestation of any form of cruelty to children to this early experience. Fortunately for him, Thomas was not one of the persecuted, but the older boys were allowed to bully the younger ones unchecked. Although not one of Mr Dundas's special victims, he cannot have come through the experience unscathed, for his brother wrote of him that 'he was never one of those "goody-goody" boys and there was never any cant about him. He gave a good deal of trouble at home as he was strong-willed and determined. He was full of mischief, thoughtless and careless; intelligent and exuberant, he gave no end of trouble to his teachers for which he no doubt suffered.'[10] Being small for his age and with poor eyesight he disliked all forms of sport, and from the earliest age made reading his main interest, an interest that was to remain with him for life.

At the time of Thomas John's birth his father was supposed to have been a relatively wealthy man, having made money not only through the fur trade but by a series of successful investments in the Wicklow and Wexford Railway Company. However, Thomas's birth coincided with the failure of the company and John Michaelis is said to have lost a lot of money in the crash; just how much was later to become a question of some importance when claims to this effect made by Thomas Barnardo were investigated during the Barnardo–Reynolds arbitration case, which will be dealt with in a later chapter. The family had lived over the shop at Dame Street from the beginning and were still there in 1860 when John Michaelis decided the time had come for him to seek British citizenship. He may have considered that his appointment as furrier to the vice-regal court, which had been gazetted earlier in the year, made this an opportune moment to make the change. His naturalisation papers confirm that at that time John Michaelis had lived for thirty years at Dame Street and that he had ten children living. A certificate was granted to him in August, but because he was travelling on business he was unable to take the oath of allegiance within the time allowed, and only became a British subject in the following November after making a second application for a certificate.

Little is known about the elder Barnardo. A portrait of him in middle life shows a good-looking man with a broad forehead, a generous mouth and a kindly if determined look. He must have been able and industrious, for arriving alone in Ireland as a young man he set up his own successful fur business and raised two successive families; apart from the famous Thomas, two of his sons by his second marriage became professional men, while the youngest son remained in Dublin to carry on the fur business. Thomas John's birth coincided with the onset of the potato blight, and the weather during July 1845 is remembered because of the dense fogs that enveloped the country for most of that month. The Irish famine and all the attendant sufferings it brought upon the Irish people in all probability had little effect on the traders of Dame Street, whose custom depended on the vice-regal court and the richer citizens of Dublin.

The religious revival that swept through Ireland in 1859, fourteen years later, probably affected John Barnardo's life to a far greater degree. Although he himself does not seem to have been much influenced by the religious fervour of the times, he could not have remained untouched by the effect it had on his wife and on his three elder sons. Abigail, like her sister Elizabeth, had been brought up in the Protestant faith, although their mother had married into a Roman Catholic family. In Dublin all the Protestant denominations enjoyed a remarkably close relationship with one another, united as only a religious minority could be, against an overwhelmingly Roman Catholic majority. Apart from the fact that she is known to have taken her religion very seriously, to have been very devout and rather narrow in outlook, Abigail Barnardo remains a shadowy figure. She had nine children, four of whom died shortly after birth, and she is said to have been musical. She died in 1890 fourteen years after her husband, at the home of her son Frederick.

The Revival, which had its origins in America, had swept down through Ulster to Dublin, and Revival meetings were held all over Ireland with increasing frequency; prayer meetings multiplied and reports of people being literally prostrated by transports of religious ecstasy began to appear in the papers. Thomas was still at the Rev. William Dundas's school when the Revival was at its height in Dublin. He had been confirmed according to the rites of the established church, and although a member of St Werburgh's Church, his association with the congregation was formal rather than actual. He was reading extensively and found the ideas expressed by the French rationalists, particularly Voltaire and Rousseau, more to his taste than the evangelical truths expressed by Dr Marrables at St Werburgh's.

There is no record of his educational achievements at the Rev. Mr Dundas's establishment. Unlike his elder brother, who had been an able scholar and had gone on to Trinity, and Fred, who went to the School of Medicine, Tom Barnardo was apprenticed to a wine merchant immediately he left school. No record exists of where he worked during the four years between leaving school and coming to London, but the business experience he gained during those years proved to be a valuable asset in later life. It was, however, during this period that his 'conversion' took place, In writing of the experience afterwards, Thomas Barnardo always referred to his religious conversion as the most momentous event in his life, one which so completely altered his attitude to the world that his life was never the same afterwards.

The Metropolitan Hall in Abbey Street which had formerly housed Classon's circus and music hall was at this time the centre of evangelical revivalist meetings, and many famous preachers spoke there as well as at gatherings in the homes of private individuals. Tom Barnardo reluctantly allowed himself to be taken to some of these meetings, but for many months he remained unmoved by the message of the evangelists and seemingly confident in his own ability to manage his life. However, perhaps the fact that he did allow himself to be taken to meetings showed that this seeming confidence was more an outward assertion of independence and that the example of his family was having a greater impact than was realised at the time. It was at the house of William Fry, a Dublin solicitor who had built Merrion Hall, a centre of Brethrenism, that Tom Barnardo early in 1862 felt his first conscious doubts about the life he was leading. From his own account it seems that it was the kindly way in which Fry himself dealt with Barnardo's youthful conceit as much as the words spoken at the time that gave him pause for thought.[11]

I know I behaved very badly. I was just as cheeky as a young fellow can be, and I thought you looked at me as if you would say: 'If I had that young fellow alone for five minutes I would take down his conceit, I'd give him a good hiding.' But somehow your words were very *kind* and not in harmony with what I thought your *looks* meant, and that was the beginning.'

There are several accounts of the events that led to Barnardo's conversion, but a letter which he wrote to Mr Lavington Dixon in 1903 describing his earliest spiritual experience, published in *The Christian* at the time of his death, is probably the closest to the truth.

I was brought to Christ in the year 1862. A gentleman, a personal friend of mine, a Dr. Hunt of Harcourt Street, Dublin, a charming man, had been the means in God's hands of awakening inquiry in the mind of my brother George, who was then at Trinity, of my brother Fred, who was at the school of Medicine . . . and of myself a little later on. Eventually my brother Fred's conversion was a great help to me, but I actually found Christ without any human intervention, when alone some few days after a special interview with my brother Fred and Dr. Hunt. At this time I was associated with Dr. Marrable's congregation at St. Werburgh's. He, as you know, was a very earnest Evangelical preacher, a man of great breadth of mind and liberality, especially of prophetic truth, and I continued for many months after my conversion a communicant and member of his congregation and a worker at his meetings.

However much the psychological and physical symptoms of the various forms of religious conversion are studied and analysed, there is an aspect of the experience which defies explanation, a movement of the spirit as mysterious as it may be profound. In many ways Tom Barnardo's experience would seem to fall into the classic mould. All through his life Barnardo maintained that ideas came to him through dreams, and the subliminal personality is one of the most susceptible to conversion. Living as he did at a time and in a place where the Revival movement was powerful, when the burning topic of the day was the state of men's souls – the subject of much prayer and exhortation – with both his mother and his two elder brothers among the converted, it is not surprising that Tom Barnardo should join the growing number of 'twice born' men. William James in his study *Varieties of Religious Experience* has defined the phenomenon of conversion as follows:[12] 'the process, gradual or sudden, by which a self, hitherto divided and consciously wrong, inferior or unhappy, becomes unified and consciously right, superior and happy in consequence of its firmer hold upon religious realities'. Accepting that there is a spiritual dimension to conversion which transcends the merely human aspects so described, Thomas Barnardo did indeed show many of the characteristics mentioned by James; his natural arrogance and assertiveness found a new base and his newly acquired conviction that his life was to be a channel for God's work reinforced these qualities.

Fragments of a diary recording his spiritual development later in 1862 show that his religious life was not untroubled by secular thoughts, and that his wish to go through with the public ceremony of believer's baptism in the Baptist chapel in Abbey Street was as much to strengthen his own resolve as to testify publicly to his changed life. His diary reveals that the day before his baptism he had not found the courage to tell his father what he was about to do, and his youthful notes reveal that he regarded his father's spiritual condition as 'terrible'. His mother, his sister Celia and his two elder brothers accompanied him to the ceremony; there is no record of how his father took the news of his baptism. His elder half-sister, when she heard of it, feared he had become a Baptist. He hastened to reassure her on that point, but it was not many months before he left the established Church of Ireland and joined the Plymouth Brethren.

The Brethren movement had become strongly established in Dublin, and it had gained more adherents as a result of the Revival than any other denomination. Brethrenism began in the 1820s as a protest against the dead formalism of the Church of England, described by one adherent as a 'sepulchre of dead men's bones'. Its members believed uniformly in the fundamentalist principle of Biblical inerrancy, and the movement reflected certain other conservative evangelical tendencies: it rejected the need for an ordained ministry and formal theological training; wanting to do away with liturgical and ecclesiastical trappings, it encouraged informality about the sacraments. Hoping to encourage a return to the simplicity of the early Church, it fostered the belief that there is only one 'true' Church, that of all believers, and that every member should be free to minister according to his ability. One of the central characteristics of Brethrenism was its preoccupation with eschatology and its interest in millennial speculation. The Brethren movement was not alone in stressing a belief in the importance of the Second Coming of Jesus Christ, held by many to be imminent, and which according to the pre-millennialists would precede the millennium. A quarrel between two of the Brethren leaders, J. N. Darby and B. W. Newton, over the way in which this was to occur convulsed the movement in the 1840s and gave rise to the division between 'open' and 'closed' Brethren. Edmund Gosse in *Father and Son* has left a profoundly perceptive account of the effect of the conflict between the high ideals and the narrow outlook implicit in Brethrenism, which Barnardo, in his turn, was to understand. In spite of the split between Darby and Newton, Brethrenism spread with great rapidity all over Britain, and communities appeared in America, Canada and Australia.

Little has been written about the millennial enthusiasms of the nineteenth century. It remains a controversial subject because of its preoccupation with so-called 'prophecy', which effectively meant the interpretation of the apocalyptic texts to provide a scenario for the Second Advent and the end of the world. There is plenty of evidence that millennialism was much more widespread than has been realised, and it was a movement in which Barnardo was anxious to play a part. There was a tremendous sense of urgency behind the message of the evangelists; they believed there was no salvation for those with no knowledge or acceptance of the Gospel truths; to them the state of the world was relatively unimportant compared to the vital necessity of saving men's souls and bringing them to salvation before it was too late.

The following three years cannot have been easy ones for Thomas. True he had the support of his mother and brothers, but his father did not approve of his religious activities. He was not being trained for any profession, and work in the wine business could not have been a very congenial occupation nor one with much future for the young man. A photograph taken at fourteen showed a bright, confident boy with a slightly quizzical look; seven years later the carefree boy had become a solemn, serious young man. He was only five foot three, and poor sight forced him to wear blue-tinted glasses, so that his odd appearance marked him out from his fellows.

Unlike Florence Nightingale who felt that God had called her for some special purpose and was content to wait until her role became clear, Barnardo wanted to give expression to his new-found beliefs through immediate action. Several years were to elapse before he found his true vocation. In seeking ways to put his faith to good use, Thomas flung himself into a multitude of new activities in the time he had to himself after work. The Brethren movement had thrown up many remarkable men, but perhaps the most remarkable, and certainly one of the most influential at this time, was George Müller, the founder of the orphan homes at Ashley Down, Bristol. Müller, of German origin like Barnardo, was greatly admired because he never appealed directly for funds to support his extensive philanthropic work but relied exclusively on the power of petitional prayer. His example was widely emulated. It was to him that Thomas first turned for guidance and help.[13]

Living in the heart of the City of Dublin, I see daily around me numbers in a dying state, dying because they have not life eternal, and I am anxious, with God's help, to do something to arrest them on the brink of ruin, but I am so very young, being a lad of only seventeen years; but I have been thinking lately that if I, in connection with young Christian friends, were to have a room for one night in the week and there with those friends hold a Revival prayer meeting the Lord would bless us. I have been bringing the matter for sometime back before the Lord, and today, after rising from my knees the finger of the Lord appeared to point me to you and to abide by your advice.

When Müller's advice came – to study the word of the Lord in private – in spite of Thomas's promise to abide by it, it was not what he had hoped to hear and a room was taken. In his letter to Mr Lavington Dixon, Barnardo explained what followed.

The meetings in Aungier Street were begun in the summer of 1863 and in them I was assisted (for I could not do much, if any, speaking myself) by all sorts and conditions of men – leading men among the Brethren, whom I was beginning to know, such as Mr. William Stokes, Mr. Thomas Ryan, Mr. Rochford Hunt, Mr. Alfred Trench and some of the clergy. Mr. Richard Whately [the eldest son of the well known archbishop] took our little service three or four times. I still possess a book, a kind of diary, showing every service held during the first eighteen months, with the name of everybody who either preached or taught at that little mission room. Among others who spoke at Aungier Street was my good friend Dr. Grattan Guinness and Dr. Marrable, who spoke twice.

No very great success attended their efforts among a population 'deeply affected by superstition, ignorance and whisky'. But if the Revival meetings in Aungier Street were a hard school for the young evangelist, they were not the only way in which he sought to use his new-found faith. He attended meetings at Merrion Hall and became a Sunday school teacher and worked at the centre. His religious beliefs were much strengthened by his friendship with the other Brethren, and through his association with them he came to believe in the imminence of the Second Coming and to understand the essential need to bring a knowledge of salvation to the unconverted.

Thomas also joined the Dublin YMCA in Sackville Street, a contact which was to be important to him when he went to London. It was with Richard Owens of Swift's Alley's Mission that Thomas was initiated into the finer points of visiting the poor and sick. Barnardo confided to Mr Owens that the reason why he no longer carried a cane or umbrella when visiting was that one day when he was taunted by boys in the street he had scarcely been able to restrain himself from striking them, which would have 'killed my work for the Lord'. A fellow worker recalling the brief time that he knew Barnardo in Dublin remembered him for the strong and aggressive quality of his religious life, which would not allow him to compromise with what he considered to be wrongdoing.

Another friend who was to play an important part in Barnardo's life at this time was Dr Grattan Guinness, a revivalist preacher with remarkable gifts who was to become a colleague and a lifelong friend. Thomas Barnardo was attending his Bible classes, held in his own home for the benefit of young men. While on a visit to Liverpool, Guinness had heard for the first time another remarkable preacher, Hudson Taylor, talking about his work in China with the Inland Mission. Guinness was so impressed that he invited him to come to Dublin to talk to his students, an invitation which was accepted with pleasure. Taylor, an even smaller man than Barnardo, was an inspired speaker, but perhaps even he was surprised when at the end of the evening all four students immediately volunteered to go to China; not only that, but Grattan Guinness and his wife discussed very seriously the possibility of themselves enlisting in the China Inland Mission. It is not difficult to understand Thomas's reaction to Hudson Taylor's appeal. The emotive words used by Taylor, 'a million a month dying in China without knowing Christ', constituted just the sort of challenge

Barnardo needed. He must have been feeling increasingly frustrated by the kind of life he was forced to lead, the greater part of his days spent on business in which he had no real interest.

Before Thomas could leave, however, there were very practical difficulties to overcome. His father was completely opposed to the idea of his going to China, and made it plain that if Thomas went to London it was without his blessing and that he could expect no financial support from him. The views of the rest of the family are not known, but when it became apparent that Thomas was determined to go to London in the hope of being accepted as a candidate for the China Inland Mission, some elders among the Brethren at Merrion Hall came to his assistance. Three of them, whose names are not known, combined together to provide Thomas with a small allowance to enable him to go to London. So carrying with him their blessing, some letters of recommendation, and unbounded faith that his ultimate destiny was to become a missionary in China, Thomas Barnardo left Dublin in April 1866 to begin a new chapter in his life.

2

Early Struggles as Evangelist
and Mission Leader

A WHOLE literature has been written about the condition of the
East End of London and its outcast population in the
nineteenth century; but when Thomas Barnardo arrived in
Stepney in the spring of 1866 twenty years were to pass before
Charles Booth even started his survey of the life and labour of
the people of London. Both the extent of the problem and the
underlying economic cause of the chronic and hopeless poverty
of the majority of the inhabitants were unknown. From the safe
distance of their comfortable homes, insulated from the harsh
realities of life by the large armies of servants who ministered to
their daily needs, wealthy Victorians had come to believe that
pauperism and destitution were the product of character rather
than circumstances. But the etchings of Gustave Doré and the
works of Dickens and Mayhew were slowly making the terrible
conditions of the East End of London known to a growing
public. Their revelations had stirred the consciences of the
wealthy with the result that charitable organisations of all kinds
had sprung up, and the giving of charity and the receiving of it
had become a recognised part of the Victorian scene on a scale
never previously known. The dramatisation of poverty meant
that for most of the wealthy the reality of the sufferings of the
poor was remote; the giving of charity stilled their consciences,
although for some it gave rise to further anxieties.

The sudden growth of charitable activity was not without its
critics, many of whom feared not only that all the beggars in the
land would be attracted to the metropolis, but that the giving of
indiscriminate charity would lead to the 'demoralisation' of the
poor and the creation of a class of dependent, idle layabouts.
Recent studies[1] show that the special isolation and social dislo-
cation of the East End was caused by a crisis in social and

industrial development. The causes and pattern of poverty in Victorian London sharply differentiated it from other regions at that time; the irregular pattern and varying size of the casual labour market had a direct bearing on the problem of poverty which was central to that crisis.

Barnardo came to the East End at a time when nearly all the middle class had already left to seek pleasanter surroundings in which to live and bring up their children. At the same time London's population had increased dramatically; between 1821 and 1851 it had almost doubled, and it was to double again before the end of century. Much of this increase was concentrated in the East End. With the departure of the wealthier classes there was no one to take over the contribution they had made to the social life of the community or to the maintenance of order and social stability. The vestries had largely been taken over by small house-owners or local shopkeepers whose main objectives were to keep the rates from rising, and for that reason they opposed any action to improve either housing or sanitation. They had no wish to encourage the growth of the casual labour market, rather the reverse, and their attitude tended to be one of indifference to the abject poverty of many of their fellow citizens. It would be a mistake to label the population of the East End exclusively working-class; it had many and distinct stratifications which were, if anything, more jealously guarded because of the small margin which separated those who survived from the unspeakable miseries that could so easily engulf the less fortunate.

London was a city of small masters and, reflecting its status as a capital city, it had an unusually large professional class whose attitudes towards the casual poor were based on their regard for property. The lure of the city had enticed unskilled rural migrants and foreign immigrants to join a labour market which was already unbalanced. Many of the staple industries such as ship-building and construction work were in decay or had collapsed, and owing to the nature of the population much of the employment was seasonal. The fashionable London season began in February and March and was at its height during the early summer. At this time tailors, shoemakers, cabinet-makers, milliners, dressmakers, saddlers, harness-makers, coachbuilders, farriers, cooks, confectioners and outdoor servants were all in demand. Parliamentary activity which coincided with the season increased the demand for printers, and all the service industries took on extra labour at the beginning of the season. Demand died away during the height of the summer and revived again, but on a smaller scale, as winter approached and the wealthy returned to equip themselves with winter clothing and Parliament reassembled for the autumn session. For those whose work depended on the needs of the wealthy, winter was a hard time, but they were not the only ones to be affected. During the cruel months after Christmas the docks were almost completely without work and the construction industry suffered similarly. Builders were unwilling to undertake work which was necessarily more costly, there being fewer daylight hours in which to work; fog, frost, rain and damp all affected the work of carpenters, bricklayers and painters, making it uneconomic to employ them during the harsh winter months, while the growing pool of casual labour made it unnecessary for employers to do so.

A series of hard winters had increased the miseries of those living in the East End, who already had to contend with appalling housing conditions, chronic overcrowding, poor health resulting from the almost complete lack of sanitation, and unemployment which led to direst poverty. Once a man, however skilled, lost his regular employment and was forced to join the casual labour force, he was seldom able to break away from it. The ever-growing casual labour market was for the most part the only means of avoiding starvation or the workhouse; men, women and children gratefully accepted the intolerably long hours and wretched working conditions that gave them a meagre income and kept body and soul together. In these circumstances the death of the breadwinner was one of the biggest single causes of poverty.

Barnardo had only been in London a few months when an outbreak of cholera swept through the East End, killing over three thousand people and leaving families not only stricken by the human tragedy but facing disaster in economic terms. Many were unable to work because of physical exhaustion and depression, many more had sold all to meet the cost of medical treatment and burial. Barnardo always said that those few months did more to open his eyes to the miseries of the poor than anything else. He was not yet a student at the London Hospital but he visited and prayed with many of the sick and dying. Following the horror of the cholera epidemic, the harvest of 1866 proved disastrous, and distress among the poor was further increased by the subsequently large increase in the price of wheat. Although Barnardo's thoughts were still fixed on China and the work needing to be done amongst its teeming millions, he had arrived in the East End of London in the spring of what was to be one of the most fearful years its population had yet had to face.

His first two years in London are not well documented. He himself had some hand in obscuring the facts as, in later years, he constantly referred to his work with children as having started in 1866, preferring to forget that in the early years he was known as an evangelist rather than as a philanthropist. References to the fact that his work started in 1866 began to appear in his reports during the 1870s, and all through his life he continued to date the beginning of his work for children from the time of his arrival in London. Not unnaturally, therefore, the Barnardo Organisation celebrated its centenary in 1966, an understandable if somewhat inaccurate assumption.

A series of letters concerning Barnardo's candidature for the China Inland Mission provide the most important evidence for this period of his life. In February 1866 Hudson Taylor had written to his wife from Belfast after his visit to Dublin[2] 'some fine young men and several females desire to go to China. Fishe, I think, is *now* too young; but may go by and by perhaps. One medical student desires to go . . .' This could have been a reference to Tom Barnardo because, as one of his letters of introduction showed, he had discussed the possibility of studying medicine before leaving Dublin. He arrived in London in company with the other candidates for China and lodged with them at 30 Coburn Street, a house just off the Mile End Road which had many associations with the China Inland Mission. As later correspondence between Hudson Taylor's representative and manager, W. T. Berger, and Hudson Taylor himself makes clear, it was Tom Barnardo's strong Plymouth Brethren beliefs – 'peculiarities' was the word used – and his unwillingness to accept the necessity of 'headship and government' in the China Mission as well as his inexperience that made it impossible for him to be considered an immediate candidate for China.

After Hudson Taylor had sailed for China with his newest party of recruits in the *Lammermuir* in May, Barnardo left Coburn Street and found lodgings of his own. He did not, in fact, register at the London Hospital until November 1867, and in tracing his medical career there are a number of unresolved problems. His sponsors were clearly concerned about his financial circumstances. They reasoned that if he qualified as a doctor he would, at least, be provided with a means of earning a living whether he went to China or not. Mr James,[3] a colleague from the YMCA in Dublin, sent him two letters of introduction to men 'who will welcome you in a brotherly way and be glad to afford you any counsel or assistance in their power. They may also be able to introduce you to some persons in the medical profession who may be helpful to you in the attainment of a knowledge of that department.' Hudson Taylor, who had been trained at the London Hospital himself, may also have helped him. But there is no explanation as to what prompted him to go to Durham in September 1867 and successfully enter the 'Registration Examination for Medical Students'[4] – which, however, did not entitle him to be classed as a student of the university – unless it was that, having tried the previous year to get into the London Hospital without success, he was insuring against the possibility of a second failure.

Barnardo's few surviving early letters reinforce the impression that his medical studies were only the means to an end and not an end in themselves; for at least three years his main objective was to get to China. The London Hospital was at that time small and overcrowded. It had only three hundred beds and although the theoretical training given to students was somewhat haphazard, on the practical side its reputation for surgery stood high, although by today's standards the conditions under which operations were performed would seem appallingly primitive. Little is known about Tom Barnardo's life as a medical student. A description by Dr W. L. Mayer, quoted in *The Memoirs*, gave an impression of him at the time:[5]

It was shortly after joining the London Hospital, I think in the winter of 1867–68 and in 1869, that I had the privilege of knowing Barnardo intimately. He appeared older in years and manner than most first-year men. The head and face indicated capacity and good sense, the mouth determination – his smile, to which his eyes often lent a merry twinkle, was generally bright and cheery, but he rarely laughed. His bearing was that of a thoughtful, resolute, obstinately persevering man. In manner and conversation he was reserved, correct rather than brilliant, but one gradually realised how mentally alert and capable he was. Gradually one observed also that his heart was not wholly in his work at the college and hospital.

Barnardo's letters to Berger in 1868 show how passionately he wished to go to China. A long letter to Berger[6] written in January of that year is of special interest because it included an account of his studies at the London Hospital.

A long time has now elapsed since first *China, its needs and claims* were laid upon my heart. Again and again I have, during the period of nearly two years, weighed calmly in the balances of the sanctuary, the motives, the desire, the fixity of purpose, in short *my whole heart*, and again and again has it come up from the depths of that unworthy heart the same deep desire that now about the beginning of another year fills and actuates me. 'Here am I, Lord, send me', and *he will send me* I feel assured ere long. As far as I am concerned I look forward, God willing, to leave about *October or November next*... And now to the progress of my studies – this *must* be interesting to you. I am now in my second winter session and with God's help I have worked hard, having up to this (3rd Jan) been enabled to dissect two complete subjects and think I am as well up as any man of my year. I have attended diligently all lectures including special courses upon eye and skin diseases. I have also attended 64 maternity cases for the hospital. You know that students go up at the end of their second winter session to pass the anatomical and physiological exam at the R.C.S. and being successful the two remaining years are given to surgery and medicine – what I hope to do is as follows – to read up with all the men and attend the special classes for them during the coming three months as if I were indeed going up with them at the April exam. In this way, I will, with God's help, know as much as those who *do* go up, the difference simply being that they will have been examined and I will not. Then I hope, D.V, to get freely, or pay, for 3 months in patient dressing in the hospital, also a few months at the ophthalmic and skin disease hospitals, attending at the same time the physicians' and surgeons' wards and clinical instruction, so that should I be let out in November I may, God willing, have that ground work which will infuse stamina to my future labours. Beloved brother – pray for me. I pray for you. I cease not in my approaches to the throne of Grace to joy with you in your joy – in that God has already given you precious souls for your love.

Writing three months later[7] in April 1868 to thank Berger for his kindness in sending him a cheque for £5, Barnardo showed that he was aware that his views had caused difficulty and said that he had rethought and modified many of the objections he had about the way the mission was run. Pleading still to be allowed to go to China, although he admitted to being emotional in the matter, he wrote, 'there is too little of mere sentiment as against real fact in my feeling as to China', and he reminded Berger that he had severed ties with his family, 'the closest tie that a man can have', for China. It was in this letter that he also mentioned that he had turned down an offer of £220 from a 'wealthy brother' who had replied to an appeal Barnardo had made for funds to build a hall for evangelistic purposes. The money had been offered him on condition that he remained in London and gave up all idea of going to China.

He again presented himself formally in September 1868 as a candidate, but there were still doubts about his suitability and he was urged to stay on at the London Hospital and become qualified. A letter from Berger to Hudson Taylor written the following April made the significant comment:[8]

Thos. Harvey gets on well with dear C. Fishe, much better than he does with Tom Barnardo, who is still with us; while he is a very talented fellow he is so overbearing that it tries some of us a little . . . He is doing a great work in the East End of London and gaining valuable experience, especially in the wise use of money, for he is naturally fast and spends his money far too freely and unthinkingly. He has been in great difficulties at times as to means for carrying on his work, and gets behind in his payments, so he will not be so forward to judge others who may do likewise. I yet hope dear Barnardo will turn out a very valuable labourer for China.

A later letter from Berger to Hudson Taylor[9] revealed that Barnardo was persuaded to take the preliminary examination and passed successfully in July 1869, and Berger hoped that he would go up for the MRCS and MD in 1870, 'so I trust he will have a means of support, whether he should ever go as a missionary or no'. By November 1870 Berger after a long talk with Barnardo came to the conclusion that neither could see how Barnardo could leave the work he had started in the East End, and it was finally agreed that he should no longer be considered a candidate for the China Inland Mission.[10] In the light of the previous correspondence this decision may have come as something of a relief to Berger. With the incentive to continue his studies removed, Barnardo's interest in his medical career evaporated completely and he ceased to attend the London Hospital. Temperamentally Barnardo was always intolerant of authority and it was his domineering personality as much as anything that seemed to have been the obstacle that prevented him being accepted as a candidate. His dislike of examinations was another manifestation of this trait, and his aversion to submitting himself to any form of outside judgement was to remain a dominant characteristic. One can see why Plymouth Brethrenism attracted him so much during his early years. The movement aimed at a return to the simplicity of the early Church. It refused to recognise any form of Church government or salaried ministry and its followers believed that every individual had both the privilege and the responsibility of ministering according to his gift and ability. It also believed that those who devoted themselves to the work of the Gospel should be supported by voluntary and unsolicited contributions; so the fact that he was dependent on the contributions of friends presented no difficulties for Barnardo.

Initially unable to register as a medical student at the London Hospital, rejected by the China Inland Mission, Barnardo's first year in London cannot have been very rewarding. Naturally he looked round for other outlets. His experiences among his neighbours during the cholera epidemic opened his eyes to the needs of the people of the East End and enabled him to understand them. He later wrote that, 'but for the cholera epidemic in 1866, I should never have known Stepney'. It was perhaps because of the frustrations he experienced during his first year in London that when he started to work on his own he worked with such concentrated energy that friends sometimes feared for his health. His burning desire to preach the word of God allied to his need to justify himself was to prove a powerful combination.

He had come to London with an introduction to the fellowship of the 'open' Brethren in Sydney Street, Stepney. With a kindred spirit from among them he had started preaching in the surrounding streets, lanes and alleys. Their attempts to evangelise the people of Stepney were not always well received and they had to put up with a fair measure of abuse. Preaching from a wooden chair Barnardo endured the indignity of having a pail of slops poured over him from a conveniently situated window above his head; mud and rotten eggs sometimes accompanied the jeers his words provoked; he himself described how once a pellet of mud aimed at him by a small boy caught him open mouthed and effectively stopped any further speech.[11] The apparently meagre results compared to the amount of abuse he had to endure never deterred Barnardo, and courage in the face of adversity was a quality which he was to show on many occasions during his life.

The first recorded announcement of his work as an evangelist appeared in 1867 in *The Revival*,[12] a weekly religious periodical, founded in 1859, that was to become almost compulsory reading in most evangelical households under the name of *The Christian* which it adopted in 1870. According to *The Revival*, Barnardo preached every Sunday on Mile End Waste, opposite Stepney Green, a site also used by William Booth at this time. This was only the first of four or five addresses he would give on a Sunday. He also started to teach in a little ragged school in Ernest Street at the end of Hertford Street, Mile End Road, one of many that had been opened during the past twenty years to give the children of the poorest an elementary knowledge of religion and of reading and writing. Barnardo's ability as a teacher and his success in keeping order among the children soon attracted the attention of the school committee. He was promoted and became superintendent of the school with a seat on the board, but the committee retained financial control. The school had been founded in 1865 and its president was the Member of Parliament, John Holmes; the Rev. Kennedy, Vicar of Stepney, and the Rev. Archibald Brown, Pastor of the East London Tabernacle, shared the office of vice-president. But it was not long before Barnardo was in trouble with his committee over the question of the school's finances, and the quarrel that led to his resignation can be recognised as typical and part of a recurring pattern of behaviour.

Anxious to start some work over which he would have complete control, Barnardo had had a letter published in *The Revival*[13] which he had misleadingly entitled 'Important Ragged School Work in the East End'. The letter drew attention to the needs of boys and girls whose ages, rather surprisingly, varied from thirteen to twenty-eight, and went on to say that though many of them could now be asked to join the ragged school in Ernest Street, 'crowding upward of a hundred persons in a low, narrow, and badly ventilated room which contains sittings for only eighty-six becomes, especially in summer, very unpleasant if not impossible'. Barnardo made it clear that though the spiritual direction and management of the school were in the hands of the superintendent, the financial matters were arranged by a committee of gentlemen who did not raise enough money to meet all the needs of the community. Barnardo went on to ask for £200 to enable him to carry out his plan which was:

To procure a large building, room, or shed, capable of holding about 600 persons; to obtain the personal and voluntary aid of about forty or fifty earnest Evangelistic Brethren and Sisters from the various chapels and churches in the neighbourhood; to commence our efforts by a large tea meeting service, the tickets for which will be carefully distributed amongst those only whom it is intended to reach; to get about six or eight large banners made, inviting them to this room, each of these banners to go out and about before the service, borne by some of my present school, singing hymns and parading the Parish, but returning at the hour of the service bringing their crowds with them.

Barnardo's letter, although it did not immediately bring him the money or the help he needed, did bring him the offer of the use of the assembly rooms over the King's Arms at the corner of the Mile End Road; it also brought him into conflict with the committee in charge of the Ernest Street school. They felt, not unnaturally, that the achievements of their school were being used by Barnardo to raise money for a totally different project. Barnardo in a further letter to *The Revival*[14] admitted that the funds he was appealing for had nothing to do with the Ernest Street ragged school, that he was hoping to establish a larger juvenile mission of his own and that as a result of this conflict of interest he had resigned from the Ernest Street ragged school. He did in fact succeed in raising £90 towards the new work and on 5 November 1867, with the aid of a few friends, gave a great free tea meeting on the same lines as the one Shaftesbury had given the previous year to boys from the ragged schools to tell them of his idea of establishing training ships. This first meeting can be seen as the beginning of Barnardo's own independent work with children, although this particular venture was short-lived.

Barnardo described the noise and tumult at that first meeting as being so terrible that the meeting could not be considered very satisfactory. Although a large amount of tea was consumed by the two thousand odd who are said to have attended, little resulted from the gathering which contained a large number of thieves and, as Barnardo put it, 'poor lost girls'. However, six more meetings were held before a new landlord, doubtless apprehensive at the possible damage such an unruly crowd might cause and probably aware of the uncertain financial backing on which the whole enterprise rested, abruptly terminated the agreement to let the rooms. This was a great shock to Barnardo who had doubtless spent all of the £90 and more to get the enterprise going and was now left with no base from which to appeal to the public. It is known that for some weeks after this he was seriously ill. There is a recurring pattern of illness during Barnardo's life, and it is noticeable that the onset of illness often occurs after a particularly difficult period or a setback to his hopes. He had an extraordinary capacity for work and drove himself to the limits of endurance. Berger writing to Hudson Taylor about him recognised this:[15] 'He is doing a great and I think good work in the East of London. I fear his physical powers will break down; he has been laid aside for the last three months or more and it was feared at one time that he would not recover. He begins to see that he must act more prudently.'

Besides the abortive attempt to found his own juvenile mission, 1867 also saw the publication of Barnardo's first story. Since his conversion Barnardo had given up reading any books except the Bible and works on the Brethren movement which were numerous, for the controversies within that movement generated an immense amount of literature, now of no more than academic interest to students of the subject. Secular newspapers were also proscribed reading, and Barnardo's views on social and political problems could only have been formed at that time by what he read in the Protestant religious journals of the day and from his own acute observation. His early writings reflect all too clearly the influence of his reading, and his letters and reports are punctuated by quotations from the Bible and exhortations thereon which make tedious reading. Yet when he began to write about the social problems of poverty and distress which he saw all around him, and as his awareness of the size and depth of the problem grew, so his ability to report what he saw graphically and in vivid terms developed and his natural gifts as a descriptive writer found scope. His first story, 'The Eleventh Hour', was published in *The Revival*[16] under his initials in July 1867 and told of a deathbed conversion he had witnessed. It is characteristic of much of his writing and demonstrated his ability to use the written as well as the spoken word to great effect. His subsequent stories nearly all concerned children. They were not only published in *The Revival* but also in pamphlet form, and Barnardo used many of them to illustrate his subsequent reports. He had started on another career: that of writer. The story of his meeting with Jim Jarvis, which he called 'My first Arab', was to become the most famous of them all.

When Barnardo recovered from his illness and the consequences of his first unsuccessful attempt to found his own mission, it did not take him long to start again. Still with China as his ultimate object, he left his lodgings in Princes Street and took a room at 5 Bromley Street in a typical early Victorian terrace house, two up two down, belonging to a Mrs Johnson, whose husband was a sailor. From there Barnardo continued his work of evangelisation in the time he could spare from his medical studies. He held cottage meetings in Pedley's Orchard, but they soon became overcrowded; so with the help of one or two friends he rented two small houses in Hope Place and here, early in 1868, he began the work of the East End Juvenile Mission.

The story of the work starting in a transmogrified donkey shed was introduced at a later date. It was first mentioned by Barnardo in 1900 in an account of his work entitled 'How it all began', but there is no contemporary evidence for it. The two cottages in Hope Place were used to house the mission, which opened on 2 March 1868, one cottage being used for boys and the other for girls. Seeing all around him the results of overcrowding and the indiscriminate mixing of the sexes, Barnardo made it a principle from the very start to keep boys and girls separate. The fact that the cottages were divided into four rooms also made discipline easier to maintain, and Barnardo allowed himself the pleasure of reporting that most visitors assured him that similar order was not attained in many other ragged schools. A contemporary report of the work appeared in *The Revival* in 1868. George Holland, who had set up the George Yard Ragged School Mission in Whitechapel a few years previously, was one of the first to commend publicly the work Barnardo was doing. After attending a meeting at Hope Place he wrote:[17]

To give some idea of the work going on, there are held weekly special services for children; Bible classes for men, women and children, mothers' meetings, girls' sewing classes, a special service attended every evening of the week by an average of 130 lads. A little church has also been formed, numbering to this date nearly 90 souls (adults). A day school is in formation and also a Refuge, to be nearly self-supporting, in which orphan lads in work will be boarded and lodged at a charge of three shillings weekly. The total weekly expenses are about £4. 10s.

A few months after the establishment of the East End Juvenile Mission at Hope Place, Barnardo issued his first report which he had printed in Dublin. The title, 'The First Occasional Record of the Lord's dealings in connection with the East End Juvenile Mission', showed that Barnardo was still greatly influenced by Müller's work. Müller never appealed directly for funds for his orphan homes. Instead he produced each year a long report entitled 'The Life of Trust, being a narrative of the Lord's dealings with George Müller'. Barnardo, however, straight away made it clear that he did not aspire to follow Müller's example over the question of appealing for money. His report covered the period from when he first conceived the plan to extend the work of the Ernest Street ragged school to the summer of 1868. It is important as, taken in conjunction with reports and letters which appeared simultaneously in *The Revival*, it gives the only account available of Barnardo's activities during his early years in London, and was the last detailed statement he was to make about his work until he published a major report on the mission in January 1876 under the heading *Rescue the Perishing*, which was to be the cause of a lot of controversy. It is also interesting because the major part of the report deals with Barnardo's work as an evangelist, and it is clear that at that time he saw this as his vocation and his work with children was, as he put it, to 'prepare them for heaven'.

The stories in the report are all of his successes as an evangelist and not, as they were to become, about the rescue of children. The courtyard outside the houses provided an ideal place for open-air services, and Barnardo and his helpers, perhaps members of the Brethren fellowship in Sydney Place, held open-air meetings several times a week including Sundays. By July Barnardo was already officiating at his second baptism, a function he could perform as a member of the Brethren fellowship. Although he did express some doubts in his report as to his pastoral vocation, he said that as his little church had no stated minister they might be judged as 'latitudinarian with regard to the great question of recognition of pastoral care'.

It is a measure of his powers of leadership that at the age of twenty-three he could persuade men who had spent the major part of their lives drinking and swearing to give it all up, to openly profess themselves Christians and in several instances to join with him as his co-workers. Frederick Fielder and Walter Notman, both to become members of his staff for many years, belonged to the select band who came under his influence in those early days.

Notwithstanding any passing doubts Barnardo may have felt about his pastoral qualifications, his church continued to grow and by October he had baptised and received into fellowship more than sixty-nine individuals. A notice appeared in *The Revival* underlining the appeal in his report for money to enable a hall to be built to accommodate the people in the winter, taking in the ground floor and yard of one of the houses. The announcement was shortly followed by another one appealing for a successor to take over the work, as Barnardo still hoped to be accepted by Hudson Taylor for service in China the following year. It was almost certainly as a result of reading these two appeals in *The Revival* that Samuel Smith wrote to Barnardo offering him money to build a hall if he would give up all thought of going to China. Samuel Smith, a successful Liverpool industrialist who was later to become a Member of Parliament, was the wealthy brother Barnardo had mentioned in his letter to Berger. In that letter Barnardo used his refusal to accept the money as evidence of his unchanged desire to go to China. However, it seems that he did, in fact, accept the money, for the balance sheet for the following year showed that building repairs and alterations amounted to £290. Obviously at that time Barnardo was still hoping that he would find someone to take over the work of the mission. In later accounts of this incident, written in 1900 like the story of the donkey shed, the sum of money had increased to £1,000 and the hall for which the money was intended had become a home for waif and stray children.

For any young man to have achieved so much would be extraordinary but to have done it while he was still studying at the London Hospital was even more so. It was almost as if Hudson Taylor's refusal to accept him as a candidate had spurred him on to ever greater activity in the East End, and all the time his flair for publicising his work was developing. Short stories, signed only with his initials but later under his full name, started to appear in *The Revival*. From these stories as well as from preaching engagements, Barnardo was beginning to earn himself a small income.

It was sometime during this period that the subject of his most famous story, the encounter with Jim Jarvis, the first destitute child he had come across, took place. The story was told many times by Barnardo during the course of his life, but the version that appeared in *The Christian*[18] in 1872 under the title 'How it all happened' is the earliest so far traced. From the internal evidence provided by this version of the story, with its definite reference to the incident occurring after the work of evangelisation had been going on for three years, it is clear that the meeting took place during the winter of 1869–70. Many later versions give the date as early as 1866, thus providing the reason for making the date of his arrival in London coincide with the start of his work for children. The story now has its own status as part of Barnardo folklore, so this early version is of particular interest especially when compared to later ones which do not have the same immediacy.

One evening, the attendants at the Ragged School had met as usual, and at about half past nine o'clock were separating for their homes. A little lad, whom we had noticed listening very attentively during the evening, was amongst the last to leave, and his steps were slow and unwilling.

'Come, my lad, had you not better get home? It is very late. Mother will be coming for you.'

'Please sir, let me stop!'

'No, I cannot, I think it's quite time for you to get away now. Why do you want to stop?'

'Please, sir, do let me stay. I won't do no 'arm.'

'Well, but had you not better get home? Your mother will wonder what kept you so late.'

'I ain't got no mother.'

'Haven't got a mother, boy? Where do you live?'

'Don't live nowhere.'

'Now, my lad, it is of no good your trying to deceive me. Come here and tell me what you mean. Where do you come from? Where did you sleep last night?'

In calling the child to our side we never for a moment believed that his tale was true. Our own three years' experience among poor boys and girls had taught us something of the cruelty with which many of the lowest class treat their children. And in addition to this, we had often met boys who were hungry because their miserable homes afforded them little sustenance; but we knew nothing experimentally of the houseless and destitute, having a general vague impression that homeless little ones were generally orphans and if very poor were taken care of by the Union. We also thought that the stories about their condition and sufferings in London which have attracted attention were mainly furnished by the vivid imaginations of certain writers, whose love for the sensational had overcome their strict regard for the truth. That this is the state of mind felt by a very large number of persons, we feel assured, although they like ourselves, labouring among the poor have never yet been brought face to face with these awful facts in our social history, which however much they may appal and shock, must nevertheless be admitted as true ... 'Do you mean to say, my boy, that you have no home, and that you have no mother and father?'

'That's the truth on't, sir; I ain't telling you no lie about it.'

'Well, but where did you sleep last night?'

'Down in Whitechapel, sir, along o'the 'aymarket in one of them carts as is filled with 'ay; an' then I met a chap as I knowed this afternoon, and he told me to come up 'ere to school, as perhaps you'd let me lie near the fire all night. I won't do no 'arm sir, if you let me stop.'

It was a very cold night, for although there had been no snow or wet during the day, the sharp and biting wind seemed to penetrate every joint, no matter how one was wrapped up; and as we looked at the little lad, whom the Lord had sent to us and noticed how ill prepared he was to resist the vicissitudes of the weather our heart sank as we silently reflected 'if all this boy says is true how much he must have suffered!' and then for the first time we asked ourselves the question. Is it possible that in this great city there are others as young as this boy, as helpless, as ill prepared to meet the trials of cold and hunger and exposure of every kind? It is possible, we thought, that there are many such in this great city of London of ours – this city of wealth, of open Bibles, of Gospel preaching and of ragged schools. Instinctively too we asked the question of the poor little fellow who stood beside us waiting anxiously the result of our cogitation and received the sad reply —

'Oh yes sir, lots, 'eaps on em! More 'n I could count!'

Barnardo took Jim back to his own room and gave him some hot coffee. Fed and warmed, the child told how he had left home after his mother died when he was about five years old. An old lady had befriended him and eventually he got work helping a lighterman with odd jobs on a barge, but 'swearing Dick', as the man was called, was often drunk and thrashed Jim constantly. Jim stayed with the lighterman for some time, afraid to run away lest the man set his dog on him as he often threatened to do, but eventually he made his escape. He helped an old lady who kept a tripe and trotter stall for a while, but he was often without money for food or lodging and was forced to sleep out. Then, he said, it was the police that were worst. Sometimes they let him off with a kick or a clout, but twice he had been before the magistrate for sleeping out and once he was locked up and sent to the workhouse. Barnardo in his serious way commented: 'He was a quaint little vagabond, and his sharp witticism disturbed our gravity more than once; but beneath all his external appearance of mirth and lightness of heart there was a sad under-current of remembrances of misery and sorrow that brought tears to our eyes.'

This same courage was noted by Shaftesbury writing some twenty years earlier about the gutter children, 'a tribe, bold, pert and dirty as London sparrows, but pale, feeble and sadly inferior to them in plumpness of outline . . . Though wan and haggard, they are singularly vivacious and engaged in every sort of occupation but that which would be beneficial to themselves and creditable to the neighbourhood.' Barnardo's first waif was almost certainly a Roman Catholic by birth. Barnardo finished his interrogation by asking the boy if he had ever heard of Jesus and received the following unexpected answer:

'Oh sir,' he said – and he looked sharply about the room, with a timorous glance into the dark corners where the shadows fell – and then sinking his voice into a whisper, he added, 'He's the Pope o' Rome.'

This startling reply gave rise to further astonished questions from Barnardo:

'Sir, you see, mother, afore she died, always did that when she spoke of the Pope' – and the boy made what is known as the sign of the cross – 'and one day when she wor a-dyin' at the 'firmary' a gent wor there in black clothes, a talkin' to her an' mother wor a cryin'. Then they began to talk about Him sir, and they both did the same.'

The confusion in the child's mind between the Pope and Jesus was too much for Barnardo and forthwith he launched into the story of Jesus' life, with Jim carefully listening and drawing parallels between the Roman soldiers and the 'perlice', appalled at the story of the crucifixion and crying out, 'Oh sir, that wor worse than "Swearing Dick" gave me.' It was after midnight when Jim and Barnardo eventually set off to find one of the 'lays', as the secret places where homeless children slept at night were called. The iron roof of the shed where Jim knew the children to be was in an old clothes market called 'the Change' off Petticoat Lane, and Jim scrambled up the well-worn grooves and handed down a stick for Barnardo to grasp so that he could help him up. Barnardo has many times described his reactions to his first encounter with the realities of destitution, but his own words written soon afterwards speak more eloquently and tell us more than any later reconstruction.

The roof was dome shaped, and adjoining and communicating with it was a large hay loft, used by dealers in china for packing their wares.

This loft was closed, but a good deal of straw had dropped from it into the gutter, and was put into use by the lads, whom we saw lying there asleep. With their heads upon the higher part of the roof and their feet somewhat in the gutter, but in a great variety of postures, lay eleven boys huddled together for warmth – no roof or covering of any kind was over them and the clothes they had were rags, which seemed to be worse than Jim's ...

We felt so powerless that we did not dare to interrupt their slumbers. Already we were oppressed with the tremendous responsibility in the charge of one little fellow, and to awaken these eleven, to hear their cries for food and help was more than we could bear; so taking another hurried glance at the boys, looking again at the eleven upturned faces, white with cold and hunger, we hastened away ...

Our own past career and future prospects came rapidly to mind, and ignorant of what was already being done for the outcast boys of London, unaware too, that the state of things we had just witnessed was a well-known, though lamentable fact, we asked ourselves again and again the question, 'Are we ready at all costs to devote ourselves to the task of finding out these poor destitutes and saving them from a life of misery and crime which must be their portion if no hand be extended to help them?' That awful night of discovery was not forgotten, for again and again the faces of those boys, their destitution and their mute appeal for help entered like iron into our soul, until leaving ourselves and our future career in the hands of Him who ruleth all men's hearts ... we were enabled to renounce a life of usefulness in another and a distant land ...

What hesitation marked the first steps taken! Of the divine character of our mission we have no doubts; and although the longer we are engaged in it the more deeply do we deplore our unworthiness, feebleness and failure, yet the abounding grace and wondrous faithfulness of our God have proved again and again the theme of our song, the sustaining source of our joy, and the incentive to renewed and holy labour.

From this account it can be seen that any doubts Barnardo may have felt about the direction his life should take were now removed. The meeting with Jim Jarvis is clearly linked to his decision to renounce his intention of going to China. Barnardo had found his mission in life and from now on all his ability, aggressive energy, zeal and flair were to be increasingly directed towards the needs of the destitute child. As his writings show, he felt that evening with Jim to have been a direct revelation from God and a personal message to him. With his inbuilt dislike of any kind of authority he had discovered a cause he could serve, a role he could fill which suited his qualities, satisfied his need for independent action and which he believed was divinely inspired. Certainly no one else could have projected the plight of the destitute child in the way he did.

His work with his schools and mission was, however, attracting the attention of other leaders in the mission field, and

Barnardo must have been encouraged to receive £25 from the Reformatory and Refuge Union, whose patron was Shaftesbury. Mr Williams gave a very concise account of Barnardo's work to his committee, who recommended that the special donation be given to aid and encourage this extensive and well-worked effort.[19]

> The Day Schools, where the scholars pay 1d or 2d per week, has 250 children present. Evening schools are free, well attended, conducted by two paid masters and two paid mistresses. Sunday Schools – morning 180 scholars, evening 700 to 800 present. Conducted in separate premises is a Refuge for boys employed in wood chopping. Three houses in Hope Place and one in Commercial Road are used, a fourth in Hope Place is about to be taken. The whole is the energetic work of one young man, Mr. Barnardo, a medical student. There is no committee. A Bank, a Library, Clothing Club, Boot Club, Parents' Meetings, Sewing class, Band of Hope Society are also usefully and fully at work.

The development of the wood-chopping brigade for which Barnardo raised loans totalling £145 was a shrewd move on his part. It provided employment for the boys and gave them an income and even in its first year made a modest profit. He had sound commercial sense and put to good use the knowledge he had acquired in the wine business. The wood-chopping brigade was the first of his commercial ventures and was closely followed by a city messenger brigade and a brushmaking and bootmaking department. The development of a home for these boys was something Barnardo had had in mind for two years. Since the boys were all in work and could pay for their keep, the running costs would be minimal if only he could raise the money to build the home.

In the two-page official report on the East End Juvenile Mission for 1870/1 Barnardo briefly reported that a home for working and destitute lads had been opened which would contain fifty boys but now had thirty-three, whom Barnardo referred to rather misleadingly as his thirty-three 'bairns'. From the even briefer statement of accounts it appeared the home cost £933. 16s. 7d. to rent, furnish and equip and that he received £53. 2s. 6d. from the lodger boys. Sundry donations for the year amounted to £2,428. 5s. 4d. During that winter Barnardo had been dangerously ill and was scarcely able to leave his room from November until February. Nothing but the bare fact of his illness is known though he himself speaks of suffering acutely during that period. It followed a time of great stress when he had finally decided to give up the idea of going to China, and raising money to establish that first home had been fraught with difficulties. At this period in his life Barnardo was still deeply influenced by the Brethren precept that to get into debt was not only wrong but that it contravened God's express ruling, 'owe no man anything'. Having spent all the capital he had at his disposal, work on the home would have to be stopped. A letter in *The Christian*[20] reveals how he interpreted the divine injunction to avoid debt in so far as it affected his work. He felt it would only be right to sign a contract if the money was readily available to fulfil its conditions, but it was permissible to employ a builder and obtain specifications, estimates and probable bills of quantity even if you had not money enough to complete the work, so long as you paid your builder's weekly statements as to labour and materials, dismissing both builder and workmen and closing the place until fresh funds were available.

R. C. Morgan, his influential friend and supporter, appealing in *The Christian* for funds to enable Barnardo to complete his work, added his personal seal of approval to this method of proceeding:[21] 'As I think of this half completed work, I scarcely know whether I am more impressed by the skill and industry in the portion already prepared or with regret that the workmen should have been for the present all dismissed because this young medical student had not funds to finish the work.' But finish Barnardo did, and the home was opened without fuss or ceremony in December 1870. A year later he was writing of plans to expand the number of places to one hundred and twenty, in spite of the enormous difficulties he and his co-workers experienced in dealing with this class of children. R. C. Morgan, in a comment appended to a further appeal by Barnardo for funds, also made the point that Barnardo's mission was not the only one dealing with distress in the metropolis.

Our dear brother Barnardo possesses, in addition to many other valuable qualifications, the gift of telling a good story well. We are very thankful therefore for his graphic accounts of his work in the needy East. But his narrative deserves an additional value from the fact, which must by no means be overlooked, that his mission is a *representative* one – that in describing his own work he is also describing, with more or less exactness, not only the work of many other faithful men and women, not only in the East but in all other parts of London, and to some extent also in all large towns and cities in the British Isles.

3

The Evangelical Connection

BARNARDO had arrived in London untried and penniless; with
only his restless energy, his dedicated sense of mission and his
own domineering personality he had remarkably soon made a
name for himself among those working in the East End. Within
five years of his arrival in London his mission would be
acknowledged as one of the largest and fastest-growing in the
East End; within ten years, without the assistance of a
committee or treasurer, he was handling sums in excess of
£25,000 a year. All his energy and determination would have
availed him little had he not had the support of the evangelical
movement, a movement which stamped its austere values on
the Victorian era and through the philanthropic endeavours of
its members left as a legacy a system of social service which
continues to make its contribution to the welfare of the country
today.

Barnardo's rapid success was so very closely bound up with
the evangelical philanthropic movement that to understand the
reasons for the one it is necessary to examine the philosophy,
background and influence of the other. In her book *Evangelicals
in Action*, Kathleen Heaseman analysed the scope and depth of
the social work undertaken by voluntary charitable institutions
in the nineteenth century. Although her assessment can only be
a rough generalisation, she estimated that of the total number of
voluntary organisations working at that period three quarters
were evangelical in outlook.[1]

There is no need to search far for the reasons behind this
figure. The evangelical revival that had swept over Ireland in
1859 had not been confined to that country alone. In England
and Scotland too, many people had experienced a personal
conversion to a living faith, finding authority for their beliefs in
the truths of the Gospel. Revival evangelicalism, with its

emphasis on the deep sinfulness of all men, taught that only through conversion and repentance could man be saved. Therefore evangelicals, with their concern for the fate of each individual soul, were profoundly convinced that their first duty was to bring salvation to all those in need, regardless of merit or social standing. Only the methods they used to achieve their goal varied. It was felt that for the majority the more traditional methods of evangelising would suffice, but as far as the poor were concerned they quickly realised that religion could not compete with hunger and despair. They therefore set to work to relieve poverty, and in so doing they founded a far-reaching and extensive system of charitable social work. Barnardo's gradual discovery of the needs of destitute children and his immediate and practical response to those needs was one of the most conspicuously successful examples of just such social work. Evangelicals responded enthusiastically to the idea that children, besides being rescued from a life on the streets, could, in a home, more easily be given religious instruction and taught the truths of the Gospel in the hope that they might also find salvation. Hence the amazing success of Barnardo's appeals for money.

The names of a small number of influential families appear constantly in the history of the evangelical and religious social movement in the second half of the nineteenth century. The extent of the missionary activities of the Victorian philanthropists and the influence they exerted on society can only be explained by the cohesive nature of their interconnected world. Membership ranged from the Nonconformist industrialist Samuel Morley to the aristocratic Lord Shaftesbury and the brilliant Lord Chancellor, Lord Cairns. Their influence, with the exception of Lord Shaftesbury's, has tended to be underestimated. This has been due partly to the conservative position they adopted over the interpretation of the Bible and partly to their special views on questions of prophecy and its related eschatology, the expectation of the end of the world. There is no doubt that millennialism, the belief in the imminent Second Advent of Jesus Christ, was more generally prevalent at this time than has been realised. It is one of the classic ways in which man reacts to the problem of evil and is a recurring phenomenon in religious history. The important role played by millennial enthusiasms in the nineteenth century has been deliberately neglected. Evangelical historians have designedly played down the millennial content of evangelicalism at that time, and understandably, in view of the fact that it is a difficult doctrine to put across today; it was also dangerous to evangelical unity because differing interpretations of prophecy led to damaging quarrels within the movement.

Belief in the millennium was an integral part of Brethrenism. Barnardo, because of his association with the Brethren movement, held definite pre-millennial views, which meant that he believed that Christ's Second Coming was imminent and would precede the millennium. (Post-millennialists believed that the Second Advent would be preceded by a thousand years of peace.) Millennial influence had a dual effect on those who believed its eschatological doctrines. In the first place they tended to believe that social change would only produce greater corruption in the world; therefore they did not look with favour on any sort of radical approach to social problems. But secondly, because they believed themselves to be living in an important age in history with only a limited time in which to achieve their objectives, their work had an urgency and a positive quality about it which was not matched by those whose time scales were longer. Barnardo's early work reflected both these tendencies, although as he came to appreciate the radical change that improved living conditions made to the children's physical health, this aspect of his work came to the fore. The early emphasis on the spiritual regeneration of the children came to be more evenly balanced with a concern for their material and physical wellbeing. But the sense of urgency that was so apparent in his early writing never left him, although it took a rather different form in later years.

Any analysis of the work of Victorian philanthropists leads us into a maze of family relationships and connections. Edwin Hodder, in his biography of Samuel Morley, quoted Shaftesbury as saying that the great givers of London could be enumerated on the fingers of both hands; the secretary of one of the largest distributing organisations declared that the disappearance of two thousand families from the world would stop or suspend all charitable work throughout Britain.[2] A useful example of relationships within this dynamic network is provided by a study of the involvement of the Kinnairds, an evangelical family of moderate liberal views, in Christian social work. Emily Kinnaird in her book, *Reminiscences*, claimed that her brother, the eleventh baron, was president or treasurer of twenty-eight different societies and on the committees of as many more. Many of these commitments were inherited from his father, who had married Mary Jane Hoare of the banking family, herself one of the founders of the YWCA and involved with social work for women. The tenth baron had been a schoolfellow and intimate friend of Quintin Hogg, founder of the Polytechnic. Emily herself was the god-daughter of Lady Aberdeen, wife of the Prime Minister. Mary Morley, Samuel Morley's daughter, was one of her dearest friends. Shaftesbury was a cousin of the Kinnairds. He, together with Lord Cairns, the Waldegraves and George Williams, founder of the YMCA, all worshipped together at the Portman Chapel, an Episcopalian church which in practice came very close to being Nonconformist.[3]

Besides the upper-class families like the Aberdeens, Kinnairds, Waldegraves, Kintores and Pelhams, many wealthy middle-class families, whose members were bankers like the Bevans, Trittons, Barclays and Dennys, were also involved in evangelical social work. Emily Kinnaird wrote that the banking houses of Barclay, Tritton, Ransome, Bouverie and Co. and of J. F. Deacon were laughingly referred to as the 'evangelical alliance' because nearly all the great and small evangelical societies banked with one or the other. Clyde Binfield in his study, *George Williams and the YMCA*, saw these families as the most important contributors to a national social policy because, in their interconnected world, so many of them were involved in the same charities that it was almost as though they could impose a consistent policy on the work undertaken. James Findlay in his biography of Dwight Moody, the American evangelist, found it little short of amazing how Moody not only met but became friends with so many leading evangelical figures during his first short visit to London in 1867, which only lasted for four months.[4]

It was through his connection with the YMCA, the Brethren movement and the China Inland Mission that Barnardo also quickly came into contact with people in the evangelical movement who were to be of the greatest importance to him in the future. The tide was running his way; he was not the only one to be appalled by the conditions he had discovered in the East End. The rapid growth of the ragged school movement, in which Shaftesbury took a great interest, had revealed to many the plight of the child population in urban centres. The Ragged School Union had already established its first permanent home in Broad Street, Bloomsbury, in 1852, and in 1858 a refuge for destitute children was founded in Great Queen Street. It was under the auspices of the Ragged School Union that Shaftesbury gave his famous supper to the homeless boys of London in 1866, which resulted in the establishment of the training ships, *Chichester* and *Arethusa*, a provision much admired by Barnardo.

The itinerant preachers of the London City Mission, founded in 1835, had also become increasingly aware not only of the chronic poverty of the East End but also of the almost total lack of religion among the population. The great increase in charitable social work in the East End which took place during the 1860s was certainly mainly in response to evangelical concern at the state of the souls of the 'lapsed masses'. The census of 1851 had revealed that less than half the population could be said to be Christian; it soon came to be realised that in the East End the proportion of those with any knowledge of the Christian religion was still smaller.

Richard Morgan, a man little known outside evangelical circles, was one of the key figures in this world. As editor of *The Revival*, which used the word 'millennium' as its telegraphic address, he was very influential. His journal was an immediate success, and when it changed its name to *The Christian* in 1870 it had a large and growing circulation. It carried frequent reports of the work being carried on by the many and varied missions that had become established in the East End, including William and Catherine Booth's East London Christian Mission, as the precursor of the Salvation Army was known.

It was at a prayer meeting at Morgan's house that Barnardo met, among others, Dwight Moody. His friendship with the American evangelist can be said to date from that time and it lasted until Moody's death in 1899. Out of this friendship there developed a mutual affection and admiration. Just before his death Moody had been asked to write something about the lives of the twelve most useful men he had known. Barnardo was his first choice, and although he died before he had completed his task E. C. Cleveland, who finished the article, which was printed in the magazine *Our Day*[5] under the title 'A Prince Among Benefactors', said Moody's choice of Barnardo for first place was not that of sudden inspiration but rather of settled conviction. In 1867 Moody was virtually unknown outside Chicago. His great revival campaigns, which were to make his name a household word, were still in the future. At forty-five he was more than twenty years older than Barnardo, but his personal qualities of leadership and a certain charisma already marked him out as an outstanding personality and one whom the young Barnardo was both to admire and imitate. They had many characteristics in common. Moody had been working with slum children in Chicago and at this meeting in Morgan's house he gave a vivid description of his experiences with the children of his Sunday school. In a report of the occasion Morgan's son wrote:[6] 'Nothing which he has spoken since then has exceeded the burning interest of the description to which we listened; to the unique and thrilling way in which he pursued his reclamatory efforts among the rough and lawless children of the Western City.' There is no doubt that this encounter with Moody made a deep and lasting impression on Barnardo. His immediate reaction was to try to emulate the work Moody was doing in Chicago and to start something of his own on the same lines.

It is hardly surprising that Barnardo should have been impressed by Moody's enthusiastic account of his work in Chicago. Moody, like Barnardo, had been relatively untutored in theology before he began his career, yet both shared the same overwhelming desire to preach the Gospel, almost learning as they went the rudiments of their craft. Both were influenced by Brethrenism, although Moody was too eclectic in his approach to religion to be bound by any sect; he had come to London to visit Müller's Bristol homes and to listen to the famous Charles Spurgeon preaching. Both were involved with the YMCA, and Barnardo like Moody had started his career in mission work as a Sunday school teacher, albeit in a ragged school not under his own control. It was only two or three weeks after Moody's departure that Barnardo's first letter appeared in *The Revival*[7] asking for financial support for his first independent venture. It was the ambiguous terms in which his letter was written that caused the rift with the committee of the Ernest Street ragged school. Moody used many unconventional methods to attract children to his school: riding round on a white donkey he distributed cakes and sweets to encourage them to come to his classes; before they were due to start he paraded through the streets with banners publicising his work. In the plan outlined in his first letter Barnardo also included the use of banners as a means of making his ideas known, and he too carried goodies in his pockets for the children, besides tempting them to come and listen by the offer of a free tea.

Two photographs exist showing Moody with his Sunday school, both taken in 1862. The first shows him with a group of ragged children over the caption, 'Moody's Body Guard. Will it pay?' The second photograph shows the same children, neat and tidy, studying their books; the caption reads, 'It does pay.' It was only two years after his meeting with Moody that Barnardo started to issue his own famous series of 'before' and 'after' photographs. They were stylistically so similar to those taken by Moody that it is difficult to avoid the conclusion that Moody had brought his photographs to London with him and that Barnardo had seen them. Recognising their powerful appeal in terms of publicity, Barnardo adapted the idea to suit his own needs. Advertisements announcing the sale of the photographs in aid of the East End Juvenile Mission first appeared in *The Revival* in 1869. The earliest known surviving photograph is that of a boy crouching in rags on a doorstep, which was used on the cover of the catalogue for the exhibition in 1974 at the National Portrait Gallery, 'The Camera and Dr Barnardo'. Barnardo said he fell over the boy huddled in that position in the street, and made him take up the pose again to be photographed.

Moody had been the guest of the Kinnairds during his 1867 visit. It was to take Barnardo longer than four months to gain the kind of influential support and friendship that Moody had found extended to him during his visit. Moody was, after all, a foreigner, and his unconventional manners could be accepted as amusingly eccentric. But although Barnardo was younger and as yet relatively unknown, it was not long before he too was able to rely on the same influential support, although never on the same terms of easy friendship as marked Moody's relationship with the evangelical leaders. The intense and self-contained evangelical circle, whose middle- and upper-class origins might appear to have precluded any close association with the lower classes other than that of *de haut en bas*, were remarkably successful in overcoming this social barrier in pursuit of their aims.

At the beginning of the century it had seemed to them that the heathen in foreign lands stood in greatest need, and they had played their part in building up the great missionary societies to meet this challenge. Barnardo's desire to serve as a missionary in China was very much part of this movement. Then, as the revelations of the city missionaries and the ragged school teachers made known the condition of the East End of London, confirming the unwelcome facts of the census of 1851, evangelicals came to see the East End as the right place to begin the necessary work of evangelisation in their own country. Baptist Noel was the chief speaker at a big Revival meeting held in 1861 to offer prayers for the success of work to be done in the East End. The Hon. and Rev. Baptist Noel was an ardent and vocal low churchman, the brother of the Earl of Gainsborough, uncle of Mary Jane Kinnaird and connected by marriage to Shaftesbury; he was also a founder member of the Evangelical Alliance. He said on this occasion, as reported in *The Revival*:

> If this work of Evangelisation is done we shall see some unknown Luthers and Whitfields excavated out of this dark mine to spread the Gospel further and wider than we have any idea of. If working men like Richard Weaver and others begin to preach the Gospel, I believe we are on the eve of greater work than England ever saw – and the East End of London is the place to begin.

Seven years later another great meeting, to celebrate the results of the prayers sent up in 1861, was also reported in *The Revival*.[8] The establishment of the Rowley Homes in Spitalfields and W. J. Lewis's gospel hall, the work of T. J. Barnardo and Miss McPherson, but above all the work of William Booth's East London Christian Mission were seen as evidence that prayer had been answered.

The part played by working-class preachers in spreading the

evangelical message is now virtually forgotten, although the names of the great preachers like Spurgeon and Booth are still remembered. Richard Weaver, referred to by Baptist Noel, was typical. An ex-collier by profession, he had the reputation of having been instrumental in the conversion of more individuals during the first twenty years of his ministry than any other evangelist. Harry Moorhouse, the young evangelist who found fame after following Moody back to Chicago and, preaching on the theme of God's love for man, is said to have caused Moody to alter his style, was just such another. Like John Hambledon, who was preaching in Dublin at the time of Barnardo's conversion, these itinerant evangelists preached the Gospel to the people on racecourses, at fairs, in tents, halls, theatres and circuses. Henry Varley, who had once been a butcher, and Joshua Poole, jailed for practically beating his wife to death, were others of humble origin who associated on equal terms with men of rank and wealth, united in the struggle to bring the message of salvation to the masses. Evangelicals knew they needed these working-class preachers if they were to reach the inhabitants of East London, and they did not hesitate to stretch out the hand of friendship. Shaftesbury's classic remark about J. W. Orsman,[9] a post office clerk who had founded the Golden Lane Mission to Costermongers, nicely delineates the width of the social gulf that had to be crossed: 'Few things are more marvellous than to see what can be done by one man, however socially inferior, if he has the love of Christ in his heart.'

So Thomas Barnardo, preaching from a chair in the streets of Stepney, found himself part of a movement already broadly based and united by a common desire to bring the message of the Gospel to the people. With his unusual background, his striking ability to relate to the people among whom he lived, his powers of leadership, his tremendous energy and boundless enthusiasm it is no wonder that his activities were watched with increasing interest by leaders of the evangelical movement, and more especially by those who shared his belief in the imminence of the Second Coming.

Apart from those who knew of his work personally and the readers of *The Revival* who had seen his appeals, Barnardo was still unknown. His first public speech came about almost accidentally. Thain Davidson, a Presbyterian minister, had inaugurated in 1868 Sunday Afternoon services for non-churchgoing people at the great Agricultural Hall in Islington. A powerful speaker himself, he had attracted many notabilities to speak at these services, including Shaftesbury on one occasion. As a candidate for the China Inland Mission, Barnardo had been invited to sit on the platform at one of these Sunday gatherings (the date is not known). The main speaker failed to arrive. Davidson, knowing Barnardo was working in the East End, invited him to talk of his experiences. Although extremely nervous to begin with, Barnardo warmed to his talk, for it was shortly after his meeting with Jim Jarvis. Speaking of the feelings he had experienced after his discovery of the problem of destitution among the children of the East End, he forgot his nervousness and his eloquence both moved and impressed his audience. As he was leaving the platform a young servant girl came up and asked to speak to him. She said she had been collecting farthings for foreign missions, but having heard Barnardo speak of his poor children she wished to give the money to him instead. Barnardo included this story among his later recollections and said that he felt 'not a little embarrassed' by the gift of a parcel of coins wrapped up in paper, and wrote that he felt himself getting red and hot all over for 'this was the first public money I had ever received'. It was perhaps the first money he had ever received so directly, but he had already received money from the public as a result of his earlier appeals in *The Revival*. However it did mark the start of a trend in the pattern of giving that was to remain constant. The twenty-seven farthings given him by the servant girl were to prove symbolic, for an analysis of Barnardo's receipts over the years showed that the bulk of his support came from a vast number of small donations, an unusual source at that date. Perhaps it was the result of his bold and broadly-based advertising campaign.

When Barnardo arrived in London Shaftesbury was, without doubt, the leading evangelical philanthropist, although that was a description he himself would have deprecated. Philanthropic agencies of all kinds sought his patronage, for to have his name as president or patron was of enormous value in terms of prestige and influence. He gave unstintingly of his time to those engaged in any work that promoted knowledge of the Gospel among the poor, although he complained in his diary that he was being hacked to pieces by engagements, chairs and committees. Two years before Barnardo arrived William McDuff had painted a picture entitled *Shaftesbury, or Lost and Found* showing two small street 'arabs' gazing through a shop window at a portrait of the Earl. It poignantly symbolised the debt street children already owed to Shaftesbury at that time. His abiding interest in their welfare sprang as much from compassion for them as from an intense concern that they should not grow up without knowledge of the love of God. He would certainly soon have been aware of Barnardo's work, if not through *The Revival* then through his own acquaintance with ragged school teachers and his personal knowledge of the work being done in the East End. Even in his old age he found time to visit and encourage those who worked in East London and walked with them along stinking alleyways and through foetid courtyards, not sparing himself the sights and smells, the inescapable consequence of the wretched housing and the miserably overcrowded conditions in which the inhabitants lived.

In his later years Barnardo liked to see himself in the role of successor to Shaftesbury, but his actual relationship with the venerable statesman during his life is not altogether without ambiguity. There is no doubt that in his later years Barnardo had a tendency to romanticise his early life, and his natural inclination to embroider the facts makes it difficult to present an accurate record of those years. Barnardo's own account of his first meeting with Shaftesbury provides a splendid example of his dramatic inventiveness. According to this story, it was as a result of his talk at the Agricultural Hall, which was reported in a religious periodical, that Shaftesbury sent him an invitation to dine with him at his home. According to Barnardo the object of the invitation was to enable him to meet fourteen or fifteen guests with similar interests who doubted that children were, in fact, living in conditions of destitution such as he had described. Barnardo wrote how after dinner he recounted yet again to the unbelieving guests the story of Jim Jarvis. To prove that it was no exaggeration, it was agreed at Shaftesbury's request that the whole party should go by cab to Billingsgate so that they should see for themselves the 'lays' where the children slept out. After searching for some time, Barnardo said, he finally discovered seventy-three boys sleeping under tarpaulins, and

Shaftesbury, supposedly seeing destitution for the first time, is said to have whispered to him, 'All London shall know of this.'

To imply, as Barnardo does in this story, that Shaftesbury was unaware of the problem of destitution among children until it was thus dramatically revealed to him, is enough to cast doubt on this version of the affair. Fortunately an account of a similar meeting in Shaftesbury's house in Grosvenor Square at which Barnardo was present was recorded in *The Christian*. The details correspond sufficiently to make it reasonably likely that this was, in fact, the same occasion that Barnardo later described so graphically. Shaftesbury had instructed Mr Gent, secretary of the Ragged School Union, to invite the leaders of fourteen or fifteen missions working in the East End to his house in Grosvenor Square so that he might discover for himself the scope of their work and how it might be extended. Shaftesbury, who had been responsible for the establishment of Sunday services in theatres as a means of bringing the Gospel to the poor and whose passionate interest in the propagation of the Gospel can be seen from the articles he wrote in *The Christian* on the subject, provided the assembled mission leaders with tea. He then addressed them:[10]

It is evident that there are several thousand people who would be destitute of all spiritual care and as lost as the tribes at the centre of Africa but for the agencies represented here. Possibly something may be done to tighten the bands that bind you, but I should be sorry for anything to hinder your individual and independent action...

Your plans and modes must be aggressive that you may go and take by storm these people in their lairs. All you want is increased agency and funds to put them into operation. I am sure a great field is left untilled because we do not send out Christian labourers by two's and three's, into the courts and alleys and amongst those who never go a hundred yards from where they live.

Calling upon each in turn to speak of his work, Shaftesbury said that he felt satisfied that more good was being done by them in bringing the Gospel to 'those portions of the population we have named than by all our religious establishments put together'. Among those who spoke were J. W. Orsman, whose work with the Costermongers' Mission had particularly interested Shaftesbury, and George Holland who, besides his ragged school work, had worked with Annie McPherson to found a boys' home in Hackney as well as helping her to establish her own 'home of industry' in Spitalfields; William Booth was unable to attend through illness, but Catherine Booth spoke forcefully in his absence. She gave a brief account of her husband's work during the six years he had been in London, and said the East London Christian Mission had now free sittings for six thousand people and that two hundred services were held every week, both in and out of doors; but in spite of reaching an estimated fourteen thousand every Lord's day, if called upon to express in a single word the condition of the masses of the people she would say they were 'awfully *indifferent*' on the subject of salvation.

Barnardo was next called upon to speak. He, like Booth, had been in London for six years and had arrived 'without a friend and without a farthing'. He spoke of his work both with adults and with children. He said the majority of the children in his ragged schools were the children of the labouring classes, and typically his account included the proud boast that his ragged school was the largest in London. He gave a little dissertation on the true meaning of the terms 'gutter' and 'arab' children, which he said should only be applied to those who were thoroughly destitute and homeless, 'nobody's children'. He told how his attention had been drawn to the plight of these children by Jim Jarvis, and the account given on this occasion varies from the more usual one used later by Barnardo. In this version he said, 'The boy was fed and kept for the night. Next evening he brought me to a street near Drury Lane, where his companions were to be found. I rescued six, two of whom are now in Wales, one in Bradford and the rest in the Home.' From this account it would seem that Barnardo's discovery of Jim Jarvis did not take place until the winter of 1870–1, as it was only towards the end of 1870 that Barnardo was able to open his home in Stepney. If the report in *The Christian* is correct – and there is no reason why it should not be – he could not have placed the three rescued boys in the home for this same reason. Barnardo concluded his talk by urging emigration as a solution to the problem of unemployment among boys. Shaftesbury intervened to say that whatever might be said in favour of emigrating boys, the same should apply to girls, considering the disproportion revealed by the last census, which showed an enormous excess of females.

There is one further reference to a meeting between Barnardo and Shaftesbury, and it seems likely that Barnardo also drew on this experience for his own story. Before Barnardo was fully occupied with his own work he used to help Annie McPherson at her home of industry, and there are references to him drilling her boys. Monthly prayer meetings took place at the home and Barnardo would have come into contact with many others engaged in mission work on these occasions. One such meeting was held after Shaftesbury, George Holland and James Atkinson, accompanied by Barnardo, had returned after making a round of the lodging houses, where they had found the children in sad condition, and had also visited the haunts they frequented in Covent Garden. R. C. Morgan and Clara Lowe were among the speakers that evening. When Barnardo rose to speak about what might be done for the outcast child, he apologised for having to speak before some who were long and experienced workers in the field. Nothing, he thought, would help boys more than the establishment of a training ship. But although Shaftesbury was undoubtedly very interested in Barnardo's work in the early days, his initial support was qualified by his doubts about Barnardo's ability to manage his affairs wisely. This was reflected early on by his consistent refusal to help Barnardo acquire a training ship despite Barnardo's repeated appeals to his Lordship to use his influence with the Admiralty. Shaftesbury relied heavily on Samuel Morley for advice as to which charitable undertakings he should support, and it is possible that Morley may have felt doubts about Barnardo's lack of any kind of outside financial accountability. It would seem that the relationship between Barnardo and Shaftesbury was much less close than might have been expected, and than Barnardo would have wished to imply.

What he lacked by way of support from Shaftesbury was more than made up for by the help given him by R. C. Morgan, which was of inestimable value. For seven years, following the publication of his first letter in 1867, he used *The Revival* and its successor *The Christian* to keep the evangelical network informed of his work and aware of his plans. Through its columns he had instant access to a committed and powerful group of people who shared his views and aspirations and who frequently gave him their not inconsiderable financial support.

4

The Fall of the Citadel of Satan, 1872

BARNARDO'S mission work in the East End, in spite of its rapid growth, had made him known to the relatively small number of people actively engaged in work with the poor. His unambiguous appeals for money to expand his work had distanced him to an extent from his more orthodox evangelical co-workers, who preferred to wait upon God and trust to the slower workings of the evangelical grapevine to meet their needs. He was discovering and using his literary gifts to stir the consciences of his readers, and since 1869 he had been selling photographs of the children he had rescued in an attempt to raise money for his growing enterprises. Packets of photographs were advertised for sale which must make him one of the first, if not *the* first, to use this medium for both fund-raising and publicity purposes.

With his missionary ambitions and his medical career cast aside, his boundless appetite for work and his restless energy made him constantly alert for new openings. With a home of his own for boys, he no longer had to wait for the children to find him but could seek them out himself. It was during this period that he made many of his midnight forays, lantern in hand, searching for the children. He had installed a 'Godly brother' and his wife to be the resident governors of the home, with their own private quarters; the five dormitories could each sleep about a dozen boys. His midnight rambles not only kept the home filled with destitute lads, barefoot and ill clad, 'whose poor wan faces and ill nourished bodies betoken their previous histories', they provided the raw material for the constant flow of stories that appeared in *The Christian* and in the pamphlets Barnardo wrote and circulated to his supporters.

Homelessness was not the only prerequisite for admission, as a printed card used by Barnardo in 1872 to advertise the home demonstrated[1] Boys of all ages needing work and having no home could apply any Friday afternoon at half past two. They were requested to bring their fathers and mothers with them, but if unable to do this, could come alone. Boys were accepted who came from the country or who were working but had no friends in town, on payment of a small sum from their weekly wages, but the greater part of the space in the home was devoted to the really destitute boys of the street.

The home was strictly regulated and the boys lived disciplined lives. Barnardo himself interviewed each boy, and upon admission they were put at the top of the house and slept on hammocks of canvas sacking and were given a blanket in which to wrap themselves. When vacancies occurred and their behaviour had been satisfactory they moved down and were allowed more privileges. The boys were taught various trades, there being brushmaking, tailoring and shoemaking shops on the premises. One schoolmaster alone was responsible at first for their education. Their religious training was undertaken in the home; the boys went neither to chapel nor church, Barnardo being 'unwilling that their earliest impressions of the truth of God should be of things hard to understand'. Indoor services for the boys were held in which the 'simplest and catholic' truths embraced by evangelical Christians were taught. Boys Barnardo judged unlikely to prosper in this country were sent to Canada under the auspices of Annie McPherson's agency if the necessary £10 could be obtained to defray the expenses of their passage.

The daughter of a Scottish Quaker teacher, Annie McPherson had been converted at a Revival meeting in London in 1861. Coming to live in the East End some years later she had been appalled by the conditions in which children were forced to work, and shocked in particular by the plight of children who laboured for intolerably long hours gluing and sticking matchboxes. On the site of an old cholera hospital in Spitalfields she opened her 'home of industry' in 1868 and the following year she took her first party of children to Canada. From then on she took parties of children to Canada almost annually.

Some inkling of the difficulties Barnardo and his co-workers encountered at this time when dealing with his boys was revealed in a letter to his supporters :[2]

No one, except those immediately engaged in the work, can form any adequate idea of the trials of faith and of earnest purpose which we have experienced ... beloved in the Lord, need I remind you that it has not been all sunshine and many a dark and heavy cloud has swept across our horizon, making the path for a season difficult to tread.

No details are given as to the nature of the difficulties Barnardo had to face, inexperienced as he was in dealing with all the problems of a boys' home, and the letter continued in the almost mystical style which Barnardo used at that time when talking of his relationship with God: 'But oh! how shall I speak of other moments of communion – the hallowed revealing of God's face – the leaning upon his arm, so that one almost blessed the trial and care that taught us so to lean.'

A practice common among wealthy evangelicals at this time was to promise a certain sum of money if, by a given date, a specified number of contributors had promised like amounts. Barnardo's first experience of this type of fund-raising occurred in February 1872 when John Sands called and, having carefully inspected the premises and assured himself that Barnardo had kept clear of debt, offered £100 if he could obtain two other gifts of £100 each and ten others of £20 each by the first of April. Little is known of John Sands except that he was a member of a firm of solicitors – Frith, Sands & Co. Wealthy and devout and almost certainly a Plymouth Brother, he spent a great part of his life and the greater portion of his money on philanthropic and religious works. His interest in Barnardo's work was to be of major importance to its future development and the deep personal friendship which sprang up between the two men, notwithstanding the difference in their ages, was to be of inestimable importance to Barnardo. He it was who suggested that the premises should be vested in trustees and who offered to become one when the time came. It was also his encouragement and support, together with the help given by R. C. Morgan, that enabled Barnardo to take his next great step forward and involve himself so suddenly and dramatically in the temperance movement.

It was only gradually that the part played by drink, the cheapest and almost only solace available to the inhabitants of the East End, in bringing about the destruction of families, the ruin of parents and the homelessness of children, became obvious to Barnardo. True, his ragged school included a 'Band of Hope', but until 1870 he himself had not been an abstainer nor during his first years in London was he even in sympathy with the temperance movement. By the early seventies the movement was reaching the peak of its influence; its supporters were to succeed in getting the Licensing Act through Parliament in 1872. It had progressed from its working-class origins and was becoming successful and respectable, attracting adherents from a higher social stratum with more money to finance its expanding activities, which included the education of children through its bands of hope and a programme for the construction of meeting halls. It had also become almost exclusively religious in character, and there were many similarities between religious conversion and the act of taking the pledge, the mark of the total abstainer. As religious converts frequently talked of the experience of conversion, so reformed drunkards would lecture in the early days on how they came to take the pledge, illustrating their talks with experiences drawn from their own lives telling of the miseries they had endured as a result of drink and of how their lives had since been transformed. Later these early 'experience' meetings began to be replaced by 'drawing-room' meetings, and paid agents were employed to spread the word. Wealthy temperance supporters began to recognise that the tavern was the greatest rival with which the Church had to contend, and by the 1870s the temperance debate can be seen as basically an argument as to how leisure time should be spent.

As Barnardo's first-hand knowledge of the evils caused by drunkenness increased, so did his interest in the work being done by the temperance reformers. He had discovered, by tabulating in columns the causes which led to the children being eligible for admission to the homes, that 85 per cent owed their social ruin to the influence, direct or indirect, of the drinking habits of their parents, grandparents or other relatives.[3] He had his own first-hand experience of public-house life. Writing several years later about his experiences in the East End, he told how one evening, pushing a barrow through the streets calling out, 'A copy of God's word for threepence and Christ's New Testament for one penny', he entered a beer house, in spite of the remonstrances of the landlord who said he could not answer for the consequences.

I pushed my way into the parlour and entered the door. At first I could hardly see who were the occupants. It was a long, narrow room, with a bench running all round it on which lads and girls of from fourteen to eighteen years of age were seated; the view was obscured by a cloud of tobacco smoke that completely filled the room. As soon as I entered a couple of big fellows jumped up and, putting their feet against the door, thereby cut off my retreat. Nothing remained, therefore, but to boldly state my case. Advancing into the centre of the room I declared that I came to sell them the word of God and announced that I would give the whole Bible for threepence, the New Testament for a penny. 'Come, old fellow, chuck 'em out', cried one. 'None of yer palaver, let's have the books' . . . I was, however, determined not to part with the books unless I received payment; and leaping upon the table in the centre of the room, I appealed to them to deal fairly by me, and added that these books cost me exactly double what I was selling them for. For the most part all in the room were under the influence of drink, and although many were girls and boys they were wild and beyond control. I presently found myself on the ground with the flat part of the table pressing upon me, its legs being in the air, whilst several of the biggest lads leaped inside it, dancing a 'devil's tattoo' to my great discomfort and injury.

As a result of that incident Barnardo had two ribs broken and it was six weeks before he recovered from the effects of the treatment meted out to him.[4] A policeman brought in the boys who had broken his ribs, but he said he would not charge them: 'I was off my own beat and trespassing on theirs. I have no charge to bring against them.'[5] He later wrote,[6] 'I had begun with the Gospel and was determined, therefore, not to end with the law.' His decision brought unexpected dividends. The lads and girls sent a daily deputation to call on him and inquire after his health, and he wrote, 'I believe this incident did more to open hundreds of doors in that particular quarter of East London, and to give me a greater influence over the rough lads and girls than I could have attained had I been preaching or teaching among them for years.'

Barnardo realised he needed a more efficient means of reaching those who frequented the pubs and beer houses. Individual visits were not only hazardous, but reached a limited audience who were for the most part, if not hostile, certainly far from receptive. Several evangelists, among them William Booth, had begun making use of tents for their Gospel meetings during the summer months. Relatively cheap to hire, they could seat thousands. Barnardo was not long in seeing the advantages of a tent, but he went one further and pitched his right opposite the Edinburgh Castle, a flourishing and notorious gin palace in the Rhodeswell Road. With his own mission church forming the nucleus of the congregation, he had thrown his cap in the ring and was directly competing with the publican for the custom of the local people.

Until the 1870s nearly all temperance societies were connected with some church or mission; the whole tenor of the Anglican teetotal manifesto passed in 1859 was that moral reform must precede religious conversion. It was a world in which Barnardo found himself immediately at home, and as a religious leader he was ideally suited to the role of temperance reformer, particularly because he so well understood that the question of how men spent their leisure was of crucial importance. 'I have always felt that to preach total abstinence to the working man while I could point to no substitute to the social advantages of the public house was worse than useless,' he wrote. The great mission tent he erected in front of the Edinburgh Castle held over two thousand people, and to keep them entertained he employed Joshua and Mary Poole, the highly popular and successful evangelists who preached nightly to packed congregations during the summer of 1872. Joshua Poole, or 'fiddler Joss' as he was known, was a splendid example of the reformed drunkard, and he and his wife were typical of the eccentric and charismatic leaders who gave the temperance movement its vitality and fervour.

When the Edinburgh Castle suddenly came onto the market in the late summer, Barnardo was quick to seize the opportunity this offered and immediately started an appeal for funds to buy 'the Citadel of Satan'. It seems probable that besides R. C. Morgan and John Sands he had the support of Annie McPherson and Samuel Morley for this new temperance work, and Morley may well have been among those who provided part of the necessary financial backing. Samuel Morley was very actively involved in the temperance movement; he was president of a large number of temperance societies as well as being a generous supporter of the YMCA. His cousin, Rebekah Wilson of Sheffield, had married William Hind Smith, who was to become the YMCA's most active provincial leader, and she had already founded sixteen temperance refreshment houses in the north which were known as 'The British Workman', short for 'The British Workman Public Houses without Drink'. William Hind Smith had known Barnardo in Ireland where he had lived before coming to Leeds, and he and his family were to remain loyal friends and supporters of the Barnardo organisation for many years. Before beginning his temperance crusade in the East End, Barnardo went to see the Hind Smiths in Leeds. His thoroughness and his desire to excel and outdo all his co-workers, both characteristics which remained with him all his life, are well illustrated in Hind Smith's report on the visit Barnardo paid them to learn about the work done by Rebekah Hind Smith.

1   Joshua Poole preaching in the Gospel Tent, Limehouse

Each refreshment house had a mission hall attached and Hind Smith declared that Barnardo was 'charmed with the idea, and declared he would eclipse our work by going in for something on a much bigger scale, but keeping to the main idea'. Barnardo's temperance crusade attracted a lot of publicity. Articles appeared in *The Christian* entitled:[7] 'The Gospel in the

Tent' which gave an idea of the prevailing atmosphere. A contributor wrote:

> The poor seem to love the simplicity of the stakes, the ropes, the curtained walls, the pavilioned roof and the earthen floor studded with its rough forms ... Another very delightful feature of these gatherings of hard worked people, is the absence of yawning and sleeping. They hear something to think about, not infrequently something to laugh about and not infrequently something that touches their hearts and draws tears from their eyes. One good lady we hear had gone to one of the meetings, and been shocked at the audience being constrained to laugh, we cannot say whether rightly or wrongly.

By late September Barnardo was becoming anxious as to how he should carry on when winter made the tent impossible to use. The proprietor of the Edinburgh Castle had refused to let the large music hall, which formed part of the building, for religious services for fear it would injure his trade. However, by October trade had fallen off so badly, no doubt affected by the success of the gospel tent, that the proprietor found himself forced to advertise the thirty-nine-year lease of the Edinburgh Castle for £4,200. The 'citadel of Satan' was for sale. By 26 September Grattan Guinness writing in *The Christian*[8] announced that £1,200 had already been subscribed, and only £840 was needed for the deposit. By 7 October, the day of the sale, Barnardo already had £2,865. 10s. in hand. Samuel Gurney Sheppard, the wealthy chairman of Sheppard's, Pelly's, Scott and Co. and a director of many companies, whose own firm had invested heavily and profitably in railways, was the first to subscribe £1,000. Sheppard had been born a Quaker, but drifting away from Quakerism had become a preacher of the Gospel in mission halls. He was a strong member of the Evangelisation Society, and any organisation whose object was the winning of men's souls for salvation had his support. His example was followed by Lord Radstock, who had abandoned the normal interests and occupations of a man of his class since his conversion as a young man; strongly influenced by Brethren principles, he devoted all his time to missionary enterprises.

Barnardo did not hesitate – he bought the Castle! Confident that with such support he could expect more, and well aware of the excited interest his venture had caused in temperance circles, he was not disappointed. On the appointed day a fortnight later he had all but succeeded in raising the purchase money. Only £110 was needed.[9] 'At eleven o'clock, a friend, deeply interested in the undertaking called, as he said, to have one of the last shots at the citadel. It was a hundred pounder! Ten pounds came from another quarter and by twelve o'clock we had the entire sum, £4,200 in hand and about £100 more toward the fittings', Barnardo wrote triumphantly. At the same time he announced that the Edinburgh Castle was to be vested in trustees, among whom were John Sands, Samuel Sheppard and R. C. Morgan. Thomas Pelham, the younger son of the Earl of Chichester, and his contemporary, Arthur Kinnaird, both young men who were deeply interested in evangelical missionary work in the East End, became trustees as well. John Deacon and John Howard, a member of the chemical manufacturing firm of Howard and Son and also a member of the Brethren congregation in Tottenham, completed the list.

Barnardo's audacious purchase of the Edinburgh Castle made him known to a far wider constituency. A great tea was held to celebrate the purchase in November.[10] Barnardo provided refreshment for five hundred at a time, then sent them on to the special service in the tent. Lord Cavan, another evangelical churchman much influenced by Brethrenism, one of the founders of the Evangelical Alliance and actively involved in many of the missionary enterprises in the East End, was to have chaired the meeting. He was unable to attend, so Samuel Sheppard presided in his place, thus beginning his long and valuable association with Barnardo's work. The publicity that surrounded the work of the Edinburgh Castle had the effect of almost eclipsing for a time Barnardo's work with the East End Juvenile Mission. His work as an evangelist was compared to that of William Booth, and his work with boys was seen as a branch of a constantly expanding mission which was beginning to extend its influence over the adult population.

When the alterations to the building were finally completed, Barnardo announced in *The Christian*[11] that the front part of the erstwhile gin palace was to be opened as a 'British workmen's coffee palace', and that he hoped to do a large and brisk trade and 'to make it a place where men can sit, smoke, read and drink and think, and return home safely'. He received the ultimate accolade when Lord Shaftesbury agreed to open the new coffee palace and the six hundred guests who bought tickets for tea paid a shilling each for the privilege. The Pooles, who had been preaching regularly for twenty-eight weeks, must have been quite a remarkable couple. It is said that during their ministry two thousand signed the pledge, quite apart from the large numbers who were converted under their influence. The Rector of Limehouse, the Rev. S. Charlesworth, who attended the ceremony, paid generous tribute to what had been accomplished, and his words throw an interesting light on the attitude of the Church of England:[12]

I am utterly astonished at what has been accomplished. It is a most grand idea, a most sublime scheme. In the history of Christianity in England there is hardly a fact to be compared with it – I had no hand in it . . .

The Established Church of England is not fitted for it; this work must be done outside of her; but I do feel the deepest reverence and admiration for those who have been engaged in it . . . I now see how groundless were my fears and I stand here to acknowledge with deepest regret that I had not the honour to stand forth at an earlier period and take part in it . . .

[Referring to the ministry of the Pooles]:

Their work is one with mine, and though I am in the Church pulpit and they on the platform of the Tent or Hall, we preach the same glorious Gospel of salvation through the blood of Christ.

Barnardo had every reason for feeling proud and pleased at what he had been enabled to accomplish; he would also have been the first to agree with R. C. Morgan who, in an editorial describing the occasion, wrote, 'Thou art the God that doest wonders; Thou has declared thy strength among the people and that only with such an acknowledgement of God can we look upon a citadel of Satan turned into a house of prayer and see literally "in flaming letters" God is love over the entrance where, not a year ago, the worst passions were ministered to.'

The acquisition of the Edinburgh Castle was Barnardo's first major success; it brought him public acclaim and gave his work a solid base. After his frustrating experience with the China Inland Mission and his abortive medical career, after all the difficulties he had experienced before the East End Juvenile Mission and his boys' home were established, the almost astonishing ease with which he had been enabled to extend his work into new fields gave him tremendous satisfaction. It also brought to the surface some of the conflicting aspects of his personality. Although a convinced and sincere Christian, Barnardo never found it easy to subdue his need to assert himself, to dominate others and to impose his will on those around him. In spite of his religious convictions he needed worldly acclaim and wanted his achievements to be acknowledged.

This side of his nature was partly reflected in his dandified appearance. His mother was evidently aware of this weakness in her son. In one of the rare letters that survive from her she had written in 1868,[13] 'Are you seeking the praise of men? Do you love to be approved by them? Do you indulge the flesh as to food, dress, frivolity, excitement?' It can only have been this need to be approved and accepted that made him decide, just after the acquisition of the Edinburgh Castle, to adopt the title of 'Doctor'. Until this time Barnardo had always been referred to as either Brother Barnardo or plain Mr Barnardo in *The Christian*. Orders were given in November that in future he was to be known as Dr Barnardo, and by early 1873 he was never referred to except as 'Doctor'. It can only be assumed that he felt he needed the authority and status a professional qualification conferred, in order to live up to his new responsibilities. His adoption of the title of Doctor was to have far-reaching consequences. It was not long before he had to answer allegations that he had no right to the title. He later asserted that he had obtained an MD from the University of Giessen in February 1872. But as will be shown, the letter he produced to support this claim was a forgery. It purported to be signed by the Dean of the faculty, L. D. Wichan. Records at Giessen show that no such person existed either as Dean or as member of the faculty at that date. Furthermore the original letter, written in German, contained words and phrases that would never have been used by educated Germans now or in 1872.[14] The legal problems and the moral dilemma which faced Barnardo as a result of this action were to affect his life and work in a way which he could not then have foreseen.

From the moment it opened, the Edinburgh Castle was a

success. Barnardo had indeed gone in for something more ambitious than the usual temperance coffee houses offered. He kept the bar as it was, regilded and redecorated it entirely, and

2   The bar of the Edinburgh Castle

installed gasoliers, still something of a novelty at that time. Although the decor, with its preponderance of framed texts, might seem distinctly forbidding to today's customers, the novelty and the amenities it offered made it a popular place of resort. It had a library, a reading and smoking room and its own club rooms; newspapers were provided and what Barnardo called 'other rational sources of information and recreation'; coffee, cocoa, tea and other harmless drinks were available in warm and comfortable surroundings. Receipts exceeded expenditure by £60 in the first year, giving a profit at the rate of 6½ per cent on total receipts of £973, a fact which Barnardo proudly recorded in heavy type in his report.[15]

The great hall of the Edinburgh Castle provided a splendid setting for Barnardo's mission church. Barnardo's activities as pastor and minister have been much less well documented than his work for children. Yet for nine years he undertook all the pastoral duties associated with his church and did all the preaching. The recent fortunate discovery of a very substantial number of his notes for sermons, spanning the years from 1870 until his death, give some idea of the time, care and methodical preparation that went into his preaching. He kept his sermon notes from the start, carefully writing across the top left-hand corner the place and date each was delivered. Written on any odd scrap of paper that came to hand, the collection must contain notes for well over a thousand sermons. Some of the notes have more than one date on them, showing that the same sermon was used on more than one occasion. The early sermons reflect something of the sense of urgency Barnardo felt; written in purple ink, the important passages are underlined in red, and the intensity of the feeling that lay behind the words is almost visibly apparent to the reader. As Barnardo's confidence as a preacher increased, the purple and red inks were replaced by a more uniform blue and the words ceased to be so heavily underscored, although he never gave up the habit of underlining passages he wished to emphasise.

For the first nine years Barnardo alone ministered to his flock at the Edinburgh Castle, and the number of sermons with

3   Sunday in the Great Hall of the Edinburgh Castle

'E.C.' neatly marked across the corner indicate the tremendous amount of work this entailed. In a letter to the Rev. S. Borton Brown whom he had invited to serve as co-pastor, Barnardo showed himself fully alive to his own powers as a preacher and very much aware of the cut-throat competition that existed between the rival churches.[16] 'If I leave off for even a Sunday or two it affects our numbers, our collections and eventually our very church life, for the best of my hearers go to Mr— where if they attend for three or four Sundays consecutively they get attached, and then it is most difficult to get them back again.'

In spite of Barnardo's own involvement with Brethrenism, the trustees of the Edinburgh Castle were determined that it should be undenominational and the trust deed was drawn up to that effect. Describing the ecclesiastical position of the Edinburgh Castle some ten years later, Barnardo said that although leavened by Brethrenism and Quakerism it was really eclectic.

Ten years after its opening the building suddenly began to show alarming signs of decay; great cracks appeared in the structure and there was no alternative but to demolish and rebuild. Such was its reputation that there seems to have been as little difficulty in raising the necessary funds for the rebuilding as there had been at the time of its purchase. The Lord Mayor, Sir Robert Fowler, was a member of the Society of Friends and in sympathy with Christian philanthropic work. As a result of his interest in Barnardo, he and the sheriffs attended in state the ceremony of the placing of the memorial stones. The Lord Chancellor, Lord Cairns, presided at the opening ceremony in January 1884, amid scenes of great rejoicing.

Although the enlarged building could accommodate over three thousand people, from now on Barnardo was to be much less actively involved in the work carried on at the Edinburgh Castle. A succession of resident evangelists helped by a devoted band of elders and deacons continued the work. Barnardo, writing to one of them soon after the rebuilding, admitted that he had become more and more in sympathy with the evangelical section of the Church of England, but this in no way prevented him from preaching when he was in London. A feature article in *The Record*,[17] a Church of England newspaper, written by a special correspondent in 1886, gives a vivid picture both of the

Edinburgh Castle and of Barnardo's abilities as instigator, organiser and preacher.

Two large electric lamps outside the building mark the site of the Mission Church for some distance, and as I approached the church last Sunday night, some half hour before the time of commencing the service I found people flocking there from all directions. The Hall or Church was brilliantly illuminated by the electric light and the people swarmed in literally by hundreds . . . The greatest part of the congregation were certainly of the lower orders, 'the masses' as we call them, the very people who are rarely seen inside a regular place of worship . . . The stewards are also drawn from the lower orders; one is, I believe, a Punch and Judy show-man, another a cat's meat man and a third a dock labourer . . .

Dr. Barnardo who conducted the whole service was attired in ordinary dress. It was interesting to note how thoroughly at home he seemed with the people and the people with him . . . The hall was somewhat hot and Dr. Barnardo recommended anyone who wanted to faint to take a back seat during the singing of the hymn. 'It will be more convenient,' he said, 'for all parties.' The service was simplicity itself and the vast congregation most thoroughly entered into it. The people are encouraged to feel so much at home that they mind not their clothes, whether they are better or worse than their neighbours'. Would to God such Evangelistic work were multiplied a thousand times in our midst.

He obviously possessed the power of adapting himself to his audience. Another account tells of his appearance at the Edinburgh Castle on a Sunday evening at about the same period, 'dressed in the latest Bond Street style, exceptionally well groomed and wearing a beard. When the address began one could not help being struck by the attractiveness of his personality, one could not but admire the boundless, restless energy which animated the man and fired his nature.'

On yet another occasion, when a large party of factory girls had gathered at the Castle for a free tea, they suddenly noticed an artist from one of the illustrated papers whom Barnardo had asked to come and make sketches of their hats and feathers. The girls objected strongly to being portrayed in this way, but Dr Barnardo addressed them with such 'felicity that it was evident from the way in which he was able to silence the romping, rollicking, boisterous crowd that they honoured and respected him'.[18]

But to return to 1873, Barnardo's great success in acquiring the Edinburgh Castle was not universally welcomed. It was not only the publicans who lost out; the congregations of other local missions and churches were adversely affected as, attracted by the novelty and publicity, people flocked to the Edinburgh Castle, its interior bright with crystal gasoliers. Among those who were to feel threatened were F. N. Charrington, whose Tower Hamlets Mission lost some supporters to the Edinburgh Castle, and an obscure Baptist minister, George Reynolds, whose small church, known as 'the cave of Adullam' had a congregation numbering less than thirty souls. It was Barnardo's plans to create yet another coffee palace in the area that sparked off the quarrel between the three of them that was to prove so potentially damaging to the evangelical cause.

Frederick Charrington was the eldest son of Louisa and Frederick Charrington, of the well-known brewing firm. In a biography of him written by Guy Thorne during his lifetime, no mention was made of his long-drawn-out quarrel with Barnardo. Nor indeed do any of Barnardo's biographers mention the fact that Charrington was actively involved in denigrating Barnardo's work for several years. It is only because the *East London Observer* carried a very full report of the closing stages of the arbitration case set up to resolve the dispute between the parties that the true story of the quarrel between Barnardo and Charrington can be pieced together.

Born in 1850, Charrington had experienced a religious conversion at about the same age as Barnardo. He was reputed to have joined the temperance movement after seeing a man knock his wife into the gutter while she was pleading for money to feed the children. The incident happened outside the Rising Sun in the Mile End Road, and when Charrington looked up he saw his own name emblazoned across the building. From that moment he is said to have given up his inheritance and prospects to become a mission leader and a temperance worker. As poacher turned gamekeeper Charrington did not undervalue his importance to the temperance movement. Aware of his drawing power, for the Strand was reported blocked for hours after he had presided at the AGM of the Band of Hope Union, he regarded the area round the Mile End Road as his particular preserve. Five years younger than Barnardo, his early career had developed along somewhat similar lines. Both men had been to the Paris Exhibition in 1867, Charrington as a young man of means, Barnardo to distribute religious tracts and gospels, his expenses paid by a wealthy evangelical friend; both worked in schools, Charrington at a night school run by the Rev. Joseph Bardsley, Vicar of Stepney, and Barnardo at the ragged school in Ernest Street; both soon set up their own establishments, Barnardo in Hope Place, Charrington in a hayloft over a stable. By 1870 Charrington had his own school, mission and home for boys as had Barnardo. It seems clear that at the time of the opening of the Edinburgh Castle the two young men were on terms of friendship with each other and that Barnardo had gone so far as to introduce some of his wealthy and influential supporters to Charrington, who was planning to build a mission hall in the Mile End Road, a plan which he abandoned when he acquired a better site in White Horse Lane in 1873.

Fired by his public success, which was reflected in greatly increased financial support, Barnardo was looking round for new worlds to conquer. In the year following the opening of the Edinburgh Castle he, in his turn, acquired a site in the Mile End Road on which he intended to build a second coffee palace to be called the Dublin Castle. Competition between mission leaders and temperance reformers was keen. Large congregations not only spelled success; well attended meetings were important financially and all mission leaders played the numbers game, reporting regularly the size of attendances at meetings as well as the number of conversions made and pledges taken.

When Charrington heard of Barnardo's plans to build in the Mile End Road, his growing disquiet at the success of the Edinburgh Castle turned from simple jealousy to open hostility. Because the headquarters of the family's brewery were situated in the Mile End Road, Charrington felt strongly about his own position in the area, and the idea that the relatively unknown Barnardo should seek to challenge his supremacy on what he considered to be his own special ground in the temperance field was more than he could endure. He not only demanded that Barnardo should give up the idea of building a coffee palace in the Mile End Road, he concealed his subsequent plan for building his mission hall in White Horse Lane and put it about that he had always been going to establish a mission in the Mile End Road and that Barnardo was being deliberately provocative in seeking to set up a rival establishment less than a third of a mile distant. He put this story over so effectively that many people did indeed think that Barnardo had behaved improperly in the matter. Notwithstanding Charrington's opposition, Barnardo did build and open the Dublin Castle coffee palace. But it is not without significance that it was not even mentioned in *The Memoirs*, apart from an entry in an appendix giving the official opening date as 1875. The Dublin Castle was never really successful in the way that the Edinburgh Castle was. Charrington finally opened his great new assembly hall in 1886, two years after Barnardo had rebuilt the Edinburgh Castle. Describing the opening ceremony, Barnardo had regretfully to admit that, although he had always considered the Edinburgh Castle as the 'largest, brightest and best', Charrington's assembly hall excelled it in almost every way: 'It could hold a larger congregation, it looked more attractive and it was much better ventilated.' Perhaps George Lansbury should have the last word. Recalling his young days in the East End, he remembered the packed meetings in the mission halls run by Barnardo and Charrington. He wrote that it seemed to him that religious life was far more passionate in those days, and that people really believed they were fleeing from the wrath to come.[19]

5
Marriage and the Development of his Work

FROM the outset Barnardo had seen his missionary work as being concerned with the needs of both sexes, and his ragged school and evangelistic work were as much directed towards the needs of girls as of boys. However, with the discovery of Jim Jarvis and the widespread problem of child destitution, a new dimension had been added to his work for the young; not only did they need saving from spiritual ignorance, but also from the damaging consequences of a precarious life lived on the streets which was physically as well as morally hazardous. The monstrous injustices under which these children lived and which a complacent society accepted never ceased to arouse Barnardo's strongest feelings. His initial belief that he was the first to discover the appalling conditions in which these neglected children eked out an existence was succeeded by the painful discovery that although others did indeed know and had been attempting to alleviate their situation, the problem of destitution was still acute. The Poor Law system of training destitute children continued to follow the policy of relieving only those who actually required it to do so, and the training given in most of the workhouse schools remained totally inadequate. Many boards of guardians treated the children in their care on the same principles as they dealt with adult paupers, so it is hardly surprising that many children preferred the precarious adventure of life on the streets to the deadening effects of the workhouse. Indeed many of those who were committed to the workhouse for vagrancy by the magistrates absconded as soon as they could.

Barnardo held, from the very first, strong ideas concerning the value of family life and the important role that woman should play. He firmly believed that a woman's place was in the home, and in his very first report in 1868 he argued in favour of either emigration or employment for men, but pointed out that when women are employed, 'they are taken away for the entire day from their families (many of whom are young) and the poor home, poor enough and wretched enough before, now becomes a place which only drives men to the public houses; and thus evil is done which no amount of money can ever really undo'.

Barnardo's midnight rambles through the streets and alley-ways very soon taught him that there were as many destitute and neglected girls on the streets as boys. Although both faced the same physical hazards and risked being led into criminal and vicious ways, girls were in far greater moral danger in that it was all too easy for them to accept prostitution not only as the most readily available answer to the problems of economic necessity but also as an acceptable way of life in itself. Limited casual employment opportunities existed for boys of the very poorest class, but for their sisters the opportunities were few, apart from ill-paid factory work and domestic service, and for the poorest this usually meant acting as maid-of-all-work. It is not to be wondered at that many opted for the money and the relative freedom which prostitution made possible rather than face the bleak and dreary life of a household drudge.

The prevalence of juvenile prostitution was an inevitable consequence of the chronic oversupply of girls in a highly restricted market. It was also the result of overcrowding and the lack of any kind of privacy. In spite of his bachelor status Barnardo was not deterred by the thought that difficulties might result from his working directly with girls, and the accounts for 1871/2 show that a fund for a home for orphan and destitute little girls had already been opened. At this time nearly a hundred people were engaged in the various branches of the work, only a quarter of whom were paid, the remainder giving their services freely. Barnardo was doubtless confident that he would be able to recruit suitable female workers to take charge of the home if he could raise sufficient funds to acquire a suitable building. He not only wanted a home for girls, he also kept open a fund which, when large enough, would enable him to apply to the Admiralty for a training ship.

It was sometime during this period that poor little John

Somers was discovered dead after having spent the night inside a large sugar hogshead. The tragic story of this unhappy child marks a turning point in the development of the history of the homes as important as the discovery of Jim Jarvis.[1] 'Carrots', so-called because of his red hair, was a singularly ill-favoured child, by all accounts. He had no father and his mother had turned him adrift on the streets to fend for himself, only making contact when she thought he had money. At the time of his death he was just eleven years old. In the course of his nocturnal rambles in the Billingsgate area Barnardo had come across an unusually large group of destitute children. He had room at Stepney for only five, so in spite of Carrots' pleas to be taken in he was told he could only be accepted when a vacancy occurred. It was soon afterwards that he was found dead, and the coroner's verdict at the inquest was 'death from exhaustion, the result of frequent exposure and want of food'.

From Barnardo's own account of the story it is clear that his determination to intensify his work among destitute children as a result of this tragedy was as much on account of Carrots' lamentable lack of any religious knowledge as because of his sad end. The new policy, 'No destitute boy ever refused admission', is first mentioned in the report for 1874/5. In this report Barnardo frankly admitted that the difficulty of making a limited number of beds provide for an unlimited number of applicants meant that he was compelled to pass boys very quickly through the home, often giving them only three to six months' training before sending them on their way to make room for others. After the establishment of the Girls' Village Home the slogan was amended to 'No destitute child ever refused admission'. It was a bold and challenging statement, and it became the principle on which the homes were run from then on. The Poor Law had proved itself unable to deal with the problem of child destitution, and if the state could not or would not take action, then Barnardo saw it as his clear duty to do so.

Barnardo was now a young man of twenty-seven, and had matured and developed a naturally commanding presence. He still wore spectacles and his expression was normally serious, but when he smiled or laughed he had an infectious gaiety about him. The tremendous energy and enthusiasm which went into everything he did made him a stimulating companion, but his increasingly autocratic and domineering attitude made it difficult for others to work with him in anything but a subordinate capacity. Constant prayer and a deepening religious awareness kept him spiritually humble, but the growing feeling that his mission was divinely inspired increased his natural tendency to dominate and indeed any opposition roused his more aggressive instincts. His life left him no time for normal social pleasures, because he was more than occupied by the work he had started and by his plans for future developments. He was living in lodgings which he seems to have changed at fairly regular intervals, but in spite of his intense preoccupation with his work he retained an interest in his appearance and was always careful about his dress.

It was sometime during 1871 that he received an invitation from a Miss Elmslie to come to Richmond and talk to the boys in a ragged school she was running. She must have been impressed at the way the young man spoke with the boys and noticed how easily he commanded their attention and how simply and naturally he addressed them. He had a natural sympathy for and affinity with the young, and the autocratic manner which could alienate his fellow men was somehow transmuted and softened by contact with children. The following day he found that by chance he was travelling in the same direction as Syrie Elmslie and her father, and rapidly changing his third-class ticket for a first, he accompanied them in the train from Paddington. During the journey he would have discovered, if he had not already known it, that Syrie owed her conversion to Lord Radstock, one of whose evangelistic meetings she had attended, and that she, like him, had found this to be a turning point in her life. Apart from Syrie, the Elmslies do not appear to have been particularly influenced by the Revival movement, so doubtless it was doubly welcome to Syrie to find in Barnardo a sympathetic listener to whom she could talk of her work with the boys in her ragged school.

Although she must have been attracted by Barnardo's tremendous enthusiasm for his work, nothing came of this first chance meeting. However, eighteen months later their paths crossed again. This time they met at the funeral of one of the most influential evangelical ministers of the day, the Rev.

William Pennefather, founder of the Mildmay Park Conference. He had been one of those responsible for the invitation to
Moody and Sankey to visit England, and his sudden death was
to leave Moody in an unexpectedly awkward situation when he
arrived. With Barnardo, decision was always rapidly followed
by action. Having met Syrie again he found himself attracted
both by her charm and by her serious manner. Knowing that
they had much in common he proposed to her. With a wife by
his side, in sympathy with the work he wanted to do, it would be
that much easier for him to carry through his plans to rescue and
care for girls. Only the previous year a little girl named Martha
had applied for admission to the home in Stepney on a dark
winter night. Her feet were cut and bleeding, her body bruised.
Scantily clothed and starving, she was fed and given shelter and
Barnardo found a poor woman whom he induced to care for her
until more permanent arrangements could be made. He wrote
after that, 'no further incidents were necessary to show me how
urgent was the need for opening a Home for Girls. It pressed
upon me day by day, until at length I had neither rest nor
comfort until I had put my hand to the work.'

Much has been written about the Elmslies' social and financial status, and they have been depicted as wealthy, influential
and socially Barnardo's superiors. An example of this is the way
in which William Elmslie, Syrie's father, has been described as
being chairman of Lloyds.[2] William Elmslie's grandfather,
John Elmslie, was indeed a man of substance, his property in
the West Indies included two plantations in Jamaica and a
sugar works. He fathered twenty-one legitimate children, fourteen of whom survived to adulthood. One of the features of the
Elmslie descendants is the great disparity between the wealth of
some and the poverty of others, notably that branch to which
William Elmslie belonged. Adam Elmslie, William's father, was
the third of the Jamaican sugar-planter's five sons and was left a
share in the Jamaica estates and a small legacy in common with
his brothers. When he died in Weston-Super-Mare his fortune
had diminished considerably and neither he nor his children
seem to have shown the ability and drive their grandfather so
obviously possessed, or perhaps with the abolition of slavery the
plantation ceased to flourish and they were not able to adapt to
their changed circumstances.

William Elmslie's three brothers all died in comparative poverty and he himself seems to have had a somewhat uncertain start in life. He was married in 1844 to Betsey Sarah Mumford, the daughter of Burton Mumford, a grocer living at Bishop's Stortford. The wedding took place at St Olave Jewry in the City of London and Sara Louise, as Syrie was christened, was born three years later in 1847. The family were living in 'Middlesex King's Bench' at the time of her birth, which probably meant that her father was at that time an undischarged bankrupt permitted to live in the rules of the King's Bench prison. If that was so, the fortunes of the family improved soon afterwards, for they moved to Hackney and William Elmslie started on his career as an adjuster of averages which was to be his avocation in life.[3] He became a subscriber to Lloyds in 1848, which enabled him to offer his services to the company. But as a subscriber he was not entitled to stand for membership of the committee. The move to Richmond, where the family were living when Barnardo first met Syrie, took place sometime towards the end of the sixties. Syrie's elder brother, William Stuart, had worked as a clerk in his father's office since he was sixteen, and in 1871 his father had made him a subscriber to Lloyds, hoping that he would enter the firm as a partner when he had passed his examinations. But this was not to be, for William died in 1873, a few months after his sister's wedding. Syrie had three other brothers, two of whom had already left home, and the younger one, Harry, was still at school.

The Elmslies did not conceal their dismay at the prospect of their daughter's marriage to Barnardo. Although Barnardo was calling himself Doctor he was not qualified and he could not practise medicine; he had no profession, no settled home and no regular income; he already had huge responsibilities and to any prudent parents he must have seemed far from desirable as a prospective son-in-law. Perhaps it was their influence that caused Syrie to refuse Barnardo's first proposal. Barnardo had grown into a goodlooking young man, had charm and was very persuasive, and it was not long before she agreed to marry him. Syrie brought Barnardo to meet her parents at their home, The Laurels in Richmond, where they lived in modest comfort. So little did Barnardo know of the family that he did not realise that the small boy perched up beside the coachman was Harry, Syrie's young brother.

Barnardo's initial idea was that they should marry by ordinary licence in an ordinary dissenting chapel in an ordinary way. He made it clear to his future parents-in-law that he wished to be married in the East End so that his own congregation and his many friends and helpers could be present. If the Elmslies had other ideas as to where and how the wedding should take place, these were swept aside. The ordinary dissenting chapel however turned out to be the most celebrated of them all, none other than Spurgeon's Metropolitan Tabernacle in Newington Causeway. Charles Spurgeon, the famous Baptist preacher, was at the height of his powers at this time. His congregation had recently raised money to build the great tabernacle, which could seat six thousand, and Spurgeon kept it filled; his renown as a preacher was worldwide. He answered Barnardo's request that he should officiate at their wedding regretting that he would be unable to act as 'joiner' on the date proposed as he would be away on holiday, and rightly surmising that Barnardo would not wish to wait until his return, hoped some 'better brother would have the honour'.

The wedding certainly fulfilled Barnardo's hopes in so far as he wanted to use his marriage to publicise his wish to open a home for girls. A large congregation filled the Metropolitan Tabernacle and Grattan Guinness, Barnardo's friend and teacher from his Dublin days, officiated at the service, which was performed according to the rites and ceremonies of the Baptists by licence. Two lay evangelists also took part in the service, Lord Radstock and Henry Varley, their presence together emphasising the breadth of Barnardo's friendships and support. If Lord Radstock was the representative of the upper classes, Henry Varley who, before becoming a successful evangelist had been a butcher, represented the lower orders. W. J. Mayers, who was later to join Barnardo's staff, left a description of the event:[4]

I was present at the wedding of Dr. Barnardo in the Metropolitan Tabernacle on 17th June 1873. A large company including many from the East End gathered and the bride and bridegroom looked radiantly proud and happy. Lord Radstock, Dr. Grattan Guinness and Mr. Henry Varley were on the platform with other friends. I well remember gathering together all the students of the Pastor's College, and arranging for them to stand on the corners of the seats and bending over the aisle, to link hands, so that the happy couple might have a living arch to pass under as they left the building.

Whether Syrie's father was unable to attend or did not wish to, the marriage certificate is signed only by Elisabeth Elmslie. None of Barnardo's family were able to come from Dublin, but his father sent him a gold watch to mark the occasion. Burnett Tabrum, who acted as chief elder of the People's Mission Church, was witness for Barnardo. Although Barnardo was now known publicly by the title of Doctor, under the heading of rank or profession the word 'gentleman' is inscribed on his wedding certificate. A reception was held afterwards, but it is not possible to identify the garden in which the wedding party was photographed.

Barnardo's flair for publicity and his instinctive use of the occasion of his wedding to attract support for the project so dear to his heart was not misplaced. As a result of the marriage Mr John Sands gave the fifteen-year lease of Mossford Lodge at Barkingside to the young couple for use as a home for girls; the gift was opportune for it gave them a roof over their heads when they returned from their six-week honeymoon in Lowestoft, as well as enabling Barnardo to realise his dream of extending his work to include girls. A fund had already been set up in 1872 and while the young couple were in Lowestoft a friend and supporter, Cheyne Brady, wrote to *The Christian*[5] suggesting that additions to this fund would be the best wedding present the young Barnardos could receive. When Syrie and Barnardo returned from Lowestoft at the end of July they were enthusiastically welcomed home by the congregation of the People's Mission Church and presented with a silver tea service. They set up home at Mossford Lodge and their first weeks in their new home were taken up with overseeing the alterations to the coach house where they decided the girls should live.

By October they were ready to make public their plans. Barnardo's hand is clearly discernible in the letter which Syrie sent to *The Christian* appealing for help. It is the only time Barnardo allowed anyone to share publicly with him in the direction of the work. It is clear from this letter that their original idea was that Syrie should be in complete control of the work for girls. Their object was very simple, and one which they believed had not been tried before. They aimed to take destitute girls from the street and with the aid of 'thoroughly good servants and the voluntary help of some Christian ladies, to train up a band of kitchen maids, house maids, parlour maids, laundry maids, dairy maids and cooks to meet the great demand existing everywhere for cleanly and instructed female servants'. Touching on the problem of prostitution, Syrie wrote with characteristic Victorian delicacy, 'How can we expect to grapple (I speak as a woman) with our greatest social sin so long as girls herd in the lowest lodging houses?', and followed this up by saying that this was a problem the state should grapple with and did not. Barnardo was unusual in recognising that the size of the problem made it one which only the state could successfully deal with. But as the state had failed to intervene, it was the duty of the Churches to take a lead in dealing with the problem.

At the same time as the Barnardos were starting their work for girls, Mrs Nassau Senior, who was to become a Poor Law inspector, was making her report on the education and training of pauper children, with particular reference to the education and training of pauper girls, at the request of the commissioners. Her report[6] came to the same conclusion that bitter experience was to teach the Barnardos – that barrack-type homes, where girls were herded together, were totally unsuited to their needs. Mrs Nassau Senior drew this conclusion by following up the lives of some of the girls who had left the workhouse, and reported that they were stunted in size, delicate in health and ill trained and that many of them ended up on the streets. Barnardo was driven to the same conclusion by the shattering experience of listening to a licentious conversation between his girls, who, he fondly imagined, had by now absorbed the Christian spirit of the home. The discovery that the system of aggregating the girls was possibly making the situation worse rather than better was a devastating blow. If Barnardo had found it difficult to assimilate boys taken from the streets into his first home, the problems that confronted Syrie Barnardo in dealing with girls who were chosen precisely because their backgrounds represented the most extreme cases of deprivation and neglect could only have been worse. Added to which Syrie had no experience of this type of work and was to prove neither efficient nor economical as a housekeeper.

A little over a year after their marriage Syrie gave birth to their first son, at a time when they were in financial difficulties. He was named William Stuart Elmslie after her brother who had died the year before. They weathered the storm, but the difficulties inherent in the situation at Mossford Lodge showed no signs of diminishing. With the realisation brought home to Barnardo by the conversation of the girls themselves that 'even sixty girls, congregated together under the same roof, however wise and careful the social laws might be which governed their domestic life, were in danger of losing that softness of manner and, above all, that individuality and force of character necessary to their future welfare'[7] the first experiment in helping girls came to an end. And with it ended also Syrie's effective official role in the work, although behind the scenes she gave continuous support to her husband.

Barnardo found it hard and embarrassing to admit publicly the failure of a project for which he had made a public appeal for funds. In a letter reporting on his work for girls he boldly announced a new plan to build thirty cottages on the freehold land adjoining their home, which should each contain twenty girls mothered and cared for by a Christian housewife, at a cost of not less than £450 per cottage. He asked the readers of *The Christian* for money to enable him to build, but the public were slow to respond to this new scheme.

Barnardo said that the idea of a village home had suddenly come to him in a dream during the night and that until then he had no idea that anyone else was working on these lines. But it is worth noting that on the same page in *The Christian* as Mrs Barnardo's original letter announcing the plans for Mossford Lodge, there had also been an appeal from Mrs Meredith for another cottage for the village she had founded and which was known as Princess Mary's Village, Addlestone. Her appeal was for funds with which to build more cottages at a cost of £400 each. Each cottage contained ten children ruled over by a housemother assisted by one of the elder girls, and the whole system was based on the family group, with the housemother as the central figure around which the family revolved. Barnardo said that in his dream he saw that:[8]

... there should no longer be a great house in which sixty of these motherless girls would be herded together, clad in some dull uniform generally divested of all prettiness, but little cottages should arise, each of them presided over by its own 'Mother' and in which all the members of the family could be clad as working people's children were under ordinary circumstances. The girls should be of all ages, from the baby of a few months or weeks to the growing girls, some of whom would be nearly out of their teens. There family life and family love might be reproduced and gentle modest ways would be made possible in the retirement of the little cottage with its four or five rooms, and under the influences of godly women whom I was sure would come to my aid in due course.

The idea of the cottage home system, which had originated on the continent, had tremendous appeal for those who had come to reject the idea of the large institution as a suitable setting for bringing up children. Dr Wichern's Rauhe Haus in Hamburg was based on this principle. Mr de Metz had founded the first reformatory institution for juvenile offenders in Mettrai, France, on the idea that children should be gathered into separate houses. The cottage home system had been advocated for the Poor Law by Mr Joseph Fletcher as early as 1851 in a paper submitted to the Statistical Society of London, but nothing had come of it. At the time when Barnardo was planning his village home for girls, Mrs Meredith's experiment at Addlestone and the home for little boys at Farningham were the only two examples to be found in England.

When there was no response to his initial appeal in *The Christian*, Barnardo began to have serious doubts as to whether this was the direction in which his work was intended to go. Nonetheless, in spite of the slow response public opinion was on his side. The barrack home system was increasingly under attack. Lectures, pamphlets and books were being written on the theme that institutional provision was positively harmful, and especially for girls. The Rev. Dr Clutterbuck, like Fletcher twenty years before him, advocated that a version of the cottage home system should be adopted by the English Poor Law. William Quarrier in Scotland, the founder of Quarrier's Homes, had already published his views on the harmful effects of large institutions on the lives of children and his advocacy of the cottage principle in 1870.[9]

At the end of 1874 Barnardo held his first public meeting in Spurgeon's tabernacle to publicise his work. He himself quoted from Florence Davenport Hill's widely read report, 'Children of the State':

> The case of the girls is far worse than that of the boys, as all the conditions of workhouse management fall with peculiar evil on their natures. To mass boys together in large numbers, with no home influence or habits, and no attempt to draw out their affections is dangerous; to do the same with girls is fatal. Among the endless paradoxes of female treatment, one of the worst and most absurd is that which, while eternally proclaiming home to be the only sphere of a woman, systematically educates all female children of the State without attempting to give them even an idea of what a home might be. Girls want affection, want personal care, want household duties, want everything which can train them to honour their bodies and keep pure the souls God has given them . . . Out of a single workhouse in London inquiry was instituted two years ago concerning 80 girls who had left it and gone into service. It was found that every one of them had gone on the streets.

It only needed some dramatic event for the tide to turn in Barnardo's favour. It occurred in Oxford where Barnardo had gone to attend a religious gathering for fellowship and consideration of God's word.[10] Dressing in his room on the second day he was interrupted by an imperious knock on the door and an unknown man came in. Having ascertained that it was Barnardo to whom he was talking and that Barnardo had as yet no money towards his projected village home, the man said, 'Put me down for the first cottage, good morning', and shut the door and went away. After inviting him back so they could 'praise the Lord together', Barnardo then discovered that some months previously Mr Dawson had lost a beloved only daughter. He wanted to perpetuate her memory in some practical way, and seeing Barnardo's letter in *The Christian*, had intended to write. He had not actually done so, but learning that Barnardo was a fellow guest at the hotel, he had taken this as a sign and come immediately to his room to make the offer. It was a pattern of giving that was to be repeated many times, for in an age when many children died young, their parents sometimes found solace by contributing to the needs of others; many of the cottages were given as memorials not only to children but to relations and friends. The first step is always the hardest, and once Barnardo had the money for his first cottage, within six months money for ten more had been promised. By 1875 Barnardo had organised a ceremony to celebrate the laying of the foundation stones, to be presided over by Lord Aberdeen, a young man the same age as Barnardo and grandson of the Prime Minister, who was deeply influenced by evangelical ideas.

Barnardo never underestimated the importance of publicity, and this allied to his sense of the theatrical was always well to the fore. He planned the opening of his first fourteen cottages in July 1876 with great care. Lord Cairns, the Lord Chancellor, had for some time past been showing an interest in the work Barnardo was doing. When Barnardo acquired the house at 19 Stepney Causeway which he used as an infirmary for sick children, he had called the main ward after the Lord Chancellor in recognition of this interest. By persuading him to perform the opening ceremony at Ilford Barnardo was able to make known his interest to a far wider public.

Invitations from Dr and Mrs Barnardo were despatched to all their friends and supporters. An enormous marquee was erected in the grounds, detailed instructions as to train times were sent to all the guests and every arrangement for their entertainment and comfort was attended to with the greatest care. The ceremony was thought out in great detail and only at the last minute did a hitch occur when a telegram was received announcing that Lord Cairns would be late as he had been detained by parliamentary duties. His absence would have been a blow to the Barnardos, for this was by far the most important event that they had yet organised. Lord Aberdeen prepared to stand in for him, but before the ceremony was over Lord Cairns arrived. As Ira Sankey, Moody's musical partner, sang 'Rescue the Perishing' with 'affecting tenderness' the village home was opened.[11] The Barnardos could well feel pleased and proud at the way things had gone, for criticisms concerning the work were beginning to be heard more frequently, and such an expression of faith and confidence was very welcome at that time.

Some idea of the difficulties the first cottage mothers had to face was given by Miss Stent,[12] the honorary secretary of the village and one of Barnardo's most trusted and loyal co-workers. Writing twelve years later in 1888, at a time when a further nineteen cottages had just been built and opened, she said that normally the little girls were introduced one or two at a time into a cottage;

> ... where order already prevailed and the children had been trained to quietness and obedience. In such surroundings the prevailing tone begins to influence the new-comers almost immediately, and the quiet formative moulding power of habit and association insensibly fits the little life into its proper niche. That has been our usual mode of family building, so that though all the inmates of a Cottage may be changed in the course of a couple of years, the life of the family may have gone on continuously and quietly absorbing, as it were, into itself the successive lives of the young tenants. But of late we have been going back to the old times, when the village was first established, and have been, in the new cottages, taking the girls to form the families just as they come. Some of the households are beginning life together with just one trained girl in each to represent the village and take the lead. The result frequently makes large demands upon the patience and perseverance of the 'Mother' for the sixteen or twenty inmates often come from utterly loveless and unhomelike homes. Many of the young girl waifs have no idea of order or of method, no notion of cleanliness or of comfort. All has to be begun afresh, and the mother has need of all her energy. If one thinks it an easy thing to win the confidence of, or to make obedience a pleasure to, these poor little girls who have been accustomed to distrust everybody, or to reconcile with an ordered life young people who have been accustomed to run wild and to claim the liberty of turning day into night, – well, let him or her try it!

Economic necessity as well as natural inclination forced Barnardo to rely on his own resources, and both boys and girls were trained from the beginning to make their contribution to the running of the homes: 'The girls are taught to act all parts and to do everything, for we are our own servants at Ilford, our own chambermaids and charwomen, our own cooks and nurses; we sew and mend, and darn, and sweep, and dust; and positive training in all these feminine arts is no light task.'

At Stepney the boys lived under what Barnardo called the 'half-time system'.[13] Their day was divided between school and training in a trade shop. Besides the educational, moral and personal advantages that such training provided, Barnardo pointed out that much of the work done by the tailors, carpenters, shoemakers, bakers and engineers was of direct benefit to the homes themselves and a 'considerable saving was thus effected'. Time was set aside for play, but all the household work was done by the boys, who were taught to cook and wait at table, to make their beds, to clean their shoes and to fulfil any other duties, such as acting as messengers to the offices, that might be required of them. Barnardo was particularly proud of the cleanliness of all the floors at Stepney, and their ritual scrubbing by the boys was surely devised by him.[14]

It is somewhat amusing to see twenty fellows with their shoes and stockings off, and their trousers turned up to the knees, all in a line scrubbing the floor to the word of command given by the assistant master who has charge of the cleaning operations. Some of my visitors make it a regular part of their journey eastward to call at our Home during the hour allotted to scrubbing, and I often go upstairs to our schoolrooms to find a number of ladies and gentlemen standing on an islet in the midst of a vast sea of soapsuds and water, looking at the manoeuvres of some twenty youngsters who take a pride in keeping their boards as white as it is possible to make them.

However the regime at Stepney was mild compared to that enforced at the labour house where Barnardo took older destitute boys.[15] Here the rule was 'plenty of hard work', and in the course of a sixteen-hour day, half an hour only was allowed for recreation. The boys were roused at half past five and started work at six o'clock; with half-hour intervals for breakfast, prayers, dinner and military drill, they finally finished at half past six in the evening. After supper at seven, classes were held until nine fifteen, and finally after prayers the lights were put out at ten o'clock.

Barnardo was always a strong believer in the moral value of hard work, both for himself and for his children. He made no secret of the fact that he put the value of industrial training above schoolwork, and thought advanced education was not in his children's interests. The three Rs were the chief subjects taught in class, with a little grammar, geography and history. Naturally the scriptures were taught and read daily. Barnardo found it hard to get his boys' schools recognised by the government because of the irregularity of the children's attendance, but by 1883 he had succeeded in obtaining government recognition at Stepney. Recognition was not such a problem with the girls, and the school at the village home had been officially inspected since 1877. Government recognition brought with it

4   The schoolroom of the Boys' Home, Stepney Causeway

the benefit of public examinations and an education grant.

The free ragged schools in Copperfield Road were Barnardo's largest educational enterprise. They had been eligible for government grants since 1875. The children who attended classes at these schools were drawn from the lowest East End dwellings of the 'labouring poor'. They often came to school in a condition of abject ignorance; they were often hungry and in general they were of feeble physique. Noting this, Barnardo made a system of organised free meals an integral part of the educational programme. A report from Her Majesty's Inspector of the Privy Council of Education in 1888 showed how successful his system had proved. In that year four hundred and fifty-two children were presented for examination, three hundred and seventy-six passed and the grant amounted to £347. 13s. 11d. The report stated:[16]

Considering the difficulties of the year, the higher grant for English may be again recommended, though Recitations in the upper Standards and Grammar in the fourth Standard fell short of good. Geography is unequal, being best in the first class and weakest in the third standard . . . The instruction of the younger infants is very bright and pleasing. The elder infants are in very good order, and make very fair progress.

6

A Scandalous Controversy

THE years immediately after Barnardo's marriage appear on the surface to be ones of continuing success and expansion. After the widespread publicity which had surrounded the acquisition of the Edinburgh Castle died down, receipts, which had more than doubled in 1873, fell back. But with Moody and Sankey at the height of their fame and their London campaign in full swing, support for Barnardo's work increased during 1875. Moody preached several times at the Edinburgh Castle and encouraged the public interest that the Girls' Village Home had aroused. As a result receipts for that year reached a new peak, amounting to over £23,000, a sum which did not go unremarked by those who were watching with a less kindly eye Barnardo's meteoric rise as a philanthropist.

Mossford Lodge was not a success as a family home. It was expensive to run, and when the servants who had been used to help train the girls were no longer needed in that capacity they became a costly liability. Barnardo found it irksome to be so far from the scene of his main activities and the family soon acquired a new home in East London at Newbury House, Bow. The Grattan Guinnesses lived just opposite at Harley House, and this may well have influenced the Barnardos' choice of home. The Grattan Guinnesses had come to London in 1870 and founded the East End Institute for Home and Foreign Missions, first working at Stepney Green before they moved to Harley House. Barnardo had been a co-director for a while, lecturing to the students on general subjects; but his own increasing work with the East End Juvenile Mission brought his active association with the Institute to an end in 1874. Nonetheless the families remained close friends.

By 1875 the East End Juvenile Mission was without question

one of the fastest-growing missions in East London, and the sudden success that had attended Barnardo's efforts blinded him to the dangers that await the overconfident. His unshakeable conviction that his work was directly inspired by God, allied to his autocratic temperament, gave him self-confidence, but his success also increased his aggressive instincts which, when thwarted in any way made him obstinate and overbearing. In spite of the large annual income, he continued to announce that he had no committee and no treasurer. He failed to see the dangers to which he was exposing himself when he proudly proclaimed that he, a private individual, was the sole honorary director and treasurer and that he was not responsible to any committee for the management of the funds committed to his trust. There were many in the East End who remembered him as an indigent student and evangelist and who wondered at his new-found prosperity and the power this gave him. Among those who most resented Barnardo's growing influence was Frederick Charrington, who having been born into a wealthy family and having renounced his inheritance found himself outdistanced by a newcomer who, starting with nothing, had rapidly attained a position of consequence which threatened his own pre-eminence in the area.

The quarrel between the two of them which started over the relatively minor matter of the siting of their respective missions was to escalate into a controversy which became both public and damaging, not only to Barnardo but to the whole evangelical philanthropic movement. Among others who were jealous of Barnardo's success was George Reynolds, a Baptist minister, about whom little is known other than that he was once a railway porter in Cardiff. His church was in the Mile End Road and he depended for his livelihood upon the subscriptions of his small congregation. It was therefore a matter of great concern to him when some of them deserted his church in favour of the more popular services that were held at the Edinburgh Castle. He lived in Barnes Street, in a house almost directly opposite the one in which Mrs Johnson, Barnardo's erstwhile landlady, now lived.

Charrington and Reynolds made common cause, and their accusations and insinuations which continued over the next three years form a disturbing counterpoint to the apparently uninterrupted progress of Barnardo's work for the East End Juvenile Mission. Their object – to discredit him with his public – came perilously close to success because, needled beyond endurance, Barnardo was provoked into responding, and by a series of unwise actions came near to losing all he had worked for.

He was vulnerable to attack on financial grounds. The financial statements relating to the East End Juvenile Mission were produced at ever longer intervals. Those for 1874–5 did not appear until January 1876, while the sums of money entrusted to Barnardo had reached well over five figures. Marriage had increased his personal financial difficulties; Syrie was extravagant and a bad manager, and with a wife as well as a baby to support the modest income Barnardo had earned for himself as a journalist and preacher proved insufficient to meet the family's needs. Besides articles in *The Christian*, *The Echo* and other newspapers, Barnardo had contributed stories for children to a little magazine called *Father William's Stories*. In 1874 he acquired the magazine, changed the name to *The Children's Treasury* and became the editor. The magazine came out in two versions, one at a half-penny for children in ragged schools and missions and one at a penny, known as the drawing-room version. It claimed to act as an advocate for the homes, but it also contained children's stories and religious quizzes and was well illustrated. It seems to have been a financial success from the beginning and there was said to have been a balance of £1,878 in 1877.[1]

The question of his right to the title of Doctor was one which his detractors used against him. But the first move in the campaign was the circulation of a scandalous rumour that Barnardo had had an improper relationship with his landlady, Mrs Johnson, when he had lodged in her house in Bromley Street during his last two years as a medical student. Reynolds was the instigator of this rumour. Since his house in Barnes Street was opposite the one in which Mrs Johnson now lived with a Mr Vane, it had become obvious to Reynolds, as a result of his observations, that Mrs Johnson had become a prostitute. Reynolds not only knew of Barnardo by repute, Barnardo had earlier lived in lodgings in Barnes Street himself. At some time during 1874 Reynolds invited Mrs Johnson into his house, obviously in the hope that she might say something that he could use against Barnardo; he so manipulated the conversation that he could afterwards contend that Mrs Johnson had said that Barnardo had had an immoral relationship with her. He later admitted that he never bothered to check the facts, nor cared whether the story was true or not. Some of the first people to hear of this were Barnardo's deacons at the Edinburgh Castle mission church. They took the trouble to interview Mrs Johnson, with her mother present as well as a medical man, and came to the conclusion that there was no truth in the story and that Mrs Johnson was suffering from a form of sexual hysteria, as they termed it.

Barnardo demanded and was given an apology by Reynolds in July 1874; but Reynolds, always preferring to attack rather than defend, contended that Barnardo had also libelled him, and his apology to Barnardo for circulating a false rumour was somehow inextricably mixed up with some further confusing counter-accusations. There the matter might have rested had not Reynolds and Charrington been brought together in 1875 at the very moment when Charrington was most incensed by Barnardo's refusal to give up the idea of establishing the Dublin Castle in the Mile End Road. Charrington had had several interviews with Barnardo on this subject during the spring of 1875, demanding that he give up the coffee palace and go out of the district.

Barnardo, fearing that his position might be misunderstood, had published a pamphlet entitled, 'A Word on Coffee Palaces'. In it he gave the history of the dispute and said that as a result of his talks with Charrington he had consulted his legal advisers as to the possibility of withdrawing, but as the iron framework of the building was already built this would not be possible. He said he was prepared to restrict the building to a coffee palace and leave Charrington to work the adjoining mission hall even suggesting, if this did not please, that they work together. Charrington was not to be placated and although he said privately that he would be willing to give in to anyone except Barnardo, he stepped up his attack by threatening to make public the rumour concerning Mrs Johnson, telling him only, 'There is something behind which you do not know of, Barnardo, and which you will be very sorry for.'

Barnardo seems to have been the kind of person, partly on account of his unknown background and partly because of his aggressive and flamboyant personality, to whom rumour and gossip were bound to attach. Having no idea what lay behind Charrington's threat, he was in Scotland on a preaching mission when the bombshell burst. A letter addressed to him at Newbury House from a Mr Hamilton, a friend of Charrington's and Reynolds', told of a conversation that had taken place between them concerning Barnardo's relationship with Mrs Johnson. As her husband was away Syrie opened the letter. Barnardo's feelings of indignation and disgust at the way Charrington was using the rumour were the more acute because it was his wife who had been the one to receive the first intimation of the accusation. His letter to Charrington vibrates with anger:

The intense indignation and horror I feel at your baseness cannot be expressed in words. I have tried and wrestled with myself all day to conceive some other feelings towards you than those which I now express; but alas, your conduct leaves me no possibility of doing so. This then was the threat which you hinted at as likely to fall upon my head upon the occasion of your visit. This then was what you ominously suggested might possibly come to the front if I ventured to interfere with your plans, and I, poor fool, giving you and everyone else credit for as much generosity as I felt myself was trying all the time to feel, and God alone knows how truly, kindly and charitably towards one whose house I have to-day discovered from more than one source, to have been for a considerable time a place in which any foul or filthy stories might be carried about another.

Charrington and Reynolds then started to circulate reports of the alleged affair and in June Barnardo again wrote to Charrington demanding an apology. Charrington replied that he did not make the statement in the report and wrote, 'I am not responsible for what I did not say, but I am prepared to stand by what I did say and even in a court of law, should you feel disposed to take it there.' Barnardo replied at once.

You say you did not make use of the expressions imputed to you. If not there could only have been a very slight literal error – one thing is quite clear – viz. that you must have implied in strong terms that there had been an immoral connection at some time between Mrs. Johnson and myself, and that Mr. Hamilton positively swears to ... Let me add, the charge is not worth the paper it is written upon, so utterly incredible and so easily refuted, but it is deplorable to think even if it were true, that you or any other Christian minister could for an hour entertain it without communication with the person accused, and not only so, but absolutely make the statement a public one when the individual was not present ... Either you did make the statement or you did not. If you did not, then all those present understood such an imputation and you ought to take as public a means of retracting your statement and removing the impression as you did in making it. If, however, you have made the statement and really proposed it then you have been guilty of uttering a gross libel, which I declare to be in all particulars absolutely false and in so doing you have brought yourself within the penalties of law made and provided for such cases.

John Sands, a friend of both men, had been initially unfavourably impressed by Barnardo's attitude over the Dublin Castle, as had the Guinnesses, who believed his behaviour had been both unreasonable and overbearing. Both had had some sympathy with Charrington's feeling that Barnardo was so puffed up with pride that he must be brought down. However, when they became aware of the way in which Charrington and Reynolds were using the rumours against Barnardo, their support for Charrington greatly lessened. Barnardo had touched on a very embarrassing aspect of the quarrel by reminding Charrington that both of them were Christian ministers, and friends of both sides were extremely anxious the quarrel should not escalate and bring discredit to the whole evangelical movement. John Sands made an attempt at mediation only to find immediately afterwards that the rumours were again circulating, this time at the Mildmay Park Conference, an annual event which brought evangelicals together from all over the country. The Guinnesses attempted to bring peace to the disputants and Barnardo himself wrote to both Charrington and Reynolds saying that if they could not settle their differences then he was willing to abide by the decision of five or seven well-known Christian men to be nominated by both sides. Charrington and Reynolds did not respond to this initiative.

Then began what has been described as 'the most melancholy part of the whole business', the newspaper warfare. The correspondence which appeared initially in the local East End newspapers would probably have remained of academic interest only, had it not included two letters, widely believed to be by

Barnardo himself, attacking Charrington and Reynolds in the most insulting terms. The whole affair would have been only a local nine-days wonder, had not the question of the authorship of these two letters subsequently assumed an importance out of all proportion to their content and become one of the most sensitive issues upon which, in 1877, a court of arbitration was called upon to rule.

The second phase of the quarrel between Charrington, Reynolds and Barnardo began with an attack on both Barnardo and Booth in the *East London Observer*,[2] from a correspondent signing himself Diogenes:

Why do Evangelists not organise committees, publish accounts and do as Ministers of Churches have to do in respect of money matters? Who cares whether Dr. Barnardo, Mr. Booth and others collect £2,000 or £200 a year and whether they have a committee and whether their accounts are audited or not? If Dr. Barnardo devotes himself to his work with self-denying energy, whose business is it but his own? Or if he 'makes it pay', as some suppose he does, this also is a matter between those who supply him with funds.

The writer lamented that the work done at the Edinburgh Castle and at Booth's gospel hall in Whitechapel should not have been done by the churches, and regretted that Protestants 'prefer to leave the young to Dr. Barnardo, just as they leave the adults to Mr. Booth'.

This was only the opening salvo. The 'Diogenes' letter gave George Reynolds the excuse he was looking for. Writing under the pseudonym of 'A Protestant Dissenter',[3] he launched into a straight attack on Barnardo, questioning whether those who supported the East End Juvenile Mission realised that Barnardo was also the pastor of a church of 'immersed believers' who, because they had no pastor to support, enjoyed a 'free Gospel'. Few dissenting ministers, he continued, 'can afford to keep a country seat equal to Mossford Lodge or a town residence equal to Newbury House, Bow, the residence of the self-denying Dr. Barnardo ... Let the truth be told; Dr. Barnardo, instead of having sacrificed all for the Lord's sake, has raised himself on a pedestal of his work.' Reynolds ended his letter by hoping 'that the Charity Organisation Society may go thoroughly into these matters and the law of the land may soon be altered, so as to enable them to grapple effectually with many of these societies'.

A Scandalous Controversy

The attempt to involve the Charity Organisation Society was a shrewd move on the part of Reynolds, lifting the attack above the mere jealous grumbles of one pastor about the successful activities of a rival, onto an altogether more serious level. The Charity Organisation Society or COS, as it was known, had been founded in 1869, just after the establishment of the East End Juvenile Mission. Records show that from the very start the COS regarded Barnardo's work with suspicion, and the subsequent relationship between Barnardo and the organisation can only be described as one of open hostility. To understand why this was so it is necessary to understand both the fears and the aspirations of the men who were responsible for the creation of the COS.

Those interested in social reform were becoming increasingly worried by the uncontrolled activities of the many new charitable organisations which had come into being in the mid-nineteenth century. Believing that the efficient functioning of the Poor Law would be undermined by indiscriminate charitable giving, they were anxious to establish some central body which could organise and control the work of charities. They also thought it essential to ensure the absolute separation of charitable activity from the work of the Poor Law. They feared especially for the system of outdoor Poor Relief which they believed should be severely restricted. They thought that indiscriminate giving would inevitably result in an increase in the mendicant population and in the proliferation of 'clever paupers' who, playing on the susceptibilities of the charitable, would be able to avoid both work and the workhouse. Their official title, 'the Society for Organizing Charitable Relief and Repressing Mendicity', clearly expressed their aspirations. Their belief that the existing machinery of Poor Law relief and limited charitable endeavour was adequate to deal with all the social problems of the day, if properly organised and professionally administered, was directly contradicted by Barnardo's discovery of the problem of destitution among children and challenged by his policy of accepting all such children into his homes. But their views found ready acceptance among many of the middle-class and professional people who felt threatened by the revelation that an 'outcast' population existed in a city which they thought of as the capital of the civilised world.

This attitude was clearly expressed by J. R. Green, the historian who had preceded Joseph Bardsley as Vicar of Stepney, when he wrote:[4]

It is not so much poverty that is increasing in the East as pauperism, the want of industry, of thrift or self-reliance – qualities which the legislation of 30 years ago has ever since then been with difficulty producing among the poor, but which melt and vanish in a couple of winters before the certainty of money from the West . . . Some half a million people in the East End of London have been flung into the crucible of public benevolence and have come out of it simple paupers.

The direct cause of this 'demoralisation' of the working class was squarely laid at the door of public and private charity. Reynolds' appeal to the cos to investigate the activities of the East End Juvenile Mission, with its scarcely veiled hint that its management was questionable, could not fail to attract the notice of that society, and in fact their files show that the activities of the East End Juvenile Mission had been monitored by them since 1872.[5]

Barnardo was again away preaching in Scotland when he heard of the fresh accusations made by Reynolds. He replied from Perth in a lengthy letter in which he attempted to bring the attacks to an end by saying that he would not be drawn further into a newspaper controversy. However this did not stop Reynolds from continuing to write to the papers and stepping up his attack. It was not in Barnardo's nature to allow accusations to go unanswered, but he had tied his hands by publicly announcing that he would not be drawn into a newspaper controversy. The thought must have come to him that an anonymous friend could not only take over his defence but also speak more freely than he himself could.

A letter signed 'A Clerical Junius' appeared on 11 September in the *East London Observer*, purporting to give the story of Barnardo's life and praising the work he was doing in the East End. Two weeks later a second letter from 'A Clerical Junius' appeared, this time in the *Tower Hamlets Independent*, whose editor was a friend of Barnardo's. Throwing discretion to the winds, the author praised Barnardo in the most fulsome terms and referred contemptuously to the activities of his opponents.

It was widely believed at the time that Barnardo had himself written both letters, and the question of their authorship was to become one of the most important issues that faced the court of arbitration of 1877. Over the next two years the letters were reprinted several times, extensively circulated and publicly discussed. The question of their authorship almost brought the arbitration case to a premature close, amid renewed public speculation as to Barnardo's involvement in their composition.

The first Junius letter began by saying that if Barnardo determined to be silent all must feel his 'dignified self-respect' had guided him aright. Clerical Junius, identifying himself as an evangelical clergyman of the Church of England, said that he had known Barnardo as a boy and that Barnardo had come to him for guidance shortly after his religious life began; since then he had watched 'with admiration and with devout thankfulness a course which, like the path of the righteous, has "shone brighter and brighter unto the perfect day"'. When the author came to live in London in 1870 he had wanted to write the life story of the founder of the East End Juvenile Mission, but as permission for the biography had been refused he now considered that for the sake of the work he must be allowed to 'let the sunshine of a noble life story chase away every shadow with which your correspondents' personalities and aspersions have essayed to befog your readers'. Details of Barnardo's family background were given, and as Barnardo admitted later that all the details in the letters were supplied by him, they therefore have a special interest.

His father's family is an old one. I have seen a carefully preserved genealogical tree in which their descent is traced back to Spain, whence in the year 1650, the family were driven through persecution.[6] One of the junior branches took root in Germany, from which the father of my friend came. Another branch went to Russia, from which there sprang one whose name has been within the past three years notable in the record of Russian politics. His maternal grandmother was a Drinkwater, his mother a cousin of Sir J. Drinkwater, Bart., the head of the family.[7] It will thus be seen, and my object in stating it will appear, that so far as blood be anything, Dr. Barnardo is not a mere unknown adventurer. His father, when I knew him some fifteen years ago, was reputedly a wealthy man, and the manner in which his family have been educated and brought up proves, at least, that they enjoyed the advantages of opulence.

Clerical Junius then traced Barnardo's own career:

Some years ago he became possessed of considerable means, which would have enabled him, had he chosen it, to live not at Mossford Lodge, nor yet at Newbury House as your correspondent so grandly sneers, but in a West End residence, surrounded by society of a refined and genial order. But this noble hearted man does the very opposite of all this, continuing to live in the East End and, dispensing largely on every side his bounty, he has made himself a name which will live in the memory of thousands long after their traducing statements have been buried in oblivion.

The second letter from Clerical Junius was written in reply to yet another attack by Reynolds which had appeared on 18 September. In this letter Reynolds had for the first time directly questioned Barnardo's right to the title of Doctor. He also threatened that he would in a subsequent letter reveal more details about the 'wicked woman' scandal, a euphemism that was always used by Reynolds to refer to Mrs Johnson's supposed relationship with Barnardo. In the face of this threat Barnardo acted. He took out a writ against Reynolds, and the second Clerical Junius letter was published. This letter, which fell into two parts, was truly explosive. In the first part the author was concerned to rebut the charges made against Barnardo. However, the long and evasive reply to the allegation that Barnardo had no proper right to the title of Doctor was an indication of the embarrassment Barnardo was evidently feeling on the subject. Seeking to ridicule the suggestion that all was not as it should be, Clerical Junius wrote:

Really, Sir, the poor gentleman's curiosity is evidently making him act so strangely, that I feel half tempted to solve his difficulties and tell him. But the impudence of the sentence is too much for me and I feel it is one of those enquiries in which one must obey the voice of the wise man, 'Answer not a fool according to his folly.' But is the Founder of the Boys' Home and Director of the *East End Juvenile Mission* a Doctor of Divinity? Perhaps he is; certainly if all accounts be true, he ought to be; for his sermons contain sound theology, which is after all, the bottom of good divinity. Is he a Doctor of Medicine? Ah! there's the rub. I fancy I see 'A Protestant Dissenter's' eyes light up with sudden fire – once more he is facing, in imagination at least, a mob of excited Orangemen, whom he is goading into fury by declamations against the 'confessional' etc. But really, whether my good friend be a

Doctor of Medicine, English, Scotch, Irish, German, Canadian, or, oh fie! proh pudor, from the United States, doth not concern your deponent; but I can assure the Pastor of Adullam that my friend does not practise medicine; nay that he is completely engrossed with the cares, duties and calls of the mission, the pastorate, and his editorship, that he does not even attempt to attend a single case among his rescued children, but employs three respectable medical gentlemen living in the neighbourhood to visit at the houses daily, to undertake the responsibility for the affairs of health. But may not my friend be a Doctor of Law? Why no? D.D. and LL.D. are now-a-days regarded as honorary and honourable distinctions, even when not earned by academic gradus. And as to physics, he may be a Doctor of Physics for aught I know.

However, it was the second part of the letter, describing a dream, that was the cause of much of the furore that resulted from the publication of the letters. Although long and discursive, for those with some knowledge of the events and the personalities described it must have made compulsive reading. The dramatis personae were Mr Brewgoose, a thinly disguised Charrington; Keepclose, Charrington's paid secretary Edwin Kerwin; Churlish, a paid worker of Charrington's called Chilton Dean, who was the author of some of the letters to the *East London Observer*; George Reynolds made his appearance as the Rev. Swino Reynard and Barnardo himself was portrayed as Dr Dogood, a character whose every action was described with fulsome praise. Clerical Junius started the dream sequence with the words:

I thought I had finished; but it seems, Mr. Editor, that the very notion of waiting for what is yet to come from the pregnant womb of Time, and from the fertile pen of 'A Protestant Dissenter', sent me off in front of my pleasant fire into a sound sleep.

I was in dreamland, transported to a theatre, and from one of the boxes, half-screened by sheltering curtains, looked out upon the drama which held the immense assemblage in the building, spellbound with attention. The curtain had just been raised, and I glanced at the perfumed programme before me to discover the title of the piece and the name of the dramatis personae. It was entitled 'The Biter Bit; or, Good always Triumphant', and the dramatis personae were few. Chief among them were a certain Dr. Dogood, a Mr. Brewgoose, a Rev. Swino Reynard, a Mr. Keepclose, and a Mr. Churlish. Dr. Dogood first entered. He had a benevolent expression of countenance, and in my dream he seemed to walk through the streets and every-where accompanied by the goodwill and esteem of others; for he was regarded as a public benefactor. The first scene showed him in a large school during mid-winter, surrounded by a number of ragged children whom he was feeding. Soon this passed away to give place to the second scene, where he and some of his friends were distributing warm garments to the poor in cold weather; while a third scene revealed him on the door-step of a large house called 'A Refuge for the Destitute', which had been reared through his own benevolent exertions, and within which were sheltered some hundreds of homeless boys. Apparently, Dr. Dogood's entire life was spent, as his name signified, in good deeds.

In one of the earlier scenes the doctor was observed to conduct a party of friends to the corner of a street where a great gin palace stood, from which issued yells and shouts of drunken revelry and bacchanalian songs. But, in a moment afterwards, the curtain rose upon the same house, no longer used for such wicked purposes, but now as a mission house and coffee palace, and showing numbers of passers-by pausing at the entrance, while others went in, attracted by the sounds of holy song and sweet melody which were heard issuing from the doors. A bystander remarked to Dr. Dogood, 'Sir, you deserve the eternal gratitude of this locality and of the rising generation, not only for the work of your house, but also for having rescued this "Citadel of Satan" from the enemy.' The good man only smiled, and quickly vanished. He did not appear to wish for the applause of men. But suddenly the scene changed, and we were introduced to the next personage, a Mr. Brewgoose; in some respects like Dr. Dogood, young, and of an interesting countenance. His forehead, however, was too narrow, and his facial conformation showed too evidently the lack of that decision of character so necessary to make even good deeds permanent. Mr. Brewgoose's great drawback was his ambition; to be thought a very good man was his great aim. But, poor fellow! he had not quite brain-power enough to succeed. He wished, like many other people we know, to be thought very good; and accordingly, although engaged to enter his father's own business, yet, as some persons thought, it was after all a naughty trade, though money-making. Mr. Brewgoose resolved to sacrifice prospects to reputation. But his desire to be well thought of still greatly influenced him, for he gave up his father's business with such a flourish of trumpets as induced many pious people to say – What a self-denying good young man to give so much up through conviction!

The letter then asserted that Charrington had not, in fact, given up a large income, he never had a fortune of £60,000, and he was still receiving an income of £400 from his father's share in the 'naughty business'. Although Barnardo later maintained that all the facts in the letter were correct, there is no way of knowing if this allegation was based on anything other than speculation. Clerical Junius continued his attack on Charrington:

For a long time it seemed as though this poor young man could not think of any means by which he should render himself famous, although he was seen going about every day looking very hard at everything, and trying to find out something new. Chance, however, favoured him; there was a good clergyman living near, whose name was the Rev. Mr. Dicksdaughter. This reverend gentleman, among other efforts made for the good of his parish, had obtained some large pictures with interesting reading, and these he had pasted on the wall near his church, where they were evidently much liked and read by many of the passers-by. He happened to mention this one day in Mr. Brewgoose's hearing, and the latter, of course, thought here at last was an excellent means of doing something. Calling to his aid a certain Mr. Churlish, he set up in the bill-sticking line, disfiguring every wall and hoarding in the entire neighbourhood with yellow, blue, red, and white bills of all sizes, containing, I am sorry to say, words taken from the holiest of books; meant indeed to arrest attention when prayerfully read under the Spirit's guidance; but never designed to mingle in the streets with playbills or business announcements.

This grand stroke of original design brought Mr. Brewgoose's name into great favour with certain good, but weak-minded people who believe so long as one tries to do good, no matter by what means, it must be right. But, alas! alas! one day Mr. Brewgoose met Dr. Dogood, and when he observed the work of the latter, he inwardly felt how small a thing was bill-sticking compared with the Doctor's deeds. Worse still, everybody was talking of Dr. Dogood. He never spoke himself, but everyone did it for him. His quiet earnestness won friends where even bill-sticking and a reputation for wealth had failed to do the same for others. The desire for religious fame grew into a mania with poor Mr. Brewgoose, and at last produced a disease which physicians call chronic jealousy of the mind. He would frown if anybody spoke favourably of Dr. Dogood, or, by little petty ways would depreciate the extent or motive of his deeds. But, in reality, all he wished to do was to imitate, and then to surpass, his copy. In this he succeeded with a great many things. If Dr. Dogood had a big house, Mr. Brewgoose would set up a little one, hoping by-and-by it might become big. Then Dr. Dogood had invented a method of giving employment to many boys whom he could not take into the Refuge. He became a wood merchant, and employed the lads in chopping wood, to be sold to the shops. Mr. Brewgoose did the same. Of course it was all original, and so very devoted of him! Mr. Brewgoose had a secretary; his name was Mr. Keepclose, and this gentleman's chief employment was to feed the fire of his master's ambition, a task for which he was particularly well fitted. Little sly words, hints, stories, when they could be got hold of – anything, indeed, it did not matter what, about Dr. Dogood was all grist to the mill which was ground so vigorously by Mr. Keepclose and his employer, Mr. Brewgoose.

Charrington did print texts and stick them up; he did open a home for boys and he did start a wood-chopping brigade. He also started a magazine which the writer of the letter said was merely a 'weak copy' of the one produced by Dr Dogood.

It would have been interesting to know more about Charrington's relationship with Reynolds, but Clerical Junius is silent on the subject. He simply wrote:

About this time he formed the acquaintance of a ministerial gentleman whose name was the Rev. Swino Reynard. This reverend gentleman first patronised and then toadied Mr. Brewgoose, whose reputation for wealth dazzled his ministerial eyes. Strange to say, the Rev. Swino Reynard was not popular. He had been, I think, several years in a neighbouring parish, but nobody cared for him. His church was empty, the building itself in a ramshackle condition. They were always quarrelling there, and you know it is said that 'like pastor like people', so that, if the people quarrelled so often, we may well ask, What must the pastor have been? In fact, you would have passed by the singular looking place in which Mr. Reynard preached without noticing it.

All of a sudden the inhabitants of the quarter were startled. For, what do you think? Side by side with some of the bills containing holy words, which Mr. Brewgoose's bill-sticker had placed on public walls, were other large placards announcing that in future the Rev. Swino Reynard would preach in the Castle Hall two evenings in each week! Most people were surprised at such an announcement, for it was generally known that Castle Hall was a preaching place which a kind gentleman lately deceased had generously given Mr. Brewgoose. From that hour Mr. Brewgoose's troubles thickened; for, although the Rev. Mr. Reynard was cunning, he was not wise; and he led the unfortunate Mr. Brewgoose into such sad trouble as he had not previously experienced.

Then followed a long account of the dispute between Barnardo and Charrington over the building of the Dublin

Castle coffee palace. From this account it seemed possible that Charrington had purchased the land in the Mile End Road for his own coffee palace before realising that Barnardo was already making plans to erect his building.

... He purchased the land, and then it came to his knowledge that Dr. Dogood owned the houses adjoining! 'Oh, dear me! what shall I do?' said Mr. Brewgoose. 'I shall never become famous. Although I try and try again ever so hard, nobody will take notice of poor me! For if Dr. Dogood only builds his house next door, then everybody will favour him as they have done in the past, and I shall not be thought much of after all!'

I ought to have said that Dr. Dogood performed most of his good deeds through the kindness of pious people throughout the land, who sent him such money as he might require for his benevolent operations; and he in return, having enough money of his own to live upon, gave up all his time and his services to his work gratuitously. Now Mr. Brewgoose knew a great many of the Doctor's pious friends – in fact, he first of all got supported by boasting of his acquaintanceship with the Doctor – and it occurred to him in an evil moment that, if he could only prejudice pious people against Dr. Dogood, he might not only prevent the latter from spreading his influence as he had done, but he, Mr. Brewgoose, would instead obtain all the fame which he thought the Doctor had got, and for which his own soul now so yearningly panted. The Rev. Swino Reynard was not very particular what he did; any mean little way of obtaining his end was not objectionable to him. He would talk, for example, to servants, to people whom the Doctor had once employed, but had dismissed for improper conduct. Or, he would, indeed, listen to any idle story concerning Dr. Dogood, in the hope that it would feed the ever-increasing mania of his patron.

It so happened that one day the Rev. Swino Reynard was conversing with a very wicked person – a person so wicked that everyone knew she was wicked, and respectable people would not like to be seen talking to her; and she told the minister a story about Dr. Dogood which, if true, would prove that the latter must be a very naughty man. The Rev. Swino Reynard clapped his hands. It was far too bad a tale not to be true, thought he! Away he went to tell his patron, Mr. Mr. Brewgoose, that 'it was all right!' 'He might reckon on becoming famous at last through his (Mr. Reynard's) means.' 'But how is it possible?' whined poor Brewgoose whose intellectual powers were not of the highest order. 'I've tried, I am sure, but it ain't no good!' Mr. Brewgoose's grammar was not always true, and although he had gone as a boy to a good school, people did say that his hand-writing and orthography might have been better. However, to make a long story short – for the dream I am describing seemed to me to occupy a long time – Mr. Brewgoose and Rev. Swino Reynard concocted a scheme which, I am sorry to say, reflected neither credit nor piety on either of them. It was this: They would add a little to the story they had heard about Dr. Dogood, and then they would go round to his pious friends, and make long faces, and turn up the whites of their eyes, and look quite sad about it, and hint they knew something, they didn't like to say what, and so at last might succeed in making people who knew Dr. Dogood feel unhappy and disturbed in mind about their dear friend. But Dr. Dogood was told about this. At first he laughed at it, treating the story as might have been expected from one whose whole life had been spent for others rather than for himself; but it grew serious. People began to think that, because he did not do something, and expose these idle tales, that therefore there might be some truth in what was said. So Dr. Dogood called a number of his oldest friends together.

Barnardo's friends had certainly investigated the story of his supposed association with Mrs Johnson and had been convinced of his innocence. Clerical Junius made the point:

Dr. Dogood was proved to be what everybody had always known him, a hard-working, earnest, good man. But besides this, the naughty acts and machinations of Mr. Brewgoose were fully discovered.

Meanwhile the conspirators found themselves foiled on every hand, and one would have thought this would have sufficed to prevent their attempting more; but O dear, no! The Rev. Swino Reynard told his patron that they might venture to go a little further; and, although they could not injure Dr. Dogood in the eyes of one class of people, they might get up an outcry against him by writing a lot of nonsense in some of the papers, and then people would think, if it were only continued long enough, that, where there was so much smoke, surely there must be a little fire. Mr. Brewgoose was delighted – anything was better than to remain a Brewgoose all his life; and as to Mr. Reynard, as by this time he had neither church nor people, he certainly could not lose anything, and it was quite possible that he might gain something in addition to whatever his patron would pay him. So they set to work. The Rev. Swino Reynard got somebody to write for him a ridiculous letter in one of the local papers, describing Dr. Dogood and his work; but not really containing one sensible or sufficient criticism in the whole letter.

Soon after another letter appeared... hinting at a great many naughty things. For example, he suggested that Dr. Dogood was not benevolent at all, and that all he did he only did for his monetary advantage, and that the great good that was alleged to have been done by the Doctor's efforts was a mere flash-in-the-pan, and would not last, and that it was necessary some committee or board should undertake to examine into the financial affairs of the institutions which, it was more than hinted, the Doctor had contrived to work to his own advantage. And so he went on, like a cuttle-fish, darkening the waters by clouds of suspicion instead of inviting pursuit. But alongside of his letter appeared another, signed by the kind-hearted and benevolent Doctor, written in a spirit which everybody who had any good feeling would at once appreciate as gentlemanly, calm, and dignified, replying in a Christian spirit to all animadversions. This was too much for the reverend gentleman; and, in a few weeks afterwards, he wrote again, repeating and even increasing his naughty assertions. The Doctor saw with great sorrow all this going on, and the more so, as he knew whence it proceeded; for on two distinct occasions Mr. Brewgoose and the Rev. Swino Reynard had together made private overtures to him, virtually saying, 'If you will give up the house adjoining the land Mr. Brewgoose has taken, so as to enable him to become famous – if you will do this, we will never say anything naughty about you any more, and, indeed, we will keep what we know all to ourselves.' But Dr. Dogood was not to be caught in such a trap, and the justifiable anger he felt prevented all further parley.

My slumber was disturbed; I partly woke up, but slept again, and seemed in my dream to hear Dr. Dogood in conversation with his legal adviser, to whom the story of the bitter persecution he endured was told. That gentleman said, when he had heard all and seen the papers, 'My dear sir, you are far too good to deal with such gentlemen as these. They will only take advantage of your kindness and benevolence, and of your well-known quiet character. You really must leave them to me, not, perhaps, for your own sake, for your name and character are not capable of being injured to any extent by such men as the Rev. Swino Reynard or his patron, Mr. Brewgoose. But the work which is so near and dear to your heart may be affected by their aspersions, and I must therefore advise you to leave them in my hands, to pursue such a course towards them as the law directs under such circumstances.'

Tears filled Dr. Dogood's eyes; but he saw the wisdom of the advice, and bowing meekly, left the papers in the wise man's hands. I cannot recall what immediately followed in my dream, but my imagination was still in action, and soon I saw a crowded court, and persons – some of them noble, and most of them distinguished – engaged in giving evidence of a personal nature in the great libel case of 'Dogood v. Brewgoose, Reynard, and others'. I could not catch all that was said on either side. I suppose my slumbers were disturbed, for only now and then did the sounds of voices break upon my ear. One thing, however, I remember: the true philanthropist was vindicated, and the mean treachery and sordid aims of his traducers fully exposed and confirmed in open court. Friends shrank from them, the jury retired, and after a long absence returned. A dead silence reigned over the judicial assembly. A voice was heard asking the foreman of the jury, 'What is your verdict?' I turned eagerly to listen: but felt the lights in the Court going out immediately and I awoke to discover that my dream was over, and that I had rolled out of my chair, and was lying on the hearth-rug in front of the fire. So ended my dream, but not the lesson. After all was it only a vision? Who can tell? Certainly not,

Your obedient servant,
A Clerical Junius

This letter caused a sensation. Barnardo began selling copies at the Edinburgh Castle, but within two days he realised that matters had gone too far. The following week a letter appeared under his signature in the *East London Observer* condemning the Clerical Junius letter as 'atrocious', specifically denying that he was the author and dissociating himself from it:

I write at the earliest possible moment to express publicly the grief and pain I felt on perusing that atrocious letter of 'A Clerical Junius' in last week's *Tower Hamlets Independent*. Well may I say, 'save me from my friends!' for such friends would ruin the best cause. My share in the transaction – a share which I now deeply deplore – was merely a passive one. I permitted all the letters, documents and papers relating to my controversy with Messrs. Reynolds and Charrington to remain in '*Junius*'s hands for a few days, and, at his request, purchased and sent him several publications; I know he was preparing a letter for the paper, but I never imagined that he would have strayed so widely from the path of decency, decorum and good taste. When I first perused it in the columns of your contemporary, its full import did not break upon me, but a second and more deliberate reading a day or two afterwards showed me its great wrong. Some good people have been kind enough to impute its whole, or partial, authorship to myself. I indignantly deny the charge. Never have I in any dispute or controversy permitted myself to forget I was a Christian and a gentleman. A number of copies of last week's paper were sent down to the Edinburgh Castle by a friend, and some were sold there; but as soon as I had carefully read '*Junius*'s letter I stopped the sale; and at a large public meeting held in the preaching hall, avowed my objection to and condemnation of, the abominable epistle.

More than this I could not do; and although in the interests of the institutions under my care, I have been compelled to commence legal proceedings against Messrs. Reynolds and Charrington, yet nothing will ever induce me, in speaking of, or disputing with them, to use language or employ terms which must be revolting to every true follower of our Lord and Saviour Jesus Christ.

In making such a strong statement about the tone of the letter Barnardo was at the same time condemning the Church of England clergyman, 'Clerical Junius', with whom he claimed to be on terms of friendship. As public attention came to focus increasingly on the question of the authorship of the letters, Barnardo found he had impaled himself on the horns of a dilemma. Two years later when the whole matter was before a court of arbitration, very much as had been foreseen in the dream, Barnardo found both horns had become increasingly sharp as further facts about the letters came to light.

7

Disaster Threatens

AT the same time as the newspaper controversy was taking place, work on the cottages at Ilford, which were to become the Girls' Village Home, was proceeding apace. The Dublin Castle coffee palace had been completed and it had been opened without any of the ceremony that had attended the opening of the Edinburgh Castle, and a new school had been brought into operation in nearby Copperfield Road. The general public were unaware as yet of the quarrel between the two Christian leaders which was to become so damaging to both, and continued to give support to Barnardo's work. Although the publication of the second Clerical Junius letter, with its well aimed insults, could only inflame an already unhappy situation and cause Charrington's resentment to burn yet more fiercely, the contents of the letter were as yet unknown outside the East End. But the quarrel was becoming more serious and it began to spread like a forest fire; as soon as friends damped it down in one place it broke out in another, until finally all concerned realised that unless the fire brigade were called in, Barnardo's work and Christian work generally might be irreversibly damaged.

Following the publication of the second Clerical Junius letter, immediate attempts were made by friends of both sides to avoid further public scandal and consequent damage to evangelical work. The situation was particularly awkward and embarrassing, not only on account of the nature of the charges brought by Charrington and Reynolds against Barnardo, but because of the closely interconnected nature of the evangelical movement. Charrington and Barnardo received support from many of the same sources. The two leaders had many friends in common and it was these friends who put pressure on them for a settlement to be reached and the quarrel ended.

As a result of long negotiations between the parties, Thomas Stone, a respected figure in evangelical circles who was known to all for his successful chairmanship of the London committee of the Moody and Sankey campaign, finally induced all three of them to sign an agreement to keep the peace. The document they signed was known as 'the Stone arbitration'. Barnardo had been most unwilling either to withdraw the writ he had issued or to sign the agreement, and he gave his reasons to Mr Stone:[1] 'I feel, dear brother, deeply humbled and in the very dust before God for the whole affair, although before men I assume the defensive because I am deeply conscious that I have been wronged by them in a most grievous way.' Barnardo had more reason than he knew to feel wronged. Scarcely was the ink dry on the Stone Arbitration before Charrington and Reynolds started secretly printing and circulating anonymous pamphlets. Twelve hundred copies of one of them, entitled 'The Great Eastern Bubble',[2] were printed and circulated and Reynolds had the effrontery to show it to Thomas Stone and ask him for his opinion as to who had printed it!

Nothing the mediators could do could prevent speculation continuing as to the authorship of the Clerical Junius letters, and the letters remained a subject for public discussion. It was at this juncture that the public intervention of two clergymen, the Rev. Main Walrond and the Rev. Joseph Bardsley, was instrumental in making the quarrel one of national rather than local interest. An anonymous letter, signed 'Veritas', had appeared in the *East London Observer* stating that the editor of the *Tower Hamlets Independent* had been told that the Clerical Junius letters had been written by a certain S. W. Walrond who had given Lowestoft as his address, but that no such person could be found in Lowestoft. This letter caused Main Walrond, Vicar of St Lawrence Jewry, to enter the controversy. In an angry letter to the *East London Observer* he wrote stating that there were only three other clergymen of his name and family beside himself:[3]

None of us wrote those letters . . . There is no other clergyman of our name, the writer, therefore, if he has stated his name as Walrond is a lying rascal . . . Dr. Barnardo has a notoriety in religious and other papers, which has made it impossible for me not to have heard his name; but I have supposed him to myself to be one of those ignorant fanatics who abound in the world, doing that combined mischief which only ignorance and fanaticism can do.

Shortly after this letter appeared he wrote to Joseph Bardsley to ask him for his help in discovering the name of the author of the Clerical Junius letters.[4] Bardsley replied that he was unable to help because Barnardo had refused to cooperate.[5] Both Walrond's letter and Bardsley's reply were printed in the *East London Observer* simultaneously, and Walrond took a further step and had the correspondence reprinted in *The Record*,[6] a Church of England newspaper which was published nationally three days a week.

Walrond may have written to Bardsley simply because he was Vicar of Stepney, but he also knew that Bardsley was a close family friend of Charrington's and that Bardsley, Charrington and Charrington's secretary, Edwin Kerwin, were all members of the Mile End Old Town district committee of the COS. Walrond himself was a founder member of the COS. He had been at Balliol with C. B. P. Bosanquet, who with C. J. Ribton-Turner shared the duties of secretary to the COS when it was first founded. Both Walrond and Bosanquet had been pupils of T. H. Green and had been much influenced by him, particularly by his belief in the value of systems. One of the basic aims of the COS was to bring order into the whole field of social welfare, emphasising the importance of organisation and of maintaining a delicate balance between the work of the boards of guardians who operated the Poor Law and those who dispensed charitable funds, and thus cutting across the very nature of the free-wheeling, individually managed enterprise that Barnardo had set up.

The hostile tone of Walrond's letter reflected not only his personal animus towards Barnardo but also his distaste for the principles on which Barnardo worked – an attitude shared by many other members of the COS. Most of those dealing with social problems in the 1860s and 1870s failed to see any link between the economic structure of London and the widespread poverty in which most of the inhabitants of the East End lived. They tended to see the problem in moral rather than in economic terms, believing that poverty was caused by the thrift-less and mendicant habits of the poor who had been demoralised by the giving of indiscriminate charity. One of the assumptions that permeated much of the thinking of the COS was that the 'demoralised' poor would always turn from labour to mendicancy, given the opportunity. From this it followed that they would naturally migrate to where charitable bodies were active or to areas where outdoor Poor Relief was obtainable. Barnardo never believed this. In his first report he wrote that it was important that there should be special employment for men,[7] 'because men would be conscious of *earning* their livelihood, and the wretched feeling and result of living on charity would be done away with'. Having had to live on charity himself for a time, perhaps he knew what it felt like to be beholden to others.

The work of the COS has been considered as part of the Victorian philanthropic movement but, as this quarrel was to reveal, there were deep ideological differences between the way in which the COS understood the use of charity and the way in which Barnardo and other evangelical philanthropists worked. The COS held to the then conventional view that there could be no economic solution to the problem of unemployment except through the free play of market forces, with charity for the thrifty and 'deserving' and the workhouse for the old, young, sick and 'undeserving'. Evangelicals, on the other hand, tended not to accept that distinction, wishing to bring salvation to all. Barnardo totally rejected the idea that the provisions of the Poor Law should be made to apply to children. His great success as a mission leader, which resulted from his exceptional abilities as a publicist, administrator and preacher, was seen by the COS as a direct threat to their ideas concerning the organisation of charitable work.

Rumour and anonymous leaflets are effective as weapons because they are difficult to refute and Barnardo, having withdrawn his writ, remained unable to counter the growing damage to his reputation. The leaflets not only attacked Barnardo over the question of the management of the homes, they made allegations of cruelty and neglect in respect of specific children there. Further, they alleged that Barnardo was misrepresenting facts by using faked photographs to exaggerate the state of the children on entering the homes, in order to demonstrate more effectively how much they had benefited by their stay in them.

The clumsy and unconvincing defence of his use of the title of Doctor in the first Clerical Junius letter showed that he was aware that his assumption of the title had made him vulnerable to attack. The Medical Act of 1858 had made it illegal to practise medicine or assume medical status unless registered;[8] the Royal College of Physicians had gone even further and had published a by-law in 1862 which held that 'no Fellow, Licenciate or Member of the College shall assume the title of Doctor of Medicine to imply that he is a graduate in medicine of a University unless he is a graduate in medicine of a University'.[9] Barnardo was neither registered nor a graduate, yet on the lease of Stepney Causeway which he signed in 1870 he described himself as a Doctor of Medicine. It was during the winter of 1872–3 that he decided officially to adopt the title, and later claimed that he had received a letter from Giessen University in 1872 awarding him an MD. This letter was a forgery, as has already been seen. From 1874 his right to the title of Doctor was increasingly questioned, notably by Charrington and Reynolds. It was doubtless in response to this pressure that late in 1875 he wrote to the University of Giessen to ask if there was any means by which he could be examined and acquire the right to put MD after his name. The only copy of this letter that exists is the one the COS obtained from the university and had printed. There can be no doubt as to its authenticity; only Barnardo could have written it, only he would have known the facts.[10]

I became a medical student at the London Hospital in 1867 and entered Durham University the previous September and registered as a medical student in June 1868. I duly attended all hospital practice, medical and surgical for four years. In July 1869 I passed the first professional examination in anatomy and physiology at the Royal College of Surgeons, England, and hope to go up for the final examination in April next. The reason why I have not proceeded to qualify fully before this is that in 1870 I abandoned the study of medicine and took up the philanthropic work of rescuing destitute children from the streets of our great cities, much of the same character of your own celebrated Dr. Wichern of Hamburg.

Although I did not proceed with my studies I am generally called Dr. Barnardo and enclose my card. I have never practised except when a student at the hospital, nor do I intend to practise medicine until I take an English diploma, which I am now reading for, and hope to gain in April next. But I am about to publish a book on our mission work among the destitute children, and wish if possible to have my name on the title page as T. J. Barnardo M.D., and therefore shall be glad to know if you can allow me to be examined by your University early in December as my book will be published about Christmas next. If it were necessary I could try to go over to your University for examination, but should be glad if that could be done by papers sent here. Kindly let me know the subjects of examination. I can give testimonials of my professional knowledge etc. by respectable English medical men, if you will kindly tell me what you require, and I enclose in proof of the truth of my first statements two certificates of registration, which please return when you reply. Also state the amount of fees required.

A postscript added the communication was a 'confidential one'.

Nothing came of this initiative and the book mentioned in the letter was published in January 1876 under the title of *Rescue the Perishing*, simply as the report of the ninth year of the East End Juvenile Mission and the fifth year of the homes for reclaiming destitute children of both sexes, with a note from Barnardo saying the book had been set up in type in October 1875 but that a variety of circumstances had compelled him to hold over its issue.

Barnardo had obviously given a lot of thought to the content of the report; it was not only a record of his achievements over the past eighteen months, it was in a sense his reply to the attacks that were being made on him. Besides containing nearly eight thousand receipts for donations, ranging from as little as two pennies for the general fund to three donations for cottages, one of the most remarkable features of the list was the very large number of donations under a pound, indicating again that Barnardo's appeal was widely based and that the servant girl who had given him his first twenty-seven farthings was typical of many of those who contributed to the mission. Barnardo had made it a matter of principle from the beginning never to print the names of his donors and was meticulous about sending a printed and numbered receipt to every one, even for the smallest sum. He took the advice of John Sands and in a short paragraph firmly stated that he received no salary or payment for his services and that he had sufficient private income to be able to do this without anxiety, but that if ever his private income did not suffice he would have no hesitation in making the fact generally known so that those who supported the work would be enabled to minister to his personal wants, as very many had already offered to do. He ended with a sentence aimed at Charrington and his friends: 'As I do not wish to be continually writing about myself, I hope that this explanatory statement will meet the eye of and be satisfactory to, all whom it may concern.'

Immediately after the report was issued Barnardo left secretly for Edinburgh, where he spent the ensuing four months studying at the Royal College of Surgeons, which enabled him to take his diploma in April 1876 and to qualify as a licenciate of the college; at the same time he obtained a certificate as an accredited accoucheur. But the strain and worry of the past four months had told on his highly-strung constitution. He had been suffering for some weeks from insomnia and he was left exhausted, ill and depressed by his efforts. But he had achieved his objective and on his return to London in April he registered as a medical practitioner. Three years later he was elected a Fellow of the Royal College of Surgeons.

The report was bought and eagerly read by his opponents in the hope that it might contain further evidence that could be used against him. It contained two photographs, one of which, captioned 'The Raw Material' and showing a group of boys as they might have been discovered by the boys' beadle, was seized upon by Reynolds as further evidence of misrepresentation. He contended that the ragged boys discovered by the beadle were not found in any such group. This turned out to be true, but it was of minor importance because the boys had in fact all been admitted on the same day.

The man photographed with them holding a bullseye lantern in his hand was Edward Fitzgerald, one of the most unfortunate appointments Barnardo ever made. For not only did Fitzgerald prove to be a drunkard and a liar, but for nearly a year, while still in Barnardo's employ, he had secretly been meeting with Charrington, Reynolds and Kerwin who had encouraged him to spy on his employer, doubtless rewarding him well for the information he passed on. Who else but he could have known how and where the boys in the photograph were found? After he was finally dismissed by Barnardo for immorality and drunkenness in October 1876, he was employed by Charrington for some months and later acted as a witness for Reynolds against Barnardo at the time of the arbitration.

In spite of the public support Barnardo received from leading evangelicals at the time of the opening of the village, the campaign of libel and slander waged by Reynolds and Charrington was having its effect. They made a dangerous combination: Charrington had money and influence, Reynolds with little to lose did not care what he did or said to injure his opponent. He was an aggressive man and enjoyed being the focus of attention. Once travelling in an omnibus past the Dublin Castle, he loudly declared it all to be a sham and Barnardo an impostor, and his words did not go unnoticed. He didn't hesitate to thrust his leaflets into Barnardo's own hands while distributing them outside the Edinburgh Castle.[11] So it continued through the summer of 1876, with more people becoming uneasy about Barnardo's work and support for the homes gradually falling off. And so it might have gone on, a damaging war of attrition which neither side could win. Then, some time in November, Reynolds decided to bring matters to a head and publish the charges against Barnardo publicly under his own name. All the evidence, which was to be made public later during the arbitration case, goes to show that this was done with the active connivance of the cos. It must further be assumed that unless he had been sure of the support of the cos Reynolds would have been unable to act, himself lacking the means, as Charrington lacked the courage, to print and publish publicly the accusations they had been circulating.

The central office of the cos was responsible for one of the best known functions of the society, that of inquiring into the affairs of the many bogus and fraudulent charities which had sprung up. Writers of begging letters were also investigated. The habit had become so widespread it had almost acquired the status of profession. Investigations were sometimes followed by prosecutions against offenders. One of the most effective weapons the cos used against suspect organisations was to warn intending subscribers of their suspicions and to circulate the names of the errant charities and individuals on lists known as 'cautionary cards'. Against this powerful weapon there was little that the individual or charity could do to prove their innocence as, financially crippled, they were usually unable to resort to the law. The damage the cos could thus inflict was often considerable, and at this time they were a very powerful body.

The man in charge of this aspect of the work of the society was C. J. Ribton-Turner, Lord Lichfield's private secretary who, when Lichfield took over the chairmanship of the society in 1869, remained with him and took on the duties of secretary to the society, duties which he shared with Charles Bosanquet and Alsager Hay Hill, the social reformer. Hill, who was later to become a vice-president of the society, was well known for his strong opposition to all forms of unorganised charitable work, and especially to religious charitable work. He would certainly have been in favour of any move to curtail Barnardo's work and to bring it under some form of control. Ribton-Turner was responsible for setting up the local district committees, but his main interest was in the repression of charitable impostors. He was later to be accused of pursuing this particular activity with undue vigour, to the detriment of the general work of the society.[12] The growth of Barnardo's work posed a problem for the COS. Fiercely independent, Barnardo would tolerate no outside direction of any kind, and the expanding activities of the East End Juvenile Mission constituted a challenge to the authority of the COS. There can be no doubt that the COS followed the development of the quarrel between Barnardo and Charrington with special interest.

Shaftesbury's involvement with the COS remains somewhat mysterious. Having been asked to preside over their inaugural meeting in 1869, he was to remain a vice-president all his life. Committed as he was to the development and unlimited expansion of charitable work as a means of bringing a knowledge of the Gospel to the poorer classes, it is difficult to understand his involvement with a society dedicated to restricting the work of the home missions. He had been a patron of Charrington's Tower Hamlets Mission since its inception, so it was understandable that he should lean towards Charrington's side in the controversy; but the public announcement by the COS that he was heading the list of subscribers for a fund to enable Reynolds to fight the case against Barnardo was a grievous blow to Barnardo.

The part played by the COS in the events leading up to the arbitration which was finally set up in 1877 has never been made public.[13] It has always been assumed, as the COS wished it to be assumed, that as charges against Barnardo had been made it was the duty of the COS to investigate those charges. Not only was the part the society itself played in making sure that the charges were made public concealed, but it flatly denied having been involved with Reynolds in any way, or having any part in the events that followed the publication of the charges against Barnardo. Evidence given at the arbitration makes it quite clear that Ribton-Turner had started collecting evidence against Barnardo early in November 1876.[14] Reynolds, who had gone to see him, found that Fitzgerald was already with him, and that Ribton-Turner had just taken a statement from him. That same day there was a meeting of the administration committee of the COS to whom Ribton-Turner reported his findings, but the committee decided that no action could yet be taken. Ribton-Turner was not the only member of the COS collecting evidence to use against Barnardo when the time came.

The photograph of a boy named William Fletcher had featured in one of the anonymous leaflets accusing Barnardo of using fictitious photographs to gain sympathy and money for the homes. Fletcher had been brought to the home by a Mr Bryant who had had charge of him since his parents' death in 1865. Bryant had recently had an accident, breaking his collar bone, which meant he could no longer work as a lighterman, and the only alternatives open to him were to bring the boy to Barnardo or to take him to the workhouse. Barnardo accepted the boy, who appears not to have been happy and absconded after eighteen months. He was brought back to the home and placed in solitary confinement, but again absconded, it seems with the connivance of Bryant who may have recovered from his illness by that time. One of the difficulties Barnardo had to contend with was boys who, coming in dressed in rags, absconded after they had been with him a while, sometimes at the instigation of friends or relatives, complete with the new suits and boots which had been provided by the homes. An entry on Fletcher's record sheet recording his final departure notes:[15] 'The man William Bryant called at the Home to-day with Fletcher's clothing and a note from the Rev. Mr. Walrond to the effect that Fletcher had been taken away at his instance and if any steps were taken Mr. Walrond's solicitor would act on behalf of the man Bryant.'

As Fletcher was one of the few boys who gave evidence

against the management of the homes during the arbitration case, it is obvious that Walrond's action in securing his release was not entirely philanthropic and that, even if the COS itself could not yet take action, some of its members were preparing for a showdown. Walrond had made sure not only that the controversy concerning the Clerical Junius letter remained alive, but also that Fletcher would be available to give evidence against Barnardo. It also highlighted a major problem that was to lead Barnardo into many disputes with parents and guardians who, recovering perhaps from a temporary misfortune or finding their children had grown to an age when their earnings could help sustain the family, wished to remove them from the homes. As a private individual, Barnardo had no right to keep the children against the wishes of parents or guardians, and Walrond, with his threat to employ a solicitor against him in the case of further interference with Fletcher, was sharply reminding him of the fact.

It was almost exactly at the time that Walrond was helping Bryant to secure Fletcher's release that Reynolds' pamphlet, which he had entitled 'Dr. Barnardo's Homes: Startling Revelations', was published and a new chapter in the warfare between Charrington, Reynolds and Barnardo began. The pamphlet itself was badly written and presented a confused mixture of accusations and innuendo. Previous charges against Barnardo which had already been circulated specifically accusing him of cruelty and neglect to the children were reissued; the major part of the pamphlet was taken up with a restatement of the controversy over the Clerical Junius letters, the letters themselves being reprinted together with many of the subsequent letters dealing with the question of their authorship, including the entire correspondence initiated by Walrond. The question of Barnardo's medical qualification was given an airing and the allegations concerning Mrs Johnson appeared under the provocative heading, 'The very wicked woman and her story'.

The pamphlet opened with the reasonable proposition that the whole of the properties in connection with the mission be vested in the hands of trustees, that a responsible committee of management be formed, that a treasurer be appointed and that some independent gentlemen should annually audit the accounts. It went on to suggest that the homes should be placed under entirely new management and that a kinder regime should be provided. It is almost as if two hands had drafted the opening passage. The first half is calm and reasonable; the second half appears to be pure Reynolds – facts are transposed, quotations are used out of context and the reader is left with a thoroughly confused impression of the situation and a feeling that something is amiss. All the allegations, previously circulated anonymously, appear in the pamphlet under Reynolds' signature. The most damaging new accusations were put forward in an affidavit signed by Edward Fitzgerald concerning the authorship of the Clerical Junius letters. In this affidavit Fitzgerald claimed that he was in Barnardo's back parlour on 18 September 1875 and several nights thereafter and,

> ... on those evenings I heard the said Thomas John Barnardo dictate to Frederick Fielder, who was then in his employ as a clerk, a letter which afterwards appeared in the *Tower Hamlets Independent*, signed *'Clerical Junius'*. The Extract from the *Tower Hamlets Independent* now produced contains the substance of what I heard the said Thomas John Barnardo dictate to the said Frederick Fielder; and in many places I recognise the exact expressions used by the said Thomas John Barnardo. I was in the house when the said Frederick Fielder left it, professedly, to take the said letter to the offices of the said *Tower Hamlets Independent*; and I saw him leave the said house dressed in such a manner as to represent the appearance of a clergyman. And I further say that this was done with the knowledge and sanction of the said Thomas John Barnardo.

In a further passage Reynolds said that Fitzgerald had called on Bardsley, Walrond and himself to tell them that he had known all along who had written the letters signed Clerical Junius. There can be little doubt that Fitzgerald made his affidavit in response to their request. Charrington and Barnardo both being, so to speak, professional Christian philanthropists, evangelical leaders were much concerned at the continuation of the quarrel. Many of them were not aware of the part Charrington was still playing, for he allowed Reynolds to make the running and took extreme care to cover his own tracks. But they were becoming concerned at the increasing interest being shown in the controversy by the COS, and by their actions showed that they were aware of the dangerously exposed position Barnardo was in. It was not surprising therefore that some of his chief supporters got together to consider what could best be done, not only to protect Barnardo himself, but also to safeguard his work against the allegations being made against him.

The Edinburgh Castle was already in trust, and Barnardo had declared that as soon as he was able he would vest both the Boys' Home and the Girls' Village Home in trustees, but as both were leasehold only, this had not so far been possible. The fact that Barnardo was dealing with large sums of money subscribed by the public and managing extensive properties with no committee and under no control was obviously unwise. John Sands, by transferring the leasehold of the land surrounding Mossford Lodge into a freehold, enabled trust deeds for the Girls' Village Home to be drawn up in November, the month before the publication of 'Startling Revelations'.

Although no record exists to show how it was agreed or what pressure was put upon Barnardo, it was at this moment that the trustees assumed managerial responsibility for Barnardo's work.[16] Knowing how fiercely Barnardo cherished his independence it cannot have been an easy moment for him, but no record remains of his thoughts and feelings on that day in November when he agreed to become a director of the East End Juvenile Mission, appointed by the trustees and able by them to be dismissed. The deed itself is the only evidence there is for this transfer of power, for no public announcement was made. The relevant part of the deed declared:[17]

It is provided that in order to dispense with the personal management of the said Homes, there shall be a Director or Directors thereof, and the said Thomas John Barnardo is hereby appointed first Director, such appointment to endure for his life, or so long as he shall be willing to discharge the duties of Director and shall in the opinion of the Trustees for the time being, or two thirds of their number (exclusive of the said Thomas John Barnardo), hold orthodox Evangelical opinions, and be in all respects competent properly to discharge the duties of Director and be resident within a reasonable distance of the said Homes and shall discharge the said duties in accordance with provisions and intent of these present on all which matters the decisions of the said Trustees 'or such majority of them aforesaid' shall be conclusive; and a power is further given to the Trustees to appoint new Directors or Director, subject to certain qualifications or limitations.

A similar trust was set up in respect of the Boys' Home in Stepney in January.

So little was Barnardo's changed status known that none of his biographers have referred to it, and he found it so hard to accept that the only reference that he ever made to the powers of his trustees at that time was in a small note he inserted four months later in his new publication, *Night and Day*[18] in reply to one of the many queries he answered as a regular feature of a page entitled 'Our Letter Bag': 'Financial – public accountants annually audit the accounts of The East End Juvenile Mission. The Trustees are absolutely responsible to the public for the management of the Homes and Finances. The Editor is only a Director appointed by the Trustees, without salary, and may be dismissed at any time.' Although he did not yet know it, Reynolds had succeeded in getting accepted one of the first points he had made. In his original letter signed Diogenes, he had asked why evangelists did not organise committees and publish accounts. This letter had associated Booth with his remarks about Barnardo, and it is interesting to note that William Booth was never subject to the control of trustees or of a committee during his lifetime.

Although John Sands who became one of the trustees doubtless instigated the move, for he had been the owner of the Mossford property, it was probably Thomas Pelham who was closest to Barnardo among his trustees at this time. Pelham, the third son of the Earl of Chichester[19] who 'was noted as a patron along with Shaftesbury and Cholmondeley of good and charitable works, especially such as were endorsed by the Evangelical party', worked closely with Barnardo in the East End and sometimes accompanied him on his midnight rambles in search of destitute children. Lord Aberdeen, another young man who had already shown interest in the work Barnardo was doing, persuaded his brother-in-law Lord Polwarth to join the trustees. Richard Moreton, son of the Earl of Ducie, had succeeded William Pennefather as secretary at Mildmay Park and his support was valuable. Arthur Kinnaird, who was to succeed his father in 1887, also became a trustee. Major C. H. Malan, the son of the orientalist Solomon Caesar Malan, was a neighbour of John Sands in Highbury. He had been one of the considerable number who had been 'converted' during the Crimean

War. With Harry Nisbet, a solicitor whose professional advice was to be of service to the homes from then until after Barnardo's death, and Richard Morgan, the editor of *The Christian*, Barnardo had a youthful, powerful and influential group of trustees, five of them within a year or two of him in age. He was going to need their help.

As soon as 'Startling Revelations' was published, members of the public started writing to the cos in considerable numbers asking for guidance, as the society had anticipated.[20] In view of the allegations made about the homes the cos felt themselves perfectly entitled to blacklist their work, and circulated the fact on one of the 'cautionary cards', ominously headed 'Institutions unfavourably known'. The cos had arrogated to itself the right to pass judgement on organisations and individuals, and the effect was inevitably damaging to the institution in question. Barnardo's evangelical trustees had no intention of allowing the cos to destroy his work. From now on the quarrel was no longer merely between two East End mission leaders, it was about to become a struggle between the leaders of the evangelical movement and the cos for the right to control the extent of the charitable voluntary movement. Barnardo was fighting in a sense with one hand tied behind his back, for his first concern had to be for the welfare of the six hundred or so children he had in his care. If, as a result of the action taken by the cos, funds were not forthcoming – and recent months had shown a worrying falling-off of support – there was no place for them to go other than the streets.

8

Arbitration

THE events of the year 1877 were to make the ensuing twelve months the most troubled and traumatic that Barnardo ever experienced. In the preface to the first volume of *Night and Day*, Barnardo revealed something of the anguish he suffered: 'The tempest is now over . . . yet it is only natural that there should remain upon the log of the well-nigh dismantled ship which came out of so fierce and prolonged a struggle, an indelible record of the soul agony experienced in the awful hours, now happily passed for ever.' Barnardo had intended his new magazine, first published in January 1877, to be a monthly record of Christian missions and practical philanthropy, but he was so overwhelmed by the events of 1877 that he used it as a means of publicising his side of the story, and afterwards apologised for allowing personal matters to obtrude, fearing quite unnecessarily that these, 'although of peculiar interest when written, may through the lapse of years seem unentertaining and unimportant'. The pages of *Night and Day* contain the only record that exists of Barnardo's feelings at the time and, although written for public consumption, provide valuable contemporary evidence. 'Startling Revelations' likewise reveals something of Reynolds' feelings for, although professing to deal with the management of Barnardo's homes as a matter of public interest, he admitted there was a personal side to the affair, and said he knew that lifting his voice against one of the most popular missions of the day could prove costly to him personally, and that he had already started paying the instalments.[1]

The first step taken by the trustees after the publication of 'Startling Revelations' was to summon Barnardo to a private meeting with them, under the chairmanship of Lord Aberdeen, to assure themselves that before giving Barnardo their unqualified support he could satisfy them that there were no skeletons in the cupboard and that he had an answer to all the allegations made against him. The only way in which the question of Barnardo's financial integrity could be verified was to call in an independent firm of auditors: Messrs Turquand, Young and Co. were instructed to make a thorough survey of the accounts of the mission and report back with all speed to the trustees. Barnardo had taken the sting out of the accusation of falsely using the title of Doctor by qualifying as a surgeon earlier in the year, and the trustees appear to have accepted the strange account he gave of his supposed negotiations with the University of Giessen. They must certainly have satisfied themselves as to the exact nature of his relationship with Mrs Johnson. The evangelical cause had been rocked by scandal only the previous year over the behaviour of the American Quaker evangelist Robert Pearsall Smith. Pearsall Smith had aroused widespread interest through his preaching of the concept of 'personal holiness', and conferences had been held in 1874 at Broadlands and at Oxford to extend the debate. What subsequently became known as the Keswick Movement grew from these early 'holiness' meetings, as Keswick replaced Broadlands and Oxford as the home of the movement. Shortly before the first Keswick meeting took place, at which Pearsall Smith was to have been the chief speaker, delegates at the annual Mildmay Park Conference were startled to hear an official request for prayer, 'for God to avert an impending calamity to his church'. John Pollock in his account of the incident in his history of the Keswick convention recorded that everyone began wondering if some calamity had befallen either Moody, Spurgeon or Pearsall Smith.[2] The pathetic truth was that Pearsall Smith had unwisely allowed himself to become involved with a young woman in emotional and spiritual distress and had put an arm round her in a Brighton hotel; the young woman had spread about a colourful story of her relationship with Pearsall Smith as well as an unorthodox version of his religious views, which had resulted in a meeting between eight of Pearsall Smith's supporters who included Lord Radstock, the chairman of the Mildmay Park Conference, and Pearsall Smith. After due consideration the committee, acting with ruthless severity but in accordance with their consciences, abruptly terminated

Pearsall Smith's ministry and he immediately went abroad. There was an obvious parallel between the situations in which Pearsall Smith and Barnardo found themselves. Barnardo's trustees must also have been aware of the similarity between themselves and Pearsall Smith's committee. Once they had satisfied themselves as to Barnardo's innocence and decided to support him, they could not afford to allow attacks to be made on him or his work – attacks which if allowed to continue would undermine and destroy the mission and homes, and which could affect the evangelical cause itself. Barnardo's defence counsel was to dispose of the allegations concerning Barnardo and Mrs Johnson with such convincing thoroughness that the rumour was exposed for what it was. In his statement to the tribunal he said:[3]

We now have it on the evidence that Dr. Barnardo went to live at 5, Bromley Street in the year 1868, when he was a young man of about 23. He lived there for some time in the company of a gentleman of the name of Fosse, a civil engineer, who was a man of thoroughly good character. At that time Mrs. Johnson was to all appearance a respectable married woman of about forty years of age, and having a family of children. Her husband though at times taken away by his avocation and compelled to go to sea, returned from time to time and lived in his own house with her. We find that she was in the habit of attending the Mission Church of Dr. Barnardo; that her children were in the habit of attending it. We find not one suggestion even by way of statement from any witness who has been called in this case that Mrs. Johnson at that time, whatever her conduct might be afterwards, was not a woman of thoroughly respectable character, and at all events, at that time, of thoroughly respectable conduct. Dr. Barnardo leaves the house in October 1870, giving the usual notice... we have it in evidence that the separation and subsequent divorce between Mrs. Johnson and her husband did not take place until the end of 1874... Mr. Reynolds has dared to propagate a slander which he himself had to say in the witness box, he did not believe.

Reynolds and Charrington were not the only ones to go in for character assassination by innuendo. One of the charges subsequently laid against Barnardo by the cos was that he had lodged in the house of an immoral woman and had also recommended his employees to lodge there.[4] When the truth about the allegations became known, the fact that the cos had associated itself with the charges was an embarrassment to it, and probably accounted in part for the very misleading record the society published later concerning its part in the affair.

The Johnson affair overshadowed Barnardo's life for three years: it was basically the cause of the second Clerical Junius letter, and without a clear understanding of the facts surrounding the 'wicked woman' scandal it is difficult to understand the background to the arbitration. The embarrassment felt by the evangelicals that one of their professional Christian workers should be so accused was only equalled by that of the COS who were castigated during the arbitration by Barnardo's defence counsel for their part in the affair.[5]

I cannot help thinking, too, that those who have got the management of an important Society called the Charity Organisation Society must feel that the Charity Organisation Society has been dragged very deep in the mire in this transaction by the fact that from the beginning two members of that body who have been mentioned (Mr. Hay Hill and Mr. Ribton-Turner) had been associated with that wretched man Fitzgerald, and had entirely made themselves part and parcel of this arbitration from beginning to end; and at the elbow of Mr. Reynolds, suggesting and participating in the acts of Mr. Reynolds was Mr. Ribton-Turner, the secretary of that Society.

It is owing to the veil of secrecy which both sides subsequently threw over the events leading to the arbitration that the role played by the COS has never been recognised for what it was, and the part played by the evangelical leadership has gone unrecorded. But the confrontation between Barnardo's trustees and the COS was in effect a struggle between the evangelical leaders and the COS for control of the fast growing Victorian philanthropic movement. Barnardo's young trustees, having accepted his explanations and made public their confidence in him, united to defend their freedom to save the souls of all the unconverted, while the COS believed with equal conviction that unless charitable activities were strictly regulated the whole concept of social welfare based on a well defined division between the work of the Poor Law and charitable endeavour would be endangered. The personal quarrel between Charrington and Barnardo which had been exploited by Reynolds became of trivial importance compared to the wider issues that were now at stake since the official intervention of the COS. Barnardo, whose name had been known only to a limited circle, was to become the subject of leading articles in many of the national newspapers and periodicals. It was against this background that the negotiations between all three parties – Barnardo, Reynolds and the cos – resulted in the setting up of what has become known as the Reynolds–Barnardo arbitration of 1877.

Barnardo's first public acknowledgement of the publication of 'Startling Revelations' was characteristic:[6] 'Through the goodness of God we are still alive! In reply to the many friends who have been "startled" by remarkable "revelations" we are happy to assure them that our hope and trust in the faithfulness of God is unshaken.' But these brave words belied the actual situation, and the financial consequences of both Reynolds' attack and the actions taken by the cos to proscribe Barnardo's work were disastrous. Nonetheless the new accountants called in by the trustees gave Barnardo a clean bill of financial health, stating that in their opinion the system of book-keeping was sound and satisfactory; that correct accounts appeared to be kept of all money received from the public; and that the list of donations which was printed agreed with the books kept at the office and the details of expenditure were thoroughly vouched for. Their only criticism was over the delay in publishing the accounts, which they considered gave a clear and concise explanation of the work of the organisation.

But the public was alarmed; the number of children in Barnardo's care had increased and the money to care for them was no longer forthcoming. In spite of the trustees' action in making themselves legally responsible for the work, taking over Barnardo's bank account and calling in an outside firm of accountants, the attacks by Reynolds and Charrington continued. Barnardo was faced with one of the most painful decisions he ever had to make. In a desperate appeal to his readers he implored them to relieve him of the debts he had incurred. 'We cannot go on, as we might do, in debt', he wrote, but in fact he had no real choice. The controversy forced him to abandon the Brethren principle, 'owe no man anything', and from then on the institutions were never to be free of the incubus of debt during his lifetime.

As the cos had rightly surmised, once the allegations against Barnardo were made public the number of people writing in to the central office, anxious for guidance as to the worthiness of the mission, increased greatly.[7] This gave the COS the excuse it needed to demand information as a matter of public concern from the trustees. A special committee of inquiry was set up, known as the Barnardo Committee of Inquiry, and among its members were Mr Russell Barrington who was a member of the Stepney district committee of the COS, and the Hon. H. R. Scott who shared membership of the Mile End Old Town committee with Joseph Bardsley, Charrington and Kerwin.[8] Ribton-Turner was secretary of the special committee, and his first letter on its behalf[9] was to invite the trustees to meet the committee at their headquarters in Buckingham Street. The COS wasted no time in immediately attempting to get the inquiry shifted onto ground of its own choosing. Harry Nisbet, acting as secretary for the trustees, was able to refuse the request of the COS because by this time the trustees had succeeded in persuading Reynolds to prove his charges against Barnardo in a court of arbitration. To persuade Reynolds to agree to an arbitration Barnardo had had to agree to raise all the necessary money to meet the whole cost of the arbitration and award, the only exception being that Reynolds had to find the fees for his own solicitor and the money to pay for his witnesses.

It has been said that the decision to submit the questions at issue to arbitration rather than to take them to a court of law was due to Barnardo's religious scruples, but it should be remembered that Barnardo had twice taken out writs against Reynolds during the course of the quarrel, and in one case had only reluctantly withdrawn the writ and been equally reluctantly persuaded to sign the 'Stone arbitration'. There was obviously some difference of opinion among Barnardo's trustees as to how best to handle the case and R. C. Morgan, the most militant of Barnardo's supporters, had no doubt as to the outcome had a criminal prosecution been brought against Charrington and Reynolds.[10]

For our part we think Dr. Barnardo has acted with too much leniency toward the miscreants who have libelled his work, and we have good legal authority for stating that imprisonment, probably with hard labour, would be the sentence passed on those miscreants if a criminal prosecution were instituted against them. A tissue of slanderous falsehoods has been printed and published about Dr.

Barnardo, and no man's reputation is safe if such things are permitted to be done with impunity.

However, wiser counsels prevailed and the trustees, probably led by John Sands, whose sister gave Barnardo £1,000 to meet the costs, used their authority to insist that the matter be settled by arbitration. The whole controversy must have been a matter of the utmost embarrassment to them, and the thought of the damage the spectacular publicity resulting from a criminal prosecution between two such prominent Christian workers would have had on the evangelical movement could only have strengthened their resolve to use the machinery of arbitration. The one person who steadfastly refused to be associated with the arbitration was Charrington, who continued to maintain that it was no affair of his. His non-participation was regretted by all concerned, and both Barnardo's trustees and the cos put pressure on him to take part; Arthur Kinnaird wrote to him; J. A. Bevan, a member of the cos Barnardo Committee of Inquiry, and Spurgeon urged him to participate. Finally he was compelled to attend by Reynolds. After the case had started Reynolds demanded that seven new heads of inquiry be included; the reasons for this demand are not entirely clear as the additional heads of inquiry were entirely concerned with aspects of the complicated quarrel between himself, Charrington and Barnardo, but it had the effect of involving Charrington who was forced to attend and give evidence. The relationship between Charrington and Reynolds was no longer so close, and it is evident that Charrington was a most reluctant witness. Had Charrington succeeded in his objective of dissociating himself from Reynolds, it is possible that the part he played in the controversy would have remained largely unknown.

The cos Barnardo Committee of Inquiry were not disposed to be so easily deflected, and although they professed themselves anxious to act in harmony with Barnardo's trustees, and therefore said they were not willing to set up an independent committee of inquiry, they requested definite answers to certain questions. Their request was based on the fact that an increasing number of inquiries had been received by the cos, and it was said that the information was needed to enable an interim report to be issued. The trustees allowed

Ribton-Turner's letter to remain unanswered. On 20 April he wrote them a stronger letter spelling out the serious nature of the accusations against Barnardo. The allegations, all of which had already appeared in 'Startling Revelations', were given in greater detail. It was alleged[11] that though nearly all departments of the homes were said to be self-supporting, nevertheless large sums were asked for in support of them; that Dr Barnardo, while professing to live on private means, was a very poor man and had enriched himself by the contributions of the charitable; that the system upon which the accounts of the homes were kept allowed for misapplication of the funds; that Barnardo had no warrant to assume the title of Doctor and had refused to state the nature of his diploma; that some of the boys entrusted to his care had been imprisoned by him for periods varying from three to eighteen days in a filthy underground cellar; that others had had their clothing removed and had been dressed in rags for the purpose of setting up fictitious and deceptive photographs; that during the mission of Moody and Sankey, Barnardo had issued bills advertising their services which purported to be printed by boys in the home but which were really printed by Messrs Field and Tuer; that Barnardo had issued under the pseudonym of 'Clerical Junius' forged letters laudatory of himself but in other respects devoid of the truth, and that he had allowed a clergyman (M. S. A. Walrond) to be pointed out as the author of the letters. Finally, that he had lodged in the house of a woman of immoral character and had also recommended his employees to lodge there. Ribton-Turner went on to lecture the trustees about their duties to their subscribers and asserted that if the allegations were untrue they could easily be refuted, knowing full well that this would not be a simple matter, as the COS already had potential witnesses in the shape of Edward Fitzgerald and the boy William Fletcher who were prepared to substantiate some of the allegations.

Harry Nisbet answered firmly the following day that

> ... as one of Dr. Barnardo's Trustees, I must decline once and for all to entertain any suggestion for holding more than one Inquiry into the charges brought against Dr. Barnardo and his Institutions. If the three gentlemen now chosen as Arbitrators, and whose names will shortly be announced, do not constitute a tribunal satisfactory to every-

one, including the Charity Organisation Society, I should despair of being able to meet the views of any such dissatisfied persons.

One cannot help but be impressed by the skill with which the trustees went about organising Barnardo's defence. Having got Barnardo to withdraw his writ and Reynolds' consent to the arbitration, they made application to the Court of the Exchequer, which under the 1854 Common Law Procedure Act meant that they could apply to make the submission a rule of court. This had several advantages: it meant firstly that any misconduct under the submission, or refusal to act on the award, became a contempt of the Court of the Exchequer; it gave the court jurisdiction over the award and the parties to the submission; and lastly it meant that the arbitrators' jurisdiction would be limited by that submission, as they were not permitted to go outside the parameters of what was submitted to them and could not of their own volition enlarge or alter the scope of the submission. This meant that the trustees, by using the mechanism of arbitration, had effectively blocked the cos from taking any part in the proceedings, as under the law they could neither raise any points of their own nor take any legal part in the case.

In making their dispositions the trustees had access to the very highest authority. The austere and detached Cairns was again serving as Lord Chancellor in Disraeli's second administration, which had taken office in 1874. The acknowledged leader of the evangelicals within the Cabinet, he was the man whose judgement Disraeli most respected. His rare intimacies were confined, irrespective of rank or station, to those who shared his views on social reform and religion. Since 1875 he had become increasingly interested in the work Barnardo was engaged in. Although unable to stand forth publicly while the dispute between Barnardo and Reynolds was *sub judice*, evidence of his concern that Barnardo's institutions should be enabled to continue their work abounds, and it is highly probable that it was on his advice that the arbitration was set up in the way it was.

The choice of the Hon. Alfred Thesiger as counsel to undertake Barnardo's defence could also well have been the result of Cairns' interest in the affair. Thesiger, the son of a former Lord

Chancellor, had become a QC four years previously at the very early age of thirty-five. Although slight and youthful-looking he was an excellent lawyer much sought after in commercial and important compensation cases. His business was so heavy that in 1877 he returned all his parliamentary briefs because he had not the time to give them proper attention, a rare instance of professional forbearance. Thesiger was noted for his integrity and industriousness and the lucid way in which he presented complicated cases, showing a complete mastery of detail. There was nothing flamboyant about him, and it was said that Cairns listened to no one with more respect. It seems unlikely in the circumstances that Thesiger would have agreed to undertake Barnardo's defence, a seemingly unimportant arbitration case which, however, was to drag on for three long months, had Cairns not indicated that there were very special reasons why he should accept the brief. He had two juniors, Francis Turner and Erskine Pollock, who later took silk. Compared to Reynolds, who was represented by his solicitor St John Wontner, the evangelicals had flexed a lot of legal muscle on Barnardo's behalf.

It was, of course, important that the gentlemen chosen as arbitrators should be above reproach and acceptable to all, as Nisbet had indicated they were. To make the selection acceptable to as broad a cross-section of Christian opinion as possible a committee of six clergymen from the East End of London joined the trustees. This joint committee asked Russell Gurney, the much respected recorder of the City of London, who had held that office with distinction for twenty years, for advice as to who should preside over the court. He recommended John Maule, with whom he had served as a commissioner at the time of the inquiry into the Jamaica insurrection. Maule, who was a QC and recorder of Leeds, accepted the assignment.

The committee chose Canon John Miller to act as one of the two lay arbitrators. Canon Miller, an evangelical divine with a reputation as an energetic pastor and a passionate speaker, had been Rector of Birmingham from 1846 to 1866. His concern for the poor, his habit of preaching in the open air and the working men's clubs he founded had gained him the confidence of the labouring classes. He was, at the time of the arbitration, Vicar of Greenwich and a Canon of Rochester. Bishop Thorold left a vivid portrait of him as[12] 'a man who to a massive understanding that rapidly absorbed knowledge added a capacity for business which many laymen might envy, and a resoluteness of nature which, while it occasionally thwarted you, it was impossible not to admire. His strong face, his broad shoulders, his ample form, his slow and stately tread were all reproduced in a will that knew no vacillation and the dignity of courage that feared neither friend nor foe.'

William Graham, the trustees' choice, had been the Liberal Member of Parliament for Glasgow; his success as a businessman came second to his interest in the arts and it is as a collector, a patron of the pre-Raphaelites and a friend of Burne Jones, that he is now best remembered. His delicate features, his deep-set eyes touched with melancholy and his spare frame accentuated the contrast he provided to Canon Miller's more robust personality. His daughter[13] described him as a man of singular beauty of character. He was a close friend of the Kinnairds, a Presbyterian, a strong Sabbatarian and much in sympathy with the evangelicals. He had played an active part in the organisation of the Moody and Sankey campaign, which would have further strengthened his involvement with the evangelical movement.

While these negotiations were in progress both sides were engaged in trying to raise funds. Balance sheets often reveal more of the aims and objectives of organisations and individuals than any number of written statements, and the financial arrangements made by both sides are interesting. Although Reynolds had only to pay for the services of a lawyer and his witnesses, he chose to call some forty-seven witnesses whose evidence took twenty-seven days to examine, and it was soon evident to all concerned that for Barnardo to make a valid defence he would have to call an equally large number of witnesses. And as in fact sixty-five witnesses eventually appeared on his behalf it became certain that the case was going to be both long and costly. The financial support Reynolds received from his small congregation would never have covered the expenses he was to incur, and his involvement in the Barnardo controversy had, in any case, still further reduced his tiny income. To understand the true significance of the arbitration case it is important to know the identity of those who now supported Reynolds.

It was only under pressure and with the greatest reluctance that Charrington was brought to admit, 'I have given Reynolds £50 or £60 to be used for his pamphlets, as I supposed,'[14] but he emphatically denied, in spite of Reynolds asserting the contrary, that he had supplied him with money for the arbitration. In an official statement issued after the inquiry was over, the COS also denied that the society contributed 'either directly or indirectly, towards the expenses of the Arbitration'.[15] This statement was, in fact, a lie. The committee had passed a resolution declaring that it was supremely important that the arbitration should not fail for lack of funds, and directed that the resolution and the appeal were to be inserted in the *Charity Organisation Reporter*, the society's house journal. The minutes of the COS Barnardo inquiry sub-committee make the involvement of the COS in the funding of the arbitration case even clearer:[16] 'The Organising Secretary be authorised to confer with Mr. J. A. Bevan, Treasurer of the Barnardo Fund, as to the best method of raising whatever funds are required to bring the Arbitration in the Barnardo Case to a speedy termination and to secure that the points of public interest should be thoroughly sifted.' There is a certain irony in the discovery that the COS, with their supposedly high standard of professional integrity, were not above a certain amount of deception themselves, doubtless in the public interest!

One result of this minute was that an appeal for funds was circulated to all members of the society, and to Barnardo's great distress it was headed by Shaftesbury and Samuel Morley. He replied instantly through *Night and Day*:[17]

Nothing has grieved us more . . . than to observe the unwarrantable use that has been made of Lord Shaftesbury's name . . . Among the many institutions that have profited at different times by his counsel and sympathy may be mentioned our own Homes . . . In the desire that truth and right might triumph and that the Inquiry should not fail through lack of the necessary means on either side, he signed a circular issued by our accusers, appealing, in extremis, for funds.

But Shaftesbury had been president of Charrington's Tower Hamlets Mission since its inception; he was also a vice-president of the COS. Barnardo later wrote of him:[18] 'It was a source of unspeakable regret to me that a few years before his lamented death I seemed to have lost his friendship, chiefly owing to causes over which I had no control.'

The COS not only set up a fund to finance Reynolds, they secretly undertook a whole series of investigations themselves in an attempt to obtain evidence against Barnardo. The minutes of the committee of inquiry show that in October 1877 they sanctioned the payment of an account from Messrs Stubbs, inquiry agents who operated from the Guardian of Commerce Institute; their account was in respect of expenditure incurred by them in investigating the financial circumstances of J. M. Barnardo and H. L. Barnardo of Dublin, Barnardo's father and brother. A copy of the report[19] stated that since Barnardo's father's death in May 1874 his mother and brother had entered into partnership and were running the business which had moved to Grafton Street, where it still is, 'and they are said to be going on well there. We have learned that the father died worth some £2,000 – he had a fair character.' The minutes also reveal that they had letters from St John Wontner and others involved in the case, whose accounts doubtless also had to be settled. A short note records that a certain Mr Richards, possibly one of Reynolds' witnesses, threatened that unless employment were found for him he would enter into communication with Dr Barnardo with a view to supplying him with information concerning the COS.[20]

If Reynolds' supporters found difficulty raising money, the problems facing Barnardo were infinitely more serious. In spite of the generous support given by the Sands family, Barnardo was forced to borrow a large sum to cover the legal arbitrators' fee, the hire of the room and the necessarily heavy expenses of his own counsel, solicitors and witnesses. At the end of the case for the prosecution an urgent appeal was circulated to Barnardo's supporters informing them that a further £2,000 would be needed before the inquiry closed.[21] The interest of this appeal lies not only in the light it throws on the financial mechanics of the arbitration, but in the names of the signatories. The list was headed by Lord Cairns, who was Lord Chancellor, followed by Fitzroy Kelly who was the Lord Chief Baron and in that capacity presided over the Court of the Exchequer. The submission to arbitration, it will be remembered, was made under a rule of the Court of the Exchequer, so had the court been called upon to adjudicate at any point during the arbitration, the position of the Lord Chief Baron might not have been as detached as it ought perhaps to have been.

The appeal was signed by all the trustees and included the names of three MPs, Arthur Kinnaird, Abel Smith and Samuel Whitbread. A letter from Spurgeon which was published with the appeal underlines the conflict of loyalties which the quarrel between Charrington and Barnardo had produced for many evangelicals.[22]

The inquiry now pending in reference to charges against Dr. Barnardo ought to be carried through to the end, and it will be a serious calamity if the investigation is hindered by lack of funds on either side. The request for funds which has already appeared asks for assistance for the accusing party, and this I by no means censure; but I should much have preferred that there had not been even the remotest semblance of a leaning to either side while the case is pending. It seems to me only fair that the defence should be supported as well as the charge, by sufficient means to make it thorough, and therefore I append my name to the present appeal. There is as much need on the side of Dr. Barnardo as on that of Mr. Reynolds, and it will be simple justice that if one be aided so should the other be.

At the end of the case Barnardo was left with a personal debt of over £2,400. Appeals were made over the following two years for money for an arbitration fund, but they met with little success. Finally the homes took over the debt and paid it, with the sanction of the newly appointed finance committee, out of the general fund.

The fact that Reynolds' accusations were now the subject of a legal arbitration in no way stopped him from continuing to circulate his pamphlets and to attack Barnardo in any way he could. He appears to have acquired what Barnardo described as a 'miserable photograph' and to have sold this 'wretched caricature' alongside a carefully posed shot of Frederick Charrington. This provoked Barnardo into responding with a letter to the *Tower Hamlets Independent*.[23] He wrote that although he had for many years refused to allow himself to be photographed, he was now 'compelled to authorise the publication of a carte-de-visite which shall faithfully depict my phiz for the satisfaction of those who are kind enough to care for the same, either from motives of curiosity or feelings of regard'. Thanks to Reynolds we have a portrait of Barnardo at a turning point in his life. Something of the fierce determination and passionate concern that marked his life stare out from the carefully posed picture, showing the finely modelled head to advantage, and the precise set of collar and tie reflect the care which Barnardo always took over his appearance. Barnardo's friend and supporter Michael Baxter, editor of the *Christian Herald and Signs of the Times*, used the photo on the cover of his journal in October in a laudatory article entitled 'Dr. T. J. Barnardo, the Devoted Benefactor of Homeless Boys'. Baxter, son of Robert Baxter, a disillusioned member of Edward Irving's congregation, first became a missionary in China before becoming an itinerant lecturer in the United States. Ernest Sandeen, in his book on millenarianism,[24] described him as a peripatetic sensationalist who for over thirty years was much given to predicting incorrect dates for the Second Coming on historicist millennial principles – as Sandeen commented, 'presumably being saved only by death from an infinite series'. His close friendship with Barnardo at this time underlined yet again the important role millennialism played in Barnardo's life.

9

In Court

THE arbitration court sat at the Institution of Surveyors in
Great George Street just off Parliament Square. William
Graham had a house in Grosvenor Street where he stayed, but
Canon Miller made the journey from Rochester to London
every day, a journey which he found tedious and inconvenient
during the hot weather and which he complained 'interfered
with his summer vacation and domestic comfort'. Maule stayed
in London over the three months the case lasted and Barnardo
came up daily from Stepney.

The trustees wasted no time once they had got the first
nineteen heads of inquiry made a rule of the High Court of
Justice (Exchequer Division) on 7 June, and the court was
convened on 11 June. A month later, on 5 July, a further seven
heads of inquiry were agreed between Reynolds and Barnardo,
which effectively brought Charrington into the case; this made
a total of twenty-six different heads of inquiry for the arbitrators
to rule on. The suddenness with which the case was launched
caused a number of difficulties. St John Wontner was somewhat embarrassed at being called upon to open the case as
prosecutor, having expected to defend Reynolds' actions. An
enormous mass of evidence was presented and, owing to the
speed with which the court acted, witnesses had to be called in
an unexpected order, as they were sometimes ill or not available
when needed. Consequently the evidence was presented in such
a miscellaneous way that even Thesiger found it difficult to
keep it at his fingers' ends.

The accusations against Barnardo could be divided into three
groups: those concerning the character of Barnardo himself,
those concerning the management of the homes, and the imputations which led to the attack on both. From the text of the

award it can be seen that the heads of inquiry were officially meant to be dealt with in a somewhat different manner, as they were split into four categories, but from the available evidence it is obvious that the case followed no very clear course.

The questions that came under category A in the official award dealt with the management of the homes and included allegations concerning the ill-treatment of children, lack of moral training, lack of proper physical care and the illegal detention of children in the homes. It also included charges concerning the circulation of photographs said to be fictitious representations of destitution, showing children before admission to the homes; among others the case of the lad William Fletcher was cited as an example.

The heads of inquiry under category B were entirely concerned with the question of the authorship of the Clerical Junius letters, a matter which came to dominate the whole inquiry, both sides recognising the importance of the question of Barnardo's personal credibility, which was neatly summed up by Canon Miller:[1] 'The *main* question – stripped of legal technicalities – is this, "Is Dr Barnardo worthy of public confidence?" If so, so in their main points are Dr Barnardo's Institutions. If not, they are unworthy so long as he continues as their Director.' The personal attack permeated both the following categories, category C being concerned with the question of Barnardo's right to the title of Doctor and the final category dealing with the very complicated personal quarrel between Reynolds, Charrington and Barnardo. It included the Johnson affair as well as the significant charges of financial dishonesty and other lesser matters such as his right to assume the pastorate of the People's Mission Church.

Unfortunately no complete account of the arbitration exists, although certain events caused comment in the press, and its sudden and controversial ending attracted a lot of publicity. It is certainly owing to this public interest that verbatim reports of the last four days of the case were printed. The most complete account of the arbitration appeared in the *Tower Hamlets Independent*.[2] From that we know that Reynolds' case for the prosecution lasted twenty-seven days and that he provided forty-seven witnesses. Thirty-three witnesses were called as to the management of the homes, among whom was William

Fletcher, one of the six boys called who had at some time been resident in the homes. Fletcher was the only boy to give evidence as to the actual management of the homes, probably coached by Walrond as to what he should say.

A graphic description of the way in which Samuel Reed had been punished for insubordination had appeared in 'Startling Revelations'. Hancorn, the man whose signature appeared at the bottom of the account and who gave evidence for Reynolds, was a former employee of Barnardo's who had been dismissed for gross indecency. He had alleged:[3]

A lad named Samuel Reed, about 18 years of age, who had for some time been employed at the Dublin Castle Coffee Palace was brought to the Home and on 2nd August treated with the greatest severity. Mr. Fielder, the Governor of the Home, summoned all the masters up to the schoolroom during school hours. He then offered a long prayer, which was followed by a lecture, after which he called Reed to the front.

After the boy had been asked to remove his clothes, which he refused to do, the account continued:

The lad was seized by the throat, when a terrible scene ensued. After a time the lad was laid on his back insensible. He was then dragged head foremost down three flights of stairs, and laid in the yard, where three pails of water were thrown upon him. This was more than his old companions could bear. They interfered, when Fielder and a lad named George Spinks had a stand-up fight. Fielder was getting the worst of it, when Mr. Notman, one of the Doctor's paid deacons, rushed at the lad Spinks, knocked him down, and when on the ground kicked him on the head and in the face in a most brutal manner. The lad was locked up in a cell for a week, at the expiration of which he was severely caned. When he came out he was flogged severely. When he took his shirt off I thought my heart would break to see his emaciated body. He reeled as he walked. Such was the treatment this poor boy received in Dr. Barnardo's Home.

Reynolds did not include the accusations in relation to Spinks among the heads of inquiry considered by the arbitrators, but the homes' report on Spinks provided an interesting sidelight. It read[4]

August 2nd 1876: Concerned with others in an act of rebellion and punished with the cane by Dr. Barnardo.
Jan 25th 1877: Conduct very much improved.

May 8th 1877: Is now treated as a lodger boy receiving all wages earned by him and paying for his board, lodging and clothing at a fixed sum of 7/– per week.

It was alleged that Reed 'after being confined in a cell, on bread and water, was brought out, beaten, and then turned adrift on the streets'.

The arbitrators found that Reed had indeed been insubordinate, had been flogged for his conduct and then confined to the tailor's shop for a few days to separate him from the main body of the boys, but they did not consider that he had been cruelly treated. They were, however, critical of Barnardo's habit of confining boys for varying periods of time in a cell formed from a coal cellar about seven feet square, and ruled that some of the periods were unwarrantably long. Barnardo claimed that it was because he wished to remove corporal punishment altogether from the disciplinary code of the homes that solitary confinement was introduced. Later reports show that both types of punishment continued to be used.

In defending Barnardo against allegations of cruelty Thesiger quoted from a letter which Barnardo had written in January 1876 to one of his recently appointed schoolmasters, Mr Turner, laying down the principles on which he wished his homes to be conducted. He wrote from Edinburgh where he was studying for his licenciate in surgery:[5]

I am feeling too poorly now to go into details, but I should like to urge upon you two or three matters which are worthy of your attention and which I am sure already receive your care. 1st. Punishments: Let them never be given in anger or at the time; always first appealing to a boy's own sense of desert, and seldom severe. 2nd. Religious work: Do seek in earnestness and prayer to get the elder boys under higher influences. 3rd. Prevention of disturbances is always better than cure. See to it that some master is always present to control and prevent passionate or unruly conduct at meals, play and half holidays. 4th. Food: never allow a boy to go without a sufficiency; the class we deal with are more appealed to through the stomach and appetites than otherwise. 5th. Music and singing: Press these as your very greatest means of civilising and humanising next to religion. 6th. Forgetfulness of evil: I mean learn to forget what a boy may have done amiss after he has been punished for it; otherwise he fancies you retain a grudge against him. 7th. Order, punctuality and respect, are I need hardly tell you, essentials in a well ordered institution. I should like to get a report once a fortnight at least from you while I am away.

Considering the type of boy the homes were dealing with and the ideas current at the time on the treatment of offences committed by children, the ideals put forward by Barnardo were both progressive and humane. Practice may at times have fallen short of these ideals, but the material Barnardo was dealing with was very raw.

Of the six parents or guardians[6] who gave evidence against Barnardo, Mrs Holder, Mrs Seeley and Mrs Wallbridge all had grievances concerning their children's treatment in the homes, and all had allowed their grievances to be the subject of some of Reynolds' pamphlets, as well as appearing in 'Startling Revelations'. Mrs Wallbridge claimed that her children had been badly fed, badly treated to the obvious detriment of their health, and had been forced to write and state the opposite to her. Deserted by her husband, Mrs Wallbridge had put her four children into the institutions because she was unable to support them. They appear to have been sickly children and suffered at the homes from sore heads and 'the itch' – complaints, the arbitrators noted, which were extremely difficult to eradicate thoroughly from homes of this class of children. Although the children seemed to have missed their mother very much, for Barnardo only allowed parental visiting once every quarter, the court decided they were neither badly fed nor badly treated. The court took the view that Mrs Wallbridge's evidence was partly due to the hysterical attitude she had shown when testifying, and that in spite of all she had said her two girls were still in the cottage home.

Mrs Holder's complaint was that her children had been specially dressed in rags and placed in a variety of poses indicating a state of misery, and had thus been photographed and placarded through the United Kingdom for the purpose of obtaining money. Eliza and Florence Holder had been sent to the homes poorly but decently clothed. It was a matter of some pride to respectable parents unwillingly forced by circumstances to hand over their children to the care of an institution that their children should be properly dressed at this important moment in their lives, and suitable clothes were sometimes begged or borrowed for the occasion. The evidence showed that it was Fitzgerald who, after he had been dismissed by Barnardo, immediately approached Mrs Holder and by showing her photographs of her daughters had succeeded in stirring up feelings of understandable outrage at the use to which they had been put. A photograph of her eldest daughter showed her with bare feet, dishevelled hair and tattered dress selling newspapers in the street, something which she had never done in her life. The younger sister's head was photographed and used on a collecting box over the words, 'A little waif six years old, taken from the streets', which appeared to indicate that she had no relations and lived on the streets.

Of the witnesses who had been in Barnardo's employ Edward Fitzgerald, the former boys' beadle, was the one on whom Reynolds most depended. He appears to have had a hand in nearly all the allegations that were made against Barnardo. A goodlooking rogue, he appeared in another of the photographs complained about, this one entitled 'The Raw Material as we find it', which had appeared as the frontispiece to *Rescue the Perishing*. He was called to give evidence to substantiate his account of the writing of the Clerical Junius letters, to tell of his involvement in the Mrs Johnson affair and to testify as to the conditions in the home. He had been dismissed by Barnardo for drunkenness and immorality before Barnardo had even realised that he was secretly in communication with Charrington and playing the role of a Judas. Charrington admitted in evidence[7] that he believed that after Fitzgerald had left his employ he then had some employment with the COS, and supposed that Reynolds' solicitor was now paying him out of the general fund. He was not only a disappointing witness for the prosecution, but positively counter-productive. He told so many contradictory stories in court that Thesiger had to ask which he wanted considered as true. Even Reynolds himself admitted that he knew him to be a liar and said that he had seen him in a state of 'beastly intoxication'. Thesiger said, 'Nobody who has heard this case, no one who has ever employed him, not even Mr Reynolds himself would say that he could be believed on his oath.' During the evidence concerning the propagation and dissemination of the rumour concerning Mrs Johnson, Thesiger pressed home his advantage: 'This man, foul as he was, had been taken into the confidence of Mr Charrington and Mr

Reynolds, and I am sorry to say, by several prominent members of the Charity Organisation Society.' Few if any of the friends of Reynolds and Charrington attended the case, and Thesiger publicly regretted that none of the noblemen and gentlemen who supported them were in court to hear the evidence: 'I cannot help thinking their eyes would have been opened and they would have been ashamed of joining these persons who have been guilty of such deliberately deceitful and wicked conduct as those two gentlemen have been guilty of all along.'

Alsager Hay Hill and Ribton-Turner representing the COS attended almost daily, and both frequently intervened during the case. They were not spared by Thesiger, who commented bitingly:[8]

I do say again that the association of Mr. Alsager Hay Hill and Mr. Ribton-Turner with Mr. Charrington and Mr. Reynolds in matters brought out in this Arbitration certainly does not reflect any great credit on the Society to which they belong. I think everyone will acknowledge that I am justified in what I have said. These gentlemen I have mentioned cannot be ignorant of what was going on, because one of them (Mr. Ribton-Turner) has attended here nearly throughout the whole of these proceedings and never once did they offer the least protest at the course taken by Mr. Reynolds.

Charrington only made his appearance as a witness after Reynolds had succeeded in getting an investigation into the personal quarrel between Charrington, himself and Barnardo included in the inquiry. This further development of the case was extremely time-consuming and tedious for the arbitrators, its only merit being that it did force a reluctant Charrington to reveal his part in the quarrel. His reluctance was understandable. Thesiger, in dealing with the part he had played, spared him nothing:[9]

There is Mr. Charrington; who is he? A gentleman who I can honestly say that I came into this Inquiry with every wish to treat with respect and esteem, if I may be allowed to use that expression. One heard of a young gentleman with an opportunity, if he thought proper, of pursuing a lucrative business, turning from that business and giving himself up to operations of a kindred character to those that were carried on by Dr. Barnardo. One only started with a feeling of respect for Mr. Charrington, and I must say it is only his own fault if that respect has been removed from the minds of those who have heard this case. I must say I shall have to comment strongly on the conduct of Mr. Reynolds, but I must say that in some particulars I cannot but feel that Mr. Reynolds' conduct contrasts favourably with that adopted by Mr. Charrington. Malignant as Mr. Reynolds has shown himself, he has come forward boldly and openly, and if I may use the expression, persecuted Dr. Barnardo. Mr. Charrington has pursued a course, which as regards the prosecution, I shall show you is identical with that pursued by Mr. Reynolds, but he has not pursued it openly; he has pursued it by means of instruments that were only discovered after a considerable amount of searching and cross-examination.

In spite of himself, Thesiger appears to have had a grudging admiration for George Reynolds. He even went so far as to say, 'there is a sort of audacious boldness in Mr. Reynolds which to some extent contrasts favourably with Dr. Barnardo. He does not care what he says; he says it out boldly, and I suppose proceeds on the ground which he has already stated, of attack instead of defence.' Reynolds made no secret of his total disbelief in any form of religious philanthropy, and when he spoke in the witness box he gave his evidence with drawling deliberation. His appearance as Barnardo's prosecutor appears to be his one claim to fame. After the award was announced he disappeared from the public eye, leaving behind no trace.

The two sides sat facing one another across a wide table. The arbitrators sat at one end and the witness box was at the other. Members of the public and witnesses sat round the room listening to the proceedings. The court was adjourned for several days while the arbitrators made a personal and minute inspection of the Girls' Village Home at Ilford, the Home for Destitute Boys at Stepney Causeway and the Infirmary for Sick Children in the same street. In the infirmary they would have been reminded, as they walked through the Lord Chancellor's Ward, of Cairns' particular interest in the institutions. They visited both the Edinburgh Castle and Dublin Castle to inspect the work carried on at both coffee palaces. Three of Barnardo's trustees were called upon to explain the circumstances under which they had held an inquiry the previous January which had resulted in their passing resolutions expressing their confidence in Dr Barnardo, and the evidence given during their inquiry was made available to the arbitrators.

On the twenty-first day of the inquiry Thesiger opened Barnardo's case, and twelve days were spent examining the sixty-five witnesses called by the defence. The first allegation to be dealt with concerned the financial management of the homes. The trustees were acutely conscious that unless public confidence in the system of book-keeping was absolute the homes would continue to lose support and might be forced to close. Messrs Carter and Clay, the paid auditors of the mission funds since 1868, gave evidence first, and the trustees then played their trump card and called in Messrs Turquand, Young & Co., whom they had commissioned to make an independent audit earlier in the year. The auditors repeated their favourable verdict, effectively silencing the opposition, although both Carter and Clay and Turquand's commented adversely on the serious delays that there had been in presenting the accounts to the public from the beginning in 1868.

Fifteen witnesses came from the Girls' Village Home at Ilford to counter the evidence given by the prosecution, especially in regard to the Wallbridge and Seeley cases cited by Reynolds in 'Startling Revelations'. The medical superintendent, Dr Sullivan, and the governor and his wife, Mr and Mrs Soltau, and some of the cottage mothers and teachers in the school as well as two girls who had previously been at the village testified as to the general management, food, clothing, education and health of the children.[10] Twelve members of staff from the Boys' Home including Mr Fielder, the governor, and eight boys, three still in the home and five who were former inmates, gave evidence for Barnardo. Three medical officers spoke about the sanitary arrangements and the health of the boys, and past and present schoolmasters, including Mr Turner, spoke about the religious and secular instruction given to the boys.

The charge that Barnardo used photographs representing children in a state of fictitious destitution before admission to the homes to attract support prompted him to issue and circulate with every packet of photographs sold a full explanation of his object in photographing his children upon admission or as soon after as convenient. He gave three main reasons for using

Dame Street in 1842 showing the Royal Exchange and Trinity College. Nos 1–6 on the right were occupied by traders and Thomas John was born at No. 4, the house where J. M. Barnardo carried on his business.

BELOW LEFT Barnardo's father, J. M. Barnardo
BELOW RIGHT Barnardo's mother, Abigail Barnardo

ABOVE LEFT Barnardo's first encounter with a destitute child, Jim Jarvis, in a ragged school. The print was first published on the cover of the *Children's Treasury* in 1874.

ABOVE RIGHT 'The Raw Material as we find it'. A group of boys found by Edward Fitzgerald, the boys' beadle, during the course of a night's search

BELOW 'The Manufactured Article – a plea for a training ship'. Boys rescued by Barnardo photographed before being drafted off to the training ship belonging to the Marine Society

Edward Wood, aged fourteen, photographed before and after admission to
the Home in 1873. This is an example of the type of photograph sold by
Barnardo in aid of the Homes.

Pamphlets written by Barnardo to publicise his work

The Williams children, removed from their home by Barnardo and photographed in the studio in Oliver Terrace as he had found them, naked and huddled under sacks

The Edinburgh Castle, Limehouse, was opened in 1872 as a Coffee Palace. It also became the home of Barnardo's People's Mission Church.

ABOVE LEFT Samuel Gurney Sheppard, generous benefactor and first chairman of the Committee of Management

ABOVE RIGHT Joshua Poole, the evangelist and temperance preacher, also known as 'Fiddler Jos'

The 'miserable photograph' of Barnardo taken in the early 1870s, acquired by Reynolds and sold by him alongside a portrait of himself in an attempt to discredit Barnardo

The carte-de-visite photograph which Barnardo had taken in 1877 to counteract the damage being done by Reynolds

ABOVE A group of staff photographed in the yard at Stepney in the early 1880s. *Left to right, back row*, Appleton, Odling, Dr Milne, Fielder (Governor of the Boys' Home) Quick; *middle row*, Rice, Langley, Onslow, Rankin, Conway, Notman, Nelson; *seated*, Ansert, Manuell, Sanders, Blades, Slater

BELOW A group of housemothers photographed at the Girls' Village Home in the 1880s

Examples of alleged 'artistic fiction': Florence Holder and William Fletcher

Children admitted after 1877: Emma Cook 5.7.87 and Albert Martin 10.6.02

ABOVE LEFT Barnardo reading to his two elder sons, Stuart and Herbert. Herbert died of diptheria in 1884.

ABOVE RIGHT Group of boys who sailed in 1884 to Perth, Australia on the ss *Charlotte Padbury*

A group of Canadian emigrants, 1897

Children involved in legal cases in the 1880s and 1890s:
above left Henry Gossage who was sent to Canada to an unknown destination; *above right* Martha Ward also known as Martha Tye who went to the continent with Madame Romand; *below left* John James Roddy who was returned to the custody of his mother; *below right* George Green who died in Canada and whose employer was accused of manslaughter

Dr and Mrs Barnardo on the steps of their home, St Leonard's Lodge

Syrie with her father after her marriage to Henry Wellcome

Barnardo presenting some of his girls to the Duchess of Teck at the Village Home on Founder's Day

The successful philanthropist

photographs, the first being 'to obtain and retain an exact likeness, which being attached to a faithful record in our History Book of each individual case, shall enable us in future to trace every child's career, and to bring to remembrance minute circumstances which, without a photograph, would be impossible'. Photographs also made recognition easy for boys or girls who committed criminal acts or absconded from the homes, or who had been stolen from their parents or left their own homes and found their way to the institution. It was the third reason, 'to aid us in advocating the claims of our Institution, now containing nearly 500 children, with the Christian public' and to sell all such photographs for the benefit of the institutions, that caused the arbitrators to examine minutely the circumstances in which the children were photographed and the claims made for the homes.

Mrs Williams, a West Indian widow whose three children had been photographed as Barnardo found them and whose story had appeared in *Rescue the Perishing* and in pamphlet form under the title 'Out of the Depths', was brought to court as one of Barnardo's witnesses. The circumstances in which Barnardo found her are vividly brought to life in his account of his meeting with her.[11]

No furniture of any kind can be seen – not even a chair nor an apology for a bed. The weary worker speaks, but without raising her head, or leaving off her work for a minute – she sits on an old broken box . . . the room is very dirty, dark and close smelling. The occupant of the tenement goes on with her work . . . she is not even curious enough or has not time to ask our business although she must wonder why we have come. She is a negress, and is dressed in the poorest rags. Her face is that of a sufferer, and her voice has unutterable weariness in its tone. 'Eh sar,' she says, 'mebbe you'll help the childer! My heart's most bruck! De good Lord forgive me!' Big tears coursed down each swarthy cheek. Greatly moved, we turned to the corner and pulled aside a sack revealing three woolly black heads. Yes, sure enough, there three little black children lay. In a few minutes they were awake, and to our surprise instead of springing out, with the usual vivacity of children, from the heap of sacks, they remained quite still, looking quiet and abashed. 'She ha'nt no clothes for 'em this while back,' explained the landlady in a low voice, 'so they keeps together under the sacks to get warm, till the mother takes her work off to the factory. When she comes back they've a new lot of sacks; but 'taint much they'd have to eat if it warn't for the neighbours who pities 'em and gives 'em a bit o' broken victuals now and then. But the neighbours 'bout here are only poor theirselves, God help 'em!'

Mrs Williams' husband (both were freed slaves) had been a sailor and had lost his life saving a companion who had fallen overboard. She had struggled to keep the children out of the workhouse and off the streets by sewing sacks for which she was paid at the rate of one shilling and eightpence a hundred. Barnardo returned the following day and before admitting the children to the home took the whole family to a photographer's establishment in Oliver Terrace, Bow Road, where the assistant photographer, Charles Collins, took a picture of the children posed as they had been found. The photograph, with its obvious appeal to the emotions, was extensively circulated and must represent one of the earliest examples of a type now made so familiar by children's charities all over the world. It is obvious from the evidence that the arbitrators did not believe the photographs to be genuine. Mr Maule went so far as to imply that the photographs were far beyond anything imagination could depict. But the pathetic account Mrs Williams gave of her struggles to bring up her family must have been moving in the extreme. The incident was reported in *The Christian Herald*[12] under the headline, 'Touching scenes and statements at the Barnardo Arbitration': 'So touching was the account given by this witness of her distress that both the Arbitrator and Canon Miller were visibly affected, and one of the counsel engaged in the case was compelled to leave the room to hide his feelings, while opposing counsel could not refrain from offering the poor woman a small sum of money.' Thesiger himself was greatly affected by the incident and said that since he had been at the bar he had never known anything like it: referring to it later, he said, 'I am sure her voice has often rung in my ears since, when I have thought of it. I confess, even at this moment I can hardly think of it without being upset.' He went on to press home the point that Barnardo had no need to exaggerate when such photographs proved to be true.

At the end of this mass of evidence Barnardo, the principal actor in the drama, was himself called as a witness. The court had already been sitting for thirty-three days all through the heat of July and August when Barnardo started to give evidence. For five days Thesiger took him through all the facts concerning his early life, the establishment of the East End Juvenile Mission, the Boys' Home, the Edinburgh Castle, the Girls' Village Home. He dealt with the allegations concerning his medical degree and the authorship of the Clerical Junius letters.

Concerning his medical degree, Barnardo repeated in court on the first day the story he had told his trustees: 'In February 1872 I obtained by examination, clinical and vivâ voce, at St. George's Hospital, a diploma as physician of the University of Giessen (M. D. Giess.).' On the third day Barnardo elaborated on this by producing a letter from a Mr C. J. Sayer[13] dated 10 August 1871, in answer to one dated 2 August asking him if he wished to proceed to prove his qualification for the degree of MD. Barnardo said in evidence that he went to St George's Hospital with Mr Sayer and a German whose name he did not know, and passed an examination occupying at most ten or fifteen minutes at the bedside of a patient, and that in February 1872 he had received the following letter:

Sir, I have pleasure to inform you that you have attained the grade of M.D. of our Faculty and the Diploma will be forwarded as soon as Dr. Sayer has received and sends me the remaining portion of the honorarium (300 marks = 15£ sterling) yours, etc.

Dr. L. D. Wichan
Dean of the Faculty

Barnardo then went on to say that in September 1875, owing to a correspondence in *The Times* and in the medical papers, he came to the conclusion that the degree he had obtained was a forgery and he destroyed it without inquiry. He said he had written to Mr Sayer, but his letter had been returned and he thought Mr Sayer had been prosecuted. He said that he had written to the authorities at Giessen in September or October 1875 to ask if he could obtain a degree *in absentia*, before finally making the point that he had received his licenciate as a Fellow of the Royal College of Surgeons in Edinburgh in March 1876.

There was never any opportunity for St John Wontner to cross-examine Barnardo on his evidence. He only began to cross-examine him after Barnardo had been taken through his evidence. The first day was largely taken up with questions concerning Barnardo's early years in Ireland and London; the fact that he had no means of his own and was dependent on the generosity of others was dealt with at length. He was questioned about the quarrel over the Dublin Castle and the ensuing newspaper controversy. Step by step St John Wontner approached the crucial question concerning the authorship of the Clerical Junius letters. It must be remembered that in his original letter[14] to the *East London Observer* Barnardo had declared that he would not be drawn into a newspaper discussion, and that only a week later the first Clerical Junius letter appeared. A number of new facts had come out in evidence about the actual production of the letters. In his original letter repudiating the second Clerical Junius letter and describing it as 'atrocious', Barnardo had claimed that his share in the transaction was merely a passive one; he had simply supplied Junius with letters, documents, papers and pamphlets relating to the controversy in the knowledge that Junius was preparing a letter for the papers. In her evidence to the arbitrators, Mrs Guinness stated that it was Barnardo himself who had taken the second letter to the offices of the *Tower Hamlets Independent* and that he had had both letters submitted to him before publication, points which Barnardo did not deny. Now St John Wontner asked for the name of the author:[15]

Q: 'Who was the author?'
A: 'I have already declined to tell.'
Q: 'But I am asking you, who was the author?'
A: 'I refuse to tell.'

Three times St John Wontner put the question to Barnardo, meeting with the same refusal each time. Wontner appealed to the arbitrator for help, who reminded Barnardo that he was under oath and bound to reply. Wontner tried again and Barnardo replied that[16] he respectfully declined to answer the question as put, saying, 'I distinctly and fully accept the entire responsibility of the authorship of the letter, but I decline to inflict an injury upon the real author by giving his name.'

Barnardo's dramatic refusal to answer St John Wontner's question threw the court into considerable confusion. The legal arbitrator made no attempt to hide his annoyance at Barnardo's behaviour and accused him of playing at hide-and-seek.

William Graham spoke severely to Barnardo: 'I do not think Dr. Barnardo is in a position to do justice, or to treat with respect and justice the Arbitrators who have made the greatest sacrifices in order to investigate this case; nor do I think he is doing his own duty to that important work which is committed to his hands, nor to his own character, by refusing to make this disclosure.' Thesiger was dismayed and said that he would certainly advise Barnardo to give up the name. Canon Miller felt even more strongly about Barnardo's behaviour: 'I feel very strongly that it is a very mournful thing, and very sad, for a man at the head of a great Christian work like this to appear in the witness-box and refuse to obey the law of the land. I do not see why Dr. Barnardo should be sheltered more than the humblest individual, if that is a principle of law – I think he is bound to answer.' Barnardo put the point that the authorship of the letter was only one of many issues and the one that least affected his subscribers, but this argument was swept aside. Canon Miller told Barnardo to remember that[17] 'it is clear that everything turns upon the confidence that is reposed in yourself – therefore when you say it is only one of many issues, I must frankly say that I regard it in one sense, as the most important issue of the whole, because it reflects confidence in you; and as we all know that if the result of any trial or Arbitration is to destroy that confidence, it would destroy the Institutions as they at present exist'.

William Graham's response showed clearly the intense interest that was being taken in the case, not only by Cairns but by the evangelical leadership as a whole:[18]

Of all the questions submitted to us, none is more important than the case of *Clerical Junius*, and that is the view which seems to be taken by the very highest authorities upon any such question of the Christian work, the very highest authority in the country, names – if I were at liberty to mention them – that would carry conviction, a conviction which I have shared and which is shared by some of the highest persons in this country, whose good opinion with regard to Christian work is paramount. I have no question, in my mind, that it is a frightful error which Dr. Barnardo will commit if he persists in withholding the name, although one may respect the motives that he now alleges.

St John Wontner made no secret of his reasons for wanting an answer to his question. He believed that if he could convict Dr Barnardo as responsible for the Clerical Junius letters it would shake his credit on the whole fabric of evidence that he had given, and in this he was fully supported by the COS who saw the opportunity offered by Barnardo's behaviour as their best means of discrediting him. Thesiger's position was extremely awkward. He was acting as Barnardo's counsel, but he had been instructed to do so by Cairns and the trustees and he found himself with no option but to agree with the observations made by the arbitrators. It was at this point that St John Wontner said that unless Barnardo answered his question he would not proceed with his cross-examination, and Canon Miller immediately said that without hearing Barnardo cross-examined it was impossible for him to make an award. He took a point Maule had made the day before, that cross-examination is the very backbone of truth, that Barnardo was, so to speak, 'the Hamlet out of the play' and that without taking into account his evidence-in-chief, which could not be done until he had been cross-examined, no award could be made.

Barnardo stubbornly refused to budge and Wontner, as was his legal right, refused to ask a single further question of the witness. William Graham made a last attempt to persuade Barnardo that it was his moral and legal duty, having taken the oath to do so, to tell the truth. Barnardo once more attempted to take refuge behind the promise he had given to the author of the letters not to disclose his name:[19] 'What are the issues before the Arbitrators? Either truth to the person who wrote this, or resting over me the reproach of untruthfulness. I cannot consent to his ruin.' This was too much for Canon Miller, who in a series of exchanges sought to demonstrate just how far Barnardo had been proved to be responsible for the contents of the letter:

'Dr. Barnardo, I think, if you will allow me to say so, you forget this. We have carried the thing on evidence up to your taking it to the paper.'
The Witness: 'Up to my sending it.'
Canon Miller: 'Mrs. Guinness said that you took it.'
Mr. Wontner: 'I think she said a cab was waiting.'
Canon Miller: 'It has been brought to this, that you furnished the materials – the substance I mean?'

The Witness: 'Yes.'

Canon Miller: 'And that you glanced over the proof?'

The Witness: 'I have not been examined as to how far I saw the proofs.'

Canon Miller: 'I am taking Mrs. Guinness's evidence and think you said that you glanced at the proof.'

The Witness: 'Yes I did and I accepted the entire moral responsibility of the letter and do so now, so far as that may be said to be the author's.'

A later exchange between Canon Miller and Barnardo revealed more clearly the difficulty into which he had got himself. In response to an observation of Canon Miller's that Clerical Junius had no right to write a letter of that kind, Barnardo enlarged upon the circumstances surrounding its publication and admitted that the author had written the letter for him to make use of and did not feel himself liable for the consequences.

Barnardo: 'The second letter which he sent to me, he did not send direct to the papers, but sent direct to me, and if I had had time I might have altered it or corrected it. In that way he put off the responsibility of the worst statement of the letter on my shoulders. He sent me the statement in the second letter which I opened and might have corrected; but not having time, I could not read it. He does not hold himself responsible in the same sense for that letter as for the first.'

The legal arbitrator's anger at the turn of events broke out again.

'We have been brought here and treated in this way. I cannot prevent it; of course I am sorry to use the phrase which Mr. Thesiger disapproves of, but that is my judgement that he is playing at hide-and-seek. We have been called here to enforce the law . . . Now this has taken place, I want to know further what I am to do.'

Barnardo: 'I deeply regret that I should have called for such an expression; no doubt I fully deserve it.'

The Arbitrator: 'I should certainly not use it if I did not think so.'

Barnardo: 'In taking the course I am taking I am urged by what appears to me to be the right and true motives.'

The Arbitrator: 'It does not matter who is right if I am all wrong. I am very sorry for it; but still, what is to be done next?'

Thesiger was highly embarrassed and said so. He made it clear that he was representing Barnardo personally but he was also responsible to the trustees and to persons 'behind the trustees'. He asked for an adjournment as 'there are persons to be consulted, and it is very important that no steps should be taken without doing so'. He regretted the inconvenience. Maule replied sarcastically: 'That follows. We undertook it and we must endure that as well as everything else. There is nothing but waste of time to be considered.' Before the court adjourned Wontner reminded the arbitrators that they were clothed with the full legal power of enforcing Barnardo's answer, but Maule wearily replied by reminding the court of the old proverb, 'Many a man may take a horse to the pond, but no one can make him drink.'

When the court met again the following day the situation was unchanged. Barnardo refused to give up the name, Wontner refused to cross-examine and Canon Miller came to court with a written statement setting out once more the insuperable difficulty he felt in making an award in these circumstances. It was left to William Graham to try to resolve the deadlock. He blamed the great wrong done to the arbitrators on Barnardo, and said his ill-judged and mistaken conduct had led to the present situation. From his words it was obvious that he had consulted with the trustees and Cairns overnight and that they had decided that there would be 'a risk of failure of justice if the charges brought against the Institutions and those engaged in Christian work in the East End of London were not answered', but that Barnardo 'should be left to take the consequences as to the charges in respect of his personal character' as a result of his failure to do what seemed to the court to be right – a decision that was reminiscent of the action taken over Pearsall Smith's indiscretion the year before.

This could have been a dangerous development for Barnardo and might have left him vulnerable to possible dismissal by the trustees, but Wontner's refusal to continue, even on these terms, prevented any development. Thesiger said everyone in the room must have been deeply moved by Mr Graham's arguments and only added that 'a very severe deep punishment – far beyond anything which Dr. Barnardo's case demands – would be inflicted upon him unless this case were brought to its conclusion'. The legal arbitrator called again on Canon Miller to set out the difficulty as he saw it in making an award, in the hope that some way round it could be found. After reading his prepared statement, in which he said that the whole proceedings were in a sense an impeachment of Dr Barnardo, the only concession he offered was not to change his judgement but to yield it to that of the other two in the interests of truth and justice, and in the interests of the institutions. Maule would not accept this offer, and although any two of the arbitrators were empowered to make an award, he knew this could not produce a satisfactory result. Leaning on Canon Miller's sense of fair play Thesiger, the legal arbitrator, and William Graham skilfully and by degrees led him to agree to suspend judgement until he had heard Thesiger's summing up of the case, which he accepted to do in a graceful interchange of courtesies:[20]

The Arbitrator: 'I mean he will only suffer by the time it occupies. Of course, it is comparatively no loss to him, when he has been here tuous, he will suffer nothing by listening to your argument, and at the end of it he can make use of it for what it is worth.'

Thesiger: 'I am afraid I cannot say he will not suffer while it is going on.'

The Arbitrator: 'I mean he will only suffer by the time it occupies. Of course, it is comparatively no loss to him, when he has been here about thirty-six days, a few hours more or less cannot add much to his toil and suffering.'

Canon Miller: 'It will be no suffering to me to hear the learned Counsel.'

So the matter was arranged. Wontner, Reynolds and Ribton-Turner all left the court at this moment, and Thesiger was left not only with the responsibility of presenting a long and complex case unopposed, but with the additional burden of doing it in such a way that Canon Miller's stubbornly held objections would be overcome.

The arbitration case had attracted little notice until this moment, but the sudden withdrawal of Reynolds gave rise to considerable comment in the newspapers. Although the cos denied that they took any part in the case, the fact that their representative, Ribton-Turner, withdrew at the same time as Reynolds was seen as confirming their involvement in the case. Without waiting to know Canon Miller's final decision, they put it about that the arbitration had broken down, underlining this by producing a circular of their own a week later re-stating their charges against Barnardo.

In the meantime Thesiger started on the marathon task of pulling together the mass of contradictory evidence that had been presented by both sides. The intense interest in the case taken by the inhabitants of the East End was reflected by the action of the editor of the *East London Observer*, who on two consecutive weeks produced free supplements to his newspaper giving the whole of Thesiger's lengthy summing-up speech verbatim. Without the help of this invaluable record containing the whole of Thesiger's argument, which ran to over forty thousand words, it would be impossible to understand the complexities of the quarrel between Charrington and Barnardo or to appreciate how finely balanced the decision to make an award had been. Thesiger was acutely aware of the difficulties that confronted him and in his opening address said he felt neither capable nor competent to cope with the matter. But his argument, summing up the evidence on both sides, was a masterpiece of lucidity and restraint – clear, logical, detailed and telling. He spared himself nothing, teasing out every twist and turn in the labyrinthine quarrel between Charrington, Reynolds and Barnardo, and fully justifying his reputation for scrupulous honesty and fairness in the way he presented the facts. His juniors were seldom called upon to prompt him. He paid special attention to the position of Canon Miller; acknowledging the difficulty 'which I have in addressing one member of the tribunal after the statement which has been made by him', he continued:[21]

I do feel that I am addressing a gentleman, not only of great experience, but that I am addressing a gentleman of such integrity that I may trust him to keep his mind open, and trust him to allow himself to be convinced if he sees that the argument which I have to present is well founded, though presented by an advocate who is in the greatest difficulty in which an advocate can be placed, namely of making a statement without an opportunity of being contradicted.

Thesiger spoke for two days, occasionally interrupted by one or other of the arbitrators. He ended simply:

I leave the case in your hands – I cannot speculate as to whether on any particular case you may not have been quite satisfied, but I submit that on the whole these Institutions have been carried on with the utmost propriety by Dr. Barnardo, that they are Institutions which have not been carried on for his own ends, but have been carried on through his own unselfish desire to benefit the class of children he has taken into his Home.

Most unfortunately for Dr. Barnardo, with a case he has been able to present so satisfactorily he has refused upon one particular matter to give an answer, the effect of which is, no doubt, to cast a certain amount of suspicion upon the whole matter ... I do ask you to take a charitable view of that. If you had been told to find a flaw in the case of Dr. Barnardo, I can quite understand the most uncharitable conclusion might be drawn from the refusal to answer, but after the full glare of the sunshine of this Inquiry has been poured, for now forty days, upon Dr. Barnardo's past conduct, whether it be as regards his private life or as regards his public life, I do ask you to say, and so say to the public, that while this Inquiry has been instituted by malice on the part of those who instituted it, Dr. Barnardo and these Institutions have come out of it unscathed.

With these closing remarks by Thesiger, the court adjourned.

10

Evangelical Triumph

AFTER the court adjourned, no public announcement was made as to when or even if an award would be made. The COS, however, wasted no time in making their views public. Claiming that the arbitration had 'practically broken down', they printed two thousand copies of a circular[1] which appeared in the form of a letter to the trustees, but which was sent to all newspaper editors. A large consignment went to the social science conference being held in Aberdeen. The circular was advertised in the newspapers under the heading, 'Mr. Barnardo's Homes – Caution to the Benevolent'. At least one newspaper[2] took up the point that until the arbitrators had either made an award or refused to do so any comment on the subject under discussion in the inquiry was *sub judice* and the COS, by publishing their circular, were in contempt of court.

The COS circular took Barnardo's refusal to answer the question of the identity of Clerical Junius as an admission that he was the author of the letters. From there they went on to say that this admission assumed a most serious character, as 'Mr Barnardo has stated on oath that he is not the author of the letters'. In making this statement the COS were both acting illegally, since the matter was *sub judice*, and also publishing assumptions which they had not sufficient evidence to prove. Relying on the evidence given by several witnesses during the case as to Barnardo's small means when he came to London, they stated 'that his subsequent rise and progress co-ordinately with the pecuniary results of his appeals to the charitable, point inevitably to the conclusion that Mr. Barnardo has not told the truth as to the sources from which he has derived his income'.

Barnardo claimed, when he was giving evidence concerning his father's wealth, that he lost £40,000 in the Wicklow and

Wexford Railway Company in 1847; the COS counterclaimed that his father was a struggling tradesman whose investment in the Wicklow and Wexford Railway Company amounted to only £75, and that he lost no more than £61 at the time. At all events, when the elder Barnardo died in 1874 the business was worth less than £2,000,[3] and in the light of this it does seem improbable that he gave Barnardo £1,500 in 1871 as he claimed. As for the £250 allowance which, it was implied, Mrs Barnardo received from her father, the trustees in their letter replying to the society – which incidentally Barnardo published without their consent – specifically noted 'that it was never stated that this was an allowance from the lady's father'; the money was most probably paid to her in the form of an honorarium in respect of her services to the Girls' Village Home, and Mr Sands could well have been the benefactor.

The COS had some justification for making these allegations. There is no doubt that Barnardo deliberately fostered an illusion of family wealth which was unjustified by the facts. Had Barnardo been able to accept that his family circumstances were modest, and acknowledge that *The Children's Treasury* was earning him a substantial income and that as a popular and successful preacher he was rewarded appropriately, he would not have laid himself open to charges of misappropriation of funds. These charges were never entirely forgotten, even after he had been cleared by the arbitrators. Nor were the COS satisfied with the way in which the accounts of the homes were kept, and claimed that the system was calculated to allow misapplication of funds. In making this accusation they went out of their way to stress that they were not casting any reflection upon the accountants who, they said, had simply certified the accounts on the vouchers presented to them.[4] The Institute of Chartered Accountants in England and Wales only received its royal charter in 1880, three years after the arbitration, and in fact Barnardo's methods of accountancy were very advanced for his time. However, this accusation and the recurring question of Barnardo's right to the title of Doctor, which occupied many pages of the circular, were to remain two of the main reasons for the COS's hostility towards Barnardo – a hostility which continued until his death. But the basic reason for the opposition of the COS to the type of evangelical philanthropy practised by

Barnardo was the more fundamental and more complex one already mentioned – the undermining, as they saw it, of the Poor Law by 'indiscriminate' charity.

The COS's hostility was heartily reciprocated by Barnardo, and he seldom missed an opportunity to attack the society through his own journal and in the press. It was not only matters of principle that caused the bitter antagonism; a strong element of personal animosity existed as well. Alsager Hay Hill, the social reformer who had been present during most of the arbitration case, was strongly opposed to all religious philanthropic work, and his friendship with Charles Bradlaugh, a militant atheist and the first Member of Parliament to be allowed to affirm, put him beyond the pale as far as Barnardo was concerned.

In 1875 Charles Stewart Loch, who was to become so identified with the COS that at his death *The Times*[5] said 'he made the COS; he was the COS', joined the society as its secretary. He bitterly resented the situation in which the society found itself as a result of the arbitration. Out-manoeuvred by Barnardo's trustees, the society had been denied any official status in the controversy and was left an impotent spectator. As the arbitrators considered their verdict Loch blamed Lord Lichfield, the chairman, and Ribton-Turner for having mishandled the society's affairs, and both their resignations followed swiftly once the award was published. Loch was left in virtual control of the society, and under his leadership it changed direction and reflected more his particular brand of social idealism. It is not hard to see that there would be little sympathy between the lofty Balliol introverted intellectual and the brash, successful, forceful newcomer, Barnardo. What is less well known is that neither Hill nor Loch ever relaxed their efforts to discredit Barnardo. Hill resigned from the vice-presidency of the COS in 1880, but Loch, right up to the time of Barnardo's death, continued to use his considerable influence to oppose the work of the Homes.

Barnardo was furious at the fresh attacks made on him by the COS in their circular. The events of the past months had put him under terrible strain, and he was suffering again from nervous exhaustion and insomnia. Without consulting any of the trustees, he dashed off an immediate answer to all the charges, and had it printed and ready for circulation within days. He announced through the press that his full reply would be published as soon as the award of the arbitrators was made known, and that advance copies could be had direct from the homes or from Messrs Haughton & Co., publishers. The award was published on Monday 15 October 1877, and after first being given to Barnardo's trustees it was made public on 19 October. Thesiger had succeeded in his task! The award was signed by all three arbitrators; Canon Miller's reluctance to adjudicate had only been overcome after exhaustive discussions with the other two arbitrators on every aspect of the evidence. This must have tried their patience to the limit; as the award itself noted, 'this had imposed an extra heavy labour and anxiety upon them all'.

The arbitrators began by saying that because of Barnardo's unjustifiable conduct in refusing to answer a question and because of the late withdrawal by Reynolds, in spite of the remonstrance of the arbitrators, the arbitration was not exhaustive in all its aspects. On the charges pertaining to the management of the homes, the arbitrators dismissed the allegations as mainly unsupported by evidence and unfounded on fact. Apart from their criticisms of the length of time Barnardo kept boys locked up, they acquitted him of all the charges of cruelty, ill-treatment and lack of religious instruction, and of the allegations that children suffered from disease because of inferior food, bad cooking and neglect of sanitary precautions. However, on the question of deceptive photographs, the arbitrators were distinctly critical and ruled that 'this use of artistic fiction to represent facts is, in our opinion, not only morally wrong as thus employed, but might in the absence of a very strict control, grow into a system of deception to the cause on behalf of which it is practised. Nor has evidence been wanting in this Inquiry, that in one or two cases it has been applied to an extent that the Arbitrators reprobate.'

Barnardo was careful to heed the warning. After 1877 he never sold photographs of the children for the benefit of the institutions, and the famous series of 'before and after' photographs came to an end. Thenceforward children were simply photographed for identity purposes, although their photographs frequently appeared in *Night and Day*; passing through the studio in their thousands, they faced the camera impassively while their features were recorded, the whole process taking no more than a matter of minutes. After 1885 the Barnardo photographer took to writing the names of the children and the dates when photographed on the face of the photograph itself, thus formalising them still further. Yet to look through those thousands of photographs is to be made more acutely aware of the innate dignity of the children in the face of their helplessness and destitution than any number of studio portraits could convey. A special album of photographs was always kept in Barnardo's office for visitors to see.

The arbitrators' ruling on the question of the Clerical Junius letters was a masterpiece of drafting. The arbitrators again censured both parties for their misconduct and said that they were unable fully to determine the question; but taking the internal evidence of the letters and such external evidence as was supplied, they were of the opinion that:

> Dr. Barnardo was not himself the actual writer, but that he having supplied the whole materials, having had both letters submitted to him before publication and having transmitted the second letter directly to the newspaper from his own hands, was as he has acknowledged, as much morally responsible for them as the writer, who betrays in them an intimate local knowledge of the details of the controversy no less original and personal than that possessed by Dr. Barnardo himself.

The verdict would be hard to improve upon, given that no conclusive evidence was available. From a stylistic point of view there are many other instances in Barnardo's writings of his use of the dream formula for putting over his views. Neither was this the only occasion on which he was accused of writing anonymous letters; but in view of the intrinsic nature of such letters, that fact is no more conclusive than is his predilection for using dreams, real or fictitious, as a vehicle to communicate his thoughts. Certainly the whole episode reflects one of the least pleasing facets of his character, and the manner in which the affair was reported in *Night and Day* does nothing to diminish that impression. Quoting only the passage in which the arbitrators asserted their belief that 'we [Barnardo] were not ourselves the writer, although so closely associated with him as

to be, as we have from the first acknowledged, morally responsible for the letters', Barnardo went on to reprint the affidavit he
swore, that 'we were not ourselves the writer or author of the
letters in any sense'. He ignored the inherent contradiction
between the two passages and suppressed the final sentence of
the arbitrators' judgement.

The arbitrators took a fairly relaxed view over the question of
Barnardo's right to the style and title of Doctor. They plainly
disbelieved the evidence about an examination having taken
place at St George's Hospital, but they noted that as a medical
student his friends called him Doctor: 'He has never had an
English diploma to give him a real title to the degree, nor has he
practised as a physician. It is thus strictly true that during the
time here referred to he had no legal right to the title and style of
Doctor. It was not until March 1876 that he obtained a diploma
at Edinburgh.' It is interesting to contrast the attitude adopted
by the evangelicals over this question with that of the COS.
Many leading members of that society were professional men
belonging to a professional elite, and their prestige rested not so
much on birth or wealth as on their ability to use skills which
education had enabled them to acquire. Therefore to them
Barnardo's attempt to pass himself off as a properly qualified
medical practitioner was a matter of the greatest concern and it
damned him, in their eyes, as a charlatan and an adventurer.
However, once Barnardo had qualified as a surgeon and registered as a medical practitioner, which he did in 1876, he was
legally entitled to call himself Doctor if he so wished, notwithstanding the views of the Royal College of Physicians. According to them Barnardo technically was never, throughout his
professional career, entitled to call himself Doctor as he was not
a graduate of any British university. Barnardo had obviously
been well aware of these regulations, hence his anxiety to obtain
a degree from Giessen. In dealing with the question in *Night
and Day*, Barnardo sought to minimise the affair. He said that
the matter was 'infinitesimally little' and that the manner in
which he was addressed was of small importance to him
personally. Barnardo's trustees, having accepted the facts as
Barnardo had presented them, had no real option but to play
down the affair in public. But privately some members of the
new committee of management were concerned at his

continued use of the title. A motion was put forward that the institutions should be known as The East End Juvenile Mission (Barnardo's Homes) and that the director should simply sign himself T. J. Barnardo, LRCS, Honorary Director. However, the views of the trustee members of the committee eventually prevailed, and it was agreed that the institutions should in future be known as Dr Barnardo's Homes and East End Juvenile Mission, which rapidly became simply Dr Barnardo's Homes, and that Barnardo should be allowed to continue calling himself Doctor.[6]

If the arbitrators were lenient towards Barnardo in their judgement over his medical misdemeanours, they also let Charrington off with only a mild rebuke. Regretting his non-participation in the arbitration, 'to which having regard to his active share in the controversy he ought undoubtedly to have been party', they noted 'that there existed on the part of Mr Charrington and some of his fellow workers, an unbecoming jealousy of the existing and extending work of Dr Barnardo . . . But for this jealousy, the scandal of the quarrel could and ought to have been avoided by mutual conciliation and concession . . .' Having been asked to rule on all the heads of inquiry submitted to them, the arbitrators were also asked to give their opinions on three matters of vital interest to the public. One cannot help suspecting that it was Cairns who drafted the questions, understanding how important it would be for the future of the homes if, from all the complexities of the arbitration award, three simple statements could be extracted and used by the newspapers in presenting the facts to the public.

First the arbitrators were asked to find out if the statements that were being circulated were true, and they gave as their opinion 'that these statements, with few exceptions, already pronounced on by us, were not justifiable, having at the first been made without due enquiry, and having been subsequently unsupported by evidence, and they must necessarily have had an evil effect upon the Institutions, and ought to be discontinued'. Then came the key question of whether the institutions were worthy of public confidence. In a much quoted ruling the arbitrators stated: 'We are of the opinion that these Homes for Destitute Boys and Girls, called the Barnardo Institutions are real and valuable charities, and worthy of public confidence and support.' This commendation was, however, followed by a recommendation that the trustees should appoint a working committee of gentlemen who would be associated with the Director in administering the institutions and who would take an active interest in the overseeing of the homes; they would also help the Director with the many questions that would continuously arise, and the deeds of trust would be altered to that effect. They said the new committee was necessary, apart from other considerations, because the authority and discipline of the homes appeared to be self-constituted and to have no legal sanction in cases where parents and guardians were not parties to a child's admission.

Again the hand of Cairns is discernible; even before the award was announced he had privately sent Barnardo[7] a carefully worded letter delicately pressing him into accepting the idea of a committee, offering in return his patronage: 'If, after the Arbitration is concluded, you wish to be helped by a committee, and are desirous of choosing one, the Lord Chancellor will be very pleased to show the confidence he has in you and in your work by taking the post of President.' Apart from a committee, the arbitrators also recommended that Barnardo's schools be under government inspection.

Finally, if George Reynolds' attacks could be shown to have been entirely malicious, then Barnardo's reputation, notwithstanding the ambiguities that remained concerning his personal behaviour, could only be enhanced. On this third question the arbitrators gave qualified judgement:

We cannot hide from ourselves that the pamphlets and leaflets which were presented to us by Mr. George Reynolds as embodying his charges against Dr. Barnardo are of a very grave character and contain statements, which must, if substantiated, have been fatal to Dr. Barnardo's character and if not substantiated were without excuse ... We find that many of these grave statements were made and published in the pamphlets without any sufficient steps having been taken to sift such as Mr. Reynolds advanced nor to test the credibility and accuracy of the persons who supplied the matter ... However, it is due to Mr. Reynolds to observe that his judgement in this matter may also have been biased by his general disbelief in the bona fides of all such religious charitable institutions and his entire want of confidence in them as frankly stated by him in the witness box.

The closing sentences of the award make it clear that the overriding anxiety of the arbitrators was to minimise the damage that the quarrel between Barnardo and Charrington had inflicted on the evangelical philanthropic movement. The part played by the COS was not mentioned, but the opportunity that the Barnardo–Charrington controversy had presented to the society to intervene in the work of Christian philanthropy, and the use the society had made of that opportunity, cannot have been far from their thoughts. The arbitrators did not specifically clear Barnardo of the personal charges brought against him, but they spoke in the strongest terms against the behaviour of both Barnardo and Charrington in allowing the quarrel between them to become a public scandal. They used the full weight of their authority to recommend that all defamatory charges should cease between the parties and to insist that acceptable standards of conduct must be observed by those engaged in Christian philanthropic work.

In closing this Award, we do so with the observation that the absence of Dr. Barnardo's cross-examination has embarrassed our judicial consideration of almost all the issues submitted to us, and we are by no means sure that some modification of the conclusions we have arrived at might not have been made had such cross-examination been carried out.

We have now only to commend to the earnest consideration of the parties affected by it our remonstrance against the spirit and temper which have pervaded this scandalous controversy. To the extent of our power WE DECIDE AND AWARD that the circulation of defamatory charges by either side shall henceforth be entirely discontinued, and we venture to add the expression of our earnest hope that all the persons implicated in this quarrel may henceforth be induced to conform more nearly in the prosecution of the work in which they are engaged, to the standards of conduct recognised amongst gentlemen, and to the dictates of Christian charity whose obligations are pre-eminently binding upon men professing to take a lead in religious and philanthropic work.

Comment in both weekly and daily papers was extensive, and as might be expected occupied many columns in the religious papers. On the whole the award was seen as favourable to Barnardo, but the extent of the interest taken in the result of the case made it obvious that the public was aware that more than the reputation of a single individual was at stake. The arbitration had developed into a confrontation between those who

sincerely disapproved and disbelieved in unorganised, free-
wheeling, religious philanthropic endeavour and those who
feared that the threat to Barnardo's work represented a threat
which could affect the whole Christian philanthropic movement and undermine all voluntary charitable work. This fear,
which William Graham had voiced during the arbitration, was
most clearly expressed in an editorial in the *Daily Chronicle*:[8]

The publication of the Arbitrators' Award will interest directly a
considerable number of persons. But it will interest indirectly a much
larger number to whom the particular persons and institutions concerned are but names, and scarcely even names. The amount of
money annually entrusted to individuals for charitable distribution is
so enormous, and the direct supervision exercised by the contributors
is so exceedingly small, that any suspicion as to its use cannot fail to
have a very disagreeable effect. On the other hand the range of these
charities is so large, the good, which if properly administered, they do
is so important to society, and the gap which would be left by their
failure is so serious, that no one who has the social welfare of the
country at heart can contemplate their restriction or enfeeblement
with equanimity.

Several newspapers commented on the excessively personal
character of the management as a reason for the growth of
opposition, and *The Record*[9] criticised the fact that Barnardo
was trying to raise money for a training ship like the *Chichester*
and *Arethusa* without considering whether his hands were
already too full! *The Echo*,[10] which had given publicity to the
case, made the same point: 'Had Dr. Barnardo obtained from
among the subscribers to his Institutions a working committee
to assist in the management of each, he would have saved the
benevolent public a large sum of money, the Arbitrators much
valuable time and himself no little anxiety and pain. At the same
time we must congratulate him that, with all the mistakes he has
made, the gravest charges against him have not been proved.'
Nearly all the papers commented on the dilemma which the
Clerical Junius letters had presented to the arbitrators, and the
Morning Advertiser[11] went so far as to congratulate Barnardo on
the way in which he had extricated himself from that impasse:
'The general effect of the Award is to exonerate the Doctor, who
may, therefore, congratulate himself on having got, as he has
got, out of a serious and delicate position.'

The opinion of *The Times* was, of course, crucial to the evangelicals. In a leading article on the subject on 19 October it gave a summary of the award without comment. On the following day a long article regretted that although much time and money had been spent the award was incomplete. The article summarised how the case had arisen; it included an account of how the Clerical Junius letters had become an important factor in the case; it explained the actions taken by the trustees and the COS; it discussed the options open to Barnardo and the course of the arbitration, and firmly endorsed the recommendation of the arbitrators that there should be a committee of management, with the words: 'The law imposes very special obligations on one who assumes for himself the winding up of the estate of a deceased person, and styles himself significantly an "executor de son tort". Exactly the same analogy applies to people who make themselves almoners of other persons' charity.' But it is the final sentences that must have made Barnardo's trustees feel that the long and costly arbitration had been worth while: 'Let us hope, then, that if no fresh incident occurs to justify them, we have now heard the last of the charges against Dr. Barnardo. If his work is a good one, we need not vex ourselves because we do not know how much money his father lost on the Wicklow and Wexford Railway Company, or who is the real "*Clerical Junius*".' The article concluded with a very severe condemnation of the way in which the quarrel had been conducted throughout:

When men professing to take a lead in religious and philanthropic work have to be exhorted to conform more nearly to the standards of conduct recognised among gentlemen and the dictates of Christian charity it is time for them to take care not to lay themselves open to any further rebuke of the kind ... The Barnardo Homes are now pronounced to be real and valuable charities, worthy of public confidence and support. This is really enough. It is just the kind of judgement the public wanted, and we trust it will be accepted as final.

The trustees immediately held several meetings following publication of the award to discuss how best to proceed. Barnardo was still furiously angry with the COS for having publicised their circular containing further attacks on him, and in no mood to listen to the advice of his trustees to abide by the decision of the arbitrators that defamatory charges from either side must cease. He was determined to have the last word and to circulate his reply, which was ready and printed. Under the chairmanship of John Sands, the trustees were driven to the extreme step of publishing the minute embodying their decision in an announcement to *The Times*[12] expressly forbidding Barnardo to make public his reply. Only when he saw their veto in cold print did he realise that he was no longer a free agent. They had appointed him the Honorary Director of the institutions and they had the power to dismiss him. By making their order public they gave notice that Barnardo would forfeit their support if he went ahead without heeding them, and at last he understood. The reply was not published. But Barnardo managed to get one small satisfaction out of the affair. The trustees had written privately to the COS restating the points which Barnardo had made at the interview they had had with him the previous January, and without their permission or knowledge and to their great annoyance, he reprinted their letter in *Night and Day*.[13]

In spite of Cairns' letter to him on the subject of a possible committee of management, Barnardo regarded the idea of any interference in the work of the mission with the greatest disfavour. Immediately the award was made public he announced that he would continue the work of the mission, 'either in connection with a working party or alone as heretofore'. When after two months' discussion a committee was formed, Barnardo gave them a cautious welcome stating that their appointment must not be allowed to destroy 'that necessary sense of individual responsibility which is the stay and spring of all real work for Christ'.

The arbitration represents a turning-point in Barnardo's life. Before the inquiry was set up he had been a relatively unknown freelance mission leader, able to direct his work according to his own firmly held beliefs, responsible to no one except the public with whom he so successfully pleaded his cause. The arbitration made him into a public personality. His work was now so strongly identified with his name that his committee accepted that it was the only realistic name by which his work could be known, and Barnardo's own favourite title, the East End Juvenile Mission, gradually fell into disuse. Although the outcome was a major success for the evangelicals, Barnardo himself paid a high price for this victory. Not only had he to give up a certain amount of freedom, but his phenomenal energy and strength had been taxed beyond their limit and the strain engendered by the weeks of uncertainty left him depressed and exhausted. As a public figure he had not escaped unscathed. Although the COS had failed to damage his work, doubts about his personal integrity lingered on. To his lasting regret the confidence and interest Shaftesbury had shown in his work was never regained; Shaftesbury's doubts are recorded in his diary:[14]

Dr. Barnardo is acquitted after a fashion by the Arbitrators. Is it a just acquittal? If so I rejoice. The pressure on funds is frightful. If he was guilty I lament that iniquity has triumphed. The language of the Report, and especially of the conclusion, is like an effort of men who dare not call him innocent, and yet are zealous not to call him guilty. What will be the public response? Will he regain lost confidence? Will the money flow in? Will the reaction make him greater or less great?

The editor of the *Pall Mall Gazette* had no doubts at all. He thought the award had done nothing to rehabilitate Barnardo, and stated bluntly that he did not approve of Canon Miller's second thoughts and considered that the arbitrators would have been wiser had they resigned their functions when it appeared they could not be adequately discharged.

The most disturbing legacy of the arbitration, so far as Barnardo was concerned, was the large debt which both he personally and the homes had incurred during the struggle. The COS was a very powerful organisation and its strength was measured to an extent by the cost of the arbitration, both in time and money. No struggling charity, attacked in the way Barnardo was attacked, could have possibly survived the COS's assault. Nor could Barnardo have done so without the support of leading evangelicals. It can perhaps be said that it needed the Lord Chancellor of England to intervene before the power of the COS was broken. Unaware of the part Cairns had played, several newspapers commented unfavourably on the way the COS made use of their powerful position and one, *Lloyd's Weekly Newspaper*,[15] went so far as to suggest that the tables should be turned and a 'searching investigation of the operations of the cos and their effect upon the charitable public and the worthy recipients of charity should be publicly undertaken'. It cost Barnardo £4,200 personally to clear his name and the work of his institutions from the allegations made by Reynolds and sponsored by the cos. Friends and supporters subscribed over £2,000 towards the costs of the case. But only after the arbitration fund had been in existence for two years and it was clear that the public would not subscribe, did the finance committee transfer the debt to the main account and pay it off from the general fund. Not only did Barnardo have to incur debt personally, but funds subscribed for special projects such as the Village Home and the Boys' Homes as well as the training ship were all diverted to the general fund to keep the work going, and the trustees had to borrow £6,000 to pay for the remaining cottages which had been unfinished when the case began. Barnardo was unable to fill the new extension recently completed at Stepney owing to lack of funds.

Barnardo's religious ideas were deeply influenced by his strong belief in Brethren principles, and his inability once again to obey that most important command – 'owe no man anything' – was one of the reasons for his gradual decision to loosen his ties with Brethrenism and return to the Church of England. This change was not to be shared with his supporters; too many of them were deeply influenced by Brethrenism, and his own mission church was based on Brethren principles. Barnardo was by nature a loner, but now his secret and gradual withdrawal from the fellowship he had hitherto enjoyed within the Brethren movement added a new dimension to his loneliness. It also changed his attitude to the public; it was almost as if he wanted to force them to share his feelings of remorse for having transgressed against a code of conduct which he had proclaimed as central to his work for so many years. In a sense he saw the public as responsible for his debt; they had not responded to his need, and it was from this time on that he began to see his fund-raising appeals in the light of a duty and to consider that it was part of his ministry to make people give and accept responsibility for the welfare of the less fortunate.

The cos did its best to minimise the damage it had suffered over its unsuccessful intervention in the Barnardo inquiry. After weeks of discussion a second circular was issued, reiterating the accusations against Barnardo personally. In it the society also took the opportunity of refuting the accusation made by the newspapers that it was in any sense the real prosecutor, and denied that it had contributed either directly or indirectly towards the expenses of the arbitration. Their own minutes provide abundant proof that this statement was a blatant untruth; an entry in Loch's diary at the time reveals how bitterly he deplored the situation in which the cos now found itself:[16]

In the cries of timid men and the eagerness, sometimes a little hysteric, of the more enthusiastic and the indecisive indolence of the clever, each talking about a specific, all fearful of applying any one specific lest the patient succumbs and this body of the cos pass away into nothingness and vanish, to their unfaithful eyes, without hope of resurrection, it is the only conclusion one can come to – to go straight on, to be true to oneself, to be strong.

Being strong meant for Loch that he had to get rid of those he considered responsible for leading the cos into its present difficulties. He had already confided to his diary, 'Turner was too detective, had grown unmanageable. Hill was too extreme. This was a difficulty; the non-compromise party seemed to be getting the upper hand.' Written in the curious convoluted style he often adopted, Loch alluded to this struggle in his diary: ' "Patience; you will win presently", was on one of the cards in a round game we used to play as boys. This is the card I have had dealt me. It is not winning; it is a sell; two counters have to be paid into the bank as fine. Well now the fine's paid; a few more rounds and the game will be won.' There can be no doubt that Lichfield and Ribton-Turner were the two counters that were paid as a fine. The cos circular closed with the admission that, although the society was satisfied neither with the way in which the financial affairs of the mission were conducted nor with the fact that the personal allegations against Barnardo had not been answered, they had decided no longer to retain Mr Barnardo's Homes in their 'cautionary circular' because there was to be a committee of management.

The evangelicals had triumphed; Barnardo remained as Honorary Director of the homes and the cos had been forced to suspend their public criticism, although privately Loch was to continue to obstruct the work of the institutions until

Barnardo's death. Barnardo's old friend, the editor of the *Tower Hamlets Independent*, let rip:[17]

> We venture to think the action of the cos in prostituting the funds and machinery at their disposal to ruin an innocent man, to convert an honest individual in the eyes of the world into a rogue, and in attempting to pull down the edifice of Christian Philanthropy which it has taken years of patient labour to build up, is such as will make the very name of the cos stink in the nostrils of all honest men.

Immediately after the award, Cairns made a very significant appointment, one which amazed the whole legal world and indeed astonished the public. Sir Richard Amphlett, a Lord of Appeal, had just retired, and Cairns nominated Alfred Thesiger to succeed him. Such rapid promotion was unheard of, and it created a tremendous stir. It was reported with amazement:[18] 'A Queen's Counsel whose silk gown is four years old and its wearer only 39 and who has never in any way distinguished himself above his fellows, has been passed over the heads of twenty judges into one of the most important judicial offices in the State', wrote one critic. The many judges who felt themselves slighted by Thesiger's elevation found Cairns' action in making such a recommendation to Disraeli incomprehensible, and many thought the Prime Minister had made a mistake both in the man he had selected and in the decided slight he was showing to those who had been passed over. The new Lord Justice was made a member of the Privy Council, further evidence of the special esteem in which he was held; for although Disraeli would have relied upon Cairns' advice in so far as the judicial appointment was concerned, nomination for the Privy Council was made by the Prime Minister. Thesiger must indeed have been a remarkable person. He died almost exactly three years after his appointment had been announced, and in that short time had vindicated Cairns' and Disraeli's hopes. As his obituary notice put it:[19] 'The young Lord Justice of Appeal at all times and on all occasions discharged the duties to the complete satisfaction of all parties, showing here, as through the preceding years of his life, a conscientious desire to play to the fullest of his power the part allotted to him.'

Looking for a reason to explain Cairns' action, subsequent

legal opinion has come down in favour of the idea that Cairns was seeking to make amends to Lord Chelmsford, Thesiger's father, whom Cairns had displaced when he was made Lord Chancellor by Disraeli in 1868. There seems little to support this theory; Chelmsford was furious at his dismissal, and although he was offered a GCB (Knight Grand Cross of the Order of the Bath) he refused it and angrily demanded that he should be given an earldom, a claim which Disraeli considered preposterous.[20] It seems unlikely that nine years later Disraeli should not only have forgiven Chelmsford his ungracious behaviour, but sought to make amends by promoting his son. Thesiger's services to the evangelical cause have gone entirely unrecorded, and although Disraeli was in no sense an evangelical, Cairns, among all his cabinet colleagues, was the man whose judgement he most respected and whose views he listened to upon church matters. There is no doubt that Thesiger had the brilliance and ability that justified his appointment; that he should have been made a Lord Justice of Appeal at such a surprisingly early age and at the conclusion of a case in which Cairns had such a particular interest does not seem merely to have been coincidental. Cairns could not have been unaware of the repercussions that would follow Thesiger's sudden elevation; the appointment has all the marks of having been conferred as a sign of approval for special services given, a fitting reward for the man most responsible for such a hard-won evangelical triumph.

11

The Years of Consolidation, 1878-86

UNDER Cairns' strong and powerful patronage the trauma of the arbitration case and its associated anxieties began to recede. Cairns was generous with his time and his name; the public were left in no doubt as to his interest in the homes, and he presided at a special Christmas meeting in 1877 held at Exeter Hall to show his confidence. At the first annual general meeting held under the new arrangements, he took the chair and was supported by fellow evangelical peers, Cavan, Chichester, Gordon and Kinnaird. Cairns' father, who was an Ulster soldier, had originally intended him to take holy orders, but his interest in the law prevailed and after studying at Trinity College, Dublin, he became a bencher of Lincoln's Inn.

His brilliant judicial mind made rapid progress up the legal ladder inevitable, but as his biographer J. B. Atlay says,[1] 'In spite of bringing the greatest intellectual force which the Bar has contributed to the Conservative ranks since Lord Lyndhurst no man ever had so few friends.' He noted that 'his rare intimacies were confined irrespective of rank or station, to those who shared his views on religion and social reform'. Barnardo's work was only one of many causes to which Cairns lent the support of his name; among others the YMCA, the Bible Society and the Church Missionary Society were all objects of his active interest. It was principally due to his support that Barnardo had come through his recent ordeal relatively so unscathed, and the Barnardo Homes were known to be his most favoured charity. There is no doubt that it was the public support he gave the homes for the next seven years that helped to establish their bona fides with the wider public. Under his restraining influence, committee and trustees were helped to check the expansionist dreams of their Director. Funds remained at a low ebb for two years after the inquiry and Cairns agreed, at the request of the committee, to sign a manuscript letter in September 1879 appealing for support after Barnardo had been forced to announce publicly that the institutions were in debt. However, when he read a few months later that Barnardo had made a further appeal for funds for the establishment of a labour house for destitute youths, he wrote angrily:[2]

> I saw by chance in *The Christian*, the announcement of your intention to aid destitute cases beyond the age of boyhood, and I think it better to write at once and say that if an organisation of this kind is added to your present Homes, I must cease to be President.
>
> I do not mean in any way to express doubts as to the urgency of such cases as you refer to in your paper, or as to its being possible to relieve in this way much distress and suffering, but you are aware that I am not by any means satisfied as to the extent to which your original undertaking has already been developed, and I could not accept a share of responsibility for a further increase.

Barnardo argued that the committee, with the sanction of the trustees, had given a positive pledge that a labour house could be established, and he already had £500 towards the cost. Always believing attack to be the best method of defence, he went even further and said he needed not only a labour house but a home for girls in grave moral danger who were too old for the village. He was authorised by the committee to go ahead with his plans for the labour house and Cairns, recognising that he had been outmanoeuvred by Barnardo's action in obtaining his committee's consent, remained as president; Barnardo had to wait many years, however, before he acquired his home for girls.

There was one venture for which the committee positively declined to take any direct responsibility without the sanction of the president. When Barnardo expressed a wish to acquire a small cottage where, under the additional provisions of the Industrial Schools Act, little girls taken from houses of ill fame could be cared for, the committee, though favourably disposed, required that Barnardo should make a direct statement to the president, informing him that Miss Ellice Hopkins already had £200 in hand towards initial expenses and that if the home were certified it could be made almost independent of the general funds. Cairns not only agreed to this new development, he took an active interest in the management of the home, perhaps because it was never officially listed as part of the institutions.

It is possible that this austere and lonely man, who in spite of his immense ability and powerful intellect so entirely lacked any kind of personal magnetism, found in Barnardo a fellowship he could not share with any of his political allies or with members of his own profession. Barnardo would have immediately understood him when he said that to hear Moody and Sankey was the richest feast he could enjoy. Cairns could not have been unaware of the motives of some barristers, not known for their piety but desirous of county court judgeships, who came to his house where the entertainment frequently assumed the form of prayer meetings: this awareness can only have increased the impression he gave of 'a dryness, a coldness, and an appearance of reserve and hauteur about his manner which repelled strangers and kept acquaintanceship from ripening into friendship'. With Barnardo, to whom prayer meetings were as natural as breathing, he could feel at ease and would have no need to make use of the frigid sarcasm for which he was noted. Although probably the only man Barnardo feared to cross, his obituary of Cairns was warm and sincere:[3] 'He was no ornamental President but a real friend to whom I could go at all times and who always responded by wise loving advice and personal help.' By contrast, Barnardo's tribute to Shaftesbury, who died later the same year, was significantly formal, and no mention was made of the special relationship that Barnardo later claimed he had enjoyed in his early days.

Working with a committee was a new experience for Barnardo and one that he had to get used to. The committee represented every shade of evangelical Christianity and included a large number of old friends. Three of his trustees, Arthur Kinnaird, Thomas Pelham and John Sands, were among its members; John Gordon, whose subscription was one of the earliest to be listed, and Samuel Gurney Sheppard, accepted invitations to serve. Sheppard, who became chairman and only resigned in 1895, had been brought up a Quaker but left the Society of Friends, perhaps on account of his marriage to a non-Quaker. He became a supporter of the Evangelisation Society and a preacher of the Gospel in mission halls. With his dual interest in winning souls for salvation and in supporting the temperance movement, his generous contribution towards the acquisition of the Edinburgh Castle was understandable. He lived at Leggatts near Potter's Bar, and it was his enterprise that set the family firm, Sheppard's, Pelly's, Scott's and Co., on the road to success. It invested heavily and profitably in the railways, and he himself was a director of many companies including the Quebec Central Railway Co. In 1881 he founded the Railway Mission. A Member of Parliament, William Fowler, who had business connections in the City, was appointed treasurer. His bank, Dimsdale, Fowler and Co., offered its services to the institutions and made facilities available for the loans that were frequently necessary. Robert Anderson, a fellow countryman of Barnardo's and a noted Brethren preacher, at this time working in the Home Office, was the remaining lay member of the committee, apart from Dr Heywood Smith.

Among the clergymen and ministers were the Rev. Archibald Brown, Pastor of the East London Tabernacle, who had known Barnardo since 1867. Now president of the Baptist Union, he was throughly millennial in outlook, a vigorous and successful preacher who forcefully expressed his belief that until the Second Coming it was useless to think that there could be any real improvement in this world. His affectionate understanding of Barnardo's qualities was based on personal knowledge. He once called him a 'frank, outspoken, loving and slightly impetuous brother'. The Rev. Aubrey Price, Vicar of St James's, Clapham, of 'Clapham sect' fame, was another noted millennialist preacher. R. C. Billing, the Vicar of Holy Trinity, Islington, who afterwards became the Bishop of Bedford, and William Tyler, minister of the Congregational church in the Mile End Road, completed the list of clergy members. Tyler had felt doubtful about the eligibility of ministers of the Church to act as committee members, but Robert Anderson as a barrister gave it as his opinion that clergymen and ministers were in no way disqualified from such service. Billing, who had had his doubts about Barnardo, soon came to appreciate his energy and ability, describing him once at a public meeting as the 'victim of divine enthusiasm'.

The first concern of the new committee, having established

their relationship with the trustees, was to set up a finance sub-committee and appoint a regular rota of members to visit the homes and to introduce some kind of control over the institutions. Barnardo was required to list the number of children in each home every month, the number who left for situations, were reclaimed by parents and guardians, or who absconded or died. Full medical reports were required, for which the committee relied on the advice of Dr Heywood Smith, the only medical representative on the committee. Heywood Smith had founded the London Medical Mission, and when Barnardo opened his own medical mission in Shadwell it was modelled on his work. The committee had been reassured by the trustees that the outstanding loans, which had reached a total of £9,000, were fully covered by the value of the properties held by them, now worth £20,000. Barnardo, who was always travelling the country to speak in churches, chapels, mission halls and whenever possible at private meetings, suggested a tour of America as a means of reducing the debt. But Moody and other friends whom he consulted were not encouraging, and the idea was dropped. He did, however, manage to persuade the committee that useful publicity would result if he was allowed to have a model of the Village Home displayed at the Paris Exhibition, and he took it over himself.[4]

The Village Home continued to expand both because of need and because the idea of subscribing for a cottage as a form of memorial was popular. New properties were acquired by way of gift; Teighmore in Jersey was given through the action of Lady Cairns' niece, Mrs McNeil; and Hillside, Hawkhurst, was made over to Barnardo by Mr Theodore Moilliet. Barnardo used the Jersey home as a convalescent home for little boys, and the Hawkhurst home, which he christened 'Babies' Castle', enabled him to care for the growing number of infants abandoned and left destitute who needed specialised care.

If the social problems of the East End had been acute during the 1870s, they intensified during the 1880s. The housing problem by 1883 had reached crisis proportions. Clearance for railways and street improvements as well as for rebuilding had left thousands homeless at a time when rents were steadily rising and the population of London increasing. Overcrowded conditions were standard for more than half the population. As a result many artisans found themselves forced to share the dwellings of the casual poor and criminal classes, and this gave rise to much social anxiety. Any blurring of the distinctions which separated the respectable working classes from their less fortunate neighbours was seen as a dangerous trend and one likely to undermine the frail social stability of the East End of London.

The housing crisis and the deepening economic crisis alarmed many political and Christian writers. Andrew Mearns, a Congregational minister, gave expression to the fears of many in his pamphlet 'The Bitter Cry of Outcast London':

> The Churches are making the discovery that seething in the very centre of our great cities, concealed by the thinnest crust of civilisation and decency, is a vast mass of moral corruption, of heartbreaking misery and absolute godlessness, and that scarcely anything has been done to take into this awful slough the only influences that can purify and remove it.

Barnardo answered in an article entitled 'The Bitter Cry of Outcast Children', saying that children were by far the worst sufferers:[5]

> To behold young men and women crowded together in pestilential rookeries without the least provision for decency, and in such conditions of abominable filth, atmospheric impurity and immoral associationship as make the maintenance of virtue impossible, is almost enough to fill the bravest reformer with despair . . . But to know that thousands of unfortunate boys and girls commence life thus, and grow up to a degraded manhood and a dishonoured womanhood . . . to know this and to witness the process being repeated from day to day – to be quite certain as to what it must all grow to and yet to be quite helpless to deal thoroughly with the evil, is absolutely maddening . . .

> Experienced as I am in the abominations of some of the worst rookeries, I have again and again almost been compelled to give up personal exploration and visitations, heart-sick and stricken as with paralysis of the brain at the sights which I have witnessed, while unable to afford adequate relief.

Chiding the Church and Christians for their apathy in the face of such needs, Barnardo, almost alone among evangelical missionaries, recognised that only the state could intervene effectively and foresaw that it would, because 'England can no longer tolerate such hotbeds of dangerous passions, such seed beds of revolution and disorder to remain among her crowded populations'.

In his furious drive to loosen the purse strings of the public, he used any argument he thought would be effective. Having now completely abandoned the principle that it was wrong to appeal for funds, he was at pains to justify his extensive use of appeals. He argued that his campaign to make the wealthy give was a form of ministry; he saw it as his duty to make people feel responsible, to stir them up; he even argued that his appeals were helpful to Christian life and that they were both moral and necessary: 'Solicitation rightly performed is simply diffusing a knowledge of human need and providing an opportunity for its supply.' He did not, however, ignore other arguments, and often contrasted the economic sense of subscribing £16 to keep a child in the homes and training him to become a useful citizen with the folly of spending £80 to keep a criminal in prison: 'What shall it be eighty pounds and a life lost, and society's laws irretrievably violated: or, sixteen pounds and a life saved, law reverenced and the deepest wounds which society bleeds from staunched.'

In the early eighties under Gladstone's Liberal government, England was relatively prosperous. It was only with the worsening of the economic situation that the reactions of the inhabitants of 'outcast London' were perceived as more directly threatening to the lives of the comfortable and secure middle classes. Articles began to appear in newspapers and periodicals about the 'dangerous classes', and the unknown size of the residuum gave rise to fears of revolution and social unrest. Barnardo, always quick off the mark, immediately appreciated the possibilities inherent in the situation and forthwith added fear of the 'dangerous classes' to his arguments for funds to support his institutions:

What are the consequences of allowing the children of the common people to grow up without religious teaching? We can unhappily reply to this by pointing to Nihilism in Russia and socialism in Germany. These are the forces of the enemy, the existence of which it would be folly to ignore: for the rapid spread of principles that would subvert orderly Government and banish the Bible from the world is not a sign of the times to regard with composure. Every boy rescued from the gutter is one dangerous man the less.

He seized on alarmist articles in the daily press to support his theory, like the one in the *Daily News* in April 1883: 'It is impossible to overrate the mere social danger that is involved in the growth of such conditions of suffering and neglect as exist among the poorer class of London. If they were ever to be drawn together by some common cry against the rich we should be within measurable distance of social revolution.' But in spite of all his efforts income only just kept pace with needs, and the debt which the homes had incurred, although reduced, was not yet liquidated.

His work restricted by the tight financial control imposed by the committee and insisted on by Cairns, Barnardo's thoughts began to turn more and more towards the advantages that would result from a more vigorous emigration policy. From the earliest times, when suitable opportunities offered, Barnardo had sent children not only to Canada, mainly under the auspices of Annie McPherson's agency, but also to South Africa, Australia and New Zealand where ladies eager to acquire cheap domestic labour offered to form committees to take on the responsibility for placing children upon arrival. He had sent an unescorted detachment of boys to Australia in 1883, but was worried by the length of the journey and the demoralising effects on the children of life on board ship. The experiences of other agencies who had sent out youngsters were not encouraging, and Barnardo decided that until they could be supervised during the journey and cared for until placed out he would send only isolated cases in the custody of friends. The financial situation facing the homes made Australian emigration on any larger scale impossible, and although Barnardo hoped for years to travel there, Canada was the obvious country in which to start up this new branch of the work.

The advantage of emigration as a policy for rescue societies, with limited financial means and a seemingly limitless number of children in need of help and protection, was obvious. It cost less to equip, transport and place out a child in Canada than it did to maintain a child for a year in a home, and a child might need to be kept in the home for several years before finding employment. For evangelicals emigration had another big advantage. Children were not only removed from the morally and physically unhealthy surroundings of overcrowded cities, they were irrevocably separated from parents considered 'vicious and degraded', and the advantages for girls, so obviously vulnerable, were even more apparent: emigration represented the final solution. Children transplanted from the slums to Canada would flourish in the pure Canadian air, living simple, healthy lives as members of farmers' families, part of a God-fearing rural community where only inherent weakness in mind or body would stand between them and the promise of a new life.

The wonder is that Barnardo had not adopted emigration as a policy much earlier. From the first he had been an advocate of emigration as a means of dealing with unemployment. In a moment of rare candour he once admitted that one of the reasons he had not undertaken systematic emigration sooner was because he had no wish to enter a field so well tilled by others. There were already several well established emigration societies in existence. Maria Rye had been the first to start emigration work on a substantial scale. A woman of extra-ordinary physical stamina from a cultivated professional family, her interest in emigration had emerged as a result of her work for women. She had taken her first party of girls across the Atlantic in 1868, and from then on a steady stream of girls found their way to Canada through her agency. She was joined in 1869 by Annie McPherson, and although both ladies were pioneers of the emigration movement they kept their distance, consulting together only when necessary. Miss McPherson's example was soon followed by her youngest sister Louisa Birt. Encouraged and helped by Samuel Smith, she opened the Liverpool sheltering homes and started sending the children she rescued to Canada, initially to Nova Scotia. Through the generosity of the citizens of Belleville in Ontario, Miss McPherson was given a large house, Marchmont, in 1870 for use as a receiving home. Seven years later Mrs Birt also acquired a receiving home, Knowlton, in the eastern township of Quebec. A third sister, Rachel Merry, together with her husband and two sons, also became deeply involved in the work of juvenile emigration started by her two sisters.

Both Annie McPherson and Maria Rye had included in their parties pauper children, sent by boards of guardians. In 1874 the Local Government Board sent Andrew Doyle, one of their senior inspectors, to Canada to investigate the transport, treatment and placement of pauper children in the care of the two ladies. At the time of his investigation Doyle, one of the architects of indoor relief, was already sixty-five; he knew nothing of Canada and all his instincts would be against the inevitable informality and flexibility of the child emigration programme. The picture Doyle painted was not entirely black: very young children who were adopted rather than indentured often received a warm welcome from the families who sheltered them, farm boys were well trained and the staffs of the receiving homes fulfilled their obligations to the best of their ability. But children taken for their future usefulness were often over-worked and not given time for regular schooling; many were returned as 'too small', and their lack of physical strength would doom them to a series of abortive placements and future failure. There was no check on the amount of physical punishment administered for 'faults of character', and the girls were unpro-tected. Because there were no poor laws in Canada, the dis-tributing homes were the only havens to which the children could turn in times of sickness or distress, and they had no facilities to care for or train a child who failed to make the grade. Most significantly Doyle noted that although one of the main aims of the philanthropists was to erase the 'pauper taint' and so enable the children to make a fresh start in life, the fact that their labour was less well rewarded than that of their Canadian contemporaries had exactly the reverse effect, ensuring the continuation of the prevalent English notion that pauper chil-dren deserved less than the best of the community.

Doyle returned and reported to the board his view that the only justification for the policy was financial, and that it left the children overworked, underprotected, unbefriended and over-come by a sense of loneliness and feelings of home sickness.[6]

To send them as immigrants can be regarded not as a way of improving their position, but simply getting rid of them at a cheap rate . . . if they can be reasonably well prepared for service it is difficult to understand why they should be sent out of the country in which one hears from every household complaints of the dearth of domestic servants and of the want of young hands in various branches of industry.

After Doyle's adverse report, which resulted in the virtual suspension of pauper emigration, the number of children crossing the Atlantic during the remainder of the 1870s remained fairly constant at about five hundred.

By 1882 Barnardo could no longer afford to be deterred either by his personal dislike of competition or by the gloomy picture painted by Doyle. The intractable problems inherent in the economic situation forced him to consider ways of overcoming Doyle's objections and, where he could not, to close his eyes to the darker side of the story. Food was plentiful – farmers claimed they could feed a child as easily as a chicken – work was abundant, and the system of rural schools for which all children were eligible even made it possible to claim that children were scholars rather than workers. Fears that children might be overworked or ill-treated were partly overcome by the know-ledge that the conditions in which they had been living were so appalling that scarcely anything could be worse.

Another influential voice, that of Samuel Smith, joined the ranks of those prophesying disaster and pressing the merits of emigration and industrial training. Smith, the successful indus-trialist, had now become Liberal Member of Parliament for Liverpool. From the floor of the house he was able to press the cause of emigration, arguing that it 'provides a safety valve to tide over the troubles at home'. He it was who finally persuaded Barnardo to take the plunge and set up his own emigration scheme, giving him a special donation to be used for that purpose only. This gesture was reminiscent of the action he had taken in Barnardo's early days, when he sent money for an evangelistic hall on condition that Barnardo gave up his plan to go to China and remained in London. In a much-quoted article in the *Contemporary Review* in 1885 he wrote,[7] 'I am deeply con-vinced that the time is approaching when this seething mass of human misery will shake the social fabric, unless we grapple more earnestly with it than we have yet done.' His solution was emigration and the extension of a system of industrial training for all children, 'which already obtains in the best of our district schools, in the reformatory and industrial schools and in very many private institutions, such as Barnardo's admirable homes in the East of London'.

Smith's offer was one that Barnardo could not resist. With more and more destitute children begging for admittance, straitened financial circumstances meant that Barnardo was now seldom able to seek out children and could scarcely even carry out his policy of unrestricted admission to all who applied to his door, even though they were absolutely destitute. His aggressive expansionist style made it imperative for him to find new outlets. The vacancies left by the children who went to Canada would immediately allow him to receive, at no extra cost, others still homeless and destitute.

Barnardo's first official party to Canada consisted of a hundred carefully selected boys. He had them photographed at Stepney, kitted out in thick jackets and trousers, their heads covered with sensible caps with ear flaps; their possessions packed in strong wooden boxes, they were led along the platform at Euston by the boys' band from Stepney. They embarked at Liverpool and crossed the Atlantic in the *Parisien* under the care of the governor of the Boys' Home, Frederick Fielder. Barnardo was lent the distributing home in Hamilton, Ontario, which had been given to Bowman Stephenson, founder of the Children's Home, by Methodist sympathisers in Canada. Soon Barnardo had the satisfaction of reporting to his committee that all the boys had been placed out and Fielder was on his way back. Encouraged by the success of this first party, Barnardo sent out another group of boys the following year. He engaged Alfred de Brissac Owen, an Anglican minister's son who had lived in Canada for several years, to be his agent in the dominion. With his help and cooperation of the dominion and provincial government agents, situations were again found for all the boys. An advisory committee was formed under the chairmanship of the Hon. S. H. Blake QC, perhaps a legal friend of Cairns, to watch over the interests of this new branch of the work.

In 1883 Barnardo's first party of girls left for Canada under the care of Miss Emily Morecroft. A month later George Cox,[8] then president of the Midland Railway Company, placed rent-free at Barnardo's disposal a spacious timber-framed house standing in six acres of grounds on the outskirts of Peterborough, a pleasant small town a few hours distant from Toronto. Barnardo regarded this gift of 'Hazelbrae', as the house was called, as an unmistakable sign that God's hand was directing the work. He had never met Cox but as he was both a wealthy and an influential citizen his support, and the support of his wife, was invaluable at this juncture. Hazelbrae served

5   Hazelbrae, the distributing home for girls, Peterborough, Ontario

first as the distributing home for all Barnardo's children, but soon he realised that he needed more space and premises were rented in Farley Avenue, Toronto, which became the head-quarters of the Canadian work. Farley Avenue served as the distributing centre for the boys and Hazelbrae was used only for girls.

Two years after his first party of boys had set out for Canada, Barnardo informed his committee of his intention of going to Canada himself to organise the work. The committee approved. Several of them had experience of Canadian affairs and were aware that, in spite of the welcome extended to the youngsters for their potential future usefulness, there was a groundswell of opposition to the idea of the wholesale importation of children, regarded as the discarded offspring of city slums and a potential medical and social threat to the communities in which they lived.

The idea of acquiring land in Manitoba not too far from the recently opened railroad terminal at Winnipeg was discussed, and Barnardo was authorised in 1884 to write to Sir Charles Tupper, the newly appointed Canadian High Commissioner, asking for a grant of land on which to start an industrial farm. Tupper was a remarkable man. The son of a Baptist minister, he was a close personal and political friend of the Canadian Prime Minister, Macdonald, and had fought long and hard to bring his own province, Nova Scotia, into the Federation in 1867. Before coming to London as High Commissioner he had been in charge first of railways and then of public works in Macdonald's cabinet. Explaining that the land was needed so that the farm under the direction of a suitable bailiff would train forty or fifty lads for a year, Barnardo wrote that on leaving they would then be bound to accept any situation that was found for them. He asked that in due course they might be given the same promises of grants of land which were made to all emigrants under certain conditions. It was a bold and imaginative plan, boldly stated:[9]

I need hardly point out the great advantages of a society like ours undertaking such work. First our lads would not be deserted and allowed to fight each one the battle for himself. In a new country like Manitoba where the weather in the winter is so very severe and where even a small amount of capital seems absolutely necessary in order to a Colonist becoming independent, it must be of the greatest possible advantage to immigrants of the class I refer to, that they should have a powerful institution as their friend who would be disposed under certain conditions, afterwards to be developed, to advance them a small capital as a loan so as to enable those who are able, to avail themselves of any allotment of land that would come to them as emigrants, to attempt work in the future on their own behalf.

We would, of course, undertake to send out no lads but those of thoroughly approved character, without vicious habits, or indeed any habits likely to be detrimental to their future. Thus in time our institution at Manitoba would, like those we have planted in other parts of the world, become noted for the character of its inmates and the thorough quality of the work done by them.

Barnardo was as always extremely cost-conscious, and asked if the dominion would be prepared to defray the cost of the fare to Winnipeg, which at that time came to something like £2. 8s. a head; for without such a subsidy the whole plan would be too expensive. He also made it clear that he was prepared to accept only the best land and, if the dominion Government was not prepared to cooperate, he threatened to look across the border for the help he needed. It is interesting to note his new relationship with the committee:

My Committee, some of whom have considerable Canadian experience, would not be prepared to accept any land which might be allotted to them by Government.

They would ask, if their proposal was favourably entertained, that they might have the option of choice as it is notorious that much of the land would be unfit for the purpose, whereas other portions of it in special localities would be exceedingly admirable. As the chief support of the Manitoba branch, if established (after the first two years), will be derived, it is hoped, from the cultivation of the land which would be granted, it would be of the greatest importance to us that such land should be of first rate quality and situated in the most favourable position. As my Committee are advised we consider that from 3,000 to 5,000 acres would probably be needed for the purpose of an institution in which from 40 to 50 lads or young men would be constantly kept while others were being passed through the Home over the province . . .

Should the Dominion Government not feel free to co-operate with us to the extent or in the manner we desire, or to such an extent as would make it advisable for us to attempt an enterprise of that character, I am instructed to make my way to the United States and there endeavour to obtain land in such positions as may best meet the requirements of our growing institutions.

Sir Charles Tupper, who was sympathetic to the idea of emigration, suggested that Barnardo should make contact directly with the president of the Canadian Pacific Railway and the Canadian Minister of Agriculture, the Hon. J. M. Pope, when he arrived in Ottawa.[10] He gave him letters of introduction to the minister, who, he thought, would be favourably disposed towards the idea of such a farm. Tupper warned, however, that in asking for five thousand acres they were expecting a lot of the Government.

Two members of the committee had taken over the responsibility for counselling the staff, and Frederick Fielder was in charge at Stepney, leaving Barnardo free to concentrate on the work to be done in Canada. He left Liverpool on 17 July and his first Canadian visit lasted over three months. The weather was fine, and Barnardo who was normally a bad sailor was able to enjoy the voyage and catch up with his work. On arrival he went straight to Hazelbrae and from there made as many visits to surrounding homesteads as he could fit into the time, to see how his children were faring in their new homes. He found much to encourage him, although, 'all employers were not equally pleased with the children, nor are all our children equally satisfactory in their demeanour and conduct ... but cases of dissatisfaction are by far in the minority; the general rule is that of great pleasure, great satisfaction, and thankfulness in having a little maid from our "Home" '.

The major part of his time was spent in the North West looking for a suitable location for the proposed industrial farm. Through the introductions given by the High Commissioner in London, Barnardo was able to travel free on the newly completed Canadian Pacific and Grand Trunk Railways. He travelled to Winnipeg and from there to the township of Russell where the endless flat tracts of prairie land were being carved into squares and allocated to settlers. Having carefully surveyed the surrounding countryside and not without difficulty chosen the land, he journeyed on through Saskatchewan across the prairies to the Rocky Mountains, noting many curious facts which he carefully recorded for future use:[11]

In travelling through Canada, one frequently sees vast tracts which have been burned over – sometimes such fires are the result of carelessness or wanton destruction. But often where wood is plentiful and labour scarce, the owners of land clear it by firing brushwood. If the wind is favourable, the flames are speedily carried to a great distance, and very often much further than was originally intended which does much harm. The strange appearance of desolation and ruin which meets the traveller on surveying immense tracts of country which have been burnt over and are covered with the charred stumps of trees is very striking.

Returning to Toronto, he started the lengthy negotiations that were an inevitable precondition of the final acquisition of the land.

Blake, the chairman of the Canadian committee, acted as his host for part of the time. Besides speaking at meetings, Barnardo was almost immediately called upon to defend his emigration policy for, as he discovered, there was widespread suspicion in Canada that emigration societies were solely concerned with collecting the debris of the great cities of England and 'dumping' them in the dominion. From Toronto, which he described as one of the most progressive cities he had visited in Canada and which reminded him of a 'flourishing English city of the second class', he went on to Chicago, New York and Boston. In New York he was looked after by Moody and took part with him in meetings which he was holding in Brooklyn and Boston. He did not waste any time while he was there, visiting nearly all the leading philanthropic institutions dealing with the care and instruction of destitute children.

In all three cities he made a point of visiting the 'worst haunts of the vicious and degraded'. A detective officer was his guide in Chicago, and although a smaller place than New York, what the Chicago 'hells' lacked in quantity and diffuseness compared with New York 'dives' they more than made up in 'quality and concentration of badness'. 'More unblushing wickedness is carried on in that city, with a high hand, without concealment or disguise, than I noticed elsewhere.' He judged both worse in some respects than the slums of London, for there at least Victorian ethics kept the worst excesses of its citizens somewhat veiled from the public gaze. Despite this stricture, Barnardo could not help but be impressed by Chicago; the thriving business community, the pushing enterprise of its citizens and their money-making abilities appealed to the entrepreneurial side of his nature. It was also Moody's home town and although the evangelist no longer lived there, having moved to North-field, Barnardo found it an emotional experience to stand on the platform in Moody's church where 'that earnest servant of the Lord had so often preached, whose voice like Peter the Hermit of old, has aroused two worlds to the new crusade'. He felt that he met some of the 'noblest Christian men' and some of the most successful philanthropists during his stay, and there is a note of envious admiration in his words: one has the feeling that he would have found himself very much at home in Chicago. But worrying news now arrived and made him cut short his visit. During his absence, not only had the financial situation of the homes deteriorated but Frederick Fielder, the man on whom Barnardo most relied, had accepted an offer to become the master of the Lambeth Union and had left his post.

On his return he was welcomed back by an enormous gathering of over four thousand at the rebuilt Edinburgh Castle and the meeting, under the chairmanship of Samuel Sheppard, listened avidly while he spoke for two hours of his transatlantic adventures. In some ways 1884 can be regarded as one of the most satisfactory years. In spite of seasonal financial problems, income was increasing, the total number of children in care had nearly doubled since the dark days of the arbitration, and the number that the organisation would be able to help in the future would be greatly increased by emigration. The devastating news that the fabric of the Edinburgh Castle was in such poor condition that the whole building needed to be pulled down and rebuilt had been turned into a triumph. As at the time of its acquisition, money was gladly subscribed and both the laying of the foundation stones and the opening of the rebuilt Edinburgh Castle were occasions for much public rejoicing. At the opening ceremony an unnamed clergyman noted 'that there were some who saw in the very presence of the Earl Cairns at the afternoon meeting one of the best arguments which could be used in support of Dr. Barnardo's Work'. He also noted that the most interesting feature and the most marked in Barnardo's own address was his acknowledgement of the assistance he had had from others, and most especially from Samuel Sheppard. Both H. W. Webb-Peploe and C. H. Spurgeon spoke, but as the unknown minister left the hall and walked towards the railway station he regretted 'that our own beloved church was not wise enough in its generation to discern the excellencies of such a movement among the masses of the people, and not quicker to lend its official approval and recognition to men so evidently qualified for the ministry of the Word'.

Emigration was not the only innovation that Barnardo introduced in the 1880s. Boarding children out in the country had long been known of in England, but it had been relatively little used either by boards of guardians or charitable organisations, although in Scotland it was done systematically and had proved both efficient and satisfactory. Barnardo had been experimenting with the system and had come to the conclusion that not only was it advantageous for the child, but it was also cheaper and if properly developed would allow him to admit more children. To begin with he only boarded out orphan children and those of tender years, but by 1886 he announced that this method of caring for children had become a separate branch of the work, one which was to grow with amazing rapidity. Within five years he was dealing with well over a thousand children annually in this way, and there was nothing haphazard about his methods. No children were ever boarded out with irreligious parents, however worthy; the districts to which they were sent had to be healthy and the sanitary conditions in the homes satisfactory. The centres chosen for boarding out were, ideally, as distant as possible from factories and railway stations, and the foster parents were in the main cottagers and working people.

Local committees were formed with a clergyman or some influential lady at their head to undertake visitation and inspection. Not satisfied with that, Barnardo appointed his own agent, a fully qualified 'medical woman' as Dr Jane Walker, his first inspector, was quaintly termed. In her first report she listed the advantages of boarding out:[12] it was the most economical way of disposing of children, the cost of £13 to £14 a year being considerably less than that of maintaining the same child in an institution; it was better for the children physically and gave them the kind of home life most of them had never known; it was a help to the villagers, making a nice addition to their wages and at the same time lessening the population in the denser parts of London.

Three years later a special auxiliary boarding-out scheme was introduced by Barnardo to help the infant offspring of unmarried mothers. This was a very enlightened step to take, for many charities and orphanages refused to accept any illegitimate children at all, for fear that it would prove an incentive to licentiousness. The mothers were offered help graduated according to their ability to pay. The scheme was set up to help young women who had 'gone astray' once and, in his practical way, Barnardo considered it a far wiser policy to help care for the child while at the same time doing all that was possible to foster the young mother's love for her baby. If however a second child made its appearance, the contractual arrangements between the mother and Barnardo were terminated. Although this policy was inaugurated in 1889, the subject was so delicate that there was no public reference to it until 1902. By using boarding out and emigration to supplement the means he already had at his disposal for rescuing children from the streets, Barnardo in five years almost managed to triple the number of children he could admit.

12

Private Interests and Public Good

As Barnardo's stature as a public personality grew, it becomes increasingly difficult to disentangle his private life from his public interests. In the year preceding the arbitration another son, Herbert, had been born to the Barnardos, and in the following year Kenward, a boy named after an eccentric Elmslie uncle, was born. In July 1879 Mrs Barnardo gave birth to their first daughter, Gwendoline Maud Syrie, who from an early age was known to her family as Queenie. She held a very special place in the affections of her father. The birth had not been an easy one and Syrie was ill for several weeks afterwards. The little house in Bow Road was now bursting at the seams with four children in the family and a full complement of servants and nurses.

Syrie's illness after the birth of her baby daughter made them decide that for the sake of the family they must move out of the unhealthy East End. They took a house not far away in Banbury Road, South Hackney, where they were to live for the next seventeen years. Hackney was at that time a fashionable suburban village and had long been a centre of nonconformity, so the Barnardos would have felt at home there. 'The Cedars' was a large, plain, rather ugly house, but it was close to Victoria Park. The children now had a walled garden in which to play and the surroundings were a great deal more salubrious than the cramped conditions in which they had lived in Newbury House. There Barnardo had often used the back parlour as his study, but after the move he decided that he could no longer work from home. Readers of *Night and Day* were told that in future all his correspondence would be dealt with from Stepney. It was at this time also that he rented business premises at number 279 in the Strand and set up an editorial office; a reading room was attached which supplied the public with suitable periodicals and books. The family were hardly settled in their new home before Barnardo was off again on his travels, delivering evangelistic addresses in towns all over England and Scotland and holding meetings wherever he could be sure of an audience, to speak of the work being done in the homes. The pleasures of family life were never allowed to interfere with the needs of Barnardo's larger family, and during the next few months he was frequently away, his preaching and appeals bringing profit to both himself and the homes.

The problem of separating Barnardo's private affairs from his philanthropic enterprises remains one of great complexity. Mossford Lodge, to begin with, was both his private residence and a girls' home, the girls being cared for in the coach house, the Barnardos living in the main building. In 1875 the house in Oliver Terrace where they had lived when they first moved to London was taken over by the mission and fitted up as a home for Barnardo's deaconesses, women who wished to devote themselves to good works, visiting the poor and, where appropriate, relieving distress. They held Bible classes for men and boys and sewing meetings for mothers and factory girls. The deaconesses in their distinctive costumes – simple dark dresses and bonnets tied under the chin with short veils behind – were immediately identifiable; serviceable and appropriate, their dress gave them protection and ensured them a welcome in the homes they visited.[1]

The deaconess movement can probably be said to have originated with Pastor Fleidner at Kaiserworth where Florence Nightingale finally persuaded her family to allow her to start her training. William Pennefather had started a missionary training college for women at Barnet, and after he moved to St Jude's the deaconesses of Mildmay Park became well known in Protestant evangelical circles. Many of Barnardo's future staff and co-workers were to come from among the ranks of his deaconesses. Barnardo has left, in the form of a dream, a good description of the kind of person he was hoping to attract to the work. The story, entitled 'A dream and a decision',[2] opened with Barnardo sitting in his armchair by the fireside, becoming drowsy and falling into an uneasy doze. He then, in his own words, 'had one of those brief and vivid dreams which so often accompany partial sleep', which cannot but have called to mind a similar occasion when Clerical Junius, waiting for what was to come from the fertile pen of 'Protestant Dissenter', was sent 'off in front of my pleasant fire into a sound sleep . . .'. On that occasion the results of the dream were devastating; this time the dream was designed to reinforce the idea that a number of Christian ladies might like to give their services free to the East End Juvenile Mission in return for a comfortable home in which to live. In his dream Barnardo described a young woman, whose father had died and whose mother had gone to live with a married sister, and who was dissatisfied with the idea of going to look after an uncle already well supplied with servants. In the dream the young woman finally decided that the only way she could be happy was to devote her life to helping and consoling the poor by becoming a deaconess.

Barnardo did not intend Deaconess House to be seen merely as a boarding house for ladies willing to work, but as a centre where a family of sisters with common interests and objects, who were willing to surrender individual freedom of action and submit to the rules of the house, would live together. Those who could afford to do so were encouraged to pay for their keep. Syrie, having given up her responsibilities at Mossford Lodge, was to have been in sole charge of the establishment, but this arrangement did not last long. Within a year a Miss Dudley was appointed 'Lady Superintendent' and took over the running of Deaconess House.

The last official references to Syrie in *Night and Day* showed that by 1878 the only public responsibility Barnardo allowed her to retain was a gospel flower mission which she ran from Deaconess House. Letters from her appealing for flowers to those with conservatories and gardens, asking that they should send them in hampers at specially reduced rates for distribution among the poor, remained a regular feature of *Night and Day* for some time. It could be that Syrie's increasing family responsibilities precluded her from taking as active a role in running the mission as had originally been envisaged. She had also shown herself to be extravagant and a bad manager at home, and these were faults which caused Barnardo much secret anxiety. Although he could equally well be charged with extravagance, his took the form of responding to needs without the necessary financial support. His administrative abilities were unquestioned. His method of accounting for funds was publicly acknowledged to be clear and concise. The detailed attention he gave to this aspect of the work is shown in the report for 1877; it lists sixteen thousand separate donations ranging from 4d. to £1,000, and it took over one hundred and forty pages to record; the auditor's report attached to this summary was given in just six words: 'Examined the books and found correct.' Even if Syrie's extravagant housekeeping had not alarmed and worried Barnardo he was constitutionally unable to share responsibility. As the stronger character of the two it is unlikely that he would for long have allowed Syrie to have complete control of any aspect of the work. He had surmounted the crisis of 1877, but the 1880s were to bring new difficulties of a more personal kind.

His increasing family responsibilities and the style of living which Syrie thought appropriate to their status imposed a terrible financial burden on Barnardo. His magazine *The Children's Treasury,* which had done so well in the early years, suffered a catastrophic decline in circulation. The magazine provides yet another example of the way in which Barnardo combined his private and public interests. Its full title was *The Children's Treasury and Advocate of the Homeless and Destitute,* and the front cover announced that it was conducted by Dr Barnardo of the East End Juvenile Mission. Yet it was a private commercial undertaking and a considerable financial success. That this was so is a tribute to Barnardo's skill as a journalist, as few if any other children's magazines were run at a profit at that date and most were heavily subsidised.

However, the advent of *Night and Day* had serious consequences for the magazine. Barnardo remained as editor of both, working long hours to ensure that both were instructive, informative and well produced. *Night and Day* was financed from the general funds of the institutions and its objectives were to publicise all the work done by the various branches, to stimulate Christians to greater efforts and to prove that Christianity was not mere sentiment but a vital energetic thing producing practical results among the sinful, sorrowing and suffering. As such it was effective and its circulation was extensive, but it was never a success in the way *The Children's Treasury* had been – although financial success in an undertaking of this kind cannot always be measured in strict commercial terms and it is impossible to know how many donations and gifts resulted from its appeals. It did, however, have the grave disadvantage of undermining the circulation of *The Children's Treasury,* on which Barnardo depended to a large extent for his income.

By 1881 *The Children's Treasury* was losing so heavily that Barnardo stopped publication and in November of that year announced the advent of a new illustrated children's magazine entitled *Our Darlings,* more lavishly produced and which he hoped would appeal to the readers of *Night and Day* as suitable for their children. This new publication, in spite of the careful thought that went into it, never began to make money. Besides editing the two magazines, Barnardo was writing regularly for the newspapers, and his accounts of life in the East End and his stories found a ready market in *The Echo,* the London evening paper, and other journals. He was intending to expand his literary activities further when something went wrong. Either his agent mismanaged his affairs or absconded with the funds – the details are not known – but Barnardo found himself throughout 1882 and into 1883 in the greatest financial embarrassment. Syrie's father, William Elmslie, had died two years previously and his modest assets had been entirely left to Syrie's mother; and as Barnardo's own father had been dead for eight years and his mother was now running the fur business in partnership with his youngest brother Lionel, there was no one within the family to whom they could turn for help. Had Barnardo's supporters known of his financial difficulties there is no doubt that there would have been many instant offers of help. After the gruelling experience of the arbitration, when Barnardo was required to account for every penny he received and to admit that during his early years in London he was dependent on the generosity of friends, such a course was out of the question. But it was only as the last resort and after nights of anguish and worry that he reluctantly wrote to his trustees. More than anything he regretted giving up his proud independence and acknowledging that if he was to continue to perform his public duties as Director his private interests must be safeguarded. The letter he wrote to Harry Nisbet speaks for itself:[3]

It is with great sorrow of heart I write to announce that I must at once give up my independent and honorary position in connection with the

'Homes' and to request you, as one of the earliest Trustees and (although now no longer a Trustee) yet as a solicitor and adviser of the Trustees, to place before them the necessity, if I am to continue my work as hitherto, of allotting me a sufficient annual stipend, for the next three or four years at all events . . . Nor could I ever bring myself to accept the gifts, which I have no doubt would be freely offered by good people all over the world if my position were known . . . Indeed I have always felt that to be for me an impossible, as it has happily been hitherto an unnecessary course. Every year I am offered personal gifts, which I invariably return to the kind donors, never once having departed from the rule laid down many years ago for the governance of my conduct in this respect. Painful and distressing, therefore, as it will be to take even one shilling from the 'Homes' on which I would, God knows, rather spend and be spent, yet no other honourable course seems open to me, if I am to recover the ground, unhappily lost, through no fault or improvidence of my own, but by the dishonesty or folly of others. Only one thing remains to be said: I ought to have written the foregoing weeks ago, but 'hoped against hope' that I might be spared the necessity. Now I see plainly there is no help for it and I can only ask you kindly to take the earliest opportunity of making so much of this communication known in the proper quarters as you think fit or to advise me otherwise if you think my application injudicious in any respect.

The trustees responded instantly with an offer of financial help, but Barnardo, having once been the recipient of alms, would never again allow himself to be put in that position, and answered firmly that he saw nothing dishonourable in asking for a definite salary even if he had to receive it from the hands of the committee; at the same time he gave vent to his real feelings about colleagues who had followed Müller's example and had frowned on those who made direct appeals:

I have always had a very strong feeling about the race of philanthropists and Evangelists generally who live 'on faith and postage stamps'.

A salary I can take, if it is granted, so long as the urgent necessity for it exists, and while doing so can lift up my head and look the world in the face, but I could not accept contributions without feelings of positive humiliation. Pray don't call this mere pride. I really don't think it deserves that opprobrious name, although I grant it may seem not easy how else to describe it, but I imagine you will understand what I feel.

Thomas Pelham, who knew and understood Barnardo perhaps

better than anyone and who was both trustee and committee member, brought the matter to the attention of the committee of management. The request was considered privately, and a note written in Samuel Sheppard's hand was added to the minutes for April 1883:[4] 'The Chairman read a letter received from T. Pelham referring to Dr. Barnardo's request for a yearly salary. It was resolved that the Committee gladly embraces this opportunity of expressing their deep appreciation of his long continued, valuable and gratuitous service and vote £600 per year.'

Barnardo was never able to revert to his former status as Honorary Director. Able and energetic as he was, there is no doubt that had he had the time to work for himself he could have been a rich man. All his energies went into raising money for the institutions. During the years while Cairns was alive, the committee invariably met his requests with the proviso that if he could raise funds then land could be bought or a new piece of work started, which put him under tremendous pressure. At this date he had no one to share the burden with; the entire responsibility for what today would be the work of an appeals department rested on Barnardo alone. There is no doubt that he enjoyed public speaking, and whether evangelising or talking of the work of the homes he derived great satisfaction from addressing large audiences; the knowledge that his appeals might not only induce his audience to give him the support he needed, but that they could effectively alter the lives of some of his listeners, gave him that sense of power which his nature demanded.

He rationalised this need to dominate by his unquestioning belief that as an instrument in God's hands he had a divine mandate, so duty and inclination together produced a formidable combination. A short-lived attempt as a diarist – the entries cover only a few days in 1882 – show that the confident, assertive exterior concealed more doubts and anxieties than the always careful, well-dressed appearance the Doctor presented to the world suggested, and that he was himself aware of this aspect of his nature. The diary was begun in November while away on a visit to friends at Westbridge in the Isle of Wight:[5]

23rd November 1882
Am greatly troubled to-day by reflections as to the want of purpose, plan or method in my life. So much is vague, diffuse and indefinite

'beating the air', the rest too hurried to be strong. Think may correct some of this by making daily entries of duties performed ...
   The Lord also give a purer life. Am too vain, idle and self indulgent. Strangely enough at times also too self conscious leading to depression – the whole doubtless springing from vanity. Yet how little to be proud of! Sometimes my conscious inferiority as a workman of any sort is overwhelming; then upon the crest of some poor wave of temporary success forget the previous humbling lesson and imagine myself as always successful.

The diary then becomes no more than a catalogue of engagements and daily routine, but it leaves an impression of almost frenetic activity. Having spoken at a YMCA meeting in Ryde the night of his arrival, he spent the next morning talking with a friend of the family who had difficulties with errant nephews. After a drive, when Barnardo was much delighted to be allowed to act as coachman to a pair of horses, he addressed a meeting of young women which lasted three hours: 'Speakers unconscionably wearisome – I also. Home at 9.30; very tired, tea; worship, reading till 2 a.m. Bed.' The number of hours Barnardo spent at meetings, speaking but also listening to the interminable speeches of his fellow orators, must have amounted to a considerable proportion of his waking time and contributed to his frequent feelings of fatigue. The final entry on 28 November after his return to London reads:

Very tired; could not rise till 9.30. Breakfast in bed. Afterwards letters and secretary till 12.30. Willis's rooms to meet engineer, how slow and inert these people are. Nisbet re Smith's action [Nisbet was his solicitor]. Burts: No N & D [Night and Day] posted. Office till 6.30; at correction; then to E.C. [Edinburgh Castle] saw candidates for church membership till 8 o'clock. Presided over temperance. Needham, Groves and H. Guinness Jnr. spoke – the latter very well; most refreshingly and wonderfully like his father; made a great impression. Numbers took pledge. Home 10.30; tired. Supper. Read till 2.30. Bed.

Syrie, co-editing Barnardo's memoirs after his death, with James Marchant, stressed what a wonderfully kind and tender husband he was but he cannot have been an easy man to live with. It is difficult to form any clear impression of their relationship, though it is obvious that the working partnership that was once envisaged did not endure. Barnardo held very strong views about the fundamental importance of family life, and in his public writings he never ceased to emphasise the importance he attached to the part women had to play in the care and nurture of young children. Because of his frequent absences from home the major responsibility for the children's upbringing devolved on Syrie. Hers must have been a somewhat lonely life, and it cannot have been altogether easy for his children to have had to share their father with such an enormous family, to whom he devoted so much of his time and energy. His own hectic schedule of work, interviews, travel and public speaking left him little time for home life and the enjoyment of his own children. He arrived home late, and more often than not exhausted. His persistent insomnia meant that he often read until the early hours of the morning. He demanded a lot from his children and expected them to be obedient, punctual and affectionate and to accept, as part of their lives, the strict evangelical discipline of family prayers and Bible reading, always hoping that they would come to share his own deep faith, and as he would have put it, 'yield their own selves unto the Lord'.

He is said seldom to have joked in public, and his brand of humour in private seems often to have been at someone else's expense, not least his wife's. If the letter to a friend quoted in *The Memoirs* is representative, he did not spare her feelings. Writing of an occasion when Syrie had obviously failed to handle a meeting to her husband's satisfaction, Barnardo appeared to imply that the very idea of her even opening a bazaar was now a subject for mirth.[6]

It is still a standing joke with us at home that my wife is to go down to open a bazaar in my place and to give an eloquent address! She turns very red in the face when I remind her of the eloquent words she uttered on a certain occasion in Leicester. After that the whole incident ends in a peal of laughter in which the poor creature has to join as heartily as I do.

He then adds with amazing smugness, 'so you may guess, however many my infirmities, the sense of humour is not yet quite dead within me'.

A photograph of Syrie taken at this time shows her as a serious young woman, her hair drawn back, wearing a dark

dress with a demure lace collar and surrounded by three plump
and solemn little boys in sailor suits with Queenie, ringleted and
round-faced, sitting on her mother's knee. Soon after that
photograph was taken Syrie became pregnant again and in 1882
gave birth to another son, Baby Tom, as he was known, who
lived only a few weeks. His sufferings during those few weeks
were watched over by his anxious family and his death was the
first of several family tragedies. Barnardo, who seldom obtruded
family concerns into the pages of *Night and Day*, sadly recorded
the death of the baby. A worse tragedy followed two years later
when Herbert, aged nine, a quiet and dreamy child, died of
diphtheria. Barnardo faced the bereavement by throwing himself even more energetically into the work of saving children
from destitution.[7]

As may be imagined, this loss has only intensified my desire to
continue with what earnestness I can, that work of child rescue
committed to my care. As my dear boy lay gasping in my arms, and I
gazed into the little pinched face, growing cold in death, hundreds of
other child faces appealed to me through his, while other wistful eyes
looked out at me by the waning light of his dear eyes. I could but
resolve afresh, as I then did, that, by God's Grace, I would consecrate
myself anew to the blessed task of rescuing helpless little ones from the
miseries of a neglected and sinful life. *Now I know the vows of God are
on me.*

Barnardo had known for some years that he had been driving
himself too hard and that his frequent bouts of ill health and the
periodic fits of depression from which he suffered were the
result of overwork. But he was temperamentally unable to alter
his way of life, and the fresh demands he made on himself
following Herbert's death resulted in a breakdown in his health,
whereupon he was advised by his doctors to give up all his work
and go to the South of France to recuperate. But as soon as he
began to recover he felt guilty, 'lingering among the idlers who
bask in luxurious ease on the Mediterranean coast', as he put it,
but salved his conscience by taking a meeting at the Hôtel
Alsace and Lorraine where he was staying in Cannes and collecting £130 in aid of the homes before returning to Stepney
after an absence of three weeks. Even when he was travelling on
the continent for recreation or for the sake of his health, Syrie
does not appear to have accompanied him. He was an assiduous

correspondent. Drawn by a sort of compulsion to investigate the less agreeable aspects of every town he visited, Rome was the one exception which he found interesting and soul-stirring. Naples he thought the wickedest city he had ever known, and describing it to Syrie he wrote:[8]

> Never in any place that I have visited have I seen wickedness of such a disgusting nature as stalks here unabashed. Horrible and revolting in character, it is moreover so brazen, so undisguised, so flaunting that one feels as if the fate of Sodom must become that of Naples. As I walked through the public places and witnessed the sights and heard the sounds which met eye and ear on every side, I could not help feeling the very curse of God were resting upon the place and wondering why it was Vesuvius did not belch forth the flame and ashes at her heart to destroy so wicked a city and cover up from common view such a nest of infamy.

Barnardo was a natural leader and he could exert authority over both adults and children seemingly without effort. An example of the effect he could make by his presence alone was given by one of his old boys. Describing a mutiny at the labour house which the superintendent had been unable to control because of the strict injunction against corporal punishment, he narrated how Barnardo arrived unexpectedly while they were all at tea.[9]

> The first intimation we had of his presence came from himself. We were making rather more noise than we were justified in doing when suddenly a sharp commanding voice called out the one word 'silence!' The voice was enough to establish his identity had we not seen the slight figure – rather below the average height – which stood motionless at the head of the stairs, and the handsome face with the bright piercing eyes glancing from behind the glasses. If anyone else had told us to be silent in our present mood we would have openly defied the order and he who gave it. With the Doctor it was different; his very presence conveyed power. Slowly he walked up the length of the dining hall, glancing with those keen penetrating eyes into the downcast faces of the boys seated at the tables as he proceeded. At the upper end of the hall stood a small platform where the master in charge used to stand. This was occupied by the Superintendent with whom the Doctor exchanged a few words, after which he seized hold of a chair, stood it on the platform and mounted it. By this time we had finished our tea and at the word rose to our feet and stood to attention, the majority of us waiting in fear and trembling for the sentence we expected and fully deserved. When the Doctor started speaking there

was not the slightest suggestion of sternness in his tone. He spoke as he might have spoken to his own children at home, kindly and easily ... suffice it to say that the most callous among us felt thoroughly ashamed and not a few of us were moved to tears by the Doctor's few simple impressive words.

After he had dismissed us we went down into the big yard and held a meeting among ourselves at which we agreed to forgo our weekly money allowance until the windows were mended and other damage repaired. Some of our members were also told off to apologise to the Superintendent for our recent rudeness to him. All this was voluntary on our part. It was not commanded or expected.

Like so many Victorian social reformers, Barnardo found himself by the very nature of his work concerned with the moral problem of prostitution. He understood more than most that prostitution was part of a larger system of economic and social exploitation of women; to him the battle against prostitution was a war against evil. Unable to escape from the double standards of the respectable Victorian world, fallen women could only be considered as vicious and degraded, so tainted by sin that they were forced to become outsiders, mixing only with their kind, their patrons and those involved in what may be called 'the social purity movement', if the disparate collection of reformers who wished to change social attitudes about sex can be so called. For most purity reformers the goal was the achievement of a single standard of sexual morality for men and women. The standard was high: men were to conform to the standards of chastity Victorian society enjoined on women. Since prostitution played an important role in the life of the East End, it was inevitable, given the conditions of chronic overcrowding that prevailed generally and the precocious maturity of working-class children, that child prostitution was widespread and that from an early age working-class girls were exploited and abused. On a political level the campaign of the 1860s and 1870s against the Contagious Diseases Act, which Josephine Butler saw as a move to bring in a degree of state regulation implying the acceptance of prostitution as inevitable, was the start of the campaign to arouse the moral conscience of the nation.

Alfred Dyer, a publisher who specialised in books and pamphlets related to the cause of 'social purity', was the first to crystallise opposition to child prostitution. He chose to attack on a narrow front, but the consequences of his assault were to be far-reaching. He produced evidence that there was traffic in English girls to state-regulated brothels in Belgium, Holland and France, and with the support of Benjamin Scott, who was at that time Chamberlain of the City of London, the 'London Committee for the Suppression of the traffic in British girls for the purposes of continental prostitution' was formed. By the early eighties the aroused reformers had pressurised the Government into appointing a select committee of the House of Lords to investigate 'the laws relating to the protection of young girls from artifices to induce them to lead a corrupt life and into the means of amending the same'. The Home Office appointed a barrister named Thomas Snagge to make an independent investigation of the allegations about the abduction of English girls to continental brothels. His report fully substantiated the allegations, and in the face of the irrefutable evidence he produced, the Criminal Law Amendment Bill was drafted. This would have raised the age of consent from thirteen to sixteen and widened police powers against brothels and procurers. In spite of all the publicity and pressure, opposition to the Bill remained strong not least because many upper-class men not endowed with a puritan conscience considered prostitution to be both necessary and inevitable. As one member of the House of Lords put it in 1884, when successfully opposing the Bill:[10] 'Very few of their Lordships ... had not, when young men, been guilty of immorality. He hoped they would pause before passing a clause within the range of which their sons might come.'

Apart from exerting political pressure, the evangelicals involved in the social purity movement used their considerable powers of personal persuasion in the fight against moral corruption. Given the double standards prevalent at the time, the unconscious motives of those engaged in moral reform may well be open to question, but that said, the strength and sincerity of the evangelical reformers is undeniable. The story of the sexual exploitation of children revealed by all those engaged in reform was irrefutable, and it remains as horrifying today as it was in the 1880s.

Barnardo's interest and involvement in the problem was

not limited to the saving of female children from the dangers that awaited them in the streets and lodging houses – it extended to their 'fallen' elders. Like Baptist Noel, whose 'moonlight meetings' were a feature of the evangelical approach to prostitution, Barnardo held special meetings and in the course of his wanderings through the East End was familiar with many of the haunts where the women lived and plied their trade. It seems doubtful that either political pressure or moral persuasion would have induced the Government to act had not W. T. Stead, who had taken over the editorship of the *Pall Mall Gazette* in 1883, produced his shock report on the scandal of child prostitution. Carefully warning his readers beforehand that they had better avoid the newspaper for a few days if they were 'squeamish and preferred to live in a fool's paradise of imaginary innocence', he deliberately made use of sensational journalism as a weapon of social reform and in doing so forcibly demonstrated the growing power of the press in the nineteenth century. The purpose of the story, 'The Maiden Tribute of Modern Babylon', was to depict child prostitution as a 'veritable slave trade'.

Stead brought the wrongs perpetrated on young girls closer home by his revelation that brothels existed not only on the continent but in London, which catered to the tastes of men who enjoyed forcing themselves sexually on very young virgins. Children had been 'snared, trapped and outraged either when under the influence of drugs or after a prolonged struggle in a locked room'. The girls, almost all from the working class, were depicted as satisfying the predilections of rich men so wicked that 'the shriek of torture is the essence of their delight and they would not silence by a single note the cry of agony over which they gloat'. The resulting publicity was not all in Stead's favour. To make the story credible, with the active connivance of several philanthropists he actually bought a child to demonstrate that his allegations were not only true but could happen. He was put on trial for abducting the child and sentenced to six months' imprisonment. His opponents denounced him as a dealer in pornography, but as he himself put it, he 'only struck the match that fired a charged mine of enthusiasm'. Shaftesbury, although old and ill, hurried to the Home Office; Cardinal Manning, Dr Temple, then Bishop of London, and most social reformers rallied to his side. The Criminal Law Amendment Act passed into law in a matter of weeks.

Barnardo's reaction to Stead's initiative is interesting. There is no doubt he was shocked by the sensational language used in the *Pall Mall Gazette*, for in writing of children rescued from brothels and low lodging houses his words were never explicit and he frequently could not bring himself to say more than that the facts behind the case were too painful to mention, writing on one occasion that his saddest cases 'are enough to make pity weep tears of blood'. He was away ill at the height of the publicity and when the November issue of *Night and Day* appeared after a gap of six months, Stead had already been tried and convicted and the Criminal Law Amendment Act had been passed. Expressing his sincere belief in the 'purity of motive, thorough uprightness and high sense of chivalrous devotion which characterised William Stead', he wrote:[11]

> We may not agree with the editor of *The Pall Mall Gazette* as to the methods he adopted in bringing to light this state of things – we may even have felt sadly troubled as to the necessity for and the manner of the publication which drew public attention to these things. Probably had we to do the work, we might have adopted a different method; but with the knowledge that these publications reveal pressing upon his soul and conscience, it was a moral necessity that Mr. Stead should do something – should take some step by which willingly or unwillingly, *the nation would be forced to act*!

The article ended with Barnardo expressing sympathy for Stead's plight in prison, which was vividly described through the eyes of the Rev. Benjamin Waugh who was allowed half an hour's visit and whose record of the visit was published:

> He appeared to have been 'cropped', but of course the visitor was allowed to ask no questions. His trousers were loose, baggy, of yellow linen of the duck type, with Government arrows stamped with ink in four places. His boots were very large and must have been uncomfortable. He wore a round cloth label on his left breast marked $\frac{R2}{8}$. Mr. Stead looked very cold, and put his hands inside his baggy sleeves as if for warmth. His dinner is suet pudding and brown bread at noon and supper at 5.30 of skilly and brown bread.

Small wonder that Barnardo was interested in Stead's fate – in another article in the same issue of *Night and Day* he confessed that he had abducted no less than forty-seven children himself in defiance of the law of the land in order to save them. Until Stead's revelation Barnardo's method in rescuing such children had been to work secretly. 'I have had to proceed, not from the shelter of the law, but hiding myself from the daylight, to steal to the rescue of the little ones by means of what may be called philanthropic abduction pursued as a fine art – an art painfully acquired by years of laborious effort.' Stead's fate brought home to him vividly the illegality of his actions and, as if not wanting to be outdone, he announced that he had at the present time four children under his care who had been secured by methods as 'distinctly illegal as if I had kidnapped them to sell as slaves'. He stated defiantly that he would 'willingly accept to the full the consequences of any such acts of mine as I have embodied in this "confession". They were deliberately performed and from the responsibility attaching to them I would not recede.'

Stimulated by Stead's example, Barnardo's article demanding an answer in the affirmative to the question, 'Is philanthropic abduction ever justifiable?', was the first shot in his campaign to get the laws for the custody of children changed. In his view the law should allow for the removal of children from the custody of their parents if these were leading infamous and immoral lives and were, by their conduct, about to inflict upon their unfortunate offspring grievous wrong. How certain clauses in the Industrial Act, the Vagrant Act, the Amendment Act of the Industrial Schools Act and the recently passed Criminal Law Amendment Act were interpreted was not always clear. In cases where these clauses were invoked against parents on the grounds that they were living immoral lives, too often the judge was given conflicting evidence by both sides, and in the majority of cases judgement was given in favour of the parent. Barnardo sought to convince his readers that there is law and law:[12] 'Are we as Christian men, always, under all circumstances to be governed by English law? Is *judicial* law always to be co-extensive with *moral* law? Does a period never arise when a higher law may compel a man to take a step which the law of the land would possibly condemn?'

Barnardo had never found it easy to accept man-made rules when they conflicted with the dictates of his conscience. A determination to go his own way had marked his behaviour from earliest times; although he did not then know it, this article was the first shot in the biggest battle he was to fight in support of his view against the law of the land. He realised that he had escaped prosecution up till now because the parents whose children he had abducted were either too poor to afford the costly proceeding of appearing before a judge in chambers, or were themselves engaged in some shady affairs and could not afford the publicity a court case would have brought. But for that fact he too might have been in a felon's cell. Admitting that his own sense of morality introduced the question of private judgement and public good he ended by stating that as things stood it was his profession to break the law almost systematically and to do so in the name of morality and decency.

Three years later, in 1888, a far worse sensation was to engulf the East End. It was a series of murders so gruesome and horrific that it focused the attention, not only of the citizens of London but of the whole country, on the mean streets and sordid alleys of Whitechapel; Buck's Row, Hanbury Street, Mitre Court, Flower and Dean Street were places that suddenly became known to many – haunts, courts and streets long familiar to Barnardo who had walked through them on his nocturnal expeditions in search of children. The dreadfully mutilated state in which some of the bodies were found, implying underlying, but at the time unrecognised, sexual motive, added to the sense of fear and shock that swept the country.

The unsolved mystery of the Jack the Ripper murders continues to intrigue both professional and amateur detectives, and many solutions have been put forward involving both the great and the unknown. Sir Charles Warren, Commissioner of the Metropolitan Police at the time of the first murders, was a man with a reputation for toughness and had been responsible for crushing the riots that had occurred in Trafalgar Square the previous November, remembered as 'Bloody Sunday'. He had just succeeded in forcing James Monro, head of the CID, to resign and had replaced him with Robert Anderson who took office the day after the murder of the first victim, Mary Ann Nichols, in Buck's Row. Anderson, the son of an Ulster soldier, had spent twenty years of his working life in the Home Office, but he was no stranger to the harsh realities of the East End. A noted Brethren preacher, it is likely that he and Barnardo had met at Merrion Hall, which they had both attended in Dublin. He had been a member of Barnardo's committee of management from its inception, and had given devoted support to the mission in practical terms. He was an active member of the committee, fulfilling his obligations to visit the homes and regular in his attendance at meetings. His knowledge of the conditions in which many of the children were living before they came into Barnardo's care would have given him a more than casual knowledge of the circumstances in which the victims lived.

At the time of his appointment he was suffering from strain brought on by overwork, and his doctor had ordered him to go abroad for two months' rest. Spending just one week in the CID, he left London for Switzerland at almost the same time as the second murder took place. Warren's handling of the murders had already begun to be criticised in the press, and Anderson's absence abroad was beginning to attract further unfavourable comment. Thinking it expedient to be nearer home, Anderson moved to Paris, arriving there the night the Ripper struck twice, killing first Elisabeth Stride and then Catherine Eddowes in quick succession. An urgent summons from the Home Secretary brought Anderson back to London. He would have liked the police to arrest every known 'street woman' found on the prowl after midnight, but this course of action was seen as too drastic and he had to be content with merely warning them that the police would not protect them after midnight.

Throughout October Warren had to face growing public opposition to what was seen as his mishandling of the case. He resigned on 8 November, the day before the killer struck again, murdering Mary Jane Kelly. The hideously mutilated state in which her body was found sent fresh waves of fear and outrage through the country. An alarmed public inundated the police with letters dealing with anything from the state of the country to the identity of the killer. In one hectic week letters to the police amounted to over a thousand, and to cope with the postal deluge the CID were forced to acknowledge their receipt on a printed slip of paper headed 'Whitechapel Murders' and signed by Robert Anderson. As murder succeeded murder the list of suspects became increasingly long and it is hardly surprising that Barnardo's name should have been included among them.[13] He was known to frequent the streets and courts where the murders had taken place, and was well known both to the police and in the common lodging houses.

Evidence given by Dr Bagster Philips concerning the second victim was of such a nature that it could only be reproduced in the *Lancet*.[14] In his opinion the way in which the incisions were made could only have been the work of someone who had knowledge of anatomical or pathological examinations, and this view gave further weight to the theory that Barnardo could have been the murderer, qualified as he was both as a surgeon and accoucheur. The suggestion that an advertisement might be inserted in *The Times* offering liberal terms to a medical man between the ages of twenty-five and forty as a means of trapping the Ripper indicates that the idea that the murderer was a medical man was a theory widespread at the time.

6   A scene in the kitchen of a Common Lodging House in Flower and Dean Street

Barnardo was probably totally unaware that his name was among the list of those suspected, for soon after the double murder of Elisabeth Stride and Catherine Eddowes on 30 September he wrote a letter to *The Times* in which he begged for public support to enable him immediately to open two lodging houses for children only, where young children of the 'casual or tramp class' could take refuge. He wanted it made illegal for young children to enter licensed lodging houses, and he also wanted the existing laws relating to the custody and companionship of children more rigidly enforced. It could be that it was the letter itself that gave rise to the suspicions concerning Barnardo, for the police had to find someone who was familiar with the area, had a certain medical knowledge and was in the right age group. Barnardo was in his forties at the time and, as his letter shows, he made no bones about his close association with prostitutes of the type the Ripper chose as victims.[15]

Only four days before the recent murders I visited No. 32 Flower and Dean Street, the house in which the unhappy woman Stride occasionally lodged. I had been examining many of the common lodging houses in Bethnal Green that night, endeavouring to elicit from the inmates their opinions upon a certain aspect of the subject. In the kitchen of No. 32 there were many persons, some of them being girls and women of the same unhappy class as that to which poor Elisabeth Stride belonged. The company soon recognised me, and the conversation turned upon the previous murders. The female inmates of the kitchen seemed thoroughly frightened at the dangers to which they were presumably exposed. In an explanatory fashion I put before them the scheme which had suggested itself to my mind, by which children at all events could be saved from the contamination of the common lodging houses and the streets, and so to some extent cut off the supply which feeds the vast ocean of misery in this great city.

The pathetic part of my story is, that my remarks were manifestly followed with deep interest by all the women. Not a single scoffing voice was raised in ridicule or opposition. One poor creature, who had evidently been drinking, exclaimed somewhat bitterly to the following effect: 'We're all up to no good, and no one cares what becomes of us. Perhaps some of us will be killed next!' And then she added, 'If anybody had helped the likes of us long ago we would never have come to this!'

Impressed by the unusual manner of the people, I could not help noticing their appearance somewhat closely, and I saw how evidently some of them were moved. I have since visited the mortuary in which were lying the remains of the poor woman Stride, and I at once recognised her as one of those who stood around me in the kitchen of the common lodging house on the occasion of my visit last Wednesday week.

In all the wretched dens where such unhappy creatures live are to be found hundreds, if not thousands, of poor children who breathe from their very birth an atmosphere fatal to all goodness. They are so heavily handicapped at the start on the race of life that the future is to most of them absolutely hopeless. They are continually surrounded by influence so vile that decency is outraged, and virtue becomes impossible.

Surely the awful revelations consequent upon the recent tragedies should stir the whole community up to action, and to resolve to deliver the children of to-day, who will be the men and women of tomorrow, from so evil an environment.

It is interesting to compare Anderson's attitude to the murder victims with Barnardo's constructive approach. Writing some twenty years later about the murders, Anderson reveals a typically Victorian attitude to prostitution:[16] 'It is enough to say the wretched victims belonged to a very small class of degraded women who frequent the streets of the East End after midnight in the hope of inveigling belated drunkards and men as degraded as themselves.' To Anderson prostitution was simply a manifestation of sin; there is no trace of pity for the victims nor any understanding of the economic and social conditions which made prostitution such a feature of Victorian London.

The murders, horrifying as they were, had spurred Barnardo, careless of his own reputation, personally to investigate the situation and to warn the public of the even more fearful dangers that faced the destitute children of the East End. A month after the publication of his letter, Barnardo was able to announce that he had acquired two houses, one in Flower and Dean Street and one in Leman Street, where for the price of a penny a child could be given rough shelter, a half pint of cocoa and a slice of dry bread. Their particulars were entered in a book which Barnardo described as forming 'a grim record of concentrated misery'.

13

The Custody of Children

ALL through the 1880s public awareness of the injustices suffered by children at the hands of their parents either as a result of neglect or because of downright cruelty was becoming more widespread. A barrister, Charles Baker, who had been a long-serving member of Barnardo's committee, wrote a treatise on the laws relating to young children in 1885, and his conclusion was that if expression were given to public opinion, more severe provisions would be found in the statute book against indecent assaults upon young girls, and more effectual powers of dealing with parents who neglected or ill used their children would be granted to courts of summary jurisdiction. That he could write in these terms is due in some measure to Barnardo, who had seen it as a duty to publicise the plight of the children on a scale never before attempted. *Night and Day*, with its circulation of over one hundred and twenty thousand contained many first-hand accounts of cruelty and neglect; and Barnardo wrote articles for other publications, illustrated his stories, and was constantly travelling and speaking of his work wherever opportunity offered. The great increase in donations – by the end of the 1880s his yearly income amounted to over £100,000 – clearly showed how successful he was.

When in 1882 Edward de Montjoie Rudolf persuaded the Church of England that it too should play its part in providing homes for outcast and destitute children, Barnardo welcomed the new institution saying that he did not 'care one fig' what denominational or sectarian views were imparted if only really Christian men and women undertook the work.[1] Curiously enough it was Barnardo's own undenominational standing that was indirectly responsible for the foundation of the Society for Waifs and Strays. Edward Rudolf, then a young clerk in the civil service, was also superintendent of a Sunday school at St Ann's, Lambeth. When two of his scholars failed to turn up one day he discovered that their father had died, and rather than send them to the workhouse their mother had turned them out into the streets. Rudolf was dismayed to discover the only home that could accept them was Barnardo's home for boys in Stepney, and that there was no guarantee that their church teaching would be continued. Organisations already existed for the children of Roman Catholic and Jewish parents, and the Methodists' Children's Home in Bonner Street had been opened about the same time as Barnardo's Stepney home; it was not long before Rudolf persuaded the Archbishop of Canterbury to agree to his scheme, and he became president of the society. Unfortunately the initial friendly relationship between the two societies did not last. Fundamentally Barnardo was jealous of his reputation as the champion of the children's cause, and as the Society for Waifs and Strays began to expand he came to resent the competition, especially as he felt that its financial growth was at the expense of his own. There were several acrimonious exchanges of correspondence on this subject,[2] and Barnardo finally established his own separate fund for Church of England children.

His relationship with the Society for the Prevention of Cruelty to Children followed a somewhat similar pattern. The society was founded in 1884, further evidence of the awakening of the public conscience to the unseen horrors endured by many children. The rights of parents over their children had for centuries been paramount, and the welfare of the child was so subordinated to that right that, by a hideous paradox, Parliament had given animals protection from abuse for more than three-quarters of a century before it considered extending statutory protection to the young child.

The story of how Thomas Agnew, a Liverpool merchant, with the support of his Member of Parliament, Samuel Smith, turned an appeal for a dogs' home organised by the Society for the Prevention of Cruelty to Animals into an appeal for the Society for the Protection of Children in Liverpool in 1883 is well known. A year later, again through the influence of Samuel Smith, the Lord Mayor of London allowed the Mansion House to be used for a meeting to launch a London society in July.

Lord Shaftesbury, presiding, moved a resolution to found a Society for the Prevention of Cruelty to Children in London. He was followed by the Earl of Aberdeen, who proposed the election of a council to carry on the business of the society. Barnardo rose to his feet to second the motion, thus establishing his right to be considered a founder member. Among those in the Egyptian Hall at the Mansion House were Cardinal Manning and Baroness Burdett Coutts, both of whom took a deep interest in the affairs of the society.

When the breach occurred between Barnardo and the NSPCC some six years later, Barnardo gave as his reason for resigning his fear that the society was coming under the dominant influence of Rome. Benjamin Waugh, the honorary director of the society, had criticised Barnardo for sending a child to Canada against the wishes of its mother, an action which had recently been the subject of a court case, and this criticism seems to have touched Barnardo on the raw. It is difficult to appreciate today the deep-rooted fear and mistrust which Barnardo with his Protestant Irish background felt towards Roman Catholics, amounting almost to paranoia. The society was obviously dismayed at Barnardo's sudden attack on its management, and hoped that a carefully worded letter sent from the committee would persuade him to rescind his resignation. But Barnardo's reply to the letter sent by the Duke of Abercorn, its president, and signed among others by Baroness Burdett Coutts saying that Cardinal Manning had never taken any active part in the administration of the society, took the form of a positive tirade against the corrupting influences of Romish apostasy. One amazingly long sentence alone reveals how deeply he felt on the subject.[3]

The very essence of Rome's success with a Society like the N.S.P.C.C. must consist in its exercising its influence with great subtlety, not ostensibly but perhaps all the more powerfully permeating your counsels, identifying itself in the public mind with the operations of your Society, so as to gain general credit for practical humanitarianism; all the time keenly watching over its own interests with unsleeping vigilance; snatching, where it dared to do so, the children you rescue from one horror, to encompass them with its own wiles; using every means, foul or fair, to absorb waif children whom your Society may have laid hands on into its system, and doing this all the time with an air of such fairness, with such a tone of 'looking after our poor children, you know' that those who like your Grace and your co-signatories, are utterly above all such underhand methods, are led to repose in the agents of Rome, as religious men and women, the same unsuspecting confidence which men of honour habitually show each other.

It was the more unfortunate that Barnardo chose this moment to rupture his association with the society as the previous year Waugh had been able to amalgamate the London society with some of the provincial branches into a national society. It was largely due to the influence of the national society and the patient and careful work of Benjamin Waugh that the Act for the Prevention of Cruelty to and better Protection of Children became law, and a first step was taken to curb the rights of parents to inflict injury on their children. The Act was not comprehensive and confined itself to dealing with acts of wilful cruelty: cases of neglect due to poverty, ignorance, drunkenness or any other cause were not dealt with.

Later the same year Parliament passed the Poor Law Adoption Act, which deprived irresponsible parents of their custodial rights over children and transferred their rights to the overseers of Poor Law institutions. But still nothing had been done to give any legal powers to voluntary and philanthropic organisations, who were caring for an increasingly large number of neglected and ill used children who could be removed by parents and guardians able and willing to apply to the courts and assert their rights. Whilst calling for a reform in the law, Barnardo did not hesitate, as has been shown, to obstruct parents he deemed unworthy from recovering their children. Although such undertakings were not legally binding, before any child was officially admitted the parent or guardian had to sign a form giving the child over to the care of the institution for an unspecified term of years:

The nearest Friend shall place the said child in the said *Protestant Homes* to be taken care of, maintained and educated therein, or in one of the Branch Establishments named at the head of the paper, or boarded-out in the country for a term of years from the date hereof, or for a less time if the managers for the time being of the said Homes think fit, during that time to be brought up in the *Protestant faith*.

The parents or guardians of children Barnardo considered suitable for emigration were asked to sign an additional form giving the organisation authority to send the child overseas, but in law these agreements were quite valueless if the parent chose to demand the return of a child.

In 1888 three children, Harry Gossage, Martha Tye and John James Roddy, were admitted into the homes upon the usual conditions. The following year the parents of all three demanded that their children be restored to their custody. Barnardo's response was typically high-handed; two were immediately bundled out of the country in such a way that they could not be traced, and Barnardo applied to the courts to support his claim for the custody of John James Roddy.

The stories of these three children were to blow wide open the question of parental rights versus the welfare of children, and to focus public attention once more on the unresolved anomalies inherent in the law relating to the custody of children. For the next three years Barnardo was to be involved in litigation, fighting three cases in the High Court, taking two of them through the court of appeal to the House of Lords. His actions involved both him and his work in a storm of controversy; public opinion turned against him and he had to endure more sustained abuse and criticism than at any other period in his career. Yet during this troubled time the Custody of Children Act passed through Parliament, and the fact that this law reached the statute book is in no small measure due to the publicity Barnardo stirred up by taking matters into his own hands. His vigorous attempt to demonstrate that as the law stood philanthropic abduction was justified and that judicial law was not always coextensive with moral law was not without effect. Certainly litigation appealed to the aggressive side of Barnardo's nature. With Cairns no longer at his side to guide and restrain him, uninhibited now by Brethren principles and dragging his committee with him, he was able to carry on the fight to the bitter end.

A study of the legal cases involving the three children illuminates the opinions and attitudes prevalent at the time. Barnardo's conduct during this period shows many of the same characteristics that he displayed in 1877, including a marked desire to have the last word and a propensity to produce lengthy and detailed affidavits relating to the case which, although not always strictly relevant then, now provide a wealth of interesting detail. Besides the controversial nature of the cases, questions of law were also involved, and both excited considerable comment in the daily and weekly press.

During this period Barnardo was subjected to sustained and widespread hostile criticism because, in the first instance, public opinion was understandably alarmed at the idea that a private individual should attempt to act according to his own interpretation of the law, in opposition to the law of the land, no matter how much 'moral' right there was on his side. Barnardo understood and accepted criticism on this point as part of the price he had to pay. But he never admitted the truth of the second reason, or felt other than bitterly hurt at the odium he incurred at this time. But without doubt, in all three cases he was fighting to retain custody not principally to prevent children returning to cruel and neglectful parents, but to prevent their being brought up as Roman Catholics. One cannot help regretting that instead of concentrating on the obvious evil of child neglect and abuse he should have chosen to fight on such a narrow front and to give sectarian religious considerations priority over glaring social wrongs.

The first of the three cases concerned a boy who was ten years old at the time. Harry Gossage had been found wandering destitute in the streets of Folkestone by a clergyman who had asked Barnardo to admit him in the summer of 1888. According to his story his father was dead and his mother had given him into the possession of an organ-grinder who had starved him, ill treated him and ultimately deserted him. According to precedent, a letter was sent to the mother, telling her that Harry had been admitted to the home and asking if she was willing that he should remain there. She replied that as his father was dead, his two brothers were in Canada and she was unable to keep him herself she was willing he should remain. She was subsequently sent a form of agreement which gave the home authority to place out the child in one of the colonies, but later evidence showed that Mrs Gossage never signed that agreement. Among Barnardo's many visitors in early November that year was a certain Mr William Norton, a gentleman whom Barnardo had never met before but who came with letters of introduction and recommendation from persons of standing in Canada. He said that he wished to adopt a boy of ten or eleven and take him to Canada. Five boys were called down to Barnardo's private room, among them Harry Gossage. Harry, a bright and intelligent boy, was the one Mr Norton chose; he expressed himself as particularly anxious that the parents or relatives should not be in a position to interfere with the child, and asked that Barnardo agree to his taking him without leaving any address. Barnardo had to make an immediate decision, and considering Mr Norton's offer in the light of Harry's past history, he rashly agreed to his condition and arranged that he should take the boy away on 16 November.

Barnardo was away ill during the interval between that first interview and the day when Mr Norton returned, as arranged, to take Harry away with him, and he had been unable to deal with the bulk of his correspondence. Lying on his desk unanswered was a letter from a Mr Newdigate, written at Mrs Gossage's request, asking that the boy be moved to a Catholic home, stating that he had arranged for the boy's transfer to St Vincent's Home, Harrow Road, and enclosing a subscription of ten shillings to the homes. This letter had been acknowledged by a clerk, but a further letter from Mr Newdigate had remained unanswered. Not until 31 December did Mr Odling, the secretary, write saying the rules of the homes did not permit them to dismiss a child on religious grounds – the subject had previously been agreed upon by the committee.

In January 1889 a further letter was sent to Barnardo, signed by Mrs Gossage, asking for delivery of her child. Only at that point did Barnardo admit that the child was no longer in his custody. The drama of Harry's departure is encapsulated in a stark sentence written opposite the child's name, in Barnardo's own hand: 'Disposed of by the Director. 14.11.89.'[4] Even the photographs were torn out of the record book, to ensure that no evidence remained which might lead to Harry's recovery. Happily the photograph taken at the time of his admission escaped destruction, and it shows a little face full of dignity and courage. One can understand both Mr Norton's choice and Barnardo's reasons for wishing to shield Harry from further exploitation. In March 1889 Mrs

Gossage issued a summons against Barnardo but Mr Justice Mathew, after reading the affidavits and having Barnardo cross-examined, refused to order the issue of a writ of habeas corpus because the child was no longer in his custody.

There the matter might have rested had not Barnardo in 1888 also admitted a girl named Martha Tye. The public account given by Barnardo of the circumstances in which Martha was found omits all mention of the fact that she took the initiative and referred herself to Müller's orphanage in Bristol; it also omits the fact that she was admitted as a Roman Catholic. The extract from the admissions register gives a précis of the remarks made by the director himself:[5]

Presented herself, in ragged clothes, at the gates of Müller's Orphanage in Bristol and begged for admission. Was found to be living with her mother and a cruel step-father in a low locality; sent out to beg or steal a certain sum every day; and beaten when she returned home with less. Has been kicked and beaten so that her body is marked and bruised, and her step-father – now living at Worcester – was bound over to keep the peace, at Bristol. Mother would only sign for two years and Canada clause omitted. (*R.C.*)

Dr Mayo, director of Müller's orphanage, himself applied for her admission. On receipt of the mother's written sanction the girl was admitted to the village home. On 14 December Barnardo received a letter from Martha's mother and step-father asking that she be returned to them; but when an emissary called to fetch Martha on their behalf, Barnardo refused to allow her to be given up. In reply to a solicitor's letter demanding that she be handed over to her mother, he replied that he needed evidence that the mother was married and in a position to maintain the child; in reply to a further letter dated 1 January, Barnardo again declined to dismiss the girl from his charge. It was only when he was threatened with legal action on 7 January that Barnardo revealed that the child was no longer under his control and probably not even still in the kingdom. In fact he had known since 22 December that Martha was no longer in the country, having been handed over to the care of a certain Madame R who had taken her to the continent.

The solicitors, a well-known Catholic firm who were acting for the Tyes, then made application for a writ of habeas corpus which came before Mr Justice Mathew, who had already had to do with Barnardo over the disappearance of Harry Gossage. In that case he had accepted the fact that Harry was no longer in Barnardo's custody. The story Barnardo told this time was that a certain Madame R, who mainly lived abroad, had visited the homes and offered to take abroad with her any two or three little girls about whom Barnardo felt anxious. Madame R had conveniently visited the homes again on 21 December and Barnardo had allowed her to take away with her Martha and two other children. Barnardo appeared personally before Mr Justice Mathew and expressed his regret that Martha was not in his custody; from what was said the judge thought that if time were given the child might be found, and he adjourned the case until 30 April. However, at the hearing on 30 April Martha was not produced and letters were put forward instead, purporting to show that Barnardo had done his best to find the child, but without success. The letters were read in court:[6]

Dear Madame Romand,
You will, I dare say, be surprised at the contents of this letter. You doubtless remember those three children I handed over to your care on 21st December last. It is of the eldest of these, Mary Ann Tye, of whom I now write. The wretched mother of this poor child, has it appears, quite lately married [Mrs Tye had in fact been married for some years]. However, this man and woman have moved the High Court for a writ of habeas corpus to compel me to produce and give up the child. I frankly told the judge I had given her over to the custody of a lady, not mentioning your name ... I have done my best to protect the poor girl; but now in view of the writ which has been issued, it seems my very plain duty to ask you to enable me to comply with it, and to cancel, if you will, the agreement which I entered into with you and to return the child to me in time to produce her in court on the day named.

The lady's reply was from Cannes, dated 27 February:

Dear Dr. Barnardo,
Your letter does indeed surprise me and you really must look on me as one who is demented. I cannot understand you one bit. I have read and read your letter and the oftener I read it the more perplexed I am. That you, the protector and defender of little children, the guardian of hundreds of poor little girls should really ask me to

return to the wretches who so brutally treated that poor child Mary Ann, passes my comprehension. However, of one thing you may be assured, I will not comply with any such request ... I am leaving here tomorrow and wandering about for a fortnight, but I shall hope to be in Brussels with my little maid on the 18th of next month, and if you write again you will address my letter to the post office for I am not quite sure where I shall stop.

But remember on the subject of Mary Ann my mind is made up and my decision irrevocable. Moreover I am very angry with you, and don't think you deserve I should sign myself as –
Very sincerely, your friend
Gertrude Romand.

Two more letters were read showing that Barnardo had known from the beginning that the child was destined for a Catholic religious sisterhood, but that even when Madame R was told of this she refused to recede from the position she had taken up. Judge Mathew made it perfectly clear that he was not satisfied with these letters, and ruled that Barnardo's return was evasive and unsatisfactory. He declared that Barnardo was in contempt of court and liable for the consequences: 'We do not direct that he shall now be sent to prison, but we direct that he shall enter into recognizances to answer interrogatories administered on behalf of the mother.' Mr Justice Grantham said that he was of the same opinion but felt even more strongly that Barnardo's conduct was exceedingly unsatisfactory. He went on to say in court: 'He is quite unworthy to be entrusted with large sums of money for the maintenance of a charitable institution, quite unworthy to be entrusted with the care of such numbers of children if he is capable of acting in such a way as he has acted in this case.' Strong language from the judge about a man who was entirely responsible for the wellbeing of nearly three thousand children, but his exasperation is understandable.

Mr Justice Grantham ruled that Barnardo had no right 'to question the moral competence of the mother to have the custody of her child, and even if he did so, he had no right to make himself the judge of so delicate a point,' although he gave him credit for the benevolence of his motives and acknowledged his disinterested efforts on behalf of orphans and outcasts. *The Times*, echoing Mr Justice Grantham, questioned whether Barnardo was 'a man to be entrusted with the responsibilities he has assumed'. Barnardo bitterly resented the way in which he was being publicly pilloried by the press. His committee, with one member dissenting, reaffirmed the view that he should resist attempts to remove children for religious reasons, but said that court injunctions must be obeyed. They did not use the ultimate sanction, and refrained from censuring him for the action he had taken. Barnardo for his part made it clear that he was only seeking the opinion of the committee, and asserted that the real responsibility of action must rest upon himself.

It must be admitted that the whole story of Madame Romand sounds improbable. The most the judges could say was that Barnardo's response to the mother's first request for her child had been evasive and dilatory and that the letters to Madame Romand were unsatisfactory. To anyone familiar with Barnardo's literary style, the letter said to be from Madame Romand has a familiar sound; there must be a strong supposition that he was the author of both the letters, to and from the lady, and that the whole correspondence was faked. An earlier report in *The Times*[7] stated that Dr Barnardo had sent the child in July to a Mrs Grogan to be cared for, and that it was this Mrs Grogan who had removed her from the jurisdiction of the court with a view to taking her to Canada; in the report of the High Court Mrs Grogan has become the mysterious and elusive Madame Romand.

The committee agreed that the matter should go to appeal and two members, the brothers William and Charles Baker, both barristers, took it upon themselves to advise and help. The court of appeal heard the Tye case in July, and their judgement went against Barnardo. They held that it was not a good answer to a writ of habeas corpus to say that 'I cannot produce the child because I have unlawfully parted with possession of it before the issue of the writ', and ordered that the writ of habeas corpus should stand. The result of this judgement was very serious for Barnardo. A direct consequence was that a fresh application for the issue of a writ for the return of Harry Gossage was made to the divisional court on 30 November 1889. This put Barnardo in a predicament; if he appealed, the court would certainly feel itself bound by the decision in the Tye case, and unless he succeeded in distinguishing the Gossage case on its facts from the Tye case, the court of appeal had to follow the Tye case and the result would be similar. With only qualified support from his committee[8] and smarting under the stinging attacks that had been made on him by the judges, Barnardo organised a public meeting in December 1889, taking Exeter Hall for the purpose. Sir Arthur Blackwood, secretary of the General Post Office and well known for his evangelical views, took the chair. The meeting was well attended and Barnardo received many messages of sympathy. Sir Arthur, a vice-president of the homes, set the tone by saying that even if Barnardo had made mistakes here and there they were all there to express their unabated confidence in him and in his work. The meeting ended with a resolution being passed to the effect that a change in the present law relating to the custody of children was urgently necessary, so that voluntary institutions and private individuals actuated by benevolent motives might have conferred upon them powers somewhat similar to those entrusted to boards of guardians.[9]

The Catholic hierarchy, however, feeling things were going their way, decided to continue the attack. A month later, in December, Barnardo received another letter from the same Catholic firm of solicitors who had been acting in both the Gossage and Tye cases, for the return of a third child, John James Roddy. The legalities in this case turned on the question of the custody rights of the mother of an illegitimate child. It too brought out the unsatisfactory state of the law with regard to the custody of children, but to avoid confusion this case will be dealt with later in this chapter.

To return to the Gossage case: on the advice of William Baker, Barnardo elected to go to the Court of Appeal in an attempt to show that different considerations applied in the case of Harry Gossage. In this instance he appeared on his own behalf, admitting that he was without legal experience or technical knowledge. Because of his deafness he asked permission for the judges' replies to be transmitted to him through his solicitor, Mr S. Daw. Barnardo's deafness made for certain difficulties, but nonetheless by appearing in person he was able to widen the scope of the argument and make known, at rather excessive length, many other aspects of the case which were to his advantage. His speech lasted for two days and was a remarkable *tour de force* by any standard. It was subsequently published in *Night and Day* and as a booklet under the title, 'Before my Judges'.[10] Quite apart from his technical mastery of complicated legal argument, it was a further demonstration of his ability to conquer personal feelings for the sake of his work. He and several members of his family had been ill with diphtheria at the beginning of the year. All had recovered except Kenward, his third and greatly loved son. Kenward was exceptionally bright and intelligent, the child in whom Barnardo saw himself most nearly reflected. His death had been a crushing blow and one which Barnardo found hard to accept. The child was buried at the cemetery at Bow, where the Barnardos had already buried two of their children. As the flower-covered coffin was carried to the grave, Barnardo noticed another child being buried. This coffin had no flowers, and Barnardo, taking a sheaf of flowers from his own son's coffin, gently placed them on the coffin of the unknown child.

He had no time to grieve; he had only three weeks in which to prepare himself for his appearance in the High Court. He believed the decision of the judges had been absolutely contrary to all known English legal precedent and practice, and indeed subsequent rulings were to prove that he was right. Barnardo was nothing if not thorough; a great deal of the court's time was taken up establishing that the mother was quite uninterested in the fate of her son and entirely unfitted to have charge of him, but the Master of the Rolls held that this was immaterial as the proposal was to send the child to a respectable institution and Barnardo had received no consent to send the child to Canada. He saw it as a quarrel between two institutions, and whichever could get the mother's consent would win. Refusing to allow Barnardo further time to discuss the moral aspects of the case, he said, 'If you have broken the law from the best of motives, you have broken the law and must take the consequences.' Barnardo thereupon came to his main argument, that it was not a proper case in which a writ of habeas corpus should be issued, because at the time of application the boy was not in his custody. He argued that the decision of the court should be absolutely and solely governed by the rules laid down for the issue of a writ. He said he had searched diligently all the records and had failed to find any authority for directing the issue of a writ against a person who had neither virtual nor actual control – 'in fact there is absolutely none'. Barnardo accepted that he had done wrong in the Tye case in sending the child away knowing the mother did not wish her to go, but said that this case was quite different.

He then made the telling point:[11]

> My Lords, I cannot help submitting to your Lordships that it is very remarkable that while the tide of public opinion and the action of the legislature are steadily proceeding towards the limitation of parents' rights and powers when parents do not perform duties, that it is at this very juncture the Courts are disposed, as illustrated in the Tye case, and in this, to extend the doctrine of habeas corpus, so as to enable parents of the very class contemplated by the Acts I have quoted [The Act for the Prevention of Cruelty to and Better Protection of Children and the Poor Law Act of 1889] to resume their powers over children whom they have so grossly neglected.

Nonetheless, judgement was given against Barnardo and the court followed its earlier decision in the Tye case. The Judges ruled that he was bound to make every effort to obey the writ; to write letters, to advertise, and if need be, to go to America to look for the boy. The Master of the Rolls frankly admitted that they were applying the law to a new combination of circumstances and said it was much to be regretted that good people, when animated by religious motives, would not act with that candour and openness which they would display in any other circumstances. 'I cannot approve of such modes of conduct. I therefore think the writ must be issued.' Barnardo immediately gave notice that he would appeal to the House of Lords.

Two years were to elapse before the case came before the House of Lords, and in the meantime Barnardo was almost immediately involved in the other case concerning John James Roddy. It was during the course of this case that the Custody of Children Act was passed through Parliament, so that the case is of special importance on that account. In all three cases Barnardo was continually making the point that philanthropic organisations which had rescued thousands of destitute and neglected children had absolutely no redress when parents, however unfit to have custody of their children, wished to reclaim them, and the public interest in the cases certainly demonstrated public awareness of this fact. There was no dispute as to how John James Roddy, the illegitimate son of a Mrs

McHugh, came into Barnardo's care. The boy was born in 1878 and baptised in a Roman Catholic church in 1880. To confuse matters he was subsequently baptised in a Protestant church in 1884; when asked why she had him baptised again, Mrs McHugh said in court, 'I thought it would do him no harm.'

In 1880 Margaret Roddy had married McHugh, who because of ill health had to give up work and entered Marylebone workhouse. She thereafter supported herself by charring and by working from eight in the morning until seven at night, earning ten shillings a week. Her rental was three shillings and sixpence a week. John Roddy was said to be neglected and half starved, and the mother was said to drink. Mrs McHugh agreed to the boy being placed in the care of the homes, and he was admitted in September 1888. However, when she tried to see him in September 1889 she was refused permission and told he was in the country. She wrote several letters to the child and ultimately received one from the institutions saying the boy was getting on nicely, and if she wanted to write to him she must send her letters to Stepney and they would be forwarded to him. Barnardo often had good reasons for wanting to protect his children from their relations, but on this occasion his high-handed action infuriated Mrs McHugh, and she became very much irritated and excited. She complained to her niece, a practising Roman Catholic, who advised her to get in touch with a priest. The priest put her in touch with the solicitors Leathley & Co., the firm which had been acting for Mrs Gossage and Mrs Tye.

The stage was thus set for another battle, the third in the series of court cases where the soul of the child rather than its body was the cause of the fight. A writ of habeas corpus was obtained on behalf of the mother in respect of John Roddy. William Baker, acting for Barnardo, appealed and the case was heard in the High Court before the Lord Chief Justice and Mr Justice Mathew, who by this time must have been familiar with the stance adopted by Barnardo. The case was deferred for a week to allow affidavits to be made, and an astonishing number of extraordinarily conflicting affidavits were eventually produced. Over twenty were produced by the appellant to show that the mother was an honest, hardworking, sober woman who never, except on rare occasions, went to the public house to get half a pint of beer for her supper; they were filed in response to the equally large number filed by Barnardo to show that she was a drunken, dissolute, and immoral woman.[12]

In an attempt to prevent the case coming to court, Barnardo had instructed his secretary to warn Mrs McHugh that if she persisted in her claim he would have to make a searching inquiry into her private life, and that the public exposure of her habits in court might have very unpleasant consequences for her.

You may be able to satisfy the Court that your life has been a perfectly pure and virtuous one and that you are a sober and moral person . . . Dr. Barnardo feels it his duty, before you rush into the law courts, to let you know what might be the result. Of course if you are willing to stop these proceedings and to write to Dr Barnardo that you do not wish your boy's removal from his care and that you will be satisfied if he is brought up to London so you can see him at the Homes, the matter will be at an end.

Counselled by her solicitors, Mrs McHugh refused to be swayed by this scarcely veiled threat. Thereupon Barnardo sent two agents, his beadle and a female missionary, to report on her daily life, and the huge number of affidavits he produced to the court were the result of their activities.

The boy was said to have been admitted covered in vermin, clothed in mere rags and looking half starved. The admission record shows a photograph of a bright, intelligent child, neatly and cleanly dressed, as the boy had in fact been – Mrs McHugh's employer having given the child a new suit for the occasion. The boy's physical condition was described as 'fairly developed'. But in presenting the admission record to the court as exhibit number one, Barnardo omitted both the photo and the note of his physical condition from the copy of the record, until forced to show the original. The two judges took a very unfavourable view of Barnardo's actions, although obviously disbelieving a great deal that had been advanced on behalf of Mrs McHugh. After hearing the evidence from both sides they decided to see John Roddy privately in their own rooms. After their interview with the child they announced that they would postpone final judgement until after Whitsun. Barnardo's solicitors and counsel considered this a very bad sign.

The case had put him under a tremendous strain and his wife had already tried to persuade him that it might be wiser to give up John Roddy. He wrote to her on 20 May while waiting for the judgement:[13]

My darling,

I wired you this morning as soon as I knew the judges intended to postpone judgement until after Whitsuntide . . . We have made out a strong case, but they are against us . . . You know I don't 'worry' over anything; but this case has *aged* me. Your suggestion is of course intolerable. I may die at my post, but I have never learned to run away. No, my darling, you must prepare for the worst if it be God's Will. I can give up my work if I know He wills it; peacefully lay down the great charge and responsibility I have received from His Hands alone. But to give up my children to such people to their ruin, never – not while life lasts. So now, dear, *never* suggest that again, as it *hurts* me in my very vitals, and I don't feel right for some time afterwards. Meanwhile to hear the odium under which I at present lie; to submit to imputations of meanness which I loathe – is a very heavy Cross indeed.

Judgement was finally announced on 6 August, but only delivered with reasons by the Lord Chief Justice on 4 November. The results of the judgement were far worse than anything Barnardo had anticipated. The judges had found the boy very intelligent, well nurtured, well clothed, apparently healthy and well taught and perfectly happy. He wished to stay where he was; he had no dislike whatever of his mother, but 'wished earnestly to see her from time to time'. He denied that she had been unkind to him or had starved him or within the limits of her power had neglected any of her duties towards him. But although the judges found that the boy was happy and well cared for at Dr Barnardo's Homes, they also found that Dr Barnardo's attack on his mother and his scandalous charge against her of unkindness to her son were without foundation. The judges considered that apart from the mother's right it would be undesirable to remove the child, but that Barnardo's conduct showed 'that he is unfit to have the uncontrolled and absolute power which he claims over Mrs. McHugh's child, and that Mrs. McHugh is entitled to insist that her son be withdrawn from his influence'. The judgement was a heavy blow to Barnardo, and he reacted immediately by lodging an appeal and deciding, as he had done in the Gossage case, to conduct his own case.

As in the Tye and Gossage cases, the application for the custody of John Roddy was not so that he should be with his mother, but that he should be permitted to go to a Catholic school of his mother's choice. Because of the recent judgement, both sides were now asking that the boy be put under the guardianship of a person of standing: a Mr Walsh had been selected by the Catholics, and Sir Robert Fowler, an alderman and former Lord Mayor of the City of London, by Barnardo.

The appeal was again heard before the Master of the Rolls, but this time with the Lords Justices Lindley and Lopes. Barnardo argued his own case at very great length, to the sometimes barely concealed irritation of the Master of the Rolls. By doing so he was again able to widen the scope of the argument, and this gave him the opportunity of commenting on the criticisms of High Court judges and of arguing against the exercise of their discretion, before he came to the main argument, on legal grounds, as to the rights of John James Roddy's mother. His speech was reproduced in *Night and Day* under the title 'Am I Unfit?', and it extended to over sixty pages. He was only two-thirds of the way through his argument when he was interrupted by the Master of the Rolls:[14]

What we have to do, as I told you once before, is to consider the law. Supposing you leave out all that about yourself and what the Judges said about you; they also said they were strongly of the opinion that Mrs. McHugh was entitled to insist that her son should be withdrawn from your Institution. Is that not so? We have now to consider whether the result of the judgement is according to the law or not. This is all we have to do.

Summing up, Lord Justice Lopes said the question was, 'whether the child is to be delivered to A or to B who both wish to have the child and the question arises how far the mother has the right to dictate as to whether it should be given to A or B. I take it, therefore, that it is solely a case where the interests of the child are to be protected.'

Although the judgement went against him, Barnardo had good cause to be pleased that he had taken the matter to appeal. The judgement of the Master of the Rolls was couched in much more favourable terms than formerly. He dismissed the idea that the case was simply concerned with a sensitive mother anxious to have her child under her own care and wounded by Barnardo's refusal to let her see it as often as she wished. He said it was between a well known organisation whose fundamental principle was to educate the children they rescued as Protestants, and a body of equally sincere and honest people who desired to bring up children as Roman Catholics:[15]

When I find that on one side one of the greatest names in the City of London – that of Sir Robert Fowler – is brought forward, and it is said that he is willing to be nominated as guardian of the child, while on the other hand a person of equal respectability has expressed his willingness to be its guardian, it becomes plain that this is not a mere dispute between the wife of a labouring man and Dr. Barnardo. It is a dispute between two sets of earnest benevolent enthusiasts . . . it is a fight over the soul, and not over the body of the child.

He went on to say that Dr Barnardo was the better scavenger of the two and picked up most of these gutter children. He also made the point that in this case the interests of the child would be safeguarded whichever side succeeded, and it would be better off than it would have been if this dispute had not arisen. The fact that the child was illegitimate made no difference in respect of the mother's right and wish to have the custody of her own child. The agreement she made with Dr Barnardo was absolutely null because a parent could not bind himself by any such agreement and, therefore, the court felt bound to give effect to the wish of the mother. The High Court did have its equitable jurisdiction to remove the child from a parent's care (or not to return it to it) where it decided that the parent was unfit to have custody. He concluded that in this case there was nothing to interfere with the mother's rights and 'Dr. Barnardo is bound to hand over the child as directed by the Divisional Court. I will only add that I do not agree with the strictures passed on Dr. Barnardo's conduct in the court below.'

Lord Justice Lindley, in his judgement, went even further in his support of Barnardo.[16]

I will only add I am not surprised that Dr. Barnardo should feel annoyed at finding his efforts thwarted, as they occasionally are, by persons who do not awake to their own duties to their children until he has rescued them from degradation and ruin. Whilst I regret that such a contest as this should ever have arisen, yet having arisen it is my duty to say that the law is on the side of the mother and that the appeal must be dismissed with costs.

Lord Justice Lopes expressed his view that the appeal be dismissed even more reluctantly. With greater insight as to the real welfare of the child, he said:[17]

I doubt if the contemplated change into a different atmosphere, with new and different surroundings, will be for the welfare of the child. It is, however, a matter of discretion ... in the circumstances the exercise of the discretion is not lightly to be set aside and for this reason, and this reason only, I do not dissent from the judgements delivered.

Barnardo did not despair. He took the case to the House of Lords where it was argued before Lord Halsbury, Lord Herschell and Lord Hannen in July 1891, but the view was upheld that the desire of the mother of an illegitimate child as to its custody is primarily to be considered. Barnardo was bitterly disappointed at the verdict and wrote that he felt that in handing over John Roddy he had betrayed a high and holy trust and asked for divine forgiveness for a cowardly and disloyal act.

Whilst Barnardo was fighting through the courts to retain the custody of children he had saved from neglect and destitution, other voices were making known their concern at the anomalies in the law as it stood. Lord Meath, who had been president of the homes in 1889, brought forward a bill for the custody of children in the House of Lords in July 1890, but the House was not yet prepared to accept such a radical reform and it failed through lack of support. The Lord Chancellor, Lord Halsbury, one of the law lords before whom the McHugh appeal would be heard, put forward proposals six months later, equally without success. An article appeared in the *Contemporary Review* in January 1891 by Robert Anderson under the title 'Morality by Act of Parliament', arguing that if children were trained in criminal surroundings almost inevitably they would become criminal or vicious. As the law stood at present it practically gave a divine right to vicious and brutal parents to make their children vicious and brutal, he said, and went on to illustrate his point by quoting the story of Harry Gossage: in this case, although the ostensible object was to transfer the child from a Protestant to a Catholic home, this was but an incidental factor of which the law took no cognisance, and its far-reaching powers were in effect being used to restore to the mother the wretched child she had neglected and betrayed. With a sidelong swipe at Mr Justice Mathew and his colleagues, he wrote: 'If some share of the money spent on judges and gaols were devoted to institutions which really rescue and reform such children, fewer judges and smaller gaols would suffice.'

Finally a standing committee of the House of Lords was appointed which came up with an acceptable measure. The Lord Chancellor spoke, forcefully demonstrating the flagrant abuses of the law that were possible as it stood. Lord Thring supported him and argued that this was not an attack upon the home and parental rights. The Act to amend the law relating to the custody of children was finally passed on 26 March 1891. There were six short clauses to the Act, which by their very nature show how much Parliament had been influenced by the publicity surrounding the Barnardo litigation. The Act gave the court, 'if it was of the opinion that the parent had abandoned or deserted the child or had otherwise so conducted himself, the right to refuse custody of the child, and in its discretion, the right to decline to issue the writ to make the order'. This clause was very widely drafted and gave an almost unlimited discretion to the court to refuse orders for custody of children. The second clause gave the courts the powers to order parents 'to repay any person or institution or guardians of such Poor Law union or such parochial board the whole of the costs incurred in regard to bringing up the child, or such sum as may be just and reasonable in all circumstances'. The main object of this clause was not merely to recompense the institutions, but to discourage parents who wished to remove their children.

Section three of the Act set out the criteria the court must employ to decide whether or not a child should be restored to a parent who had deserted or abandoned it. This clause is of special importance in that the parent had to prove to the court that, although unfit to have custody in the past, he was now fit to have custody of the child. Parental rights were subordinated to the overriding consideration of the welfare of the child. It was probably this clause more than any other that enabled Barnardo to frustrate more than eighty attempts by parents to regain custody of their children in the years that followed.

With the memory of the Barnardo litigation in mind, a lengthy clause, dealing with the rights of parents to ensure that the child be brought up in the religion that the parent had the legal right to require it to be brought up in, was inserted in the Act. The final two clauses merely defined what was meant by parent and person and gave the Act its official title, the Custody of Children Act, 1891. Although at the time it was sometimes referred to by Barnardo's opponents as 'the Barnardo Relief Act', until the monumental Children's Act of 1908 was passed establishing separate juvenile courts, it was one of the most important contributions to the growing body of statute law dealing with the rights of the child.

However, Barnardo's court appearances were by no means at an end. The Court of Appeal had ruled in the Tye case that Barnardo was in contempt of court, and he was only bailed, the question of sentence being adjourned until the results of his appeal to the House of Lords in the Gossage case were known. It was not until 1892 that the case was finally heard before the Lord Chancellor, Lord Halsbury, Lords Herschell, Mcnaghten, Morris and Hannen. The results were both a victory and a defeat for Barnardo. Lord Herschell said – and he had the support of three of his fellow law lords – that to use a writ of habeas corpus as a means of compelling one who has unlawfully parted with the custody of another person as a means to regain that custody, or of punishing him for having parted with it, struck him as being a use of the writ unknown to the law and unwarranted by it. This was the point of law which Barnardo had been anxious to establish. Unfortunately for him, Lord Herschell went on to say that where the court entertained a doubt as to whether this was the fact, it was unquestionably entitled to use the pressure of a writ to test the truth of the allegation that the defendant was no longer in possession or control and to require a return to be made. Opposing counsel immediately made use of this statement to say that in the case of Henry Gossage doubt did exist, and that he and his colleagues had not had an opportunity to cross-examine Barnardo. Although successful on the point of law, Barnardo's appeal had failed to succeed against the issuing of the writ. On 25 July 1892 he was given a further three months in which to make a return and ordered to pay costs.

As at the time of the Arbitration case, a special law costs fund was set up to defray the legal expenses of the various court cases. William Baker had given his services free, but nonetheless costs must have been substantial. It was not a popular appeal. Barnardo insisted that not a shilling of the law costs had ever been charged against the institutions, but it is more than probable that the expenses incurred at that time contributed to the financial crisis of 1893. Although personally responsible for the costs, he must have been helped by a circle of friends who were both wealthy and felt the cause to be worth fighting for.

He did not make life easier for himself by writing an article in *Night and Day* giving his account of the appeal to the House of Lords. For this he was taken to court by his opponents and fined £25 for contempt, a fine which, although 'poor as a churchmouse', he paid himself. When the case finally ended in 1893 Barnardo announced the issue of a special supplement to the May issue of *Night and Day*. If it was ever printed it is no longer to be found; it may well have been suppressed by the committee, fearful that it could give rise to yet more litigation. One is reminded of the action taken by the trustees at the end of the Arbitration case, when they publicly forbade Barnardo to print his reply to the COS.

According to A. E. Williams in his book *Barnardo of Stepney*, Barnardo eventually re-established contact with Mr Norton and discovered that Harry Gossage was doing well in Canada. Nothing else is known about the lives of the three children who caused such fierce controversy.[18] They were the agents of change; the fight between Barnardo and the Roman Catholics for the right to instruct them in the Christian faith acted as a catalyst which lit up whole areas where an unjust law could be used against the true interests of children. Perhaps only religious fanaticism could have caused the litigants to go to such lengths. In the short term the unfavourable publicity Barnardo received at the time and for some time afterwards certainly harmed the reputation of the homes. But in the long term Barnardo's courage and tenacity in fighting for what he believed to be the true interests of his children brought its own reward.

14

Emigration - the Golden Bridge

'Over the Golden Bridge – from the slums to the Fair Land of hopes
and promises'

Night and Day

HAD Barnardo had the physical strength and the necessary
financial support, his Canadian emigration scheme would only
have been the first of several. South Africa, Australia and New
Zealand had all been receiving a steady trickle of children, and
he nurtured the hope until near the end of his life that he would
be able to establish branches in Australia and South Africa
which would enable him to send supervised parties of children
to those two countries as well as to Canada.

Historians have only just begun to study the phenomenon of
juvenile emigration, yet from the last third of the nineteenth
century to the first quarter of the twentieth century between
eighty and a hundred thousand children from the age of five
were removed from the slums of London, Liverpool and other
large urban centres to isolated and lonely homesteads in rural
Canada, under indenture as agricultural labourers or as domestic servants in Canadian households, the younger children
being boarded out with families. Occasionally the children were
adopted, but this was the exception rather than the rule. More
than a third of the children sent to Canada during this period
went under the auspices of the Barnardo organisation. The
success Barnardo achieved, in so far as juvenile emigration can
be seen as a successful policy, was due to the fact that the work
was carried out according to definite principles. The children
were carefully selected and trained before they left England;
they continued to be supervised after they had been placed out
in Canada, and the Barnardo organisation was unusual in paying the boarding-out costs of the younger children. Barnardo
selected his staff with great care, and with his outstanding
administrative ability allied to his attention to detail, the whole
operation was as soundly based as it could be.

From the start the policy of emigrating children had its critics, but opposition to what has come to be seen as a 'flawed' policy did not become effective until the mid 1920s, long after Barnardo's death. At that time opinion on both sides of the Atlantic, concerned at the quality of the home children's lives, succeeded in convincing their respective Governments that 'fourteen years of childhood was the right of even the least of Her Majesty's subjects', and from then on only children above school-leaving age could be emigrated, thus effectively ending the emigration of all juveniles to Canada.

For Barnardo the years following Cairns' death were years of expansion. The policy of boarding children out had become a distinct branch of the work and had grown rapidly. A new hospital called Her Majesty's Hospital had been commissioned to celebrate Queen Victoria's jubilee; nineteen new cottages had been opened at the Girls' Village Home. Barnardo had wanted to go to Canada in 1886, but financial problems prevented him from leaving England. His building activities had overtaxed the financial capacity of the organisation and a large mortgage had had to be raised to meet the costs. However the following year, in spite of having to rely on an overdraft to keep going, Barnardo insisted that he must go to Canada as new super-intendents had been appointed to Hazelbrae whom he wished to see before confirming their appointment. Arrangements concerning the farm also needed to be finalised. Syrie accompanied her husband to Canada on this occasion, taking eight-year-old Queenie with them too. They visited Toronto and Peter-borough, but Syrie and Queenie remained at Hazelbrae while Barnardo was away in the North West. During this visit Barnardo succeeded in concluding all the complicated negotia-tions involved in acquiring, by purchase and grant, land and buildings for the industrial farm in Manitoba which had been begun in 1884.

Upon his return he triumphantly announced that he had now secured over seven thousand acres of land in the Birtle district, not far from the town of Russell. He had appointed A. E. Struthers, an experienced farmer, as manager, and local architects had been commissioned to erect the necessary plain wooden farm buildings. Ever since Barnardo had acquired his labour house for older boys, finding suitable work for these untrained lads had presented formidable problems. Even when sent out to the province of Ontario they soon drifted back into the cities and resumed their old way of life, so that the idea of sending them to the North West of Canada where they would be far from any town appeared to be the complete solution. There were plenty of farmers anxious to take on extra labour, and there was always the possibility that a boy with sufficient initiative might ultimately be able to become a homesteader in his own right.

Financial worries and the litigation with the Roman Catholics prevented Barnardo returning to Canada again until 1890, but during an interval between the court cases he took the opportunity of spending three months both in Canada and the United States, this time taking with him his son Stuart, who was at Fettes College. Stuart was destined for Cambridge where his father hoped he would study medicine. The party consisted of Barnardo, Stuart, his tutor (a Mr Marriott), a secretary and an amanuensis. Besides letters written to his wife, Barnardo also kept a diary which has survived and which gives a vivid impression of how he and his party spent their time. He reported with satisfaction that he was given the place of honour next to the captain at table, and that the captain had given him his room to work in. The day after they left Barnardo celebrated his forty-sixth birthday and wrote:[1]

Assuredly reason for great thankfulness to God for all His mercies and Providential care ... I greatly value the gifts I received to-day, although Stuart seems to have left two parcels behind him, one being from Queenie, and the other from you. Please don't let Queenie know: she will break her heart. Keep it safely till I return, if it is not in my leather portmanteau which is gone down to the hold ... Please don't forget, I am badly wanting a young Christian girl to fill the post of Assistant Secretary, or rather, Assistant to the Secretary. She must be a Christian, if possible she must be a *lady*, but quite as important, she must write a really beautiful hand, clear well formed letters, good figures, and be in the habit of rapid calligraphy. Shorthand is *not* required.

The diary does not relate if Mrs Barnardo found such a paragon, but she was asked to consult with Miss Westgarth who would know the kind of work the new assistant would be required to undertake.

The steamship *Polynesian* obviously justified her nickname of 'Rolling Polly', for the following day the diary recorded:

We had favourable breezes, and the sails which were spread to catch them, although they steadied the ship from pitching, increased her rolling, an increase which we all felt we could have cheerfully dispensed with. I pass over the next twenty-four hours, preferring to draw a curtain over our feeling and experiences which were bad enough to the subjects of them and can never be *adequately described*! Sunday was indeed to most of us a *dies non*.

It did not take Barnardo long to sum up his fellow passengers.

We have a Jewish Rabbi, the Rev. B. A. Elzas and his wife, Mrs. Elzas, on their honeymoon, and I think I may say he is the very least desirable of all our fellow-passengers. I hate applying the word 'cad' to anybody, but I don't think in my life I ever met a man who more worthily deserved it, and who may be more fitly described thereby than the Rev. B. A. Elzas.

There was also a clergyman by name of Williams on board, who had once met Barnardo years ago in East London. He had come from China and was on his way to Banff. Barnardo said that though he had nothing against his personal character, he thought little of his ability as a minister:

I can only express my feelings by a note of interrogation? *What* he did when he was in China I don't know because I am at a loss to conceive what he could do. That he has some general confused ideas of religion I have no doubt. It was quite painful on one occasion to stand by his side when he conducted a service for the emigrants. The Gospel he preached was summed up in a single sentence: 'Let every man do his best and God will do the rest.'

On 10 July Barnardo wrote:

We have not forgotten that to-day is our dear Queenie's birthday, and Stuart, Marriott and I have talked of the dear little puss, whose photograph stands on my table. God makes it a very happy blessed anniversary to the dear child, and may her future life be spent in His service! No doubt you have given her our letters and my present. I shall look forward to hearing from her on arrival.

By the time the vessel was off the coast of Newfoundland, making slow progress because of icebergs, Barnardo had finished most of his work and was able to spend a little time reading. He described Stanley's book *In Darkest Africa* as full of thrilling interest, but it would have been improved if

... the writer would only give his readers credit for being able to see things themselves and not to be perpetually needing explanation. His endeavour to depreciate Gordon by comparison with himself, his contemptuous review of Emin Pasha, whom yet he is compelled to recognise as having great qualities, and whom until the last he hoped to secure either for the Congo or for British service, are types of what I mean.

Mixing his metaphors with splendid abandon, Barnardo concluded: 'They flavour strongly of the old fable "sour grapes" and indeed may be said to be the dead flies in the vase of otherwise sweet ointment.'

A revealing little incident occurred towards the end of the voyage. Barnardo, to his evident pleasure, had been asked to preside at a ship's concert, and having looked over the programme he accepted. But alas, two of the songs were such that

... I was compelled to rise and make a short protest against such pieces being included in the programme. I was very glad when the business was over. Perhaps the most melancholy thing to me in the whole of it was this, that some of the Christian men present thought everything was right, with perhaps the exception of a single song, and evidently did not feel that there was anything inconsistent in sharing in a scheme so unworthy of the followers of Christ.

However, old as I am, I ought not to have needed such a lesson. I yielded to their invitation simply with a desire to please them and as I hoped to prevent the occurrence of that which has occurred; but I ought to have known there is only one position that a servant of the Lord can honestly and happily take on such an occasion, and that is, *to be outside of it all.*

The party stayed on board the steamer until it reached Montreal, where the heat was intense. They were met by de Brissac Owen, Barnardo's representative in Toronto, and did some sightseeing before travelling on to Peterborough. The Annersleys, appointed as superintendents of Hazelbrae in 1887, had proved most unsatisfactory. Barnardo was anxious to see for himself that Miss Woodgate, the lady appointed to replace them, was up to the job.

Miss Woodgate has effected such improvements and changes here, as you who remember what Hazelbrae was, would hardly realise or believe. The servants are respectful; they wait upon us properly, we never see or hear the nineteen children in the house except at morning Prayer. Miss Woodgate has everything like clockwork, is scrupulously methodical and clean, and very thoughtful and capable. Except her slight mannerism, which one soon gets over, there is no possible point at which we can criticise her unfavourably. The grounds are delightfully cool after the broiling heat of the last few days. The grass was green and verdant, the trees in full leaf, and flowers everywhere and Marriott says 'it is just as sweet a spot as he has ever seen in Canada'.

Birthdays were always special occasions in the Barnardo household. The day after they arrived at Hazelbrae Barnardo was writing:

To-day was our dear boy's 16th birthday, and as I was in his room calling him at a little before seven, I gave him your gifts and dear Queenie's and our birthday wishes. My gift consisted of the duplicate legs for his camera which I had to buy at Montreal. He is very pleased both with the brushes and with the prayer book and delighted with Queenie's gift.

Need I add that we have had prayers together, and I have had a quiet happy talk with him; and I do really think the dear boy sees the importance of the better life, although he is so very shy and timid at revealing the secrets of his heart. As you may imagine, tonight I did not let him go to bed without seeing him again, and having the last little word and prayer with him as I tucked him in on his first night at Peterborough and on his birthday night. God bless the dear lad! He has been very amiable and good throughout, quite obedient – we have not had the least trouble and I need hardly say, he often talks of you.

Adolescence cannot have been an easy time for any of Barnardo's own children. There was no escape from the intense religious pressure to which they were subjected. One has the impression that with Stuart it was neither shyness nor timidity that prevented him sharing confidences with his father, but rather a healthy desire to retain some independence of thought, a defensive measure in the face of the strong pressure he was under to conform to his father's wishes.

Hazelbrae had apparently been left in a disgusting state by the Annersleys, and although the capable Miss Woodgate had coped with the downstairs rooms she was baffled as to how to deal with the top rooms. Not so Barnardo:

Tonight I had two or three pounds of sulphur got, and several hours were spent in sealing up windows and every aperture, the girls' mattresses being taken down to the schoolroom where they are to sleep for one night. When I was ready I set fire to the sulphur and then retreated sealing up the last door. While we were at work the wretched vermin actually fell from the ceiling on to me. Happily I observed them and shook them off; but it will show you how infested the place has been, and how necessary a new regime was.

However, this time we have given the creatures their *coup de grace*, and I hope tomorrow we will be free of them for ever. I am having all the woodwork (and you know the place is filled with woodwork) washed as soon as we open the doors with strong carbolic laid on very much like paint.

Obviously the Annersleys' unsatisfactory conduct had affected the proper supervision of the girls, and Barnardo wrote that it was a wise and providential step to have sent out Miss Stent, an experienced and valued worker: 'She thoroughly grasped the exigencies of the position and I have no doubt that in a little while, every girl will have been visited, privately talked to and warned of the dangers before her and assured of rapid assistance in any extremity.' Some of the dangers the girls might face were apparent from Barnardo's instructions concerning their placement: girls must not be left alone unchaperoned when the mistress was away; neither were they to be left alone in distant outhouses milking cows!

An invitation to old girls to visit Hazelbrae resulted in about forty coming in

... the queerest kind of buggies, gigs, waggons and other primitive vehicles, often driven by their employers, sometimes by the mistress only, and of course, in holiday attire. No doubt the staff here see a great deal of the seamy or dark side of Canadian life; but occasions of this sort bring to us not those who have done ill, but those who have done well, and the visits were most encouraging and comforting to us ... We have had many confabulations in which the whole staff have had a share; and I hope that we are beginning to see the gloom that has recently fallen on us clearing up and some hope and prospect of better things. God grant it!

This glimpse of what life was really like on the other side of 'the golden bridge' was rare. The articles in *Night and Day* in which Barnardo wrote of his work in Canada were designed to encourage his supporters to contribute the necessary £10 it cost to equip and place out each child. The articles were frequently illustrated by a whole series of pictures of the children showing them as they were on admittance and as they now appeared, happy and prosperous in Canada, accompanied by a brief résumé of their stories. Barnardo had hoped while he was at Hazelbrae to persuade the Coxes, who now lived in Toronto, to make over the house by deed of gift to the institutions, but he very much feared, owing to all the unpleasantness consequent upon the departure of the Annersleys who had been friendly with the Coxes before their departure, that this would not now be possible. George Cox had become president or director of a large number of important financial and mercantile organisations, and his active support would have been most helpful to Barnardo. The roof at Hazelbrae needed repairing and Barnardo found himself obliged to organise fund-raising events to meet the cost.

As Barnardo's emigration programme became more successful and the number of children he sent to Canada increased, his work started to attract support from a wider field. The Marquess of Lorne, who had been Governor General of Canada for five years, was the first man to succeed Cairns as president. Both he and the Earl of Meath who, as Lord Brabazon, had caused a certain amount of controversy by his advocacy of state-directed colonialisation, as well as Lord Brassey, were interested in emigration, and all three became presidents of the homes in turn. Sir Charles Tupper, the Canadian High Commissioner, attended the annual meeting of 1893 and spoke in terms of the highest praise of the emigration work being done. But in spite of such support and all the success stories Barnardo could quote, there was a continuing current of opposition to juvenile immigration in Canada. Fears about the mental and physical characteristics of the children, 'the offal of the most depraved characters in the cities of the old country' as they were once described, found continual expression, particularly among doctors. But the most vocal opposition came from the Toronto Trades and Labor Council, later known as the Dominion, Trades and Labor Congress. D. J. O'Donoghue, a printer by trade and chairman of the legislative committee of the Toronto Trades and Labor Council for eighteen years, had some experience with Canadian orphans through his work with the Ottawa St Patrick Orphan Asylum.[2] He kept the issue of juvenile immigration before his colleagues and castigated the whole movement as a 'gross injustice to the people of Canada and in particular to the working classes'.

The system of bonuses whereby the Dominion Government paid $2 *per capita* for all but pauper children to the responsible agency, the subsidised transatlantic passage and the free railway transport inland were all, it was alleged, a drain on the public purse, and aided entrants who were not only unsuitable but detrimental to the proper advancement of the dominion. Labour leaders argued that Canada already had an ample supply of pauper and orphan children in its own institutions, and the addition of 'little paupers', often sporting a fair growth of whiskers and with a marked inclination for life in urban centres, during the years of deepening depression in the 1890s could only be seen as a threat to the native unemployed who received no public assistance. Any adverse publicity immediately stirred the suspicions of the populace, and in 1896 two events occurred which illustrated just how easily this could happen.

One of the lads from the farm at Russell was charged with indecent assault and was tried before a grand jury at Brandon. The jury disagreed over the charge and in the event the lad was sentenced to only one month's imprisonment, but because the foreman of the jury made some remarks reflecting on the work of the Barnardo organisation, his comments were taken up by all the leading Canadian newspapers; their comments were transmitted by cable to England and reproduced by the press all over the English-speaking world, inflicting, as Barnardo pointed out, 'an undeserved and almost irreparable injury upon a section of the Canadian Community'. The Brandon jurors in effect expressed the opinion that, in view of the case they had just dealt with, there should be legislation to prevent the further importation of the class of children now being brought out from the slums of Europe to industrial schools and farms in Canada. Barnardo interpreted this representation as an attack on his work and took the opportunity of replying at length[3] with a formidable array of facts and figures, to the underlying implication that his children were vicious criminals and a menace to Canadians. His letter restated the principles upon which his work was conducted:

(a) That only the flower of our flock shall at any time be emigrated to Canada – that is, only those who are in robust physical and mental health; those who are thoroughly upright, honest and virtuous; and those who, being boys, have been industrially trained in our own workshops, or who, being girls, have had careful instruction in domestic pursuits.

(b) That continued supervision shall be exercised over these children after they have been placed out in Canadian homesteads; first by sympathetic visitation, second by regular correspondence. Emigration in the case of young children without continuous supervision is in our opinion presumptuous folly and simply courts disaster.

(c) That in the case of the total failure of any emigrants, the Colonies shall be safeguarded by their *return* at our expense wherever possible.

The foregoing conditions form the basis upon which alone our emigration work has been erected; it follows, therefore, that if we have loyally carried out these provisions we have done our utmost to ensure that no young person is sent out by us to Canada who is known to have had any serious blot upon his or her past record, to have been tainted in morals, or to have any marked tendency to disease, mental or physical ... What the public estimate of the character and value of our young emigrants has been and still is, is shown by this one fact, that whereas during earlier years of our work every child sent out was applied for twice over, now we have five applications registered in our books for every individual boy or girl who is fit for employment.

Barnardo's letter contained tables of figures which enabled him to show that in the past ten years, out of a total number of six thousand, one hundred and twenty-eight emigrants, there were fifty-two recorded convictions, making a percentage of ·136 convictions per thousand as compared with convictions among the general population of Canada recorded at ·755. Barnardo admitted that there were a further sixty-six of his children whose careers had been deemed unsatisfactory from his point of view, but claimed that even with a total figure of a hundred and eighteen failed emigrants this represented less than 2 per cent of the total number emigrated. By using Canadian criminal statistics he turned the tables on his detractors:

Reviewing calmly and dispassionately the successes and failures of the 6,128 young people sent out from these institutions to Canada, and judging the same by the criterion of the criminal statistics of the general population of Canada, published under official authority, it would appear that, taken as a whole, 'the class of youths brought to the Barnardo Home from the old country' are much more free from crime, vice, general profligacy or vagrancy than is the population of the Dominion generally, or any particular section of it considered separately.

Not all the agencies dealing with the emigration of juveniles were well organised, nor were all children so carefully supervised. With the increasing number of children arriving in Canada, reports of ill treatment began to appear more frequently, and the actions of the emigration agencies were used to demonstrate that 'the Great British Nation' was 'so lost of all morals and Christianity that they would lose the soul of a child for a few dollars'. Attention naturally focused on Barnardo's work because he was by this time the undisputed leader in the field.

When one of Barnardo's boys, George Green, died and his employer was tried on a charge of manslaughter, the tragedy added fuel to the fires of controversy. According to a letter written by de Brissac Owen[4] to the Secretary of State for the Interior in January 1896, Green had been sent to a farmer named Cranston for a month on trial and had been returned as he had defective vision and was unable to perform the work required. Three days after being returned to the home he was placed with a Miss Helen Findlay, a member of a family with whom Owen had for several years past placed boys. She had kept house for her brother, George Findlay, and when he died in 1894 she was left in charge of the farm, in spite of much opposition from the family. It was to her that the boy was sent and nothing more was heard from the boy by Owen, although he had two addressed and stamped postcards in his possession, until the notice of his death through neglect and cruelty appeared in the paper.

The trial at Owen Sound ended in a disagreement of the jury, and there was much conflicting medical evidence. On the one hand Owen admitted that the boy had short sight and had only one eye, and although he denied that he had used the words 'of weak intellect' he had stated that he was 'not brilliant but that he was neither imbecile, or a lunatic or an idiot or insane'. For this he was castigated by the Trades and Labor Council as 'Dr. Barnardo's versatile agent in Toronto who can, when it suits his purpose, travel on the outside edge of truth without trouble of conscience'. A witness for the other side spoke of the boy as being 'lame, knock-kneed, hump-backed and cross-eyed; that his mouth was crooked and he was short-sighted and of weak intellect'. But whatever the true facts about the boy's physical condition, his case was used to exemplify the weakness of the system of medical examinations which were supposed to prevent the entry of medically unfit children. The minutes of the legislative committee of the Trades and Labor Council also reveal the extent of trade union hostility to Barnardo personally:[5]

Your Committee are astonished at Dr. Barnardo's lack of his usual audacious shrewdness in rushing into public print in England with a denial that he is sending imbeciles out to Canada and asserting that the medical examinations of his protégés are 'stricter than is the examination of soldiers in the British Army' before he had time to read the sworn testimony of his man Owen. Although Dr. Barnardo is a preacher of the Gospel – at least he 'holds forth' when he visits this city in more than one of Toronto's Christian churches – he must have intended this statement 'for the marines' as nobody else will believe it. Still the Doctor must be accredited with at least one other very prominent characteristic and that is – *bare faced effrontery*.

The fact that Barnardo had just received a purse for £3,000 in recognition of his work in founding homes for destitute children in London and Canada added to the committee's sense of outrage: 'Dr. Barnardo was well entitled to this recognition at the hands of the London people for his work in ridding its parishes of thousands of undesirable children (and landing them in Canada at a dollar a head) whose maintenance otherwise would be a direct tax upon London ratepayers.'

The Owen Sound tragedy was the occasion for a further spate of hostile press comments. 'All we have to say is that if Canada has been getting "the flower" of Dr. Barnardo's flock, our people have good cause to congratulate themselves that they have not had the rest,' was how one paper put it. The *Toronto Evening Star* wrote that 'Canada has had enough Barnardo boys – even the best of them. This class of assisted immigrants should be banned outright.' In a long article admitting that Dr Barnardo was animated by good motives, the paper said there was plenty of room to question the wisdom of planned juvenile emigration, both for the children themselves and for the community to which they were sent. It argued that if the children were the offspring of physically sound parents their introduction into a new country might be beneficial to them and to the country, but the writer of the article feared that many children had been shipped to the country with inherited and ineradicable diseases and been placed on farms, and had grown up and married into the families of Canadian farmers. Such unions must propagate disease and lower the physical standard of the people. 'Let England look after her own paupers and not continue a practice which tends to the physical corruption of a pure blooded people.' It was not only country doctors and labour leaders who tried to bring pressure on the Dominion Government to end the immigration programme. Urban child-welfare workers, who saw the more fortunate British immigrants usurping rural placements which they felt should have belonged to needy Canadian orphaned and dependent children, added their voice to the chorus of opposition. But preoccupation with more pressing domestic concerns left the Dominion Government no time to concern itself with the immigration programme, funded and staffed from abroad, which provided the country with 'the most valuable . . . and least costly of all immigration'.[6]

Ironically the very fears being voiced in Canada became reasons for the increased support given in Britain to the juvenile emigration movement. Continuing prosperity based on trade within an expanding Empire had quieted middle-class fears and doubts about the dangers of the casual residuum. But in the 1890s chronic poverty was the dominant social problem, and social reformers and others concerned about the condition of the poor and unemployed continued to seek for solutions. Increasingly the idea that the condition of the masses was caused by generations of urban slum living rather than their moral failings came to be accepted. The theory of urban degeneration took hold. Barnardo's concept of 'the golden bridge' had obvious appeal for those who were seeking answers to this problem. The ideas put forward by Brabazon and Booth for state-directed colonialisation had found little practical support, but as the ideas of the social imperialists became increasingly influential towards the end of the century, Barnardo's emigration work, as it grew in size, gained support both because it removed slum children from their unhealthy environment and because it forged links between the dominion and the mother country. The flood of imperialist sentiment that swept over the nation at the outbreak of the Boer War in 1899 further stilled the earlier anxieties of revolution and unrest.

But as the war dragged on and newspaper revelations about the low standard of recruits were made public, the spectre of racial degeneration and physical deterioration raised its head. There were fears that unless measures were taken, the physical condition of the casual poor would so weaken national efficiency that the Empire itself could be endangered. Barnardo was not slow to exploit this change in the climate of public opinion. His was the first among the children's rescue societies to assert the claim that emigration was the answer to the threat posed by the degeneration of the casual poor. He saw at once that if juvenile emigration could be seen by the charitable to be advantageous not only to the child but also to the concept of Empire, support for the work would be enormously increased. By the use of slogans like 'How to think Imperially' he led the way in popularising a programme of philanthropic imperialism which was designed not only to save the child but to strengthen the Empire. The success of this policy can be seen from a study of the receipts; support for the institutions increased dramatically during the first years of the twentieth century.

Barnardo made his fifth and final visit to Canada and the United States in 1900, a visit which lasted all of four months. He had been in failing health for more than a year and wrote to his wife:[7] 'I have been rather seedy twice, but I am better now, but I find I have to take great care. I am reminded twenty times a day, that there is at least sixteen years between me and the man who came out here to settle in this spot in 1884.' The visit was in a sense a triumphal progress. Wherever he stayed old boys and girls came to see him; 'Very often the hall of the hotel would be inconveniently crowded with young men, for the most part well grown, stalwart, muscular fellows, bronzed and bearded and altogether so changed that I usually quite failed to recognise in them the puny, half starved, homeless waifs that had come under my care in England, twelve, fifteen or twenty years before.'[8] He was deeply touched by the loyalty of most to their old associations and their gratitude for past help, although he came across a few of his former girls who occupied positions of real distinction and preferred to break all ties with the homes. He met over a thousand of his children. An annual agricultural exhibition was taking place in Toronto and open house was kept at Farley Avenue, the receiving home, where several hundred fellows called to register their names in a book at the home. At every halting place on the way to Winnipeg he was greeted by groups of lads many of whom had come from great distances to welcome him. He was pleased at the way in which they had developed and noted the free and familiar way in which they talked: 'Some might think their manner betokened a lack of respect ... but theirs was respect without servility, and with that conscious sense of independence which grows and flourishes in the atmosphere of Canada.' He thought that many more were Christian and took their religion seriously than would have been the case with a comparable group in England, and some had remained total abstainers. Of the eleven thousand children who had been emigrated only eighty had been in trouble with the law, and as Barnardo pointed out with satisfaction, this represented less than 2 per cent. Yet even among those he met there were, as he put it, 'hints of trouble, of trial, of sadness and even temptation yielded to'. Of the ten thousand he did not meet, no one will ever know how many found that 'the land of hopes and promises' lived up to their expectations. Only letters from those who were happy found their way into print.

Not content with his work in Canada, Barnardo had long hoped to establish branches in Australia and South Africa. Over the years he had received much support for the homes from Australia, particularly from New South Wales, and from New Zealand. Several groups of children had gone out to both countries either in small parties or under the care of friends. Non-conformity flourished in both countries, and Barnardo's old friend Henry Varley had made several trips to Australia to preach the Gospel. Barnardo was confident that if he could raise money to finance the venture there would be no difficulty in finding homes and work for his children. But he did not want to send them out unaccompanied, fearing that during the course of the long journey they would come into contact with undesirable emigrants travelling steerage. Barnardo had a correspondent in Queensland who had already placed out one party of boys and another small group were sent to him in 1896. Owing to the influence of Lord Brassey, who had gone to Australia as Governor-General in 1896, a scheme had been submitted to Sir John Forrest,[9] Premier of Western Australia, which was discussed when he came to England in 1897. But in spite of Australian interest and the offer of land from Lord Brassey,[10] then president of the homes, for the establishment of an industrial farm on the lines of the one in Manitoba, nothing came of this initiative.

Barnardo had also had many requests for trained children from South Africa, and he had been seriously investigating the possibility of setting up an industrial farm there as well. But with the outbreak of hostilities between the Boers and the British, nothing could be done until the war was ended. When peace was finally concluded in 1902, he had to hand a personal envoy to make the necessary preliminary inquiries. Stuart, having decided against medicine as a profession, had qualified as a mining engineer in London and gone out to Canada to work for the Arlington Mining Company in the far North. He had visited the Manitoba farm several times and so had first-hand experience of the work carried on there. He and his father had spent some time together at Russell in 1900, and Barnardo had been able to reassure his wife at that time that 'Stuart was strong and vigorous and simply enthusiastic about his work. I am quite certain he will do well. He has one or two very advantageous offers, one of these he may in the end accept.' Although Stuart took part in the gold rush in the Klondike, this cannot have been a very successful experience, for he had returned to England by mid-1902. In commissioning him to go to South Africa to investigate what possibilities there were of obtaining government aid towards establishing a training institution for boys in one part of the country and for girls in another, Barnardo agreed to pay him his expenses and a small salary.[11] Stuart set sail in RMS *Scot* on 4 August, where he met the South African Alfred Beit, millionaire, and Dr Jameson, who both expressed sympathy with the object he had in view. Sixteen days later the ship reached Cape Town and for the next four months Stuart travelled all over South Africa seeing and meeting with a wide variety of people in government, industry and agriculture.

His regular written reports of all he saw and everyone he met, sent to his father at intervals, provide a fascinating glimpse of the country as it then was. He was very thorough and determined; although it took him a long time to get an interview with Lord Milner, who had recently been made Governor of the Transvaal and Orange River Colony, he persevered, writing to his father while he was kept waiting: 'Everybody out here seems to be born tired. The whole country is in a sort of paralysed condition, waiting, like Mr. Micawber for something to turn up.' When he finally met Lord Milner he found him sympathetic to the idea of juvenile emigration in principle, but suggested that it might be best for Barnardo to send a few of his boys to a government model farm before attempting to acquire a farm of his own. The Duke of Argyll, who had been president of the homes both as Marquess of Lorne and after he succeeded to the dukedom, was also anxious to help. He owned a considerable tract of land which was administered by Henderson's Transvaal Estates, and he was willing to put any one farm on his lands at Barnardo's disposal. Stuart had been supplied with a list of possible farms, but he often found the greatest difficulty in visiting them as public transport was practically non-existent and horses impossible to hire, so expensive and scarce had they become as a result of the war. When he did succeed in reaching his objective, the land was often totally unsuited to any kind of farming, although he thought that a few farms had possibilities. His final assessment of the situation was not unhopeful. He made little of the political aspect of the emigration question, in spite of the strong Dutch opposition he had encountered to the idea of any further British emigration, but warned his father that he could expect little government support at the present time. He was also very aware of the different social conditions that prevailed in South Africa compared to Canada.

Unlike Canada, in South Africa nearly all domestic servants were natives and nearly all the land privately owned, for the most part by Dutch farmers who had become accustomed to cheap native labour and were basically opposed to further immigration.

Boys and girls should be of as superior a class as possible in view partly of the fact that white servants of both sexes have not proved a success when brought out here; in part because the South African colonist is an aristocratic person, or thinks he is, and does not want to be saddled with children of the criminal class ... Boys and girls sent out must be kept away from mixing with the natives in any way and you must not send out children with the least trace of colour in them ... the great danger to young immigrants to South Africa is that of getting down to the native level and forgetting they are whites and consequently the superior race.

The other great danger seemed to be that, 'no matter what the social rank or position of whites in the country where they originally come from, yet as soon as they set foot in South Africa they find themselves one step higher in the social scale owing to the native populations. This in a great number of cases causes them to look down and refuse to undertake hard work of the kind they had previously been willing to do.' Nonetheless Stuart believed his father could succeed. His report ended simply with the words: 'I hope I have done satisfactorily. I have done my best for you out here and I think you will meet with success.' His mission accomplished, Stuart did not return to England but went back to Johannesburg where he had decided to strike out on his own and resume his career as a mining engineer.

The financial situation facing the homes at this time would have precluded any further expansion of the work without outside funding; no one but Barnardo could have set up a satisfactory emigration scheme in South Africa, and he no longer had the energy and resilience to grapple with all the problems such an initiative would involve. But even if he had been fit and money had been available, it is to be doubted whether Barnardo would have wished to proceed. There was only one further mention of South Africa in *Night and Day*[12] in early 1903, and nothing in the minutes. One of Barnardo's principles had been to accept all destitute children of whatever age, sex, creed or nationality, believing them all equal in the sight of God. He had been delighted at the way Canada had fostered in many of them a spirit of true independence; he might well have felt that the social conditions prevailing in South Africa would not be so conducive to the interests of many of his children. The lack of financial support was certainly the principal reason that Stuart's report was not implemented.

Thus Canada remained the only outlet, and consequently for

the next few years the number of children going to the dominion never dropped below a thousand. The speed with which the
children passed through the English homes increased accordingly. Barnardo never had the least doubt that his emigration
policy was beneficial to the children and a source of wealth to
Canada, whilst it enabled him to rescue and place out in life an
ever greater number of children. He made clear his views on the
question of heredity versus environment on more than one
occasion. By 1904 more than fifty thousand children had passed
through his hands, and he could write with confidence that
'heredity is not fate, it is only one factor . . . good environment
granted certain conditions is as powerful a factor in neutralising
tendencies which one might suppose would be all potent in life'.

There is no doubt that the dramatic increase in the number of
children being sent to Canada after 1899 brought pressure on the
Canadian side of the organisation, already working under tight
financial constraints; the quality of the supervision offered to
the children inevitably suffered and debts began to accumulate
on both sides of the Atlantic. Sadly, one of the first actions
forced on the council which took over the running of the institutions after Barnardo's death in 1905 was to arrange for the sale of
the farm in Manitoba, which in spite of all the care and money
lavished on it had never paid its way. The phenomenon of
juvenile emigration is now attracting more interest; as more
research and analysis becomes available a more systematic
assessment of the long-term results of emigration will be possible. Barnardo himself certainly had no doubts about its value to
his children and to the nation. He was not alone in this. In its
obituary notice the *Daily Mail* wrote of him as 'A real Empire
Builder':[13]

Starting in a slum, he became a real empire builder, whose influence and work reach the shores of the Pacific. Beginning with one
miserable young Stepney waif he became the father-in-charity of sixty
thousand of the fatherless and destitute. These would have filled the
workhouse and the prisons. He transformed them by the thousand to
makers of the Great Britain beyond the sea.

15

The Financial Crisis

THE first public hint that all was not well with the financial situation of the homes made its appearance in the annual report of 1889, the same year that saw the start of the court actions concerning the custody of children. By the time the court battles were over, the incipient financial crisis had come to a head.

Since the establishment of the committee of management, Barnardo, as founder and Director of the homes, had always each year written his own personal report which preceded that of the committee, they first having approved its contents. The report of the committee invariably started by carefully defining their relationship with the Director and setting out their specific responsibilities, which were to sign cheques, approve a monthly audited statement of receipts and expenditure, undertake an audited statement of receipts and finally to inspect the various English establishments to ensure adequate standards were maintained. Barnardo did not take kindly to criticism from visiting members, and some found that resignation was the only effective means of marking their disapproval. Samuel Sheppard, as chairman, had the ultimate responsibility of interpreting how far the committee was entitled to interfere with the 'fulness and freedom of the Founder's action so as not to neutralise his effectiveness'. The committee was unique of its kind at the time, and its relationship with the dynamic and inspired creator of the institutions for which it had responsibility was fraught with difficulties. The idea of such a committee had been Cairns' brainchild at the time of the arbitration, and while he was alive he effectively held the balance between the two sides. The trustees possessed the ultimate sanction of dismissing the Director, a sanction which they could now no longer invoke without endangering the work of the organisation itself. They took no part in the direction and management of the homes, requiring only to be consulted over matters financial.

In 1887 William Baker and Howard Williams, two men who were to exercise great influence over the institutions during the following years, joined the committee. William Baker, whose elder brother Charles had been on the management committee since 1880, was an Irishman from Lismacue, Co. Tipperary. He was a distinguished and successful lawyer deeply interested in evangelistic work who since his arrival in England in 1875 had worked at the Chancery bar and had acquired a flourishing practice. Howard Williams, a son of Sir George Williams, the virtual founder of the YMCA, had both business and administrative experience. His father was not only deeply involved with the affairs of the YMCA, he was also head of the very prosperous firm of Hitchcock and Williams in the City, and Howard Williams was actively involved in the work of both organisations. That the homes survived the financial and legal crises of the nineties is no doubt largely due to the financial acumen and business experience of Williams and to the legal expertise of Baker, who were to become Treasurer and Director of the homes respectively in 1905, after Barnardo's death. Cairns had been succeeded as president by the Marquess of Lorne, a man of much less forcible character, and Barnardo was able to persuade both committee and trustees that his work could not be carried on effectively in the old inconvenient buildings he had been using. The following year Queen Victoria would be celebrating her jubilee, and to commemorate the event he proposed not only to build a new hospital for children, to be called Her Majesty's Hospital in honour of the Queen, but to rebuild at Stepney, Hawkhurst and Jersey. Although not luxurious, the buildings were well and solidly finished and no expense was spared to make them fit for the children.

The debt that had been incurred at the time of the arbitration, when money had had to be advanced to finish paying for the building of the village, had never been completely liquidated. Now fresh mortgages were created and further overdrafts were arranged to finance this new burst of building. Although by 1889 the committee was able to announce that the planned programme of reconstruction was nearly complete, they also

7 The boys' playground at Stepney, showing the south end of the Bower Street building

had to point out that the mere cessation of building would not discharge the liabilities thus created. Repayment of the loans and interest on the mortgages had to come from income, as the jubilee fund, set up to meet the cost of the new building work, had petered out, swamped by the many other jubilee appeals launched that year. At the same time they noted that in the past five years the work had almost tripled, necessitating further expenditure. However, to reassure their supporters they pointed out that the value of the properties was now almost treble the indebtedness of the institutions.

Behind the scenes Sheppard was becoming increasingly worried by his Director's apparently insatiable desire to spend more money than he could raise. When the manager of the London and South Western Bank wrote to say that the banking statement had long been overdrawn and now stood at £18,000, and either the account must be put in order or securities supplied,

Sheppard immediately convened a special meeting. A further overdraft of £22,000 was arranged, and the deeds of Leopold House, 18 Stepney Causeway, Bower Street and Teighmore, Jersey, were handed over by way of security. It was decided that the running audit should not be in the hands of Carter and Clay, who were responsible for the general accountancy of the institutions. Messrs Turquand, Young & Co., who had been doing an additional annual audit since the arbitration, were instructed to take over the running audit as well. The account standing in the Director's name was changed and renamed account number two. When the Earl of Meath was asked to take on the presidency of the homes in 1888 he had demanded as a condition of acceptance that an independent audit should be made. The committee in agreeing to his request stipulated that it should be done at his own expense. Meath resigned the following year, but in the meantime the committee had come to see that his request was more reasonable than they had at first supposed.

While Cairns was alive, the committee would habitually sanction new work provided Barnardo was able to raise the money for it, or at least for a large part of it. In his early days Barnardo recognised that by making outright appeals for money he was offending many evangelicals. To go some way towards meeting this point of view Barnardo's appeals appeared at first only in *The Christian* and other religious papers, but as he became aware of the extent of the need he had uncovered, he saw no need to restrict his appeal to Christians alone. Soon he was asking for support through his magazines and postal appeals, through advertisements, the sale of photographs, pamphlets and booklets; he was raising money through bazaars and sales of work, and by talking, preaching and lecturing the length and breadth of the land. He came to regard appealing for funds as part of his ministry. Until 1888, apart from the help given by his committee and supporters at public functions, he carried out single-handed his duty, as he saw it, to awaken the conscience of the wealthy to the needs of the poor.

In 1885 Barnardo had been very ill – the nature of his illness is not known – and he had been forced to take a prolonged rest, a warning of things to come. The demands the organisation was making on his time and the state of his health made it obvious that he could no longer be solely responsible for raising money, more especially as the amount needed to keep pace with his work was increasing yearly. In 1888 five lecturers were appointed who were known as deputation secretaries; two were clergymen, two were Non-conformist ministers and one was a layman. One of the ministers, the Rev. W. J. Mayers, had been a friend of Barnardo's since his earliest days in Stepney. Barnardo was nothing if not enterprising in the use he made of his deputation secretaries. In 1891 Mayers took a party of 'musical boys' to Australia on a fund-raising tour which lasted all of four months.[1] Nothing was left to chance; special costumes were designed for Mayers and the boys, and £2,000 were set aside for their expenses. They travelled extensively and succeeded not only in making known the work of the organisation in New Zealand and Australia, but in raising more than £10,000 for the institutions. Barnardo's hopes were more than justified. On his return each boy was presented with a watch and a letter of commendation for his services; Mayers received a present of £100. Barnardo planned to repeat the exercise in the United States, but unhappily the train taking the boys from Toronto to their first engagement in Chicago was involved in an accident in which two of the boys were killed, and the experiment was never tried again. Nearer home performances by the 'musical boys' became a regular feature of the fund-raising calendar. The boys travelled all over the country and they revisited Australia on more than one occasion.

In the same year that the 'musical boys' went to Australia, Barnardo put before his committee yet another idea to increase his income: the creation of a league of boys and girls from the well-to-do classes, 'to extend practical sympathy and support toward the sick, crippled, blind, deaf and dumb and ailing children of the waif classes, especially those under Dr. Barnardo's care'. The Young Helpers' League, as it was to be known, would not only be an effective means of replacing many of his old friends and supporters who had died or moved away, but it would also, he hoped, greatly extend the scope of the work. Thoroughly Victorian in its uninhibited emphasis on the 'two nations' theme, it was immediately popular. Mrs Everard Poole was appointed chief warden, a magazine was launched and Princess Mary, Duchess of Teck, became its first president. Within a year the League had attracted eleven thousand members, but despite its popularity the amount raised was disappointingly small in proportion to the effort needed to raise it.

It would be a mistake to mention the Young Helpers' League without referring to the fact that it too is said to owe its birth to a dream Barnardo dreamed while dozing in his chair. In this one he saw himself walking beside a fast-flowing stream when he heard a cry for help and saw a boy struggling in the water. Running ahead of the boy, he stretched out a hand as far as he could, but was unable to reach him. Calling for help to some children playing a little way on he made another attempt to save the boy, succeeding this time because the children held on to his legs and clothes and he could thus reach further. The symbolism is obvious: the contributions of the league were to be used specifically to help maintain sick and suffering children.

The same year saw another important new development. At this time a third of all children admitted to the homes came from the provinces. Barnardo argued that it would be much cheaper and more effective if provincial centres were opened so that all the children's case histories could be checked on the spot. A receiving centre to be run by a married agent and his wife which could accommodate eight to ten children was all that was required. The committee could not but agree to the scheme, stipulating only that each centre should cost no more than £250. Barnardo promptly opened seven centres in Bath, Cardiff, Edinburgh, Leeds, Liverpool, Newcastle and Plymouth which were known from the beginning as the 'ever open doors'. He was later to maintain in their defence that these centres had been one of the most effective ways of maintaining his support, and that money, legacies and gifts from the provinces had noticeably increased as a result.

However, in the short term the 'ever open doors' had the inevitable effect of adding to the number of children who came into his care. By 1892 the number had risen to well over four thousand. A year later more money was needed and a further loan of £10,000 from the United Kingdom Provident Temperance Association had had to be raised.[2] In exchange another title deed was handed over, and a policy for £5,000 was taken out on the Director's life. Mr Anstis Bewes, a fairly recent member of the committee, found the situation alarming and wrote privately to Samuel Sheppard:[3]

As you know, these last four months have been bad for income, and the expenses are going up steadily. The £10,000 second mortgage was absorbed immediately with none of the expected beneficial results of buying cheaper and the overdraft at the bank is as big as ever, £23,000. There seems absolutely no limit to the increasing size of the work, hundreds of children, enough for a separate charity being added every year ...

The bane of the Institution is what Dr. Barnardo most prides himself on: 'No absolutely destitute child ever refused admittance.' I can only think of two plans, one to stop the increase absolutely and tell the Doctor he must not entertain more than the present number until the debt or the greater part is paid off, or instruct him to do the same thing by raising the standard of the absolutely destitute. What would you and Mr. Fowler say to this?

Samuel Sheppard, in forwarding Bewes' letter to Barnardo, wrote that it had only been for his sake personally that he had avoided raising doubts, but that he now felt that unless expenditure was limited he would no longer be able to hold the committee together. The possibility that a situation might arise which would make Sheppard and his colleagues personally liable for the debts incurred by the institutions made membership of the committee an increasingly hazardous occupation. A joint meeting of trustees and committee took place in March, and they sent Barnardo a letter making definite demands. Only children who were in dire need were to be admitted; boarded-out cases were to be reduced until the numbers fell to below five hundred; old debts were to be paid off at an average of £1,000 monthly; tradesmen and other persons accepting orders were to sign a form indicating that the funds of the institution alone were liable and that creditors had no claim against any individual except Dr Barnardo; and finally an insurance of £20,000 on the Director's life was to be effected as soon as possible.

Barnardo reacted characteristically. He wrote a passionate appeal to the readers of *Night and Day* for help:[4]

A great crisis has arisen in the history of our work – a crisis the gravity of which cannot easily be exaggerated ... I stand face to face with the most serious problem which has ever met me during my twenty-seven years of labour among destitute children ... shall I partly close my doors and meet the need of every second destitute child who appeals for aid?

Ironically, this crisis came at a time when Barnardo himself was relatively prosperous. He had acquired a substantial house, Ardmore, at Buckhurst Hill. Although it was well supplied with guest rooms he had built on a large room in which he held regular evangelistic services. He had at that time a penchant for stained glass, which he had inserted into many of the windows.[5] His children were being expensively educated. Stuart had left Monckton Combe and was in his last year at Fettes. Queenie was at an exclusive and strictly religious school at Eastbourne, from which she was to be expelled for sliding down the banisters on a tea tray. Cyril, born four years after Baby Tom's death, was at a prep school and was to go on to Repton, popular at that time among top evangelical families. Even so Barnardo was uneasy about the effect school life might have on his youngest son, and wrote a letter which he asked him to keep, warning him against doing mean things and stressing the importance of honesty, of keeping his mind and thoughts pure and remembering to pray daily. The letter ends: 'Remember you are my boy – Dr. Barnardo's own boy – and keep from everything wrong and dishonourable for my sake and Mother's.' In the original letter the word 'own' has been inserted afterwards, which must have had a certain poignant significance for Cyril, who had to share his father with so many other boys.

Only one child remained at home, a little daughter, Marjorie Elaine, born in 1890 some months after Mrs Barnardo had become seriously ill with a complaint which was to impair her health and force her to rest for several hours daily for the next few years. It was soon clear that little Marjorie would never develop normally, but Barnardo loved her with that particular tenderness he showed to all disabled children. He was writing steadily. His children's magazine *Our Darlings*, which had succeeded *The Children's Treasury*, was doing well, and he was preparing to launch yet another children's magazine, *Our Bubble*. Magazine articles flowed from his pen in a never-ending stream.

Always a natty dresser, Barnardo now looked even more the part of the benevolent philanthropist. He had put on weight, and deafness forced him to use an ear trumpet, but if his coat was at times a trifle tightly buttoned his linen was always immaculate. His cuffs were specially made to button on to his shirt and he always carried a spare pair with him so he could change them in case of need. With his cane, top hat and the grey frock coat he liked to wear on public occasions, he looked successful and flourishing, a far cry from his early impoverished days. Although he still preached at the Edinburgh Castle, his religious allegiance had altered and his reconciliation with the established Church was made explicit when he received his licence as a lay reader of the Church of England from the Bishop of St Albans.

He was becoming an increasingly lonely man. Many of his friends had died, and writing of the death of Spurgeon he said he felt the desolation of personal loss. But he was not only losing friends through death; his actions were alienating even his closest colleagues. William Baker, whose affection and admiration were sincere, felt it necessary to write a strongly worded letter in which he said that he believed that by allowing debts to mount he was placing himself in opposition to the will of God. Even William Fowler, the generous and long suffering treasurer of the homes, felt that the organisation had become too large for any one person to manage. But as usual Barnardo would not accept criticism. Deeply grieved that Baker should write in such terms, he was not to be deflected from doing what he felt to be right. Nor would he accept that there was any irresponsible management or improper administration, arguing that his many journalistic, sectarian, political and professional critics would have soon exposed it had there been. The real cause of the debt was the £200,000 that had been borrowed to acquire and build property. Had the British public recognised the importance of the work at that time and come forward with a capital sum, he would have had sufficient income now. In a desperate attempt to stave off the necessity of retrenching, Barnardo appealed directly to many of his old friends for help.

A letter from him to Lord Radstock, whom he had not seen for fifteen years, highlighted his changed attitude, a change that Radstock noted with regret. Radstock and Barnardo had met at the Mildmay Conference that summer, but owing to Barnardo's deafness Radstock had been unable to get over to him the reason why he felt he could no longer support the homes, and had written to say that he believed that Barnardo was following his own wishes rather than doing God's will; he saw the mounting debts as evidence of this, and felt that Barnardo had been 'tempted to lean more on man to get the help of people who were influential with the world rather than with God'. In his reply Barnardo for the first time admitted openly that his views had changed and that he had rejoined the Church of England.[6]

> I am bound to tell you that within the last fifteen or sixteen years I have personally been led to resume my communication with the Church of England, although I am deeply sensible of her grave defects ... Of course, I do not talk of this for it only refers to my personal feeling ... but I felt it would be uncandid to you, who have written me so kind, so unexpectedly friendly and brotherly a letter after a silence of fifteen years, not to tell you frankly ... for your private ear only, that which concerns me so deeply.

It is interesting to note that this change was one he felt might damage his public image and how consciously he lived at two levels, one private and one public. The letter continues:

> I feel most tempted to add, that sometimes I feel dreadfully alone so far as human friendship is concerned; all my old friends and counsellors have passed away; hardly one is left. One dear old man who lives abroad is my only link with days gone by ... Of those of my own age who have survived, almost all have withdrawn their friendship – I think that is the correct term – or are so absorbed, I suppose, in other matters that old friendships seem to have died out.

Could he have but realised it, his loneliness sprang in part from that stubborn intransigence which had marked his behaviour throughout his life. The central message of his letter to Radstock was clear: no matter what others thought, he believed that he was right. 'I may be very, very wrong; you may be wholly right; but at present, from the standpoint from which I write, I think the position is a sound one, and one pleasing to God; in fact, I have no doubt of it.' It was not, however, pleasing to his committee.

Although the initial response appeared encouraging, his supporters were only replying sooner rather than later to his appeal, and by the end of the year it was evident that the extra £10,000 the committee felt they must have would not be forthcoming. The Director's life was insured, Deaconess House was closed, the number of deaconesses was reduced and less relief work undertaken; his publications were all slimmed down and appeared less frequently. The most painful economies were those affecting the children: the number boarded out fell by five hundred, the number admitted was reduced by six hundred, and the number emigrated alone increased in 1893, but after that numbers in all categories remained below the 1892 figure until 1899 when the organisation, after lengthy negotiations, became incorporated. The committee did not get things all their own way. The number of children boarded out always remained at more than double the figure originally stipulated, and the size of the debt never decreased for long. Formal resolutions were passed by the finance committee and sent to the bank stating that the overdraft would be reduced by £2,000 within a matter of months. Come the date the size of the overdraft would be virtually unchanged. With these resolutions went statements from the committee placing on record the fact that they neither individually nor collectively accepted any personal liability for the overdraft which was secured on the property.

It was obvious the situation could not continue unchanged. But a curious incident, which occurred the following year, forced the committee to continue as it was for fear that any sudden resignations might jeopardise the work. In a letter entitled 'A Romish Plot',[7] Barnardo had written to his subscribers urgently begging them to send him £7,000 immediately to prevent a Roman Catholic sisterhood from buying land at Barkingside adjoining the village home, which had been occupied on lease and free of cost by the institutions ever since 1873. Barnardo wrote:

Thus, not only may I lose the house, Mossford Lodge, and land hitherto occupied and still so sorely needed, but I may also be opposed in the very centre of our work by a hostile community, who, I regret to say, have for ten years past left no stone unturned to hinder and to harass my operations . . . if the property is to be saved to our Institutions, it must be bought without delay, or else the fruits of years will be jeopardised by the action of Romish proselytisers who never seem to want money when it is required to make converts or to hinder a work of true Evangelisation, although funds are conspicuously lacking when the rescue of the children of Romish parents from slum land is in question.

The appeal came at an awkward moment, following so closely his passionate appeal for funds launched only the previous year.

It unfortunately united two aspects of Barnardo's work about which there was public disquiet, and it did not pass unnoticed. Although evangelicals quickly rallied to his support and money was put at his disposal for the purchase of Mossford Lodge, Labouchère, in an article in his influential journal *Truth*, questioned both the appeal and the attack on the Catholics. The article elicited an immediate response from Barnardo in the form of a letter couched in the most violent terms. Labouchère did not print Barnardo's letter but replied to it in a further article. The trustees, worried by this renewed adverse publicity, called one of their special meetings. After hearing Barnardo's side of the story they passed a resolution approving both his statements and his actions. Unfortunately, the memory of this angry exchange of views between Labouchère and Barnardo was to linger on in the mind of Wilfred Short, the man who became private secretary to Arthur Balfour when he was Prime Minister, with unhappy subsequent results for the organisation.

Cardinal Vaughan had succeeded Manning two years previously, and although he wrote to protest at the terms in which Barnardo had written, negotiations were proceeding to overcome the troubles surrounding the admission of Catholic children to the homes. Even this curious episode did not upset the negotiations, and eventually an agreement was reached stipulating that in the case of children whose fathers were Catholic, or in the case of an illegitimate child whose mother was Catholic, notification was to be sent immediately to the Archbishop's house in Westminster. If no action had been taken at the end of a fortnight, Barnardo was free to keep the child. Cooperation was to be mutual and Barnardo was to be informed if a Protestant child had been admitted to a Catholic home on the same terms. The agreement was very thorough – Barnardo had insisted that it should be personally agreed by Vaughan after his previous experiences. It finally brought to an end the bitter wrangles between both sides.

But if the mid-nineties brought the religious controversy to an end, it did not solve the financial crisis. Samuel Sheppard had been chairman of the committee of management for eighteen years. He had given generously not only of his time but, over the years, he had given large sums to the work, although he had begun to question the financial wisdom of incurring increasingly large debts. When Dr Heywood Smith, one of the original members of the committee, decided to resign, Samuel Sheppard, whose own firm had not been unaffected by the economic difficulties of the times, decided that he could no longer continue as chairman. His letter of resignation thoroughly alarmed the committee and Howard Williams, the vice-chairman, wrote begging him to reconsider his decision, fearing that the news of his resignation might do further damage to the organisation. Sheppard was adamant and refused to change his mind, although he accepted the invitation to remain as vice-president. For the next four years Howard Williams, who succeeded him, together with William and Charles Baker, had to carry on the business of the organisation virtually alone and unaided. One of their first decisions was to investigate the possibility of becoming incorporated, either by royal charter or through the Board of Trade.

During this time, unknown to them all, the Charity Organisation Society, officially silenced by the verdict of the arbitrators in 1877, had been steadily and secretly opposing the work of the organisation. There is no doubt that during the eighties and nineties the effective power of the COS had been declining, but this was somewhat concealed by the immense personal prestige and influence of its secretary, C. S. Loch, and also by the fact that many of its members were called upon to serve on royal commissions and government committees. Members of the public were in the habit of writing to the COS to ask their opinion as to the merits of the different charitable organisations, and sometimes their views on individual applicants for charity. Relying on very imperfect evidence, the COS had no hesitation in giving an opinion or, to be more exact, that of its secretary, but since the arbitration these views were always given in confidence. Barnardo had never ceased to oppose the work of the COS, and the pages of *Night and Day* are sprinkled with attacks on their methods and their policy. In a characteristic passage he wrote:[8]

People sometimes ask me why I trouble to refer to the C.O.S. in these columns at all. They need not go far to find an answer, and especially if they reflect for a moment upon the needs and sorrows of the London poor. It almost makes one's blood rise to fever heat to know that hundreds and thousands of pounds, given by godly people for the furtherance of a real work of relief, have been spent under the shadow of grand names and high-sounding titles in a vexatious officialism, that wounds and degrades almost everyone it touches. The Society is, I admit, capable of good work, but does not do it. The little excellence that comes from it is traceable to the merits of devoted and good men on the district committees, who are like lumps of salt, preserving the body corporate from corruption ... if here and there a little good is done at great expense, and duly advertised in misleading press paragraphs, credit is given to the whole organisation which it in no wise deserves, whilst hidden away in official pigeon holes are stories of hearts broken, homes destroyed, of domestic happiness ruined, and of commercial credit even lost, as the results of a system as detestable as it is heartless.

Barnardo's blood would have doubtless boiled right over had he known of the damaging reports that were being circulated with regard both to his policy for admitting destitute children and to the financial management of the homes. Those members of the public who sought guidance on the merits of the Barnardo Homes received an official-looking report stating that it was confidentially communicated. After describing the scope of the work the report continued:[9]

Different opinions exist with regard to the soundness of the principles by which the admission of applicants to the [Barnardo] Homes is regulated; but the C.O.S. do not consider it desirable that indiscriminate admission should be given to what are properly Poor Law cases – such as the children of unworthy parents – unless those safeguards to which the Guardians would resort are brought to bear ... We are therefore unable to recommend support to the Barnardo Homes.

This advice continued to be offered to the public all through the nineties, with even greater emphasis being placed on the desirability of neglected children being cared for through the machinery of the Poor Law:

It should be remembered that the Poor Law provides specially for the maintenance and education of children who are destitute from any cause whatever, so that as a matter of mere economy and wise co-operation, it is better for charitable people to direct their efforts to the well considered treatment of cases of distress arising from exceptional misfortune which industry and providence have failed to avert. This rule applies with greater force when the destitution of the child is attributable to neglect or misconduct of the parent ...

The cos's report was also critical of the way in which the accounts were rendered:

The accounts rendered by the East End Juvenile Mission are not of a nature to satisfy the just and reasonable claims of contributors. The wholesale lumping of items renders it impossible to distinguish the official from the charitable expenditure, or to form an opinion as to the merits of the administration from a financial point of view.

For the cos to attack Barnardo on this point had a certain irony. He had frequently attacked them for their excessive administration costs, claiming that while they appealed for funds to relieve distress they spent at least fifteen or sixteen shillings in the pound on establishment charges:[10]

... or what is more euphoniously termed 'Organisation Expenses'. When an Association, making such high professions of reform in the matter of charitable expenditure, is guilty, not once or twice, but for successive years of such breaches of the first elements of what may be termed the scientific laws of charitable economics, we and others may be pardoned if we think and say that the Society seems to us to need 'organisation' itself.

It is impossible to know, in terms of donations lost, how much damage was done by the circulation of these reports. The very fact that they existed must have contributed to a certain feeling of unease about Barnardo's work, an unfortunate result of his many controversial court appearances. Apart from a spectacular rise in the receipts in 1894, the result of the special Mossford Lodge appeal, funds did not continue the steady upward trend they had shown throughout the eighties. A foundation fund was set up by the committee to try and build up a reserve to be used to pay off debts, but it was not a success. Two new schemes, Waif Saturday and Founder's Day, were started in an attempt to stimulate new sources of income. Waif Saturday was presented as an opportunity for the poor to help the poor. Even the very poor could spare time to collect from others, and the first street collection held in London in 1894 raised £203. The idea took root and spread rapidly to other towns, soon becoming a permanent and successful feature, popular and cheap to administer. The following year Barnardo invited his supporters to celebrate his birthday at Stepney Causeway where they could inspect the homes, watch the children at work and play and listen to an address by the Director, all for the price of a shilling ticket. In the event Barnardo was not well enough to attend, but the number of supporters attending encouraged him to turn this into an annual event.

Negotiations were now proceeding with the Board of Trade as to the possibility of the institutions becoming incorporated. There were difficulties about the name by which the organisation was to be known. The committee was anxious to depersonalise the work, but at the same time the founder was adamant that he must continue to direct the work on the same individual lines as he had always done. All could see the obvious advantages that would result if the work could be seen to be national in character rather than the work of a single man. The difficulty lay in finding a means of combining these two seemingly contradictory elements. The result, arrived at after months of negotiations, was that the well known name, Dr Barnardo's Homes, was abandoned in favour of the impossibly clumsy title, 'The National Incorporated Association for the Reclamation of Destitute Waif Children, otherwise known as Dr. Barnardo's Homes'. Likewise *Night and Day* became the *National Waifs' Magazine*. Neither title ever became popular with the public, and the homes continued to be known by the name of their founder.

The certificate of incorporation was issued on 20 April 1899, and Lord Kinnaird was the only one of the original trustees to become one of the first seven subscribers; William Fowler and Barnardo had been members of the first management committee; two more recent members of the committee, H. W. Webb-Peploe, Vicar of St Paul's, Onslow Square and James Mathieson, joined Howard Williams and William Baker on the first list of subscribers. Incorporation brought with it several major advantages. Without incorporation it would have been very difficult, if not impossible, to find people willing to take on the responsibilities and liabilities that Barnardo and the trustees and committee carried. Now the properties of the institutions under the Act were vested in the new association, and only after an appeal to the High Court could they be used for any purpose other than those set forth in the memorandum and articles, thus providing as far as possible for the continuity of the work.

Incorporation limited the personal liabilities of the council and trustees, and with this disadvantage removed the committee had far fewer reservations about allowing the work to expand and debts to accumulate. The five years from incorporation until Barnardo's death show the most astonishing increase in all branches of the work, with new homes and receiving centres being opened as well as the establishment of a naval training school at North Elmham. The liabilities of the organisation escalated to an alarming degree. Barnardo had succeeded in retaining his personal power to direct the work and he was also given the further power of selecting a successor, if he so wished. The mounting debts show that the committee no longer saw any reason to limit the work. It was almost as if, having been restrained since the crisis of 1893, nothing was now to be allowed to stand in the way of further expansion, and the committee had neither the will nor the wish to prevent a new crisis arising. By 1905 the organisation had liabilities amounting to £120,000. Feeling the work being done was truly national in character, the committee, with considerable public support, launched a national appeal to celebrate the founder's sixtieth birthday. Before the appeal had time to get under way Barnardo died, and the true extent of the liabilities was seen to be £249,000.

16

The Last Decade,
1895-1905

BARNARDO's need to find new ways of attracting public support to his work and fresh sources of income had been intensified by the financial crisis of the early 1890s. Although he never lost his faith that God would provide him with the means to carry on his work, there was an underlying note of disillusion to his appeals as he found the burden of always begging for funds increasingly wearisome. However there were compensations: there is no doubt that he found the great annual meetings, which since 1890 had been held at the Albert Hall, thoroughly enjoyable occasions. Until then the annual meetings of nearly all the evangelical societies were habitually held at Exeter Hall, that great stronghold of Protestant Victorian social life. It was a bold decision for Barnardo to change from those familiar surroundings in the Strand and hire the Albert Hall.

He had long hoped to attract the great preacher Spurgeon to be guest of honour at one of his annual meetings, recognising him as the most influential platform speaker of the day. When he finally succeeded in 1890, through the good offices of his deputation secretary the Rev. W. J. Mayers, who had long been a friend and associate of Spurgeon's, it was at Mayers' suggestion that the Albert Hall was taken for the occasion. The meeting was carefully prepared and rehearsed; speeches and reports were to be enlivened by the children singing and performing elaborate musical and military drills, and by limelight reproductions taken from the photographic records. Although the hall was not full, the success of this first great meeting encouraged Barnardo to exploit the possibilities of developing this method of making his work known. Barnardo knew he was not in the same class as Spurgeon as a platform speaker. He spoke too fast, and although eloquent, his public speeches tended to be more in the nature of confidential chats. He tried to analyse how Spurgeon achieved his success, how he conveyed so much power, and could only conclude that 'it was the simple sincerity of the man and the spirit of God behind him'.

However, as a showman Barnardo had few equals. In 1894 he not only hired the Albert Hall for the annual meeting, he decided that the Young Helpers' League should also hold their annual birthday fête there. By 1895 he was filling the Albert Hall twice a year, once in January for the YHL and again in July for the annual meeting. In spite of the enormous amount of extra work that was involved in putting on these performances, for there is no other word for them, Barnardo found the greatest satisfaction in their planning and production, thoroughly enjoying the role of showman. As one admiring critic said, the way in which the exhibitions were directed would have done credit to a professional entertainer. Rehearsals took place in the great hall of the Edinburgh Castle and in the yard at Stepney. Barnardo was at his happiest and most relaxed directing and organising these events. A revealing story told by A. E. Williams, who was his devoted secretary for the last seven years of his life, conveys something of the atmosphere. Barnardo had come down to the Edinburgh Castle to supervise a rehearsal and to make sure that each child knew exactly what he or she was supposed to be doing. A young master, unused to Barnardo's ways, was fussing around distracting the children's attention. He was called to the Director's side and given a cord to hold. In a manner which implied that the matter was of vital importance he was told to hold on to the cord, which was attached to a toy horse, until given further instructions. The rehearsal then proceeded and the unfortunate young master was left helplessly attached to the toy.

As Barnardo got older he had even less time for those he considered incompetent, and his autocratic ways gave rise to many stories about him, not always favourable. He had always had a well developed dramatic instinct, and it is interesting to compare his theatrical ability with his strict views on the theatre as a source of amusement. He was on record as saying that theatrical performances of any kind were vicious and instrumental in promoting much individual and public evil. His children and his family were never permitted to attend a theatre, and if he accepted money that had been raised as a result of a dramatic performance, the sender would be certain to receive a letter setting out his views on the subject in no uncertain terms. Even a dance, 'however innocent its character', came into this category:[1] 'I don't say that other people might not be able to engage in a fancy dress dance with good conscience, but I could not be party to it . . . Rightly or wrongly Christian people regard dancing as somewhat outside of those pleasures which are consistent with a profession of following our Lord.' Obviously his Albert Hall extravaganzas allowed him to indulge a natural instinct for drama which his religious beliefs had forced him to suppress, untroubled by the thought that his girls dancing round a maypole were engaging in a ritual whose origins were far from Christian.

The physical and mental demands Barnardo made upon himself in the early nineties were more than most men meet in a lifetime. He had always been subject to bronchial trouble and had periods of illness; as has been seen, he suffered from insomnia and bouts of depression; the first signs of heart disease had already made their appearance. Now the demands his new fund-raising activities were making on his time and energy were to prove more than even he could cope with.

Two months before his fiftieth birthday he was suddenly seized by a violent paroxysm of pain in the chest, which his doctors diagnosed as *angina pectoris*. Barnardo had always prided himself on his medical knowledge and he was certainly aware of the implications of the disease. He knew that for the sake of his health he should avoid mental and physical strain, that undue exertion and stress could bring on a further attack and that repeated attacks could prove fatal. But it was not in his nature, with his excitable energy, to relax or to abandon any project to which he had put his hand. Resting only when he was physically unable to keep going, Barnardo drove himself on, making only minimal alterations to his lifestyle. Although forced to give up work for a period of several months after this first attack, he had no intention of relinquishing control of the organisation. Writing from Ilfracombe where he had gone to recuperate, he acknowledged the debt he owed to his staff in a personal message which was read to them at a party held to celebrate his fiftieth birthday.[2]

I do not believe that any philanthropic or Christian work anywhere has more enthusiastic and single eyed servitors than ours; nor has any chief of a mission enterprise more loyal colleagues and comrades than I. I take this opportunity, therefore, of placing publicly on record my sense of great indebtedness to all my faithful fellow labourers at Stepney, and elsewhere, whose names are seldom heard of, but to whose continuous and unceasing toil any success which God has given us is chiefly due. Credit is often given me that really belongs to them, and it is in no spirit of mock modesty that I add that I am often ashamed at the prominence given to my personal share in an undertaking, the great burdens of which have been silently and heroically borne by a great company of splendid workers . . .

I desire to add that although the suddenness and alarming character of the attacks during the last two months have compelled me to relinquish my share in my beloved work for a season . . . I confidently expect, by the blessing of God, to be able to resume my usual duties after a while and . . . to continue to occupy the position it has been my privilege and joy to hold for so long.

To the world at large he never allowed any sign of weakness or strain to show, but as the years passed, public meetings or services would often leave him prostrate and utterly exhausted by his efforts. Always a prolific letter-writer but now increasingly cut off from his fellow men by his deafness, he came to rely more than ever on the written word. The number of letters he dictated daily both from his home and from the office became legendary. A good shorthand writer became one of the necessities of life. He dictated in trains and cabs, in bed as well as at the office. When he was not sitting at his table, very much the autocrat, surrounded by telephones, speaking tubes and electric bells, and giving rapid orders to an army of men and boys ready to do his smallest bidding, his favourite method of dictating was while walking round the room, a method which he found cleared the head and quickened the brain. This system had its disadvantages as the room was large and the proximity of the trains often made it difficult for the shorthand writer to catch the exact words; the resulting errors sometimes led to ridiculous blunders, causing him to remark on one occasion that shorthand as an art 'was chiefly the medium for mistakes'. As the size of the organisation increased, so did the number of letters requiring his attention. It was a burden from which he never escaped.

Always quick to exploit the opportunities which anniversaries presented, and as, according to his calculation, 1896 marked the thirtieth anniversary of his work among the waifs, Barnardo was determined that it should be celebrated appropriately. The Duchess of Teck, encouraged by Angela Burdett Coutts' example, had for many years taken an interest in charitable work in the East End. Despite her size – she had been fat since girlhood – her face was kind and beautiful and her interest in the poor genuine, and she was affectionately known by East Enders as 'fat Mary'. She had been the guest of honour at the opening of Babies' Castle in 1883 and Barnardo, who could be a charming host and a captivating talker on such occasions, had obviously won her sympathy for his work. She had recently accepted the presidency of the Young Helpers' League. When her daughter Princess Mary became engaged to Prince George, the future George V, trustees and committee met together and sent her a special telegram of good wishes. Perhaps because of this link, the then Prince and Princess of Wales, later to become King Edward VII and Queen Alexandra, accepted an invitation to preside at the thirtieth anniversary meeting at the Albert Hall, and the princess agreed to receive purses containing gifts towards the establishment of a foundation fund. For the first time the Albert Hall was completely full.

No effort had been spared by Barnardo to make this a truly spectacular success. In a series of tableaux of astonishing diversity the work done by the homes was exhibited to the public. Over three thousand children took part, with Barnardo introducing his report and the children illustrating his words. At one moment the centre of the hall was filled with boys representing bakers, blacksmiths, carpenters, cooks, engineers, harness-makers, mat-makers, printers, shoemakers, tailors, tinsmiths, wheelwrights and wood-choppers. Minutes later babies filled the space: cots, tea tables, rocking horses and even a miniature hayfield were provided to show them at play, at tea and at bedtime. This was probably, as Barnardo noted, 'the prettiest and most pathetic episode of the afternoon'. This was followed by flag drill, battalion drill and a display of life and work at the Village Home. Then it was the turn of the cripples. To have kept them away would have been to admit that they were inferior to other children, Barnardo said, anticipating criticism, as they made their appearance and prepared to demonstrate their abilities at cricket.[3]

It was a short innings and the interest lay in the players and not in the game. Most of the players had two crutches and when they batted they dropped one crutch, leant firmly on the other and held the bat in the disengaged hand. One little fellow had no crutches at all. His legs were folded beneath him and he moved about in an upright position on his hands and knees. Nevertheless he got about very quickly, fielded a ball smartly and threw a man out . . . The cripples appeared to enjoy the game immensely and the sympathetic onlookers loudly applauded them. The display opened the eyes of the audience to some of our difficulties, our problems, our nuts to crack and it suggested the hard question, 'what door other than this stands open to such as they?'

Every aspect of the work was represented. Boys and girls already selected for Canada came on stage dressed as for the journey. When they marched off the leading girl hoisted a banner with the word 'Goodbye' on it, while the band played and the remaining children waved their handkerchiefs. Finally the stage was filled by four hundred old boys and girls who had come to claim their prizes for having kept their situations with credit.

The Prince of Wales spoke briefly, but Barnardo could not have wished for more. 'It must be our great wish that continually increasing success may attend the operations of this beneficial and national work,' he said, and asked that the public contribute to the foundation fund to remove the debt from the homes. But in spite of royal patronage, publicity and a full house, the results were very disappointing, amounting to less than in the previous year, and did nothing to improve the financial position. However, the memory of what she had seen at the Albert Hall must have remained with the princess, for seven years later as Queen Alexandra she became patron of the homes and later gave her support to the idea of establishing a national fund in their favour. And at the time of Barnardo's death she expressed the hope that his work would be kept up as an everlasting tribute to his memory.

The following year the Barnardos left Ardmore. The grounds had been frequently used for fêtes and bazaars in aid of the Homes during the few years they lived there, but it must have been expensive to run. Queenie was now out of the school-room, and perhaps Mrs Barnardo felt she needed somewhere more convenient to entertain and for her daughter to receive her friends. The nephew of his old friend and supporter from his early Plymouth Brethren days, John Eliot Howard, bought the house from Barnardo. Eliot Howard was one of the first members of the association to sign the articles after the organisation became incorporated, and one has the feeling that in taking on the house he might have been relieving Barnardo of a burden which had become financially onerous. It was some time before the Barnardos found a house to suit their tastes, but finally they settled on a large and singularly unattractive red-brick Victorian house standing in its own grounds in Surbiton. Mrs Barnardo is said to have been happier at St Leonard's Lodge than at any of their previous homes. Because of her husband's frequent absences and the long hours he worked, and because of the very nature of the organisation, their social life had been very restricted. But with a lively and attractive daughter at home, even Barnardo was sometimes prevailed upon to come home early to attend the occasional parties she gave. Frederick Barnardo, his brother George's son, lived with the family, and his exuberant personality enlivened the household. .

However, the journey from Surbiton to Stepney was more tiring for Barnardo and he often spent the morning working at home, arriving at the office in the early afternoon. Not that this meant he spent any less time at his desk when he was well. A special evening staff came on duty at six p.m. and worked on until past eleven. This uninterrupted time was used for the composition of letters and magazine articles which were dictated to one particularly good shorthand writer. His notes went at intervals to the chief of the typewriting corps for transmission, so that by the time dictation was finished almost all the notes were transcribed and ready for Barnardo to check and sign, which he did with a flourish after adding or altering words and underlining passages of special importance. To keep going he drank cups of strong black tea unadulterated either by milk or sugar. He was fond of his food and a hearty eater, but often had no time for proper meals. He was very hard on the physical side of his nature. When he arrived home after midnight, he would find in his study a beef sandwich held in a book press so that the juices were absorbed by the bread, an idea he had evolved for himself. Only Peer, his coachman, and his daughter are said to have shared the knowledge that towards the end of his life, in the solitude of his study, he would pour himself a drink before retiring to rest in the early hours of the morning. If this seems at variance with his views on temperance, it should be remembered that he had become a temperance advocate only because he had seen at first hand the devastating effects that drink could have on the lives of the poor. Both Shaftesbury and Spurgeon spoke in favour of temperance reform, but neither saw any reason why they should not privately enjoy a drink; apparently neither did Barnardo, who by then was often ill, always tired and overworked, yet feeling a duty to cram yet more into the time that remained to him.

The late nineties had seen the work of the homes again expanding, although receipts had been almost static during that period. Incorporation had relieved the committee of their personal responsibilities, but it was not until the end of the Boer War in 1902 that receipts began to improve, and by that time Barnardo had become increasingly a sick man. Notwithstanding the lack of funds, the number of children in residential care had been going up steadily, largely as the result of the work of the 'ever open doors'. New 'ever open doors' had been established in Notting Hill, Belfast, Brighton, Portsmouth and Southampton; a new school was added to the Girls' Village Home; and other specialist establishments, including one for incurable children at Bradford, were acquired to add to the long list of those already filled with children. It almost seemed as though the new council which had replaced the trustees and committee of management no longer saw any reason for opposing Barnardo's wishes, believing that the work of rescuing destitute children must be seen as a national responsibility, and that the financial problems the organisation incurred should be solved nationally.

Although the finance committee made some attempt to hold expenditure to within certain limits, debts mounted and the overdraft grew steadily larger. There was only one occasion when Barnardo's actions produced a real clash of opinion: in 1901 he bought the freehold of the Cairns Mission Hall without first getting sanction for the cheque, and certain members felt that he had acted *ultra vires* and that they were not bound to sanction the cheque. It was decided that counsel's opinion should be sought, but the Director had the backing of Robert Anderson, William Baker and Howard Williams, and by the following meeting it was clear that opposition had evaporated and council duly confirmed the purchase.

Although Barnardo was to be away ill for the major part of 1901, fortunately the year started well. Since the early seventies Barnardo had wanted to have a training ship of his own to which his boys could be sent. When the county school at North Elmham, Norfolk, failed in 1899 after only a few months, the whole property came on the market. Barnardo went to inspect it and realised at once both its potential and the reasons for its failure. It had no heating system and no baths, and although it was lit by oil lamps there was no means of escaping from the upper floors in case of fire. But properly equipped the premises would make a superb training school. With funds already stretched to the limit there could be no question of buying the property at that time. H. W. Webb-Peploe, the popular preacher and Vicar of St Paul's, Onslow Square, had been a friend of Barnardo's since the days when they had worked together as members of Moody's London campaign committee. A convinced evangelical, millenarian in outlook, Webb-Peploe's preaching reflected his views. He had been a vice-president of the homes for some years and was one of the seven signatories of the articles of association. Among his fashionable congregation were E. F. Watts, a wealthy shipowner, and his family. Knowing of Barnardo's wish to establish a naval training school and of Watts' interests, Webb-Peploe arranged for the two to meet. It took Barnardo some time to persuade Watts that his plan to transform the derelict county school into a naval training establishment was not only practicable, but that a regular supply of boys trained in seamanship would be of benefit both to the Royal Navy and to the mercantile marine.

Once convinced that the plan was possible, Watts was a generous benefactor. Not only did he buy the property and make it over to the council of the homes, but when the enormous estimate for conversion was finally presented he agreed to pay half the £9,000 the alterations would cost. The conversion of North Elmham into a 'ship on land' inevitably entailed a lot of complicated planning and time-consuming work, and Barnardo would never have willingly delegated such an enterprise to a subordinate. It is therefore all the more surprising that he should choose this moment, when negotiations were taking place for the acquisition of the school, to stand for the Essex County Council. It was not only difficult for him to hear what was said at public meetings, his deafness made it difficult for him to control his voice at times and he did not always know when a whisper had turned into a shout. Did he perhaps feel that with incorporation his role within the organisation was diminished and that membership of the county council would give him added prestige?

He stood for the Hainault Ward against Mr R. Stroud, a member of the urban council. The campaign was a lively one. At one meeting Barnardo accused his opponent of coercing the electors to vote not as they wished to but as their employers would like, and denounced such interference with the rights and liberties of the people.[4] The voting was very close and there were three recounts. The final count gave Mr Stroud a majority of one. It will come as no surprise to learn that Barnardo lodged a petition demanding a scrutiny. It was unsuccessful. This appears to have been his only serious attempt to stand for public office. His only other known involvement in politics is when Joseph Chamberlain and Arthur Balfour came to the East End in 1903 and spoke by invitation at the Edinburgh Castle. Barnardo was seen rather pathetically trying to hear what was said through his ear trumpet.

The month following his defeat he had another severe attack of angina. When he was sufficiently recovered he was urged by his doctors to go for treatment to Bad Nauheim, a little village some twenty miles north of Frankfurt, which had been known since the fourteenth century for its thermal waters. In recent years it had become fashionable as a spa, and a course of baths in its water was thought to be beneficial to those suffering from rheumatism and heart disease. Barnardo went to Nauheim reluctantly. He was always worried at being out of the country when funds were low, but at this time he had a more personal reason for anxiety. Henry Wellcome, the American-born founder of the chemical firm of Burroughs and Wellcome, had fallen in love with Queenie and had telegraphed from Florence on his way back from Khartoum his intention of marrying her. There was much that could have made this seem an ideal marriage. Wellcome with his religious background, his interest in medical research and his wealth might have seemed the perfect son-in-law. In a famous letter to his parents, written when he was twenty-one, he had told them that he wanted to make a lot of money so that he could pursue medical research for the good of humanity and to the glory of God. He was a great admirer of Barnardo's work and his firm provided medical supplies for the homes. He was, however, twenty-five years older than Queenie.

Henry Wellcome had stayed with the Barnardos in 1897 as a paying guest, and seemed at that time still to be the confirmed bachelor he thought himself to be. At the time of Burroughs' engagement to Miss Chase he had written to him giving his views on marriage, which he believed was not for him, but he thought that almost certainly he would come to envy Burroughs' domestic happiness. But Queenie, or Syrie as she came to be called, after her mother, was seventeen in 1897, beautiful, lively and clever. If Wellcome did not fall in love with her then, when he met her again in Khartoum in 1901 he was bowled over by her charm and beauty. He was probably there to set up the Wellcome Tropical Medicine Laboratory which he founded in Khartoum the following year. Syrie was there with a group of English visitors. The romance must have blossomed quickly, because it was on the return journey that Wellcome sent his telegram. Mrs Barnardo or 'the Begum', as she had become known to the family, had no doubts about the matter. Not only was money always short in the Barnardo household, Mrs Barnardo was worried about the education of her two remaining children and Syrie's marriage to Henry Wellcome could solve that problem. Syrie herself would seem to have had some doubts about the marriage, well founded as it turned out, but she was overborne by her mother. Barnardo is said to have been saddened at the idea of his daughter's marriage to Wellcome, a man so much her senior, and he was ill and away from home at the crucial time. The marriage took place at Christ Church, Surbiton, on 2 June while he was still at Nauheim. Syrie and Henry Wellcome spent their honeymoon going round the world. To members of the family who wrote disapproving of the marriage Barnardo answered defending his daughter's decision. When a son was born to them two years later, Barnardo was proud and delighted at being a grandfather, keeping photos of the baby in the place of honour on his writing table.

But when he returned from Nauheim in 1901, although he was certainly better for the treatment, he was still far from well. His doctors sent him back to Nauheim in August, and it was not until the end of the year that he began to resume work on a regular basis. All his branch homes were inspected regularly by lady visitors to ensure that proper standards were being maintained. A long and detailed memorandum dictated in November giving rules and suggestions to visitors of branch homes shows he had lost none of his appetite for work and his zest for detailed administrative organisation.[5]

In visiting the Branches it is important that the Lady Visitor should minutely inspect *everything* and report thereon. Naturally she would pay attention to the appearance of the household, the condition of the staff (i.e. their suitability for their work), their general happiness, the concord between each member of the staff and the appointed Head; also the appearance of the children in health, dress, cleanliness, a careful examination such as only a woman can give to underclothing, bed linen and bedding. A bed should be unexpectedly opened in each bedroom so as to see if the sheets are kept too long on the beds ... Opportunities might be taken, if any individual girl looks untidy, to quickly get her into her own bedroom and make her remove part of her dress, so as to be assured that the underclothing she has on is neither too large nor too small, that it is warm enough for the season, that it is in good repair, and that buttons, hooks and eyes and tapes are not missing and simply replaced with a pin ... It is suggested that the Visitor should abstain from giving orders which will involve any change in administration ... In other words, it has been found by experience that *duality of control leads to confusion*. Changes of the staff which may be necessary must not, therefore, even be hinted at on the occasion of the visit. The recommendations of the Visitor will always have the Director's careful consideration ... Needless to say, all such reports should be on one side of the paper only; that as far as possible the paper used should be ruled quarto; that each new item in the letter should have its underlined heading at the left-hand corner of the paragraph, and a catch word at the foot of the page, so that there will be no doubt as to which page follows.

The final pages contained instructions to the visitors to make it clear to any candidates whom they might be interviewing on behalf of the Director that the decision as to their appointment 'lies absolutely' with Dr Barnardo and they have 'no power in the matter at all'. This inability to delegate was one of Barnardo's few weaknesses as an administrator and in his last years led to difficulties. He refused to adopt the filing system suggested by his secretary, Williams, and to the end continued to bundle his unanswered letters into his own black bag, resolutely ignoring Williams's protests that this was how letters got mislaid.

1902 and 1903 were both busy years. Mr Watts unfortunately died before the work on the Watts Naval School was completed, but his son, Fenwick Watts, took over his father's responsibilities and with equal generosity not only furnished the establishment but gave it an endowment of £10,000. Many delays occurred before the extensive alterations were complete, and in spite of the Watts family's generosity, a substantial financial burden fell on the homes. Barnardo took a close interest in the whole project, and the thought that he would at last own a naval establishment gave him great satisfaction. He planned to have a grand opening in the summer of 1903, but his hopes were to be frustrated. Sandringham was only thirteen miles distant from North Elmham as the crow flies, and Barnardo had hoped that the Prince and Princess of Wales might perform the opening ceremony. When they were unable to do so he asked his old friend Mr Hind-Smith to try to get General Baden-Powell for June. Instructing Hind-Smith on how to persuade the General to accept, Barnardo wrote:[6] 'Don't write him a letter. I always think that is such a stupid thing to do if you can make a call, for a letter invites a refusal from a busy man. But go and see him, grip him by the hand, look him in the face, and ask him to help this splendid work for uplifting these little chaps from misery and wretchedness and giving them hope of a better life, at the same time making them into strong and sturdy citizens of the Empire.' But although Barnardo promised that 'the Dean of Norwich and all the County will turn out to give General Baden-Powell a welcome', in the end there was no grand opening. Batches of boys simply continued to arrive at the school until all three hundred and twenty places were filled.

He had to make another visit to Nauheim in 1902 and the treatment seemed to give him relief for a while, but from the pressing financial problems of the institutions there was no let-up. He sometimes replied to demands for payment in jocular fashion:[7]

Advertising Agents are like the Horse Leach's daughters. You will remember he had four and they all cried 'give! give!' You are only one but you have the voice of eight. I think I did very well to send you £150 when you expected £300. I do not think you will get any more money this week; in fact I am sure of it, but I think very likely some time before the end of the month we will send you another £150. That will complete the £300 that you wanted at the 1st of the month. I am afraid until the millennium comes you must not expect that you will get a cheque on the 1st of every month.

But a series of letters written early in 1905 to his old friend Mrs Kirkpatrick, whose meeting he addressed at the end of February, shows the trouble he took to ensure that such a meeting was successful and the price he paid:[8]

Owing to my own illness, and weariness which is sometimes worse than illness, I have been prevented from promptly dealing with the meeting at Harrow ... Now, my dear friend, just a few weary words as to how to carry out my views about the meeting ... I sell every ticket for a meeting several days before the meeting takes place, so that it gets about there is not a seat to be had – the place is crowded. A certain number of people won't come unless they hear they can't get in, then, British like, they say, 'can't get in? Well, we'll see. I shall.' And they come down, and they do get in. We make them pay more on the night, but the result is a feeling of such heartiness and enthusiasm and warmth that when I rise to finally endeavour to get a good collection for the night I get two or three or four times as much as I used to do in the old days with a comparatively free meeting and just a few seats at 1/-d or 1/6d.

He wrote to Mrs Kirkpatrick afterwards:

I must send you just one line of acknowledgement and thanks for your most encouraging letter. I very seldom get such a letter as yours. Remember the poor Director sometimes needs a word of encouragement as much as any of his colleagues, and your letter has quite cheered me. I do not think the meeting has done any *serious* damage to me, but certainly I have not been well since and am now enjoying a mild attack of lumbago in addition to my other ills; Mr. Hallam's letter was very kind; but I don't like your friend's view who said that my way of 'extracting money was like a conjuring trick'. *That* is what might well be termed a doubtful compliment. I should be sorry to think there was any 'trick' in it. However, people must form their own opinions upon such matters.

He had been involved in a serious railway accident the previous July when a train travelling between Birkdale and Liverpool crashed. He escaped without injuries, but the bruises and shock did nothing to improve his condition. He went twice more to Nauheim in 1904, and it was evident to his friends and family that he was no longer responding to treatment. The slightest exertion now brought on feelings of prostration and the marvellous powers of concentration began to fail. With the arrival of the milder weather in the spring of 1905 he was advised that complete rest and quiet were essential. His wife and family decided that the only way to ensure him freedom from worry and correspondence was to go abroad. Syrie with her cousin Gladys, Cyril and a friend took him to Venice where they stayed for about three weeks. A letter written to his staff from there, headed 'A desert place', showed how difficult he found it to detach himself from the cares and responsibilities of the institutions:[9]

Here I am at last! I have obeyed physically the 'come ye apart and rest awhile'; but it is not so easy to yield obedience *spiritually* and *mentally*. That I hope will come. My thoughts are with you day and night. For what little sleep I get is visited by dreams of the Homes, of my dear children and my fellow workers on the staff; so that I wake often, greatly perturbed by difficulties and calamities which I hope have no foundation except in my disordered thoughts.

And looking back he wrote:

What a wonderful experience mine has been during these thirty-nine years! What inexhaustible supplies have been vouchsafed to the work in my hands. How amazing to mere unaided human reason have been the answers to prayer, even when Faith has almost failed and our timidity has begotten distrust instead of love and hope! And *He* has not failed us once!

From Venice the party went on to Lucerne and Paris. They met Queenie in Paris and lunched with her twice. Barnardo wrote sadly to Stuart of the change he saw in his daughter since her marriage to Henry Wellcome; he was deeply distressed by it, and wrote of his fears for her future happiness. The April issue of *Night and Day,* which was produced in his absence, carried a banner headline message from him to his readers:[10] 'I cannot disguise from myself or from my readers that the task is growing more and more difficult as the years roll on. But I feel and know that this is God's work carried on in obedience to God's call and I cast the burden upon Him in assured hope and confidence.' In the last 'personal notes' he was to write in the July issue of *Night and Day,* he said that in the last seven years he had lost twenty-one thousand donors and pleaded for others to take their place.[11]

We are, alas, no longer able as of yore to devise and carry out fresh and vigorous plans for the revival of interest, or to make new friends by personal advocacy! Every attempt at such sustained efforts during the past twelve months has been followed by days or even weeks of prostration and illness . . . Although only sixty years of age, we have in the exigencies of our work 'burned the candle at both ends' and we are, in consequence, now being forcibly reminded of our limitations.

While Barnardo was asking his supporters to make the coming Founder's Day a memorable one, the committee were making determined efforts to have Barnardo's work recognised as of national importance. Howard Williams had been forced to resign because of his father's failing health, and had been succeeded by William Baker. In spite of a yearly increase in the income, the number of destitute children coming into care was increasing even faster and by 1905 numbered over eight and a half thousand. The committee used all expedients open to them to meet the needs of the children: overdrafts, mortgages, loans, loans on reversionary legacies, all were authorised in a desperate attempt to keep the 'ever open doors' open. On 1 July under the heading, 'A Claim upon the Nation', a letter was sent to *The Times* signed by peers, bishops and clergy, Members of Parliament and the Lord Mayor of London, and names as diverse as those of W. T. Stead, Edmund Gosse and Marie Corelli were among the forty-eight signatories. The letter asked for a founder's birthday fund of £120,000 to lift from the council of the National Waifs' Association the burden of their accumulated liabilities:

From this gigantic homestead which has 121 distinct branches no fewer than 16,800 children have been planted out in the colonies in the last few years, of whom less than 2% have failed to do well. From this point of view Dr. Barnardo may be regarded as a great Imperial asset. He has only had the residuum – the poorest, the most desperate, the most forlorn of the children of the gutter and the slum. Of the 8,500 whom he is feeding to-day, 1,300 are either cripples or afflicted with various deformities and diseases. Nevertheless, with the worst of material to deal with, he turns out results which beat the record of all colonising agencies that have the pick of the basket. This man has rendered services infinitely greater and more lasting than most of the exploits which are rewarded by national grants, by Parliamentary votes of thanks, or by titular honours – is it not true that the nation should recognise the services of one of the most useful and well deserving of its souls?

If we could restore Dr. Barnardo's health to what it was even ten years ago we should provide far more effectively for these Institutions than if we raised a million as a Founder's Day Fund. That, however, is, alas, beyond our power.

The letter ended with the information that the Lord Mayor had convened a meeting at the Mansion House the following Monday. There was much private canvassing of support for the appeal, and some Members of Parliament approached the Prime Minister, Arthur Balfour, in the hope that he would give the meeting his official blessing. It was Wilfred Short's duty, as Balfour's secretary, to advise him on the merits of the case, and remembering the articles that had appeared in *Truth* under Labouchère's signature ten years previously, he wrote to Loch at the Charity Organisation Society for his views:[12]

10 Downing Street, s.w.   June 26th 1905
I send you the enclosed papers in confidence. The Prime Minister has not yet replied but he ought to do so without further delay. It is, of course, indisputable that Dr. Barnardo has done an enormous work; but did not Labouchère make certain charges in connection with financial matters against him some years ago? I only ask because, if so, this national movement to recognise his work may perhaps revive those charges, and, as you will understand, the Prime Minister ought therefore to proceed carefully in the matter. For any observations you are able to send, I am sure the Prime Minister will be very grateful. They will, of course, be treated confidentially.

From the point of view of the organisers of the appeal, Short could hardly have chosen a worse source from which to seek advice. Loch had never forgiven or forgotten the events of 1877, and as the COS papers on the Barnardo Homes show, he had followed closely the development of the work since then. A secret stream of adverse reports had been his only reaction to the growth of the organisation, and his response to Short's letter was only too predictable. However, he took his time over replying, and in a further letter on 29 June Short wrote: 'I should be very glad if you let me have a reply during the course of the morning to my note about Dr. Barnardo. They are pressing for an answer and we have one or two letters from M.P.s on the subject.'

The Mansion House meeting duly took place on 3 July. The Queen sent a telegram of support, but the Prime Minister did not attend, presumably as a result of 'all the trouble' Loch had taken. How far Loch alone was responsible may never be known definitely, but the episode gives an indication of the personal power and influence he still commanded at a time when the influence of the COS itself was declining. The particular irony of the story in this instance was that Labouchère's articles in *Truth,* to which Short referred, were never meant to be construed as an attack on Barnardo's work. Unaware of the impression he had made at the time, writing three months later, at the time of Barnardo's death, Labouchère made this quite clear.[13]

The late Dr. Barnardo deserves a foremost place among those who have devoted their lives to philanthropic work. A few years ago, some small detail in connection with his charities having incurred criticism in *Truth*, he astonished me by writing a violent letter, in which he expressed his belief, from information received, that I was on the look out for making some attack on his work. I do not know how he got hold of this idea; but in point of fact I have always had a great admiration for his work, and should have been the last to say or do anything that might injure it.

Nothing demonstrates more clearly C. S. Loch's obsessive dislike of Barnardo than the letter he wrote to the Medical Defence Union after his death,[14] when the question of a national memorial fund was being discussed, in a final attempt to discredit him. In this he was disappointed, for the Medical Defence Union replied that there was no record to show that Barnardo had ever practised medicine before he was legally registered, but confirmed that his qualification was purely surgical. As is known, Barnardo never received any official recognition for his work during his lifetime. The evidence shows that Loch would have used his considerable influence to prevent any such move.

At his last public appearance on Founder's Day, which was held at Ilford, Barnardo to all outward appearance seemed his normal self. But he was ill for days afterwards. When he was somewhat recovered, doctors advised a further course of treatment at Nauheim and he set off alone, except for a secretary, in August. He was taken ill in Cologne on the way there but was able to continue his journey. On arrival he knew he was too ill for treatment, and asked that he be brought home. Travelling with a nurse he reached Paris, but there he had such a severe attack of angina that he was not expected to recover. His wife was sent for and, accompanied by his brother Frederick, a doctor in Southport, and his son Cyril, she came over to be with him. He recovered sufficiently for them to start the slow journey back to England by ambulance carriage. They arrived at St Leonard's Lodge on Thursday 14 September. Over the weekend he had several further intensely painful attacks, but on Monday he had recovered sufficiently to look over the letters which had accumulated in his absence. On Tuesday he spent some time dictating letters, and among those written that day was one to his nephew Wilfred, his brother Lionel's son. Wilfred had written to his uncle from Dublin in June asking for advice about emigrating to America, and had received a long helpful letter in reply. In this final letter Barnardo promised to obtain a free passage on a ship going to Canada for his nephew and ended, 'Be sure to tell your father all that I have written. Yours affectionately, Uncle Tom.'

A few hours later at six in the evening, while he was looking over the letters he had dictated and eating a light meal, he had another sudden attack and died. The family kept the news from the organisation that evening. The following morning all the papers carried long notices of his death and many spoke of him as a national benefactor, the famous philanthropist and friend of homeless children. Tributes, appreciations, recollections and stories of his life's work filled many columns. To allay public anxiety William Baker almost immediately announced that the work would be continued by the council upon the original principles. The King and Queen sent messages of condolence to Mrs Barnardo. The Queen's message expressed the wish that his 'splendid life-long work may be kept up as an everlasting tribute to his memory'.

It was obvious that special arrangements would have to be made for the funeral in view of the great public interest. Henry Wellcome offered his help, which was accepted, and he took over the management of the funeral. The body was to lie in state at the Edinburgh Castle from Sunday 24 September until Wednesday morning, to give the children and staff of the Homes as well as the public an opportunity of paying a last tribute. On Wednesday a procession consisting of council, staff, officers and children would follow the coffin borne on an open car to Liverpool Street Station, where it would be met by family and friends. The cortège was to go by special train to Barkingside station and from there the procession would go to the Girls' Village Home. A colossal marquee was erected to accommodate the huge crowd of mourners who attended the funeral service, held on a rainy afternoon. After the service the coffin was to lie in state at the village church before it was finally interred at a spot in the village already chosen by Barnardo. He had left instructions in his will that his remains were to be cremated, and although this was not made public at the time in spite of demands to know if cremation had taken place, this was done before the final interment took place.

Not only are there many accounts of the moving scenes that occurred in the East End and at Barkingside during the funeral procession – and many photographs exist of the lying in state, the processions and the service – a ciné film was also taken of the event. It is very fitting that one of the earliest examples of a news film should be of the funeral of Dr Barnardo, a man who had himself made so much use of the photographer's art.

17

The Legend and the Legacy

FROM the moment that Barnardo's death became public knowledge, his legend started to crystallise. All the major national and provincial newspapers carried a statement issued from St Leonard's Lodge giving an account of the circumstances leading to his death. The statement also included some vague references to his family background: he was said to be of Spanish descent, and his mother was mysteriously referred to as an Englishwoman living in Ireland. No mention was made of the fact that his father had been a Prussian subject for the major part of his life. With the publication of *The Memoirs* two years later came the first reference to the family name of Drinkwater, and the reader was allowed to assume that Abigail Barnardo had been a Drinkwater. James Marchant, co-author of *The Memoirs*, wrote the article on Barnardo for the Dictionary of National Biography. There was no escaping the necessity of supplying a few essential facts, and there for the first time Barnardo's mother's maiden name was officially given as Drinkwater.

Only after Mrs Barnardo's death could Norman Wymer reveal in *Father of Nobody's Children* that Barnardo's father had married the two O'Brien sisters in succession, the social stigma that this had been thought to imply being no longer of any consequence. In fact John Michaelis' marriage to Abigail had always been perfectly legal, there being no impediment in Prussia to a man marrying his deceased wife's sister. The revelation that the family had close Roman Catholic connections through the O'Briens could then also be acknowledged. It was probably Mrs Barnardo who was mainly responsible for this carefully constructed version of the family history, because there is no doubt that she was the more socially ambitious of the two.

Although Mrs Barnardo may well have been responsible for the creation of the family legend, Barnardo himself had taken care to tailor the story of his early years in London to correspond with his version of the events that took place during his first four years in the East End. The first full-length biography of Barnardo had appeared the year before his death. Entitled *Dr. Barnardo, Foster Father of Nobody's Children,* it was written by the Rev. John Batt with the explicitly expressed hope that it might enlist further support for the homes. It is not known how far Barnardo cooperated with the author, but even if he did not actually help with the book it seems likely that he gave his approval to it. In any case Batt quoted extensively from Barnardo's own published accounts of the way in which the work began. These accounts, as has been shown, throw the dates of the early work back by three or four years, so as to enable the beginning of the work to be seen as almost coinciding with Barnardo's arrival in London. Batt's book appears to have been the source upon which all the newspapers relied for information about Barnardo's early life. They described Barnardo's meeting with Jim Jarvis in the mythical donkey shed and give the date as 1866. Nearly all the articles included long extracts of the conversation that took place between Barnardo and Jim as rewritten by Barnardo at a much later date. In an attempt to correct part of this misconception, W. A. Cater wrote a letter to *The Standard* saying that the Ernest Street ragged school, which had been founded by his father in 1865, was never housed in a donkey stable.

In an effort to make the facts fit these dates, the opening of the home in Stepney was given as having taken place in 1867. Given that his medical career was also said to have started in 1866 and that during this time he was actively preparing himself for missionary work in China, the picture emerged of a young man who in the space of one short year had recognised and started on his great work of rescuing the destitute child. The fact that Barnardo did indeed do all this is hardly less remarkable even when it is known that he had been in London for over four years before his first home for boys was opened.

What makes the subsequent growth of his work the more astonishing is that, unlike his contemporary, Bowman

Stephenson who under the auspices of the Methodist Church founded his first home for destitute boys marginally ahead of Barnardo in 1870, Barnardo's work was never part of any established Church. The Waifs and Strays Society was supported by the Church of England, and when Roman Catholic work for children was more directly coordinated through the Crusade of Rescue, which was founded in 1899, it remained very much Church-orientated.

The man whose work is most nearly comparable to that of Barnardo is J. W. C. Fegan, who like Barnardo belonged to the Brethren fellowship and was sustained and supported by many of the same people. It was owing to John Sands' generosity that the lease of the industrial home in Deptford was acquired, and Sands provided Fegan with a modest salary to run it as a home for destitute boys, paralleling his gift of Mossford Lodge to the Barnardos a year later. Like Barnardo, Fegan also wrote up the story of his first meeting with a street 'arab', Tom by name, whom he discovered at Bognor. He too searched the streets at night, lantern in hand, seeking homeless children, and he too preached the Word. On more than one occasion police had to be called to his gospel hall to control the crowds, and among those who spoke there was also Joshua Poole. Fegan and Barnardo crossed the Atlantic together on their way to Canada in 1884, Fegan escorting a party of emigrant boys, Barnardo making his first visit. But there the similarities ended. Fegan did not share Barnardo's love of drama and publicity, being of a quieter disposition.

It is in keeping with Barnardo's flamboyant personality and central to his need to be the dominant figure that the story of his invitation to meet Shaftesbury at his home was romanticised. According to his version of the story, he was no longer one among fourteen other mission leaders invited to a meeting to discuss their mutual problems, but the guest of honour at a dinner party; he was no longer just one among a concerned band of workers who, after a prayer meeting at Annie McPherson's Home of Industry, accompanied Shaftesbury on a tour of lodging houses and other haunts frequented by destitute children at night, but the man who took them all to Billingsgate after a grand dinner and dramatically discovered seventy-three destitute boys asleep under a tarpaulin. It is interesting to note that Barnardo made use of the story of these seventy-three boys again in his description of his meeting with 'Carrots', the boy whose subsequent death was to have such a far-reaching effect on his work. Through constant repetition Barnardo's account of his meeting with Shaftesbury thus became part of the legend of his early years.

If Barnardo felt it necessary to embellish the legend of his early days, there was no need for him to add anything to the monument he left behind him. Almost without exception the newspapers marvelled at the extent of his work. *The Times*[1] said that 'it is impossible not to be astonished by the magnitude of his work and its diversity', and said that he had 'raised up a noble monument of philanthropy and usefulness'. Many of his friends and supporters regretted that it was only after his death that his achievements were so universally honoured. They knew how much it would have encouraged him had he known that it would be said:[2] 'He has left behind him such an enduring monument to noble self sacrificing effort, such a legacy of good deeds well done, such a claim upon the reverence of the nation as few men among us will leave.'

W. T. Stead, whose initial suspicion of Barnardo's work had given place to unfeigned admiration, saw him as[3] 'a man with the personal force, tenacity of purpose, brain power and diplomatic skill that might have reaped the greatest rewards of human ambition'. Describing him as a 'moral genius of the supremely great order', he said: 'Only the most absolute self-abnegation could have carried him through the trials and discouragement and the unworthy detraction that marked the earlier stages of his undertaking ... Everyone now sees what Dr. Barnardo saw from the beginning, the shame, the folly, the sin of letting a steady stream grow up in a predestined progress of misery and crime.'

Today destitution is no longer a problem in this country. The word used to describe the under-privileged child is 'deprived', and the present-day concept of a cycle of deprivation implies that the recurrence of social problems through successive generations is still with us. The existence of a programme of research into the causes of this so-called transmitted deprivation shows that it is still not clearly understood why some people manage to break out from this potentially limiting cycle while others do not. Stead drew attention to Barnardo's 'positive conclusions' on the subject, and said that they should be taken note of, as the research on which they were based covered a period of forty years and fifty-five thousand experiments. Stating that Barnardo believed that the condition of the children could not be put down to inheritance but that it could be transformed by proper environment, Stead concluded: 'Let us then have it clearly set down, that the attribution to environment *alone* of practically all the physical unfitness in our cities is based upon the most positive and extended evidence of every kind.'

The Times, too, drew attention to Barnardo's work in terms of an experiment in psychology, and noted that the records of the organisation would repay study on the part of those interested in such problems better than some other sources of information. The article mentioned the two main features of his work which stood out as supremely important – religion and the workshop. It noted that religious training was the cardinal point from the beginning and remained the foundation of the influence exercised by the Homes. Many other papers referred to Barnardo's faith, including the *Morning Post* which said:[4] 'His was a faith that removed mountains; it was the secret of his success.' *The Record* went so far as to say:[5] 'No one will ever be able to understand the secret of the success of Dr. Barnardo's work who does not allow for the spiritual relationship which existed between him and the children.' Bowman Stephenson of the National Children's Homes said: 'No other man has touched and shaped the lives of so many children by his own personal effort. Although he could not know intimately the majority of his family they all knew him, his name, his face, his voice and they felt in some way which they could not quite understand that he was caring for them, controlling and comforting their lives.'

The most tangible element, the workshops, were singled out for their share of praise. Although the children received schooling as required by law, the fact that they were given the opportunity to acquire manual training in a workshop rather than at school was seen as positively advantageous. *The Times* thought the experience of real work under real conditions quickened their intelligence and self-respect. It noted with approval that fourteen trades were carried on at Stepney and that the girls learned 'woman's work' at Ilford. Considering that the parents of those children were at best inefficient and at worst degraded, vicious and criminal, the successful results of his training schemes were 'positively astonishing'. In today's changed circumstances, the Barnardo School of Printing at William Baker House, Hertford, is the last remaining such establishment to apprentice and to teach a trade.

The realisation of the sheer magnitude of the work undertaken by Barnardo brought home to many the inadequacies of both the Poor Law and the education laws with regard to the health and welfare of children, and the general lack of social reform. The *Local Government Journal*[6] in an unwitting tribute noted that it was the very lowest stratum which they should have been dealing with as a primary necessity, but which none of the acts of parliament appeared able to reach. 'Yet men like Barnardo and Booth have done it single handed; why should not our Poor Law administration with its millions of money be able to do likewise?', it asked. One correspondent writing in *London Opinion*[7] said that he saw not one sign of the shame that both individuals and the nation should feel in reviewing Barnardo's work: it should not have had to wait for private enterprise. Destitute children should have been the concern of the state, as well as of prisons and the Poor Law. The shame was shared, however, by the writer of an article entitled 'Barnardoism or Socialism' in the *Labour Leader*.[8] The writer paid tribute to the heroism of Barnardo's work and honoured him for it, but lamented its necessity: 'Consider what it implies – it implies that but for Doctor Barnardo these 20,000 children [the figure was in fact nearly 60,000] would not have been rescued – what a revelation of the state of the nation. Words cannot express the crime and shame of it.' And commenting on the appeal that was being made, the article continued:

Now he is gone something must be done to keep his work going. *His* work, mind you, not the nation's work – for the nation does not yet recognise that it has any duty to save 20,000 waifs and strays. The work should be kept going, but how infinitely better indeed it would be if the nation dealt with the social disease of uncared for children, not by mitigating the effects of the disease but by removing the cause of it.

Perhaps not realising what the local government board with its millions had failed to achieve, the writer continued: 'Consider what amount of labour and money is spent upon public philanthropic schemes ... consider too if all these efforts were organised and economised into one whole national system for the prevention of destitution and degradation how great would be the result. Only by socialism can the nation do that.'

The sudden realisation of the extent of Barnardo's work not only stirred up public disquiet over the inadequacies of the Poor Law and the education acts. Several papers also commented unfavourably on the fact that Barnardo, who had done so much for the nation's children, had received no fitting recognition for his work.[9] Accepting that Loch may have had some responsibility for this (Loch was knighted in 1915), Barnardo embodied certain contradictions within himself. With his mutton-chop whiskers, he was described as looking more like a merchant than a philanthropist. There was a less flattering description of him in *The Star*:[10]

In appearance he scarcely looked the part he played so successfully. His figure was short and round and his clothing was nearly always too tightly buttoned. His complexion was florid and his cheeks were puffy, his eyes somewhat fierce, and he did not favourably strike the visitor, who would not unnaturally look for someone with a kind and sympathetic countenance. Even his moustache was martial!

Photographs taken during the last years of his life show clearly enough what was meant, although those of his staff who knew him well would certainly not have agreed: 'All we workers', wrote Walter Notman, 'were bond slaves, linked to him by loving devotion.'

Barnardo's work, as he himself fully recognised, depended for its success on the qualities of his staff. He is on record as saying that the achievement of which he was most proud was to have gathered round him such a fine body of dedicated men and women. No teacher training colleges or social work courses existed, but he seems to have been able to attract to his service many educated Christian men and women who were prepared, for a very modest return, to devote their lives to his children. Unfortunately the register containing the detailed staff records has been destroyed. It would seem that many had links with the

Keswick movement and that the evangelical network provided him with educated and highly motivated workers. This was especially true of the many women he employed as cottage mothers and superintendents of his other establishments. There was no doubt that he could be hard on his staff. Long hours and low pay were the rule, and tremendous pressure was exerted on any who murmured at the demands made on them. He exploited the example he himself had set; the majority submitted willingly for the sake of the children, and carried on the work in a spirit of dedicated service. Times were hard and employment not always easy to come by, factors which served as a spur to the less enthusiastic. No one was ever left in doubt as to who was in charge. His need to dominate partly explains his reluctance to delegate. He once rebuked one of his cottage mothers for writing to him about one of 'her' children. 'Not yours,' he wrote, 'she is mine, *mine, mine!*'

The tributes of his committee expressed a very real sense of desolation at the loss of their Director. Nearly all the long-serving members had had their differences with him, but his had been the inspiration and driving force which had carried the work forward. William Baker had increasingly borne the daily burden of running the institutions in recent years. It was perhaps fortunate that as the man picked to succeed Barnardo as Director he should have had 'kind eyes which twinkled with humour' and a 'gentle fatherliness of manner'. His new responsibilities meant that he had to abandon a lucrative practice at the Chancery bar. This was opportune in a sense, for not only did Barnardo's physical appearance attract comment, his lifestyle and apparent wealth were also the subject of some speculation. George Reynolds' early jibe that Barnardo had 'raised himself on the pedestal of his work' had never been entirely forgotten. His wife's family was sometimes mentioned as having made some contribution to his fortune, but this seems unlikely. William Elmslie, Mrs Barnardo's father, had died in 1880 leaving his small estate of under £2,000 to his widow; Harry, his younger son, had been appointed chief steward of the Homes in 1890, and as such had been one of the senior members of staff. When the appeal was launched William Baker made the point that from 1866 to 1883 Barnardo had served the Homes in an honorary capacity, maintaining himself by his private medical practice and by his pen. This was to put the matter in a slightly misleading light, as Barnardo would only have been entitled to practise after 1876. Although figures are not available, remembering the success of his first magazine, it may fairly be assumed that his later ventures as an editor and publisher were equally successful and that his literary career was a profitable one. *The Children's Treasury* belonged to Barnardo personally, although it was advertised as an advocate for the destitute child. His magazine *Our Bubble,* which was used to publicise the work of the Young Helpers' League also belonged to him personally. Doubtless it was this overlap between his personal interests and those of the homes that was the cause of the speculation. The outspoken comment of a correspondent writing in *London Opinion*[11] reflected this feeling:

> Let us suppose, for the sake of argument, he cleared ten thousand for himself – I for one will – why shouldn't he? His work is true imperialism and the results would be worth far more than ten thousand a year. I don't know if the Organisation paid him anything, but I hope it paid him well for he deserved it.

When his will was proved the value of his estate attracted considerable notice. He left £13,485 gross and £10,732 net. His gift of one-tenth of his fortune to the Homes, 'established by me which I have directed during my life and loved to the last', made headlines. He had asked that his ashes be buried with the least possible expense to his estate; it was his son-in-law, Henry Wellcome, who organised the elaborate arrangements for the lying in state at the Edinburgh Castle, the impressive funeral procession through the East End of London and the great service at Barkingside. The fine monument that was subsequently erected over his grave was the work of the well known sculptor George Frampton, who gave his services as a tribute to the founder of the Homes. The simple words that Barnardo had used in his will, 'I hope to die as I have lived, in the humble but assured faith of Jesus Christ, whom I have so imperfectly served, and whom I acknowledge to be my Saviour, my Master and my King,' were inscribed at the base. An annual service of rededication and commemoration is held at the church in September, attended by staff and old boys and girls, who walk in procession to the grave for the final prayers.

Barnardo left all his private letters, correspondence and papers – both at Surbiton and Mossford Lodge and in his private rooms at Stepney Causeway – to his wife, to be dealt with as she thought fit. He left his Kodak camera, his bound copy of the *Encyclopaedia Britannica* and a presentation grandfather clock to Stuart, who was then living in Trinidad. Syrie, his daughter, and Cyril also received specific bequests, but his youngest handicapped daughter Marjorie Elaine was not mentioned. His library of over four thousand books was immediately sold and the house at Surbiton given up. Barnardo's salary was paid to his widow until the end of the year, when the council decided to give Mrs Barnardo an annuity for the following five years so that the education of her children could be completed.

Two months after Barnardo's death a national memorial appeal was launched for £250,000 to be applied for the purpose of extinguishing the financial liabilities of the homes. It had been hoped that the national appeal, launched in July, would raise £120,000. It was not a success. Barnardo's death two months later had, however, created a great wave of sympathy for his work; its scope and variety were seen to have been far greater than most people had realised. In launching a national memorial appeal the council must have felt that they had a very strong case to make, and that never again would they have such an opportune moment in which to make it. The liabilities which the new Honorary Director, William Baker, inherited were enormous. They included £100,000 for mortgages and £12,000 for special loans; Canadian liabilities amounted to £14,000; tradesmen's accounts, builders' contracts, bills payable and interest created on mortgages totalled £99,700. With the overdraft at the bank at £22,800, the total amount came to £249,000.[12]

In an article in favour of the appeal *The Times* made a strong plea that Barnardo's work should be supported as a genuine service to the community, saying that the sole conditions for admission were destitution and grave moral danger: destitution accounted for two-thirds of the admissions and moral danger for the remainder.

It went on to say that it was hardly necessary to argue in favour of this remarkable institution, 'which has so recently received world wide recognition'. More than half the children

applying for admission came from outside London, principally
through the fourteen receiving centres which now included all
the large English seaports and Belfast. An important element in
Barnardo's success was the careful discrimination he exercised
in accepting children. Had he not done so he would have been
accused of being a pauperising machine, and the principles he
followed to distinguish the merely needy children from the
destitute were clearly laid down in an annual report, providing a
further example of his methodical approach to his work:[13]

There must be real elements of actual destitution to qualify for
entrance, and we take careful and minute precautions, which prevent
or at least minimise deception and imposition. We distrust mere letter
appeals from unknown correspondents, and, wherever possible, we
institute instead direct personal enquiries relative to each candidate.
Twenty expert enquiry agents are constantly engaged in investigating
the life stories of those boys and girls who apply . . . The door is always
thrown wide open to the really destitute; but there are competent
'keepers of the gates' who see to it that none is admitted who has no
proper claims to urge.

Just under a third of the applicants were actually admitted. The
others were assisted with free meals and free lodgings; some
were restored to friends; others were sent to situations or
recommended to other homes. Eighty-five per cent of the total
admitted in 1904 were orphans, 51 per cent having lost their
fathers, 13 per cent their mothers and 21 per cent both parents.
The way in which the information concerning the children was
recorded is an object lesson in itself. Apart from the obligatory
photograph and details of age, height and physical condition,
the child's story together with that of the adult who made the
request was noted. The work of the inquiry agents was no
sinecure. The names, addresses and occupations of all the
child's known relatives were always listed at the foot of the
form, and they might include grandparents, cousins, aunts and
uncles as well as brothers and sisters.

After an initially encouraging start, the response to the appeal
was disappointing, and within two years it had virtually ceased
to attract funds, while still a long way short of its initial target. It
was fortunate, in the circumstances, that legacies and donations
were not affected by Barnardo's death. In fact they continued to
increase steadily. Nonetheless, to keep going the council was

forced to cut expenditure to the bone. All additional work not contracted out was stopped, the farm in Manitoba was sold, and gradually over the next few years, by the exercise of tight financial control, the liabilities the council inherited were slowly reduced.

In appraising the qualities which brought Barnardo success, all his contemporaries were agreed that it was his common sense, his amazing and untiring energy and his ability to follow his ideas through down to the most minute detail that made him outstanding both as an administrator and as a leader. His sound common sense gave him the necessary elasticity to adjust his work and methods to each individual and to the conditions prevailing at the time. Among those who reviewed his achievements, Bowman Stephenson was the most percipient.[14] He noted that some aspects of Barnardo's work should be carefully analysed before it was all accepted as a model for others. Admitting, with perhaps a tinge of envy, that it was his energetic and ingenious advertising that had brought him nearly £3,000,000 in his lifetime, he said that the percentage of children Barnardo had kept out of police hands was enormous, but he thought that a much smaller number of them had become well rounded and stable Christians. Warning of the dangers that could result from the sheer size of the organisation, he pointed out that size alone was no guarantee of success and that it carried within itself certain disadvantages, the most obvious being an inability to give sufficient time and attention to the needs of each individual child. He also thought that it might be difficult for Barnardo's successors to maintain the work because it was not organically connected to a great Christian Church and might sink into a formal and mechanical routine, although he fully appreciated that the fact that Barnardo had been undenominational had brought him certain advantages.

His professional pride asserting itself, though admitting that Barnardo worked with astonishing energy, Stephenson noted that he followed familiar methods which had been invented by others; he did not pioneer emigration; his boys still wore uniform and lived together in large establishments; the advantages of the cottage system and boarding-out were. all well recognised before Barnardo made the Ilford Village Home famous and used boarding-out to such good effect. Strictly speaking he was correct in his view of Barnardo's work. He failed to recognise, however, that no one individual, until Barnardo himself did so, had ever before attempted to work with children on such a large scale. Barnardo devised, set up and administered a system for the recording and management of his work which was unique in its day, and when compared to present-day methods, set standards which make it a model of its kind.

He may not have been the first to recognise the value of the boarding-out system, but the use he made of it and his energy in implementing this method of caring for children was outstanding then and remains so now. In many ways Barnardo followed Poor Law practice; his foster homes were supervised by lay committees and subject to unannounced visits by official inspectors whose terms of reference were strict and precise. Miss Mason, the local government board inspector, admitted that Barnardo's inspections were more thorough and said she thought the precautions were on the safe side.[15] He differed from Poor Law guardians in never allowing a child to be boarded out with irreligious parents, no matter how respectable, and on occasion children were removed from areas where the local incumbent was thought to have introduced unacceptable high church practices. He was also able to ensure that all the boys returned to Stepney by the time they were twelve or thirteen for training, so that when they came to leave they had all acquired a skill in some trade which would enable them to earn their livings.

The departmental committee, under the chairmanship of A. J. Mundella, was appointed by the Local Government Board in 1894 to inquire into the Poor Law schools, and it strongly recommended in its report of 1896 boarding-out as a method of care, saying that it was:[16]

> ... the small details of everyday life that help to bring out the character of the child, and as it grows up enable it, though unconsciously, to develop self dependence, resourcefulness and thriftiness; it learns by the example of its elders ... no amount of teaching by direct information could give a child that particular class of experience which it gets in everyday home life – the rubs and frictions that come from brothers and sisters and elders and youngers; the self denial that

it sees its parents going through when times are bad, the happiness when times are good.

Barnardo had been aware of the advantages of the boarding-out system since 1886, when he had made that part of the work a distinct branch of the organisation. With the exception of the years when financial stringency forced him to decrease the number of children boarded out, he had increasingly made use of this method of care. In the ten years that followed the setting up of the committee, Barnardo had boarded out more than twenty-three thousand children[17] which, when compared with the eighty thousand children boarded out during the same period by unions,[18] who had more than ten times as many children in their care, was a remarkable achievement. It is a measure of Barnardo's administrative ability that, in spite of the hazards inherent in the boarding-out system at a time when standards of child care varied greatly, by 1900 he was successfully boarding out babies. By 1902 Babies' Castle was no longer being used for its original purpose and had become a home for a group of younger children for whom boarding out was not suitable. By 1904, of the seven thousand eight hundred and eighty-five children in care, three thousand, nine hundred and sixty-seven, rather more than half, were boarded out.

When the departmental committee started its work in 1894 criticism of Barnardo was at its height. As has been shown, his attacks on the Roman Catholics, his court appearances and his desperate appeals for money had given rise to much adverse comment in the newspapers and elsewhere. The committee in the course of its investigations inspected not only Poor Law institutions but many voluntary organisations as well. The Barnardo Homes were among those inspected. Several members of the committee, including Mundella himself, Sir John Gorst, MP for Cambridge, and Mrs Barnett of Toynbee Hall all admitted later they they had felt considerable prejudice against Barnardo and his system. Mrs Barnett[19] said that she and Canon Barnett had been strongly opposed to Barnardo's methods of drawing attention to the needs of the poor, but they had been so greatly impressed by the Barnardo children they had met in Canada in the course of a world tour in 1890 that their attitude had changed. At a meeting in aid of the homes after his death, she described Barnardo as 'the man of the last century, who thought for the children as well as fought for them', and she condemned the attitude of the British public which compelled men like Barnardo to beg for money. 'He had the force, the energy, and the brain capacity to put into practice his thoughts, not only for the children, but for the nation, for it must be remembered that his work is a national work'; she ended by quoting Sir John Gorst's remark that the committee 'came to inspect, they returned to learn and they humbly tried to follow'.

Shortly after the report had been published, Mundella, speaking at a public meeting chaired by the Duke of Marlborough, said that the committee had felt it their duty to investigate Dr Barnardo's methods.[20]

I can only say to you, without in the least flattering Dr. Barnardo, that at the conclusion of our enquiry I came to the opinion which was shared, I think, by all my colleagues, that we could wish that in the Local Government Board there was a department for the Poor Law children of this country, or what are called the children of the state, and that we had a Dr. Barnardo to place at the head of them.

Nothing astonished me more than the magnitude of Dr. Barnardo's undertaking, and the faith, I may say the daily Christian faith, on which that undertaking seemed to be resting. It is a marvellous work that he has done in the Homes during the last thirty years, and its growth is entirely due to his wonderful energy, determination and character. I think I may say without the least reserve that Dr. Barnardo is not only a born administrator; he is a born master of method . . .

Most of the reforms that the Committee has recommended, Dr. Barnardo has anticipated, and put into practice in the administration of his institutions. We owe him much for what he has done. I think we owe him more for the example he has set us of how to do it. It is only fair to make this acknowledgment, and I do it all the more heartily because I confess that when I started upon the enquiry I had grave doubts about Dr. Barnardo's methods. I am here to say publicly that I would to God the same methods were introduced into the system of the administration of the whole of the Poor Law children of the country.

The manner in which Barnardo split families by his policy of keeping his children segregated by sex and by his energetic emigration programme did not pass unchallenged. He was particularly criticised in Catholic circles for this disregard for family life. An article in *The Universe*[21] opposing emigration as a social policy, criticised his use of transportation and exile as a means of combating destitution. This insensitivity to the claims of kinship, the tearing apart of brothers and sisters and the breaking up of homes was held to be a typically Protestant response to the problem of poverty, and both Barnardo and Booth came under attack for their schemes of wholesale depopulation. In fairness it must be remembered that the Roman Catholic rescue societies had also sent their children to Canada, although not in such large numbers, and that it was only in 1899 that Cardinal Vaughan made the public pledge, reminiscent of Barnardo's famous declaration made more than a quarter of a century earlier, 'that no Catholic children, really destitute or in danger with regard to their faith, and for whom no other provision could be made, would be refused admission to our Homes'.

If juvenile emigration can now be seen to have been a 'flawed' policy, the flaws were not so obvious then when the alternatives were so bleak. Barnardo responded to the plight of the destitute children in a positive manner which he believed must, in the long term, be beneficial to them. He may be criticised in retrospect for implementing his policy of emigration in a high-handed manner, but what none of his contemporaries seemed to have noted and what may perhaps be considered as his greatest achievement was the universality of his help to the destitute child. The two great principles upon which his work was based – that no destitute child should be refused admission and that all children of whatever creed or nationality, irrespective of any physical infirmity, were eligible – made his work unique. It underlined his view, publicly expressed in 1873 and 1883, that the problem of destitution was one for which the state should have assumed responsibility. It was in response to the failure of the state to take up the challenge that Barnardo took the decision, as an individual, to assume that responsibility. The principle of giving to all destitute children some form of shelter and care was the public expression of that decision, and the debts he incurred in so doing, he believed, should properly be the debts of the nation.

It was obvious by the middle of the nineteenth century that the Poor Law had become a relief agency rather than a means of dealing with destitution. It had become more punitive than positive in effect, its measures acting merely as a palliative; in so far as children were concerned, it had proved totally inadequate to deal with the enormous growth in destitution.

Thomas Coram had been one of the earliest philanthropists to attempt to change society's attitude to the abandoned child, through the establishment in 1739 of the Foundling Hospital where desperate mothers could bring their unwanted babies, in the knowledge that they would be cared for and educated. The babies were accepted with no questions asked, but in return the mother surrendered all her rights to the child. The Philanthropic Society, with its prison school for young convicts, its workshop for the employment of destitute boys and its training school for pauper girls, was followed by Mary Carpenter's enlightened work for what she called 'the children of the perishing and dangerous classes'.

The ragged school movement started as a rescue operation for destitute and neglected children, but perhaps its most lasting contribution to the welfare of the outcast child was to open the eyes of the many humane and compassionate reformers, from all ranks of society, who gave so much time and service to the movement, to the vacuum that existed in so far as the provision of the most basic necessities of life were concerned. Barnardo was only one of many who had come to realise the extent of the problem of destitution through their practical experience of working in ragged schools. Orphanages and charitable institutions of all kinds came into being in response to the knowledge of the existence of these needs, but nearly all followed some form of self-restricting policy which enabled them to limit their intake. Müller's orphan homes accepted only legitimate children, as did Spurgeon's Stockwell orphanage. Barnardo, taking care not to give offence, contented himself with the comment that he did not see his way clear to follow this practice. Many other charities catered for special categories and many required part payment by relatives or friends before they would admit a child. One of the most common ways in which entry could be controlled was by means of the voting system, which meant that a child could only be admitted if its sponsor was able to secure a sufficient number of votes of subscribers to the charity in question. The size of the subscription governed the number of votes each subscriber was entitled to hold, and Barnardo had no hesitation in denouncing the system as both cruel and wrong. Under such a system the most urgent cases could be refused by default if no votes were forthcoming. The most celebrated case of this kind was the discovery by Edward de Montjoie Rudolf that Barnardo's Homes were in fact the only ones that would admit his destitute Sunday school scholars immediately and with no strings attached, and that questions were asked only after the children had been given shelter. The foundation of the Church of England's Society for Waifs and Strays, a dozen years after Barnardo had opened his first home, was a direct consequence of this discovery.

Not only was Barnardo's famous public proclamation that no destitute child should be refused admission one of the most positive and enlightened statements of his time, the principles that lay behind it guarantee him a foremost place among social reformers.

Barnardo's concern for the children has all but eclipsed the other side of his work. To evangelise among the masses of the East End and to attempt to heal the sick and to relieve the deserving poor rank second and third in the list of objectives which formed part of the groundplan of his enterprise. The Edinburgh Castle was not only the home of his mission church; the annual Waifs' Supper took place in its great hall, and it was used to give free meals for other groups, including factory girls, unemployed men, the aged poor and even 'rogues and vagabonds'. His medical mission and the work done by the deaconesses in visiting and relieving the poor together represent the means he employed to meet both their physical and spiritual needs.

If the debts must go on the debit side of the account in financial terms, the fact that at the time of his death Barnardo was maintaining the largest children's hospital in London must go, unquantified, on the credit side, together with the fact that of the seven thousand, nine hundred and ninety-eight children in care, over one thousand, three hundred were crippled or handicapped. There was no public money to pay for the continuous care and treatment they needed, there were no grants for their maintenance and no possibility that they could join the growing number finding independence and a new life in

Canada. Yet Barnardo and those associated with him never shrank from adding to their number. One of the greatest legacies Barnardo bequeathed to those who have carried on his work is the example of his selfless concern for the wellbeing of all deprived and handicapped children.

Barnardo stands out as a great social reformer. He had identified the need for the state to take responsibility for destitute children long before the climate of public opinion changed and made such a reform possible. It was not until the Children's Act of 1948 that the local authorities were given a clear and inescapable duty to receive into care all homeless children and those children whose parents were unable to care for them. When Barnardo started his work there were said to be more than thirty thousand destitute children roaming the streets. At his death few of these 'arab' or 'gutter' children were to be seen. His public campaigns against cruelty and neglect had certainly played a part in getting the acts for the prevention of cruelty and the protection of children made law. The act relating to the custody of children was passed largely as a result of his campaign against cruel and neglectful parents. When the Education (Provision of Meals) Act was passed the year after his death, it was only implementing a policy Barnardo had recognised as essential more than thirty years before. Barnardo had not only made known the needs of children in a way never before attempted, he had endeavoured to meet those needs on a scale no one individual had ever before tried to do.

Autocratic and paternalistic by nature, believing himself to be acting under a divine mandate, he could see no way of re-establishing any kind of family life for the majority of his destitute children in the conditions that existed in most cities in the late nineteenth century. It is easy to criticise some aspects of his work with hindsight. It is only relatively recently that the importance of the role of the family in the life of a child has again come to be appreciated and more fully understood, and social policies developed to foster and improve the quality of family life. Even had such knowledge existed in Barnardo's day, attitudes change slowly and social policies cannot be implemented overnight. The problem Barnardo faced was immediate and urgent; he saw himself as working to save the next generation from the miseries of destitution by training his children to work for their livings and by giving them a fresh start in new surroundings.

How successful was Barnardo? No comprehensive studies have been made of the records, and so any assessment can only be based on what little knowledge does exist. It is not easy to generalise about the feelings of the thousands of children who passed through Barnardo's hands. Inevitably the letters of those who were grateful were the ones to be printed. Obviously there were those who resented the discipline and were critical of the treatment they received; there were those who over-identified with the organisation and failed to find their own independence. For the more sensitive the almost aggressive publicity to which they were subjected was hurtful; not all of them came from the gutter as the 'before' and 'after' style of the public presentation of the work of the homes implied. Many were deeply saddened by the forcible separation from family and friends. Nonetheless, it is probably fair to say that the vast majority seem to have felt a sense of gratitude for the care they had received and the chance they had been given. There seems to have been a large measure of understanding among the children of the reasons that governed the policy of the organisation, and a thankful acceptance that they had been given a fresh start in life, even among those who found life almost unendurably hard in Canada. From its earliest days the organisation has received support from those who were formerly in its care. No records exist to show the extent of that support, but it has remained steady and constant.

Social reforms are implemented in fits and starts. For many years after Barnardo's death the state was content to leave the care of many homeless and deprived children to the voluntary organisations who had first identified their needs and responded to them. When, in the aftermath of the Second World War, the state assumed responsibility for such children and new insights and new knowledge made previous forms of care seem inappropriate, it became fashionable to disparage the work of the voluntary childcare organisations and to see their role as no longer relevant. Yet in spite of an enlightened state welfare system children are still neglected, abused and deserted. Parents still batter their children, some still pass their lives in large subnormality hospitals, and the handicapped are too often denied opportunities of developing to the full their capabilities. The growing number of juvenile delinquents serves to remind society that increased prosperity has brought its own problems as well as solving others.

Barnardo's most enduring legacy is the organisation which he founded. It survived his death and two world wars and today is still the largest voluntary childcare organisation in the country. Barnardo always believed that the state must take greater responsibility for its children, which it has now done, although he did not believe that the state was capable of exercising that care, which he thought should remain in the hands of the churches and voluntary organisations. Inspired by the example Thomas Barnardo left his successors, the organisation that carries his name has grown and developed. Stephenson's fear that it might sink into a formal and mechanical routine has proved unfounded. Alive to the changing patterns of social need, and working now with children and their families, the organisation has adapted to changed conditions. It has seen that Barnardo's fears as to the state's ability to provide good child-care were unfounded, but it has never abandoned his view that the individual, also, has a role to play in the relief of distress and suffering. Today it is becoming increasingly apparent that the mere satisfaction of material wants does not meet people's deeper needs. The increase in voluntary and community work shows that serving and giving are as important as the act of receiving, and that the one without the other will remain an incomplete response. The Barnardo organisation has now worked for many years in cooperation with central and local government. Nourished by its own great tradition of service to children and based firmly on Christian principles, the contribution it has made and continues to make to the welfare of children and young people has been welcomed and praised by Labour and Conservative ministers alike. For many it provides the medium through which they can express their own desire to serve the community and, because of its voluntary status, it is able to deploy its resources with a freedom and flexibility that statutory authorities may well envy.

Stepney Causeway has been sold. The new headquarters building, Barnardo House, stands in the grounds of what used to be the Girls' Village Home at Ilford, where some of the remaining cottages are still used as family homes for mixed groups of children. Mossford Lodge, too, has disappeared, but New Mossford, one of the finest residential schools in the country for severely handicapped children, has been built on a nearby site. It is a living witness to a continuing tradition of care; to Billy and the other children who live there this book is dedicated.

Today the work of the Barnardo organisation is concentrated throughout the country in areas of most need. From the eight divisional offices situated in Cardiff, Birmingham, Liverpool, Edinburgh, Newcastle, Leeds, Belfast and London children and their families are helped in a great variety of ways. There are branches in Australia and New Zealand, and the independent Kenya Christian Home was started under Barnardo auspices. Deprived children remain an inarticulate minority. Thomas Barnardo proclaimed his unalterable belief that all children have an inalienable birthright to kind treatment, decent surroundings and a good education. He devoted his life to fighting for that right. He aimed high within the confines of his vision and, in so doing, he created an organisation which has made his name synonymous with a great tradition in childcare.

Appendix

THE Charity Organisation Society, unwilling to allow any opportunity of exposing Barnardo's unprofessional conduct to go by default published a Circular on 15 September 1877 in which they took up, among other matters, the question of Barnardo's right to the title of Doctor. The COS in their Circular stated that they had obtained a press copy of Barnardo's original letter of 2 August to Mr Sayer which made it plain that the letter referred to an American University for which alone Mr Sayer was authorised to grant diplomas, and that it had no reference whatever to the University of Giessen. Mr Sayer said that no degree was ever granted to Mr Barnardo through him and that the letter of 26 February 1872 was a fabrication in illiterate German, on English notepaper. The letter in the original German read as follows:

Herrn T. J. Barnardo,

Ich habe das Vergnügen Ihnen mitzutheilen dass Sie den Gratt von Doctor der Medecin von unserer Facultat erlangt haben. Das Diploma wird geschickt sobald als Dr Sayens den Rest der Gratification 300 Mark = £15 erhalten und mir gesandt hat.

Ihr, etc.

L. D. WICHAN, Decan der Facültat

There can be no doubt that this letter from Giessen purporting to award Barnardo an MD was a forgery.

Mr Sayer denied that he had ever been to St George's Hospital and according to the COS Circular the authorities of St George's Hospital stated that 'there had not been a German on the medical staff since 1870; further, that examinations are not in any way conducted in the loose manner described by Mr Barnardo, and that no paper whatever is granted by the Hospital Authorities which could in any way influence the authorities of the University of Giessen to believe that Mr Barnardo had passed through the hospital with credit and honour. Medical gentlemen have the privilege of walking through the hospital, and may, if they like, bring a medical student with them, but such visitors must be introduced by one of the staff who then takes charge of them in his round. The name of Barnardo was quite unknown there.' The COS Circular also made the point that the notice in *The Times*, which Barnardo never produced, appeared in March 1873 and not in 1875 and quotes the warning notice which appeared under the title 'Forged University Diplomas'. 'Another batch of about forty of these worthless documents have been distributed to greedy buyers in absentia in various parts of the United Kingdom, who are now disporting themselves in their illgotten plumage as proudly as if the feathers had been stuck in their coats after honourable University competition. This time the MD, PhD, BA, MA, etc. have been forged upon the Marburg and other German Universities, the authorities of which, to their credit, be it observed, have telegraphed the news to this country. Our readers, therefore, must exercise some little caution before accepting the ipse dixit of newly fledged Doctors in their neighbourhood.' The COS obtained a copy of the letter Barnardo had written to Giessen in 1875 together with a note from the Pro-Rector of the University who remarked that Mr Barnardo seems not to have found the conditions proposed to him either convenient or acceptable.

The COS published a final letter they received from Mr Sayer: 'I wrote three letters in all to Mr Barnardo in the months of July and August 1871. The first letter, dated 7th July, was written in consequence of information that I had received, and in it I stated that on giving proof of his qualification he might be promoted to the degree of MD from a fully chartered American University. I received a reply, a short note requesting further information and wrote on the 2nd day of August a second letter, the first sentence of which is as follows: "the medical diploma of MD, respecting which I wrote to you a short time ago, is from a fully chartered College and University in one of the principal cities in the United States". The third and last letter of our correspondence, dated 10th August, was produced in Court, and a copy of it is in your possession. No other letters have ever passed between Mr Barnardo and myself – no mention was ever made of the University of Giessen, or of any other – no interview took place between us, and in fact I have never seen him in my life. Every word of what he states passed between us subsequent to that date, as reported in the shorthand writer's notes with which you have kindly furnished me, is totally and entirely false; and the extraordinary statement he has made as to my own personal history is a mendacious fabrication, destitute of the least particle of foundation or truth.' Had the case continued St John Wontner would doubtless have been instructed to question Barnardo further concerning these matters.

Notes

Abbreviations

HTP Hudson Taylor Papers
PAC Public Archives of Canada
FWA Barnardo Papers. Papers concerning Dr Barnardo's Homes in the ownership of the Family Welfare Association.

1 Birth and Boyhood

1 Marriage certificate in the possession of the late Mr H. Barnardo of Dublin.
2 I am indebted to Miss Smith, archivist of the Hudson Bay Company, Winnipeg, for this information.
3 See Hyman, *The Jews of Ireland from Earliest Times to the year 1910*, p. 111.
4 *East London Observer*, 11 September 1875. See letter signed 'A Clerical Junius'.
5 I am indebted to the curator of the Religious Society of Friends in Ireland for this information.
6 Information from a document in Sophie Ryder's writing giving 'details and dates connected with Grandpapa Barnardo's family'.
7 Information from *Reminiscences*, written by Sophie Salbach and Abbie Fulwood, children of J. M. Barnardo by his first marriage.
8 Wheeler and Craig, *The Dublin City Churches of the Church of Ireland*, pp. 38–41.
9 The School for Collegiate and General Education run by the Rev. William Dundas was also the St Patrick's Cathedral Grammar School in Dublin. Information from prospectus giving examination results for Christmas 1854.
10 Barnardo and Marchant, *The Memoirs of the Late Dr Barnardo*, pp. 2–3.
11 Ibid., p. 12.
12 James, *Varieties of Religious Experience*, p. 189.
13 Barnardo and Marchant, op. cit., p. 13.

2 Early Struggles as Evangelist and Mission Leader

1 Stedman Jones, *Outcast London: a study in the relationships between the classes in Victorian Society*, Part I.
2 HTP, Hudson Taylor to his wife, 23 February 1866.
3 Barnardo Archives, letter from Joseph James to T. J. Barnardo, 9 May 1866.
4 University of Durham Calendar 1868, p. 192. Registration examination of medical students, September 1867.

Notes

5 Barnardo and Marchant, op. cit., p. 37.
6 HTP, T. J. Barnardo to W. T. Berger, 3 January 1868.
7 HTP, T. J. Barnardo to W. T. Berger, 30 April 1868.
8 HTP, W. T. Berger to Hudson Taylor, 21 April 1869.
9 HTP, W. T. Berger to Hudson Taylor, 13 July 1869.
10 HTP, W. T. Berger to Hudson Taylor, 25 November 1870.
11 Barnardo and Marchant, op. cit., p. 37.
12 *The Revival*, 11 July 1867.
13 *The Revival*, 25 July 1867.
14 *The Revival*, 8 August 1867.
15 HTP, W. T. Berger to Hudson Taylor, 6 March 1871.
16 *The Revival*, 1 July 1867.
17 *The Revival*, 1 October 1868.
18 *The Christian*, 22 August 1872; 29 August 1872.
19 I am indebted to the Shaftesbury Society for allowing me to quote from the minutes of the management committee of the Ragged School Union, 10 June 1870.
20 *The Christian*, 26 October 1871.
21 *The Christian*, 16 June 1870.

3 The Evangelical Connection

1 Heasman, *Evangelicals in Action. An appraisal of their Social Work in the Victorian Era*, chapter 1.
2 Hodder, *The Life of Samuel Morley*, p. 301.
3 Binfield, *George Williams and the YMCA*.
4 Findlay, *Dwight L. Moody, American Evangelist*, pp. 237–43.
5 *Our Day*, Vol. XIX, April 1900, No. 4, pp. 181–9. I am indebted to Mr Walter Osborn, librarian of the Moody Bible Institute, Chicago, for drawing my attention to this article.
6 Morgan, *Mighty Days of Revival: R. C. Morgan, His Life and Times*, p. 171.
7 *The Revival*, 25 July 1867.
8 *The Revival*, 29 October 1868.
9 Battiscombe, *Shaftesbury: A Biography of the Seventh Earl*, p. 292.
10 *The Christian*, 28 March 1872; 4 April 1872.

See also Murray, *The Puritan Hope: A study in Revival and the interpretation of prophecy*; Sandeen, *The Roots of Fundamentalism, British and American Millenarianism, 1800–1930*; Orr, *The Second Evangelical Awakening*; Barr, *Fundamentalism*; Orchard, *English Evangelical Eschatology 1790–1850*, unpublished thesis. For further information see Pickering, *Twice Born Men* and Coad, *A History of the Brethren Movement*.

4 The Fall of the Citadel of Satan

1 *The Christian*, 13 June 1872.
2 *The Christian*, 8 December 1870.
3 Barnardo, *Something Attempted, Something Done*, p. 13.

4 Williams, *Barnardo of Stepney*, p. 62.
5 *The Christian*, 28 September 1905.
6 Barnardo and Marchant, op. cit., p. 103.
7 *The Christian*, 22 August 1872.
8 *The Christian*, 26 September 1872.
9 Barnardo and Marchant, op. cit., p. 102.
10 *The Christian*, 31 October 1872.
11 *The Christian*, 13 February 1873.
12 *The Christian*, 20 February 1873.
13 Barnardo and Marchant, op. cit., p. 46.
14 I am indebted to Dr John Bourke of the University of Munich and to Dr Anderhub, archivist of the University of Giessen, for this information.
15 Barnardo, *Rescue the Perishing*, p. xcv.
16 Barnardo and Marchant, op. cit., p. 104.
17 *The Record*, 15 November 1886.
18 *The Record*, 21 November 1905.
19 Lansbury, *Looking Backward and Forward*, p. 8.

See also Harrison, *Drink and the Victorians*; Hind Smith, *William Wilson Hind Smith, Ambassador for Barnardo's 1869–1961* (Barnardo Archives); Thorne, *The Great Acceptance, The Life Story of F. N. Charrington*.

5 Marriage and the Development of his Work

1 Barnardo and Marchant, op. cit., pp. 353–5.
2 Wymer, *Father of Nobody's Children*, p. 84.
3 I am indebted to Sir Anthony Wagner and Mr Thomas Woodcock for information concerning the history of the Elmslie family.
4 *The Sword and the Trowel*, September 1905.
5 *The Christian*, 30 October 1873.
6 Third annual report of the local government board 1874, pp. 343–4.
7 Barnardo, *Rescue the Perishing*, lxiv.
8 Barnardo and Marchant, op. cit., p. 121.
9 Quarrier, Occasional Paper No. 1, 'The Cottage Principle'.
10 Barnardo and Marchant, op. cit., pp. 122–4.
11 *The Children's Treasury*, July 1876.
12 Barnardo, *Something Attempted, Something Done*, pp. 97–8.
13 Barnardo, ibid., p. 40.
14 *Night and Day*, Vol. VII 1883, p. 78.
15 Barnardo, *Something Attempted, Something Done*, p. 65.
16 Barnardo, ibid., pp. 174–8.

6 A Scandalous Controversy

The background to the quarrel between Charrington and Barnardo over the building of the Dublin Castle and the history of the rumour concerning Barnardo and Mrs Johnson were given during the course of the arbitration by

Alfred Thesiger, Barnardo's defence counsel, in his summing-up speech. This was published in two free supplements to the *East London Observer* on 8 and 15 September 1877. An article in *The Christian Herald* on 31 October 1877 entitled, 'Dr. T. J. Barnardo, the Devoted Benefactor of Homeless Boys', provides additional information about Barnardo and George Reynolds. The correspondence between Reynolds, Barnardo and their supporters started in the *East London Observer* on 28 August 1877 and continued in that paper and in the *Tower Hamlets Independent* until the end of the year. The first 'Clerical Junius' letter was published in the *East London Observer* on 11 September 1875 and the second was published in the *Tower Hamlets Independent* on 25 September 1875. For further discussion of the subject see Wagner, *Dr. Barnardo and the Charity Organisation Society: a re-assessment of the Arbitration Case of 1877*, pp. 93–111 (unpublished thesis). See also Thorne, *The Great Acceptance, The Life Story of F. N. Charrington*.

1 The *Charity Organisation Reporter*, 20 December 1877.
2 *East London Observer*, 28 August 1875.
3 Ibid., 4 September 1875.
4 Green, *Stray Studies*, Second Series, p. 127.
5 FWA Barnardo Papers.
6 No member of the family to whom I have spoken has any knowledge of such a genealogical table, which would surely have been preserved by J. M. Barnardo and be known to other members of the family.
7 This claim cannot be authenticated.

7 Disaster Threatens

1 *East London Observer* (supplement), 8 September 1877.
2 I have not been able to trace any copy of 'The Great Eastern Bubble', but references to it appear in the evidence given during the course of the arbitration.
3 *East London Observer*, 9 October 1875.
4 Ibid., 15 November 1875.
5 Ibid., 16 November 1875.
6 *The Record*, 26 November 1875.
7 Barnardo, 'The First Occasional Record of the Lord's dealings in connection with the East End Juvenile Mission', p. 43.
8 According to the *Lancet*, 1860, p. 524. The Medical Act of 1858 had been put to the test in 1860 when a man named Herbert Kelly was taken before the Court of the Exchequer for having styled himself Doctor, having qualifications of MRCS and CSA. The appeal was dismissed by the judge who said, 'if a man is registered he may call himself what he pleases and the Act [Medical Act of 1858] is to prevent any man practising medicine who is not registered'.
9 Annals of the Royal College of Physicians of London, 1862.
10 COS circular of 15 September 1877.
11 *East London Observer* (supplement), 15 September 1877.

12 *Charity Organisation Review*, Vol. XII p. 58.
13 For a more detailed account see Wagner, *Dr. Barnardo and the Charity Organisation Society; a re-assessment of the Arbitration Case of 1877* (unpublished thesis).
14 *East London Observer* (supplement), 15 September 1877.
15 Barnardo Archives.
16 There are no known records of any of the meetings held by Barnardo's trustees.
17 Barnardo Archives.
18 *Night and Day*, Vol. I p. 36.
19 *Complete Peerage*, Vol. III p. 196.
20 FWA Barnardo Papers.

8 Arbitration

1 Reynolds, 'Dr. Barnardo's Homes: Startling Revelations', p. 56.
2 Pollock, *The Keswick Story, the authorised history of the Keswick Convention*, p. 34.
3 *East London Observer* (supplement), 15 September 1877.
4 'The Charity Organisation Society and the Reynolds–Barnardo Arbitration', 28 November 1877 (circular issued by the COS).
5 *East London Observer* (supplement), 15 September 1877.
6 *Night and Day*, Vol. I p. 29.
7 FWA Barnardo Papers.
8 Minutes of the administrative committee of the COS 1876–8.
9 Preliminary correspondence between the COS and the trustees of Mr Barnardo's Homes, 31 March–21 April 1877 – circular of 15 September 1877.
10 *The Christian*, 7 June 1877.
11 COS circular of 15 September 1877.
12 Simpkinson, *Life of Bishop Thorold,* p. 89, quoted by Balleine, *A History of the Evangelical Party*, p. 241.
13 Horner, *Time Remembered*, chapter 1.
14 *East London Observer* (supplement), 15 September 1877.
15 'The Charity Organisation Society and the Reynolds–Barnardo Arbitration', 28 November 1877, p. 5.
16 Minutes of the COS Barnardo committee of inquiry, 28 June 1877.
17 *Night and Day*, Vol. I p. 100.
18 *Night and Day*, Vol. XXIV p. 32.
19 I am indebted to the late Mr H. Barnardo who allowed me to quote from this report dated 25 October 1877.
20 Minutes of the COS Barnardo committee of inquiry, 29 October 1877.
21 *Night and Day*, Vol. 4 p. 100.
22 *Night and Day,* Vol. I p. 100
23 *Tower Hamlets Independent*, 25 August 1877.
24 Sandeen, op. cit., p. 59.

See also Redman, *A concise treatise on the Law of Arbitration and Awards with appendix of Precedents and Statutes.*

9 *In Court*

I have relied on three main sources for the evidence upon which this chapter is based:

(a) The *East London Observer*'s two free supplements of 8 and 15 September 1877, giving a verbatim report of Alfred Thesiger's summing-up speech which lasted two days and ran to over forty thousand words.

(b) The Charity Organisation Society's account of the last two days of the arbitration, printed in the form of a pamphlet entitled, 'The Barnardo Investigation: Report of the last two days' proceedings'.

(c) The *Tower Hamlets Independent*, which on 20 October 1877 printed the award of the arbitrators in full. It also published a detailed account of the way in which the case had been conducted.

1 'The Barnardo Investigation', p. 27.
2 *Tower Hamlets Independent*, 20 October 1877.
3 'Startling Revelations', pp. 7–8.
4 Barnardo Archives.
5 *East London Observer* (supplement), 8 September 1877.
6 *Tower Hamlets Independent*, 20 October 1877.
7 *East London Observer* (supplement), 15 September 1877.
8 Ibid., 8 September 1877.
9 Ibid., 8 September 1877.
10 *Tower Hamlets Independent*, 20 October 1877.
11 Barnardo, *Rescue the Perishing*, pp. LXXIV–LXXV.
12 *The Christian Herald*, 6 September 1877.
13 For a fuller account of Barnardo's dealings with Mr Sayer see Appendix, pp. 315–17.
14 *East London Observer*, 4 September 1877.
15 'The Barnardo Investigation', p. 3.
16 Ibid., p. 4.
17 Ibid., p. 7.
18 Ibid., p. 7.
19 Ibid., p. 12.
20 Ibid., pp. 29–30.
21 *East London Observer* (supplement), 15 September 1877.

10 *Evangelical Triumph*

1 Circular issued by the Charity Organisation Society, 15 September 1877.
2 *Tower Hamlets Independent*, 29 September 1877.
3 Evidence taken from the findings of the inquiry agents, Stubbs, 25 October 1877.
4 FWA Barnardo Papers, Confidential report on Dr Barnardo's Homes, 1883.
5 *The Times*, 25 January 1923.

6 Barnardo Archives, Minutes of the committee of management of Dr Barnardo's Homes, January 1878.

7 *Night and Day*, Vol. IX p. 45.

8 *Daily Chronicle*, 20 October 1877.

9 *The Record*, 26 October 1877.

10 *The Echo*, 19 October 1877.

11 *Morning Advertiser*, 20 October 1877.

12 *The Times*, 23 October 1877.

13 *Night and Day*, Vol. I p. 138.

14 Shaftesbury's diary, 20 October 1877, in the possession of the trustees of the Broadlands Archives, National Register of Archives.

15 *Lloyd's Weekly Newspaper*, 28 October 1877.

16 Extract from typewritten copy of C. S. Loch's diary.

17 *Tower Hamlets Independent*, 27 October 1877.

18 *The Law Times*, 23 October 1880.

19 *The Times*, 21 October 1880.

20 Blake, *Disraeli*, pp. 487–8.

11 The Years of Consolidation, 1878–86

1 Atlay, *Victorian Chancellors*, p. 332.

2 Bready, *Dr. Barnardo, Physician, Pioneer, Prophet. Child Life Yesterday and Today*, p. 232.

3 *Night and Day*, Vol. IX pp. 42–7.

4 Barnardo Archives, Minutes of the committee of management, 1878.

5 *Night and Day*, Vol. VII pp. 140–3.

6 Doyle 1875 p. 35 Br. PP. 'Report to the Rt. Hon. President of the Local Government Board by Andrew Doyle Esq., Inspector as to the Emigration of Pauper children to Canada 1875', CXIII 255.

7 Smith, Samuel, 'The Industrial Training of Destitute Children', *Contemporary Review*, Vol. XLVIII pp. 108–10.

8 Cox: see *Encyclopedia Canadiana* and *Dictionary of Canadian Biography*, 2nd ed. (1945).

9 PAC Letter from T. J. Barnardo to Sir Charles Tupper, 26 June 1884.

10 PAC Letter from Sir Charles Tupper to Dr Barnardo, 2 July 1884.

11 *Night and Day*, Vol. VIII pp. 156–60.

12 Barnardo, *Something Attempted, Something Done*, pp. 168–71.

See also Parr, *Home Children, Juvenile Immigrants to Canada 1869–1924*, (unpublished dissertation); Birt, *The Children's Homefinder, The Story of Annie McPherson and Louisa Birt*.

12 Private Interests and Public Good

1 Barnardo, *Something Attempted, Something Done*, pp. 219–23.

2 *Night and Day*, Vol. I pp. 9, 16, 48, 54, 76, 98.

3 Barnardo and Marchant, op. cit., pp. 151–2.

4 Barnardo Archives. Minutes of the committee of management, Dr Barnardo's Homes, April 1883.

5 Barnardo and Marchant, op. cit., pp. 311–13.
6 Ibid., p. 315.
7 *Night and Day*, Vol. IX p. 115.
8 Barnardo and Marchant, op. cit., p. 267.
9 *Weekly News*, 13 September 1905.
10 Hansard, House of Lords 2nd series, Vol. 289 Col. 1292, quoted in Gorham, *The Maiden Tribute of Modern Babylon Re-examined: Child Prostitution and the Idea of Childhood in Late Victorian England.*
11 *Night and Day*, Vol. IX p. 158.
12 Ibid., p. 149.
13 Private information.
14 Rumbelow, *The Complete Jack the Ripper*, p. 65.
15 *The Times*, 6 October 1888.
16 Anderson, *The Lighter Side of my Official Life*, p. 136.

13 The Custody of Children

1 *Night and Day*, Vol. VI p. 28.
2 *Night and Day*, Vol. VIII, April 1895; 'Our Waifs and Strays', June 1895.
3 *Night and Day*, Vol. XIV p. 115. Letter from T. J. Barnardo to the Duke of Abercorn, 17 May 1890.
4 Barnardo Archives.
5 Barnardo Archives.
6 *The Times*, 24 May 1889.
7 *The Times* law report, 16 May 1889.
8 Barnardo Archives, Minutes of the committee of management, May 1889.
9 *Night and Day*, Vol. XIII pp. 145–69.
10 A special supplement to *Night and Day*, Vol. XIV pp. 1–56, entitled 'Before my Judges', was printed by Barnardo. It was a verbatim report of his speech on the Gossage case, delivered on Friday 24 January and Monday 27 January 1889, with a summary of the judges' decision.
11 'Before my Judges', p. 44.
12 The Roddy case was extensively reported in *The Times* on 8, 16 and 17 May 1890.
13 Bready, op. cit., pp. 202–3.
14 *Night and Day*, Vol. XIV pp. 1–66. 'Am I Unfit?', a verbatim report of Dr Barnardo's speeches in the Roddy case, p. 39.
15 Ibid., p. 61.
16 Ibid., p. 63.
17 Ibid., p. 63.
18 If Barnardo kept in touch with any of the children it was not officially noted in the Barnardo records.

See also law reports on Tye case, Queen's Bench Division 1889 pp. 310–16; Gossage case, Court of Appeal, 24–7 January 1890, pp. 283–302; Gossage case, House of Lords, 25 January 1892, pp. 226–341; (Roddy) McHugh case, House of Lords, 30 January 1891, pp. 388–400; Custody of Children Act,

1891. I am much indebted to Mr Andrew Munday, barrister-at-law, for the skilful way he steered me through the legal complexities surrounding Barnardo's actions.

14 Emigration – the Golden Bridge

The material for this chapter is largely based on the research embodied in Dr Joy Parr's unpublished dissertation, *Home Children, Juvenile Immigrants to Canada 1869–1924*, which she generously allowed me to read and make use of.

1 Extract from a diary in the possession of Mr Kenward Barnardo, to whom I am much indebted for permission to quote from it.
2 Parr, op. cit., pp. 102–3.
3 PAC RG 76 Vol. 94. Letter from T. J. Barnardo to the Secretary of the Department of the Interior, Ottawa, 4 April 1896.
4 PAC RG 76 121/23624. Letter from A. de Brissac Owen to the Secretary of the Department of the Interior, 18 January 1896.
5 PAC RG 76 121/23624. Report of the legislative committee presented to and approved by the trades and labour council at its meeting, 10 December 1895.
6 Parr, op. cit., p. 145.
7 Letter in the possession of Mr Kenward Barnardo.
8 *Night and Day*, Vol. XXIV pp. 51–6.
9 *Night and Day*, Vol. XXIV p. 35.
10 Barnardo Archives, Minutes of the committee of management, July 1897.
11 MS letters from Stuart Barnardo to his father, Barnardo Archives.
12 *Night and Day*, Vol. XXVII p. 8.
13 *Daily Mail*, 21 September 1905.

15 The Financial Crisis

Background information for this chapter comes from the minutes of the meetings of the committee of management and of the finance sub-committee during the years 1890–1905.

1 *Night and Day*, Vol. XV pp. 62, 84, 110; Vol. XVI p. 45.
2 Barnardo Archives, Minutes of the finance committee, 16 December 1892.
3 Barnardo and Marchant, op. cit., pp. 224–5.
4 *Night and Day*, Vol. XVII p. 31.
5 Howard, *Upstream*, p. 50.
6 Barnardo and Marchant, op. cit., pp. 231–4.
7 *Night and Day*, Vol. XVIII p. 39.
8 *Night and Day*, Vol. V p. 188.
9 FWA Barnardo Papers.
10 *Night and Day*, Vol. VIII p. 97.

16 The Last Decade

1 Barnardo Archives. Letter from T. J. Barnardo to Miss Reynolds, 12 October 1898.

2 Barnardo Archives.
3 *Night and Day*, Vol. xx pp. 51–9.
4 *Essex Weekly News*, 15 March 1901.
5 Barnardo Archives.
6 Barnardo Archives. Letter from T. J. Barnardo to W. Hind Smith, 23 May 1903.
7 Barnardo Archives.
8 Ibid.
9 Ibid.
10 *Night and Day*, Vol. xxviii p. 1.
11 Ibid., p. 22.
12 fwa Barnardo Papers.
13 *Truth*, 28 September 1905.
14 fwa Barnardo Papers.

17 The Legend and the Legacy

1 *The Times*, 21 September 1905.
2 *The Manchester Evening Chronicle*, 21 September 1905.
3 *Pall Mall Gazette*, 21 September 1905.
4 *Morning Post*, 21 September 1905.
5 *The Record*, 21 September 1905.
6 *Local Government Journal*, 28 September 1905.
7 *London Opinion*, 29 September 1905.
8 *Labour Leader*, 29 September 1905.
9 *English Churchman*, 21 September 1905.
10 *The Star*, 21 September 1905.
11 *London Opinion*, 20 September 1905.
12 In todays terms £249,000 is worth £3,784,000. I am indebted to Barclays Bank, bankers to Barnardo's for over a hundred years, for this information.
13 Thirty-ninth annual report of Dr Barnardo's Homes, 1904.
14 *Wesleyan Methodist Magazine*, 1905, p. 106.
15 'The Report of the Departmental Committee appointed by the Local Government Board to inquire into the existing systems for the maintenance and education of children under the charge of managers of district schools and boards of guardians in the metropolis and to advise as to any change that may be desirable, C. 8027.' p. 2.
16 Ibid., p. 2.
17 Thirty-ninth annual report of Dr Barnardo's Homes, 1904.
18 Thirty-fourth annual report of the Local Government Board, p. lix.
19 *Islington Daily Gazette*, 21 November 1905.
20 Quoted by Williams, *Barnardo of Stepney, The Father of Nobody's Children*, p. 174.
21 *The Universe*, 7 October 1905.

Bibliography

All books published in the UK except where otherwise stated.

Books, Reports, Articles and Pamphlets

Allan, Anne, and Norton, Arthur, *N.S.P.C.C. This is your child* (1961)

Anderson, Robert, *The Lighter Side of my Official Life* (1910)

Atlay, J. B., *Victorian Chancellors*, 2 vols (1908)

Baker, C. C. M., *The Laws relating to Young Children* (1885)

Balleine, G. R., *A History of the Evangelical Party* (1908)

Barnardo, Mrs, and Marchant, James, *The Memoirs of the late Dr. Barnardo* (1907)

Barr, James, *Fundamentalism* (1977)

Batt, John, *Dr. Barnardo, Foster Father of Nobody's Children* (1904)

Battiscombe, Georgina, *Shaftesbury: A Biography of the Seventh Earl* (1974)

Binfield, Clyde, *George Williams and the Y.M.C.A.* (1973)

Birt, Lilian M., *The Children's Homefinder, The Story of Annie McPherson and Louisa Birt* (1913)

Blake, Robert, *Disraeli* (1970)

Blumenfeld, Simon, *Doctor of the Lost* (1938)

Booth, Charles, *Life and Labour of the People of London*, 17 vols (1902)

Booth, William, *In Darkest England and the Way Out* (1890)

Bradfield, William, *Life of Thomas Bowman Stephenson* (1913)

Bradley, Ian, *The Call to Seriousness: The Evangelical Impact of the Victorians* (1976)

Bready, J. Wesley, *Dr. Barnardo, Physician, Pioneer, Prophet. Child Life Yesterday and To-day* (1930)

Broomhall, Marshall, *The Jubilee Story of the China Inland Mission* (1915)

Chesney, Kellow, *The Victorian Underworld* (1970)

Coad, F. Roy, *A History of the Brethren Movement* (1968)

Coutts, General Frederick, *No discharge in this war: A History of the Salvation Army* (1975)

Cruikshank, George, Our Gutter Children (1869)

Findlay, James F., *Dwight L. Moody, American Evangelist* (University of Chicago Press 1969)

Fraser, Donald, *Mary Jane Kinnaird* (1890)

Gorham, Deborah, The Maiden Tribute of Modern Babylon Re-examined: Child Prostitution and the Idea of Childhood in Late Victorian England. Paper given at Canadian Historical Association, 1977.

Bibliography

Gosse, Edmund, *Father and Son. A Study in two temperaments* (1907)

Green, J. R., *Stray Studies*, Second Series (1904)

Guinness, Joy, *Mrs. Howard Taylor, Her Web of Time* (1949)

Harrison, Brian, *Drink and the Victorians* (1971)

Harvey, Colin, *Ha'penny Help. A record of Social Improvement in Victorian Scotland* (1976)

Healey, Edna, *Lady Unknown: The life of Angela Burdett Coutts* (1977)

Heasman, Kathleen, *Evangelicals in Action: An Appraisal of their Social Work in the Victorian Era* (1962)

Heywood, Jean S., *Children in Care: The development of the service for the deprived child* (1978)

Hobson, J. A., 'The Social Philosophy of the C.O.S.', *Contemporary Review* Vol. LXVIII (1896)

Hodder, Edwin, *The Life and Work of the Seventh Earl of Shaftesbury*, 3 vols (1887)

Hodder, Edwin, *The Life of Samuel Morley* (1889)

Horner, Frances, *Time Remembered* (1933)

Howard, Elizabeth Fox, *Upstream*

Hyman, Louis, *The Jews of Ireland from Earliest Times to the Year 1910* (1972)

Inglis, Brian, *Poverty and the Industrial Revolution* (1971)

Inglis, K. S., *Churches and the Working Classes in Victorian England* (1963)

James, William, *Varieties of Religious Experience* (1971)

Kinnaird, Emily, *Reminiscences* (1925)

Labouchère, Henry, 'Dr. Barnardo and The Pope', *Truth* (1894)

Lansbury, George, *Looking Backward and Forward* (1931)

Loch, C. S., *Charity Organisation* (1890); 'Charity and Charities', article in the *Encyclopaedia Britannica*, cloth ed. (1902); *Charity and Social Life* (1916)

Longman, Norman, *The Workhouse* (1974)

Low, S., *Charities of London* (1891)

Mackay, Thomas, 'The Anti-Socialist Philosophy of the C.O.S.', *Essays in Labour History*, ed. K. Brown (1974)

Mcleod, Hugh, *Class and Religion in the Late Victorian City* (1974)

Macpherson, John, *Henry Moorhouse, the English Evangelist* (1881)

Marsh, M. C., *Brief Memories of Hugh McCalmont Cairns* (1885)

Mayhew, Henry, *London Labour and the London Poor*, 4 vols (ed. 1961)

Mearns, Andrew, 'The Bitter Cry of Outcast London: An enquiry into the condition of the Abject Poor', Congregational Union (1883)

Moore-Anderson, A. P., *Sir Robert Anderson, A Tribute and a Memoir* (1919)

Morgan, George, *Mighty Days of Revival: R. C. Morgan, His Life and Times* (1922)

Mowat, C. L., *The Charity Organisation Society 1869–1913: Its ideas and works* (1961)

Müller, George, 'The Life of Trust, Being a Narrative of the Lord's dealings with George Müller' (1878)

Murray, Iain, *The Puritan Hope: A study in revival and the interpretation of prophecy* (1971)

Newman, A. R., *Dr. Barnardo as I knew him* (1914)

Orr, J. Edwin, *The Second Evangelical Awakening* (1949)

Owen, David, *English Philanthropy, 1660–1960* (1965)

Owen, H. J., *Days in London, Mildmay Park* (1876)

Pickering, Henry, *Chief among the Brethren* (1931); *Twice Born Men* (1934)

Pierson, Arthur T., *George Müller of Bristol* (1902)

Pinchbeck, Ivy, and Hewitt, Margaret, *Children in English Society*, 2 vols (1973)

Pollock, J. C., *The Keswick Story, the authorised history of the Keswick Convention* (1964)

Quarrier, William, 'The Cottage Principle', Occasional Paper No. 1 (1870)

Redman, J. H., *A concise treatise on the Law of Arbitration and Awards with appendix of Precedents and Statutes* (1884)

Reynolds, George, 'Dr. Barnardo's Homes: Startling Revelations' (1876)

Roberts, David, *Victorian Origins of the Welfare State* (Yale University Press 1961)

Rooff, Madeleine, *Voluntary Societies and Voluntary Policy* (1957)

—— *A Hundred Years of Family Welfare 1869–1969* (1972)

Rumbelow, Donald, *The Complete Jack the Ripper* (1975)

Sandeen, Ernest, *The Roots of Fundamentalism, British and American Millenarianism 1800–1930* (University of Chicago Press 1970)

Shaftesbury, 'The Mischief of State Aid', *Nineteenth Century*, Vol. XXIV (1883)

Stedman Jones, Gareth, *Outcast London: A study in the relationships between the classes in Victorian Society* (1971)

Stroud, John, *13 Penny Stamps: The Story of the Church of England Children's Society from 1881–1970* (1971)

Sutherland, Neil, *Childhood in English Canadian Society* (University of Toronto 1977)

Taylor, Dr and Mrs Howard, *Hudson Taylor and the China Inland Mission: The Growth of a work of God* (1919)

The Complete Peerage, 2nd ed. (1905–59)

Thorne, Guy, *The Great Acceptance, The Life Story of F. N. Charrington* (1913)

Tiffin, Alfred, *Loving and Serving. An account of the life and work of J. W. C. Fegan* (undated)

Trotter, Mrs Edward, *Lord Radstock* (1914)

Varley, Henry, *Henry Varley* (1925)

Webb, Beatrice, *My Apprenticeship* (1926)

Wheeler, H. A., and Craig, M. J., *The Dublin City Churches of the Church of Ireland* (1948)

Williams, A. E., *Barnardo of Stepney, The Father of Nobody's Children* (1943)

Wilson, Bryan, *Magic and the Millennium* (1973)

Woodroofe, Kathleen, *From Charity to Social Work in England and the United States* (1962)

Wymer, Norman, *Father of Nobody's Children* (1966)

Unpublished Theses

Orchard, S. C., *English Evangelical Eschatology, 1790–1850*, Ph.D. thesis, Cambridge University (1968)

Bibliography

Parr, Joy, *Home Children, Juvenile Immigrants to Canada, 1868–1924*, Ph.D. thesis, Yale University (1977)

Wagner, Gillian, *Dr. Barnardo and the Charity Organisation Society: A reassessment of the Arbitration Case of 1877*, Ph.D. thesis, University of London (1977)

Woodard, C. S., *The Charity Organisation Society and the Rise of the Welfare State*, Ph.D. thesis, Cambridge University (1961)

Newspapers and Periodicals

The Baptist
The Christian
Coming Events
Contemporary Review
Daily News
Daily Telegraph
Eastern Post
East London Observer
The Echo
The Globe
Islington Gazette
The Lancet

The Law Times
Lloyd's Weekly Newspaper
Morning Advertiser
Nineteenth Century
Pall Mall Gazette
Quarterly Review
The Record
The Revival
The Times
Tower Hamlets Independent
Truth
Weekly Times

Archive Collections

1 *Goldsmiths' Library, University of London*

Papers and reports of the Charity Organisation Society
Annual reports of the COS, 1870–97
Charity Organisation Reporter, 1872–84
Charity Organisation Review, 1885–96
C. S. Loch's diary (typescript copy only), 1876–92
'The Barnardo Investigation: Report of the last two days' proceedings' (5–6 September 1877)
Annual reports of district committees, Mile End Old Town and Stepney

2 *Greater London Records Office*

MS minutes of the council of the COS, 1876–9
MS minutes of the administrative committee of the COS, 1876–8
MS minutes of the mendicity sub-committee of the COS, 1876–8
MS minutes of the committee of inquiry into Dr Barnardo's Homes, COS, 1877
MS inquiry sub-committee of the COS, 1878–87

3 *Offices of the Family Welfare Association*

MS papers, letters, reports and press cuttings concerning the Barnardo organisation in two packets dated 1883–90 and 1904–43

4 *National Register of Archives*

Shaftesbury's diaries – in the possession of the trustees of the Broadlands Archives

5 *Public Archives of Canada, Ottawa*

MS letters and reports and printed matter concerning the emigration and d welfare of Barnardo children in Canada

6 *Provincial Archives, Manitoba*

Papers concerning the Industrial Farm, Russell, Manitoba.

Barnardo Archives

Annual reports of the East End Juvenile Mission, 1867–77
Annual reports of the East End Juvenile Mission, Dr Barnardo's Homes, 1877–82
Annual reports of Dr Barnardo's Homes, 1882–1905
MSS minutes of committee of management of Dr Barnardo's Homes, 1877–1914
MSS minutes of finance committee of Dr Barnardo's Homes, 1877–1914
Property ledgers and deeds of trust from 1870
Account ledger books from 1870
Photographic records from 1874
Records and case histories of children from 1870
Canadian record books

Night and Day, edited by T. J. Barnardo, 1877–1905, 27 vols. (There was no *Night and Day* in 1901, owing to Barnardo's illness.)
The Children's Treasury, edited by T. J. Barnardo, 1874–81
Our Darlings, edited by T. J. Barnardo, 1881–94
Our Bubble, edited by T. J. Barnardo, 1894–1900
Rescue the Perishing, an extended report of the work of the East End Juvenile Mission, 1874–5, published in 1876
Something Attempted, Something Done (1888), an extended report of Barnardo's work up to 1888, published in 1890

East End Juvenile Mission leaflets, published by Morgan and Scott (undated), first series 1–13 (some missing)
 1 'Sunset'
 2 'Sunrise'
 5 'Winter Experiences'
 6 'The Poor and Needy'
 8 'Waifs and Strays'
 9 'A Midnight Ramble in East London'
 11 'On the Tramp'
 12 'Where and how we find Poor Boys'
 13 'Lost Tommie'

'Labours of Love among our East End Arabs' (1871)'Nobody's Children: A brief account of what is being done to save the Arab children of our great city' (undated)

A series of undated pamphlets published by F. J. Shaw and Dr Barnardo:
'Done to Death'
'Episodes in Humble Lives'
'Kidnapped!'
'The King's Business Requireth Haste'
'A Little Street Heroine'
'The Message of the Bells: a true story of Christmas'
'My first Arab'
'Never had a Home'
'Out of a horrible Pit'
'A puir Scotch Laddie'
'Rescued for Life: the true story of a young thief'
'Saved from Crime: incidents in the life of a waif and stray'
'The seed of the Righteous'
'The Shilling Baby'
'Twelve Sheep from Australia'
'Worse than Orphans: How I stole two girls and fought for a boy'

Index

Index

Index